M

TEACH YOURSE

p

DATE DUE

panjabi

Surjit Singh Kalra

Navtej Kaur Purewal

with

Sue Tyson-Ward

TEACH YOURSELF BOOKS

For UK orders: please contact Bookpoint Ltd, 39 Milton Park, Abingdon, Oxon OX14 4TD. Telephone: (44) 01235 400414, Fax: (44) 01235 400454. Lines are open from 9.00–6.00, Monday to Saturday, with a 24 hour message answering service. Email address: orders@bookpoint.co.uk

For U.S.A. & Canada orders: please contact NTC/Contemporary Publishing, 4255 West Touhy Avenue, Lincolnwood, Illinois 60646-1975, U.S.A. Telephone: (847) 679 5500, Fax: (847) 679 2494.

Long renowned as the authoritative source for self-guided learning – with more than 30 million copies sold worldwide – the *Teach Yourself* series includes over 200 titles in the fields of languages, craft, hobbies, sports, and other leisure activities.

British Library Cataloguing in Publication Data

A catalogue record for this title is available from The British Library

Library of Congress Catalog Card Number: On File

First published in UK 1999 by Hodder Headline Plc, 338 Euston Road, London NW1 3BH.

First published in US 1999 by NTC/Contemporary Publishing, 4255 West Touhy Avenue, Lincolnwood (Chicago), Illinois 60646-1975 U.S.A.

Typeset by Pure Text India Ltd, Pondicherry
        http://www.puretech.com

Printed in Great Britain for Hodder & Stoughton Educational, a division of Hodder Headline Plc, 338 Euston Road, London NW1 3BH by Cox & Wyman Ltd, Reading, Berkshire.

Impression number	10	9	8	7	6	5	4	3	2	1
Year		2004	2003	2002	2001	2000	1999			

CONTENTS

ACKNOWLEDGEMENTS

The authors would like to thank a number of people who were involved in different capacities throughout the inception and production of this book. Thanks first go to Dr Virinder S. Kalra, Lecturer in the department of Sociology, Leicester University, England who gave invaluable guidance, moral and technical support and advice each step of the way. To Balbir K. Kalra and Amarjit K. Purewal for their patience and understanding during the entire process. Also, to J. S. Bhogal, Neelu Kalsi, G. S. Bhogal, Jaswinder Kaur and T. S. Nahal from California for their help and encouragement.

ABOUT THE AUTHORS

Surjit Singh Kalra is founder and director of the Panjabi Language Development Board in Birmingham U.K., a voluntary organisation dedicated to the promotion and development of the Panjabi language. He is the author of over twenty Panjabi teaching aids. He is a prolific writer and is widely published in the Panjabi press as well as having two books of short stories published. He retired in 1992 as head of the Community Language Service for Birmingham Education authority. He is presently the Sikh representative on the Inner Cities Religious Council.

Navtej Kaur Purewal is a lecturer at the University of Manchester in the Department of Sociology. She teaches Development and South Asian Studies. Her doctoral thesis was on Panjab.

Sue Tyson-Ward was formerly Subject Officer for Community Language examinations at a National Exam Board.

SYMBOLS AND ABBREVIATIONS

🔲	recorded cassette	m.	masculine
💬	dialogue	f.	feminine
✅	exercises	v.	variable adjective
🔲	language points	sing.	singular
🔑	key words	plu.	plural
		lit.	literally

INTRODUCTION

Geographically, the present day area of Panjab is divided between the nation states of India and Pakistan (see Map 1). This division took place in 1947 upon the departure of the British from colonial rule of the sub-continent. While the language and culture of East and West Panjab are similar, there are religious differences, with Muslims being the predominant group in Pakistan Panjab, Hindus and Sikhs in Indian Panjab, and a substantial Christian minority in both parts. Panjab has come to some prominence in the West because of the long history of migration from the region to the four corners of the world.

1. Map 2
2. Pakistan
3. India
4. Nepal
5. Bhutan
6. Sri lanka
7. Bangladesh

Map 1   Indian sub-continent

Map 2   Panjab and the 'Five Rivers'

Source: Mawi and Tiwana, 1990

There are, therefore, mainly three areas of the world where Panjabi is spoken; in East Panjab (India) where it is a state language, in West Panjab (Pakistan) where it is most widely spoken and in the diaspora, particularly Britain, North America, East Africa and Australasia. This wide geographic spread of the language is ironic given the fact that the word Panjabi – also spelt Punjabi – designates the language of the 'Panj – ab', the 'Five Rivers'. These are the Jhelum, Chenab, Ravi, Beas and the Satluj (see Map 2).

No accurate figures are available on the number of Panjabi speakers, either as a first or second language, but if the three Panjabs and various dialects are taken into account an approximation of 100 million would not be too far from the truth. One of the main problems with designating the exact number of Panjabi speakers is the presence of a large number of distinct dialects that are spoken across the large geographical area of East and West Panjab. There are some eleven recognised dialects of Panjabi: Majhi, Bhattiani, Rathni, Ludhianwi, Doabi, Patialwi, Powadhi, Malwi, Multani (Siraiki), Putohari and Hindko. The last three can arguably call Panjabi a dialect of themselves and are all spoken in the Pakistan part of Panjab. In the diaspora the most spoken form of Panjabi is the Doabi, and encompasses those speakers from the Jalandhar area of East Panjab.

Given the great variety of Panjabi there is some debate as to what is standard. This book is based upon the Majhi dialect which is the everyday form used in Lahore and Amritsar. The most important point is that once you have mastered the language using this book you will be understood across the Panjab. The language used here is neither the colloquial rural nor the urban literary, as the focus of this course has been on developing an ability to communicate in as many different situations as possible.

One of the more interesting facts about the Panjabi language is that where it is numerically the most widely spoken, in Pakistani Panjab, it is hardly written at all. Panjabi is most often written in East Panjab in the Gurmukhi script. It is also possible to write the language in the Persian script often referred to as Shahmukhi in this context. However, in the last one hundred years or so, Panjabi has become closely associated with Sikhs and Sikhism, thus Gurmukhi has also become associated with Panjabi. Gurmukhi literally means 'proceeding from the mouth of the Guru', and it is widely acknowledged that Guru Angad, the second Sikh Guru

(1504–1552 AD), began the process of modifying existing scripts of the time laying the basis for the modern Panjabi alphabet that is used in this book.

Despite the modern day usage of Gurmukhi, the first Panjabi literature was written in Shahmukhi, and popular history associates this writing with Shaikh Farid and Goraknath. However, the literary period of the language begins with the sacred scriptures of the Sikhs, the *Guru Granth Sahib*. This collection of writings by the Sikh Gurus is probably the first manuscript of the Panjabi language. After the period of the Gurus, it was the Sufi poets who developed the Panjabi language. In fact it is the folk literature developed by the Sufis, and particularly the Quissa – love ballad form – which has had a long and lasting impact on the development of Panjabi literature. The stories of Heer-Ranjha and Mirza Sahiba are deeply embedded in the everyday life and culture of Panjab.

During the period of British colonial rule, the advent of the printing press saw the proliferation of the Panjabi language in the Gurmukhi script. Pamphlets, journals, novels and short stories all began to appear at the beginning of the twentieth century using the Panjabi typewriter. However, the official language of the time was either English or Urdu. The division of Panjab in 1947 between East (India) and West (Pakistan) and subsequently of East Panjab in 1966 led to the formation of the State of Panjab in the Indian Union. Panjabi is the official language of communication in East Panjab and the modern development of the language has been greatly accelerated by state patronage. Indeed, the development of Panjabi University in Patiala is one such example of state sponsorship.

Language may be the basis of culture, but there are many other aspects of Panjabi society and everyday life that impinge on the use of language. We have included a Commentary section in each unit which will introduce various aspects of the social and cultural life of the three Panjabs, although these are by no means exhaustive discussions of the rich culture of Panjab and the Panjabi diaspora.

HOW TO USE THIS COURSE

Who is this course for?

This course in Panjabi has been designed for the absolute beginner who may or may not have studied a language before. The course will be useful for people who want to learn Panjabi in order to speak with their Panjabi friends and relatives, to communicate with Panjabi communities in relation to their work, to learn about aspects of Panjabi culture and society or to travel to Panjab itself. The course will also be useful for those who already know a little Panjabi but who may not have the confidence to speak and even for those fluent in spoken Panjabi but who wish to learn to read and write the Gurmukhi script. Throughout the course you will come across a number of different situations in which you will learn how to make requests, ask and give information and to express your feelings. The units include dialogues, language points and background information about Panjab and Panjabi people both in the region of Panjab as well as in other parts of the world where Panjabi communities have settled.

The course is divided into two parts. The first part (Units 1–10) is specifically designed for those who want to learn the basics of grammar and vocabulary in order to communicate in a simple manner and also enable you to read and write simple sentences. The second part (Units 11–16) will help you to expand your knowledge of spoken Panjabi further and is designed for those who are committed to becoming proficient in the Gurmukhi script.

Overall, the course introduces you to a wide range of vocabulary and covers the basic grammar of Panjabi. By the end of the course, you will be able to understand the spoken language, communicate in Panjabi in a number of everyday situations while also having a sufficient level of understanding of the written language to begin to read newspapers and to write letters. We hope that this course will be the beginning of your journey into the world of the Panjabi language.

How to use this course

The structure of the book is outlined in the contents pages. It is recommended that you read the introductory chapters before proceeding with the course. The Panjabi script and sound system follows this section and it is advisable to work through this section regardless of whether you intend to learn the script or not. Through this section you will gain practice of listening, speaking and reading which will help you for the rest of the course. After the script chapter, the book is divided into sixteen units. The pattern of each unit is as follows:

- First there is an outline in English of what you will learn in the unit.
- ਗੱਲ ਬਾਤ gall baat̲ (Dialogue): Each unit has two or three dialogue passages containing situations and commonly used speech which include the vocabulary and grammar to be covered in that unit. In the first part (Units 1–10) the dialogues use Gurmukhi, Roman script and English translations. In the remainder of the book (Units 11–16) the dialogues are only in Gurmukhi and English. However, Roman is maintained in the vocabulary sections throughout the book.
- ਸ਼ਬਦਾਵਲੀ shabd̲aavalee (Vocabulary): The vocabulary sections follow each Dialogue and include all new words, and sometimes key expressions, which appear in the dialogue text. All nouns are denoted according to their masculine or feminine (m/f) gender in parentheses and all adjectives which vary according to gender and number are identified with a (v).
- ਅਭਿਆਸ abhiaas (Exercises): These follow the vocabulary and often make reference to the dialogues that they follow. There is a range of different exercises including true/false, matching, comprehension, 'fill in the blanks' and crosswords.
- ਬੋਲੀ ਬਾਰੇ bolee baare (Language points). These sections cover the main grammar points which appear in the dialogues.

Each new grammar point is explained clearly using examples to illustrate. Often, English equivalents to the Panjabi are given alongside the explanations.

■ ਵਿਆਖਿਆ viaakhiaa (Commentary): These sections introduce you to various aspects of Panjabi culture which have been touched upon in the content of the dialogues. These will help you to become acquainted with colloquial speech, social etiquette and Panjabi history, traditions and customs.

■ ਅਭਿਆਸ abhiaas (Exercises): Further exercises come at the end of each unit and review some of the main vocabulary, content and grammatical elements that were introduced in that unit. While the exercises that come after the dialogues in the units do not contain references to grammar, the exercises at the end of the units may test you on your ability to use the grammar you have learned.

At the end of the book there is a key to the exercises so that you can check your answers. The course concludes with a Panjabi–English glossary which will be of use to you throughout the course in referring to the English definitions of Panjabi words which appear in the units.

How to study each unit

■ Read the summary at the beginning of each unit to learn about what will be covered.

■ Study the dialogues using the vocabulary lists for words that you do not understand and then read the dialogues aloud.

■ Read the commentary section which will give you the relevant background to the dialogues.

■ Complete the exercises which follow the dialogues and vocabulary. Check your answers with the key to the exercises at the end of the book.

■ Go through the grammar sections to understand the new grammar points introduced.

■ After learning the grammar, read the dialogue again to make sure that you fully understood the content.

■ Go back to the dialogue and repeat it as often as you can, acting out the roles of the different characters.

■ Complete the exercises at the end of the unit, checking your answers with the key to the exercises at the end of the book.

How to use the course with the cassette

The book is accompanied by an audio tape which will help you to recognise and distinguish the Panjabi sound system and also to improve your listening and speaking abilities. While the book is in itself a complete course, the audio tape will be an added advantage for all Panjabi learners as it contains pronunciation exercises, dialogues from the units and oral comprehension activities based on the ਅਭਿਆਸ abhiaas (Exercises).

As you begin to go through the first part of the book (Units 1–10), you should listen to the recording of each ਗੱਲ ਬਾਤ gall baat (Dialogue) as you read it. Listen to it again without looking at the book once you have understood the general meaning. This will allow you to pay attention to the pronunciation and intonation of the speakers. Imitating the speakers in the dialogues is a useful way of picking up the language quickly. As you progress through the course to the second part (Units 11–16), you should try to listen to the dialogue on the tape without reading it in the book.

THE PANJABI SCRIPT AND SOUND SYSTEM

Introduction

Panjabi is most commonly written in the Gurmukhi script which is the most complete and accurate way to represent Panjabi sounds. Unlike English, the Gurmukhi script follows a 'one sound–one symbol' principle. There are a few exceptions to this rule and these will become apparent throughout the book. However, with some practice you will be able to recognise the characters and know their names and sounds. Ultimately, with even a basic knowledge of the sound system, you will be able to read and write Panjabi in the Gurmukhi script.

The Gurmukhi alphabet has forty letters including thirty-seven consonants and three basic vowel sign bearers. There are ten clear pure vowels and three auxiliary signs. The most striking characteristic of the Gurmukhi script, in comparison with English, is that, with the exception of five, all letters are joined by a line across the top. Like English and other European, Latin-based languages, it is written and read from left to right. However, there are neither capital letters in Panjabi nor articles such as 'a' and 'the'. Panjabi spellings are, for the most part, regular and relatively simple to learn, though you may come across variations in spellings of some words. However, as is the case in English, Panjabi spellings are not fully standardised.

Handwritten Panjabi, as with any script, differs from person to person in style. Some people prefer to write Panjabi without lifting a pen, making curves and having an irregular top line. It is up to the individual as to what sort of style he or she wants to adopt. Our advice to new learners is to follow the simple, clear style of lettering. There are a number of Panjabi fonts available on computer disk which have differing typefaces, some of which are very clear, attractive and decorative.

Equivalent sounds which have been given in romanised (English) script are only approximate since the Gurmukhi alphabet has many unfamiliar sounds to the English speaker which often may not be exactly represented by the English alphabet. It is hoped that you will use the cassette, attend classes, or seek help from a native speaker so as to perfect your pronunciation and to familiarise yourself with the sounds. In order to learn any language it is important to follow these basic rules: listen carefully, repeat aloud and distinctly, and do not worry about making mistakes. Apart from unfamiliar sounds, there are nasal and double sounds, intonation, stress and different dialects which might initially dishearten the student. However, with a little practice, you will begin to enjoy learning Panjabi.

Transliteration

The standard modern system of transliteration (the writing of Panjabi in the Roman alphabet) is used in this book with some modifications. As there are forty letters, ten vowel sounds and three auxiliary signs in Panjabi, it is necessary to adapt the standard English alphabet. You will note two ways of distinguishing letters:

1 by a combination of two English letters such as rh, kh, bh, nh, etc. In those few cases where these letters appear together but *not* in combination, for instance, a 'r' and 'h' appear together, a '-' is shown between those letters.
2 by underlining, for example, the letter n (<u>n</u>) indicates nasalisation or underlining ch (<u>ch</u>) indicates an aspirated sound.

Consonants
The Panjabi alphabet

South Asian languages are richly endowed with sounds and consonants. Sanskrit may have been one of the first languages to group the letters according to their sounds. At one time there were only thirty-five letters in the Panjabi script, but later five more letters were added in order to accommodate Urdu sounds correctly. This need arose because of the many loan words from Urdu used in Panjabi. More recently, an extra character (.ੜ l) was introduced, though it has not become popular and hence will not be included in this book. The complete Panjabi alphabet is given in Table A.

Table A Panjabi alphabet

ੳ	ਅ	ੲ	ਸ	ਹ
—	a	—	s	h
ਕ	ਖ	ਗ	ਘ	ਙ
k	kh	g	gh	ng
ਚ	ਛ	ਜ	ਝ	ਞ
ch	<u>ch</u>	j	jh	nj
ਟ	ਠ	ਡ	ਢ	ਣ
t	th	d	dh	nh
ਤ	ਥ	ਦ	ਧ	ਨ
<u>t</u>	<u>th</u>	<u>d</u>	<u>dh</u>	n
ਪ	ਫ	ਬ	ਭ	ਮ
p	ph	b	bh	m
ਯ	ਰ	ਲ	ਵ	ੜ
y	r	l	w/v	rh
ਸ਼	ਖ਼	ਗ਼	ਜ਼	ਫ਼
sh	<u>kh</u>	<u>gh</u>	z	f

It is quite possible to learn the characters of the Gurmukhi script (ਗੁਰਮੁਖੀ ਲਿਪੀ gurmukhee lipee) and sounds of the language at the same time as, by and large, Panjabi is a phonetic language. It is more accurate to call the Panjabi writing system a syllabary because each character represents a syllable. It is important to note that two phonetic features of all North Indian languages are the system of contrasts between aspirated and unaspirated consonants and the contrast between retroflex and dental consonants. These do not occur in English. Aspirated consonants are accompanied by an audible expulsion of breath, whereas non-aspirated consonants are those produced with minimal breath. The letter 'k' in the word 'kit' and 't' in the word 'top' come close to Panjabi aspirated consonants. The problem for English speakers arises with non-aspirated consonants. To get an idea of the difference between the two, try saying the words 'kit' and 'top' while holding your breath. In dental consonants the tongue touches the upper front teeth, whereas with the retroflex consonants the tip of the tongue curls upwards against the palate (see diagrams in Appendix) The nearest approximations to English are the 't' sound in the word 'eighth' which is dental-like and the 'd' in the word 'breadth' which is retroflex-like.

There is a range of technical terms used to describe the pronunciation of Panjabi consonants. For those who are interested in technical, and linguistic matters these can be found in the Appendix. The important thing is to be able to distinguish between the different consonants. The audio tape or the help of a native speaker are invaluable tools in this process.

Panjabi syllabary

The syllabary in Table B gives the Panjabi letters in groups, according to pronunciation.

Table B   Panjabi Syllabary

Gurmukhi	Translit -eration	Pronunciation
ਸ	s	as 's' in 'sun'.
ਹ	h	this 'h' sound as in 'ahead' is the simplest form, although there is considerable variety, which will be discussed later.
ਕ	k	as 'k' in 'sky', but with less release of breath.
ਖ	kh	as 'k' in 'kit' but with stronger release of breath. No English equivalent .
ਗ	g	as 'g' in 'go' but with less release of breath.
ਘ	gh	as 'gh' in 'ghost' said quickly. No English equivalent.

ਙ	ng	as 'ng' in 'sing'. No English equivalent.
ਚ	ch	as 'ch' as in 'cheese' but with less release of breath.
ਛ	<u>ch</u>	strongly aspirated form of 'ch'. No English equivalent.
ਜ	j	as 'j' in 'jeer' but with less release of breath and with the tongue against the lower teeth.
ਝ	jh	the stronger aspirated counterpart of the above, somewhat like 'bridge'. No English equivalent.
ਞ	nj	representing the palatal nasal sound. No English equivalent.
ਟ	t	as 't' in 'train' but with the tongue further back and with less release of breath.
ਠ	th	the strongly aspirated counterpart of the above. No English equivalent.
ਡ	d	as 'd' in 'drum' but with tongue further back and with less release of breath.
ਢ	dh	strongly aspirated form of the above. No English equivalent.
ਣ	nh	representing the retroflex nasal sound. No English equivalent.
ਤ	<u>t</u>	unaspirated soft 't'. No English equivalent.
ਥ	<u>th</u>	as '<u>th</u>' in 'thermos', strongly aspirated form of the above.
ਦ	<u>d</u>	as 'th' in 'then' with less release of breath.
ਧ	<u>dh</u>	strongly aspirated form of the above. No English equivalent.
ਨ	n	as 'n' in 'nice' but with the tongue flatter against the front teeth.

ਪ	p	as 'p' in 'spin' but with less release of breath.
ਫ	ph	as 'f' in 'fund', aspirated form of the above, though many Panjabi speakers pronounce 'ph' as 'f'.
ਬ	b	as 'b' in 'bin' but with less release of breath.
ਭ	bh	as 'bh' in 'club-house' spoken quickly. No English equivalent.
ਮ	m	as 'm' in 'mother'.
ਯ	y	as 'y' in 'yet'.
ਰ	r	as 'r' in 'motor.' This sound is always fully voiced and never lost like the English 'r'.
ਲ	l	as 'l' in 'life'.
ਵ	v/w	this sound lies between the English sounds 'v' and 'w'. However, unlike the English 'v' the lower lip hardly touches the upper teeth; unlike the English 'w' there is no lip-rounding. For transliteration purposes we only use 'v'.
ੜ	rh	no English equivalent.
ਸ਼	sh	as 'sh' in 'ship'.
ਖ਼	<u>kh</u>	similar to 'ch' in Scottish 'loch'. No English equivalent.
ਗ਼	<u>gh</u>	no English equivalent.
ਜ਼	z	as 'z' in 'zip'.
ਫ਼	f	as 'f' in 'find'.

Consonants with a dot

It is also important to note the distinction between plain consonants and those consonants which are marked by a dot, as shown in Table C.

Table C   Consonants with dots

ਸ	ਸ਼	ਖ	ਖ਼	ਗ	ਗ਼	ਜ	ਜ਼	ਫ	ਫ਼
s	sh	kh	<u>kh</u>	g	<u>gh</u>	j	z	ph	f

These letters are named by adding the words ਪੈਰੀਂ ਬਿੰਦੀ **paireen bindee** to the name of the letter, so ਸ਼ is called ਸੱਸੇ ਪੈਰੀਂ ਬਿੰਦੀ **sasse paireen bindee**, which literally means sassa with a dot in its foot. Many Panjabi speakers do not make a distinction between ਖ ਖ਼, ਗ ਗ਼, and ਫ ਫ਼. There are two main reasons for this, first, their pronunciation is quite similar and second, they are used to differentiate borrowed words from Urdu, the knowledge of which is decreasing in East Panjab. You may come across written texts in which writers have not used the dot. In this book, however, we have maintained its use.

Subjoined consonants

Some Panjabi words require consonants to be written in a conjunct form, which takes the shape of a subscript to the main letter. The second consonant is written under the first as a subscript. The reason for this is discussed after we have looked at Panjabi vowels. There are only three commonly used subjoined letters (see Table D) and to distinguish them from their normal forms the word ਪੈਰੀਂ **paireen**, which means *belonging to the foot*, is attached under the letter.

Table D Subjoined consonants

Full letter	Name of full letter		Subjoined letter	Name of subjoined letter		Transliteration
ਹ	ਹਾਹਾ	haahaa	੍ਹ	ਪੈਰੀਂ ਹਾਹਾ	paireen haahaa	h
ਰ	ਰਾਰਾ	raaraa	੍ਰ	ਪੈਰੀਂ ਰਾਰਾ	paireen raaraa	r
ਵ	ਵੱਵਾ	vavvaa	੍ਵ	ਪੈਰੀਂ ਵੱਵਾ	paireen vavvaa	v

For the purposes of transliteration there is no special sign for the subjoined character so you will have to pay careful attention to the Panjabi spelling.

Nasalisation

There are five nasal consonants in Panjabi:

■ ਙ ng   ■ ਞ ng   ■ ਣ nh   ■ ਨ n   ■ ਮ m

As shown in the syllabary, the nasal consonants belong to the five different classes of consonants. Nasalisation is produced by directing a substantial part of the breath towards the nasal cavity as the letter is being uttered. In addition there are two nasalisation signs in Panjabi which accompany consonants:

■ ਬਿੰਦੀ   bin<u>d</u>ee   •   ■ ਟਿੱਪੀ   tippee   ੰ

These will be dealt with in detail later.

Pronunciation of consonants

Most letters in Panjabi have a fixed pronunciation, however some are variable and this depends on their position in a word. Consider the letters in Table E.

Table E Pronunciation of consonants

	ਘ	ਝ	ਧ	ਧ	ਭ
	gh	jh	dh	<u>dh</u>	bh
Sound at beginning of word	ਕ	ਚ	ਟ	ਤ	ਪ
	k	ch	t	<u>t</u>	p
Sound in middle or at end of word	ਗ	ਜ	ਡ	ਦ	ਬ
	g	j	d	<u>d</u>	b

Perhaps the most variable pronunciation of a single consonant in Panjabi is that of the letter ਹ *h*. Words beginning with ਹ *h* and those where no vowel precedes or affects it, carry the *h* sound as it would be used in English. For instance:

ਹਕੁਮਤ hakoom<u>t</u> *government*   ਹਕੀਮ hakeem *doctor*

However, when ਹ *h* is used in the middle of a word following consonants and vowels its pronunciation is varied. We will return to this point after considering the vowel symbols and sounds.

Vowels

There are ten vowels in Panjabi in contrast to the English five (*a, e, i, o, u*). Panjabi vowels are generally pronounced as they are written, following the one sign – one sound rule. They are pure vowels making only one sound. However, there are two forms that vowels can take. The independent vowel form which does not require a consonant and the dependent form which is attached to a consonant. All consonants use the dependent form of the vowel. Tables F and G show the dependent vowels on their own and combined with the letter ਸ *s*.

Table F   Dependent vowels on their own

	Vowel sign		Name of vowel	
1	invisible	a	ਮੁਕਤਾ	mukṯaa
2		aa	ਕੰਨਾ	kannaa
3	f	i	ਸਿਹਾਰੀ	sihaaree
4	ੀ	ee	ਬਿਹਾਰੀ	bihaaree
5	▬	u	ਔਂਕੜ	aunkarh
6	≋	oo	ਦੁਲੈਂਕੜੇ	dulainkarhe
7	◝	e	ਲਾਂਵ	laanv
8	◠	ai	ਦੁਲਾਂਵਾਂ	dulaanvaan
9	◟	o	ਹੋੜਾ	horhaa
10	◝	au	ਕਨੌੜਾ	kanaurhaa

Table G   Dependent vowels in combination with *s*

Consonant and vowel sign		Pronunciation
ਸ	sa	*a* in ahead
ਸਾ	saa	*a* in part
ਸਿ	si	*i* in it
ਸੀ	see	*ee* in see
ਸੁ	su	*u* in put
ਸੂ	soo	*oo* in food
ਸੇ	se	*a* in cake
ਸੈ	sai	*a* in man
ਸੋ	so	*o* in show
ਸੌ	sau	*o* in bought

You may note that the vowels are divided into five pairs. In the first three, the distinction is between a short and long sound, for example between *u* and *oo*. In the last two pairs the distinction is between closed and open sounds so *e* is closed and *ai* is open sounding.

Short *a* sound – muk̲taa

We have seen that in Panjabi there are ten vowels and they are represented by nine symbols. The vowel **muk̲taa** has no equivalent sign to be used with consonants. The individual consonant expresses its own sound and also implies an *a* sound with it. This means that, unlike English, words can be formed with consonants only without using any visible vowel. Each consonant has an inherent sound, making it a syllable on its own. However, there is no symbol for this sound in Panjabi, though we have chosen to represent **muk̲taa** with the letter *a* for purposes of transliteration. Examples of the use of **muk̲taa** can be found in many borrowed words from English, for example: ਕਪ **kap**, *cup*, and ਮਗ **mag**, *mug*.

The inherent *a* is not pronounced in three main positions:

■ at the end of a word, e.g. ਕਾਰ **kaar**
■ with a subjoined consonant, e.g. ਸ੍ਰੀ **sree**
■ at a syllable break, e.g. ਗਰਦਨ, ਗਰ–ਦਨ **gar–d̲an**

Independent vowels

The independent form can occur in three ways. First, when the vowel comes at the beginning of a word or a syllable, second in those instances where two vowel sounds are required as a consonant cannot support two vowels, and third, in a dipthong – when two vowels are present in one syllable. In fact one of the features of Panjabi is the presence of many dipthongs, sometimes with three vowel sounds in one word with no consonants, for instance ਆਇਆ **aaiaa**, (*he*) *came*.

Independent vowels are represented by dependent vowels carried by the first three letters of the Panjabi alphabet.

ੳ ਉੜਾ **oorhaa**   ਅ ਐੜਾ **airhaa**   ੲ ੲੀੜੀ **eerhee**

They are never used on their own and do not represent any consonant sounds. They *must* be accompanied by their allocated vowel signs. Their main function is to denote their own respective vowel sounds. They are founder, basic or parent vowel bearers representing the ten sounds.

However, the pronunciation of both independent and dependent vowels is the same (see Table H).

Table H   Independent vowel

Formula	Example word	Trans-literation	Meaning
⌐ u is added to ੳ to give ਉ	ਉਪਜ	upaj	*production*
≈ oo is added to ੳ to give ਊ	ਊਠ	ooth	*camel*
⌐ o is added to ੳ to give ਓ	ਓਟ	ot	*shelter*
Invisible sign 'a' is added to ਅ	ਅਮਰ	amar	*immortal*
⌐ aa is added to a to give ਆ	ਆਟਾ	aataa	*flour*
≈ ai is added to ਅ to give ਐ	ਐਨਕ	ainak	*spectacles*
⌐ au is added to ਅ to give ਔ	ਔਰਤ	aura<u>t</u>	*woman*
f i is added to ੲ to give ਇ	ਇਨਾਮ	inaam	*prize*
ੀ ee is added to ੲ to give ਈ	ਈਸਾ	eesaa	*Jesus*
⌐ e i5s added to ੲ to give ਏ	ਏਕਤਾ	ek<u>t</u>aa	*unity*

Silent vowel signs

In English there are some silent or soft spoken consonants, for example *r* and *k*. There are no such consonants in Panjabi, however there are silent vowels. These are not often found in modern Panjabi but occur often in the sacred language of Sikh religious texts. Silent vowels give special meaning to the word they are referring to. The most common use of the silent vowel you will come across is in the Sikh greeting ਸਤਿ ਸ੍ਰੀ ਅਕਾਲ **sa<u>t</u>(i) sree akaal**. Note that the **sihaaree** in the word ਸਤਿ has no effect on the pronunciation, however its presence does alter the meaning:

■ ਸਤ sa<u>t</u> *extract*   ■ ਸੱਤ sa<u>tt</u> *seven*   ■ ਸਤਿ sa<u>t</u>(i) *true*

In this example we have included the silent vowel in brackets for purposes of illustration, however throughout the rest of the book the silent vowel is not included in the transliterated text.

Tones

One of the unique features of Panjabi, in the variety of modern South Asian languages, is the presence of pitch contours. These change the meaning of the word depending on the way it sounds. In technical terms these are called 'tones' and there are three types: low, high and level. The Panjabi tone system is far less complex than Chinese, the best known tone language. The low tone is characterised by lowering the voice below the normal pitch and then rising back in the following syllable. In the high tone the pitch of the voice rises above its normal level falling back at the following symbol. The level tone is carried by the remaining words. Tones are not represented by any letters or symbols in the Gurmukhi script. In this course we are not marking words with tone signs, as we believe this will create confusion. The best manner to learn tonality is from repetition from the audio tape or listening and imitating native speakers.

Table I illustrates how tone can change the meaning of a word.

Table I   Tone illustrations

Low tone			Level tone			High tone		
ਝਾ	jhaa	*peep*	ਚਾਅ	cha-aa	*desire*	ਚਾਹ	chaah	*tea*
ਘੋੜਾ	ghorhaa	*horse*	ਕੋੜਾ	korhaa	*whip*	ਕੋਹੜਾ	kohrhaa	*leper*
ਘੜੀ	gharhee	*watch*	ਕੜੀ	karhee	*link of a chain*	ਕੜ੍ਹੀ	karhhee	*turmeric curry*

Return of ਹ haahaa

We have already noted the variable pronunciation of the consonant ਹ *h*. Now that we have covered vowels and tones, we can return to look at some of the other varieties of **haahaa**'s pronunciation.

1 When ਹ is preceded by a **sihaaree** the pronunciation of the vowel changes to resemble **dulaanvaan**. For instance the word ਸਹਿਰ **shahir** is pronounced ਸ਼ੇਹਰ **shair**. The pronunciation of the word is therefore converted into a high tone.

2 When ਹ is accompanied by **aunkarh**, the pronunciation of the word changes to resemble **kanaurhaa**. For instance the word ਬਹੁਤ **bahut** is pronounced ਬੌਹਤ **bauht** once again changing the word to a high tone.

3 In a similar manner, when the letter preceding the ਹ has either the **aunkarh** or **sihaaree** vowel attached, then the

pronunciation of the word changes so as to produce the **haurhaa** and **laanv** vowels respectively. For example: ਸੁਹਣਾ **suhnhaa** is pronounced as ਸੋਹਣਾ **sohnhaa** and ਸਿਹਤ **sihat** is pronounced as ਸੇਹਤ **sehat**.

Subjoined consonants revisited

As we previously noted, a few Panjabi words require consonants to be written in a subjoined form, which takes the shape of a subscript to the main letter. The reason for this is to indicate that the inherent **muktaa** vowel is not present. Where vowels are present on the first letter, these are meant to be applied to the subjoined consonant. Therefore, in the word ਪ੍ਰੇਮ **prem**, there is no *a* symbol in the transliteration indicating the absence of the **muktaa**. The **laanv** vowel is applied to the *r* in the foot of the *p*. Note that the pronunciation of the subjoined consonant is the same as the normal consonant.

Auxiliary signs
The double sound ਅਧਕ **adhak** ੱ

The function of the ਅਧਕ **adhak** ੱ is to allocate a double sound to the particular letter that it is assigned to. It should be placed above the preceding letter that is to be read twice, however, in practice it is placed between the two letters. Therefore, when the **adhak** occurs between two letters, it is the second of the two that is to be repeated. For example, in the Panjabi word for **thigh**, ਪੱਟ **patt**, the **adhak** affects the letter ਟ *t* changing the sound of the word from **pat** to **patt**. In some cases another vowel sound may come in between the two letters, but the **adhak** still affects the second letter, for example in the word ਬੱਚਿਓ **bachchio**, the **adhak** comes before the **sihaaree** vowel but still affects the letter ਚ **ch**, so it is pronounced **chch**. The **adhak** is a very important, though subtle device, as two letters without an **adhak** give rise to completely different meanings. For example ਪਗ **pag** means **foot**, whereas ਪੱਗ **pagg** means **turban**. A similar effect can be seen in English with the words **super** and **supper**.

Nasal sounds: ਬਿੰਦੀ **bindee** ੰ and ਟਿੱਪੀ **tippee** ੰ

The **bindee** and the **tippee** both serve to add a nasal sound to a particular vowel. The **bindee** is used with **kannaa, laanv, dulaanvaan, bihaaree**,

horhaa and **kanaurhaa** and the independent forms of vowels where ੳ is the bearer. For example: ਗਾਂ gaan *cow*

The tippee is used with the muktaa, sihaaree, aunkarh and dulainkarhe. For example: ਖੰਡ khand *sugar*

The sound of the **tippee** and **bindee** is almost equivalent to the *n* in *pound* or *bangle*. However, their sound varies from the almost totally nasalised to a more fully pronounced *n* sound. For transliteration purposes the letter n is used for both the **tippee** and **bindee**.

Panjabi loan words

The Panjabi language has a substantial number of words which have been borrowed from the English language, for example *school*, *college*, *telephone*, *bus*, *pen*, *pencil*, *chalk*, *ticket*, and *computer*. Moreover, some Panjabi words have been adopted by English including *chutney*, *pandit*, *kebab*, *samosa*, *saree*, *dhobi*, and *guru*. Some English words borrowed by Panjabi have also been altered by Panjabi pronunciation and you will notice in the transliteration that English words and names have been written with this in mind.

Dictionary order

The letters in Panjabi dictionaries are arranged in the order of Table A, reading left to right, as are the order of words within each letter. The exceptions to this rule are those letters which are distinguished by a dot that is ਸ਼, ਖ਼ , ਗ਼, ਜ਼ and ੜ, as these letters occur within the non-dotted form. Subjoined letters are not differentiated from the full form. Dictionary order in the Gurmukhi script is based upon phonology as vowels precede consonants. Therefore, the vowel signs follow **muktaa**, **kannaa**, **sihaaree**, **bihaaree**, **aunkarh**, **dulainkarhe**, **laanv**, **dulaanvaan**, **horhaa**, **kanaurhaa**.

Writing

Panjabi words are made up partly of consonants and partly of vowel signs. Letters are written first and then the sound symbols. Panjabi punctuation is similar to that used in English. However, one distinct difference is that in Panjabi a vertical stroke is used at the end of a sentence to mark a full stop. For example: *My name is Ritu.*   ਮੇਰਾ ਨਾਮ ਰਿਤੂ ਹੈ ।

There are ten vowels represented by nine signs. Their positions relating to consonants are as follows ⌣ are written beneath the letter: ⌐ ⌐ ¬ ¬ are written above the letter; f is written on the left of the letter while ' and ੀ are written on the right. The three auxillary signs, ੰ ੱ ੰ are written above the letter. Panjabi is best written on lined paper initially. In English the letters rest on the line, whereas in Panjabi the horizontal headstroke is written upon the line, the characters then hang from the line, in much the same way as clothes hang from a washing line.

Panjabi alphabet ਪੰਜਾਬੀ ਵਰਣਮਾਲਾ ਗੁਰਮੁਖੀ ਲਿਪੀ
panjaabee varanhmaalaa gurmukhee lipee:

Letter	Name of letter		Sign of letter
ੳ	ਉੜਾ	oorhaa	—
ਅ	ਐੜਾ	airhaa	a
ੲ	ਈੜੀ	eerhee	—
ਸ	ਸੱਸਾ	sassaa	s
ਹ	ਹਾਹਾ	haahaa	h
ਕ	ਕੱਕਾ	kakkaa	k
ਖ	ਖੱਖਾ	khakhkhaa	kh
ਗ	ਗੱਗਾ	gaggaa	g
ਘ	ਘੱਗਾ	ghaggaa	gh
ਙ	ਙੰਙਾ	nganngaa	ng
ਚ	ਚੱਚਾ	chachchaa	ch
ਛ	ਛੱਛਾ	<u>chachchaa</u>	<u>ch</u>
ਜ	ਜੱਜਾ	jajjaa	j
ਝ	ਝੱਜਾ	jhajjaa	jh
ਞ	ਞੰਞਾ	nja<u>nn</u>jaa	nj
ਟ	ਟੈਂਕਾ	tai<u>n</u>kaa	t
ਠ	ਠੱਠਾ	thaththaa	th
ਡ	ਡੱਡਾ	daddaa	d
ਢ	ਢੱਡਾ	dhaddaa	dh
ਣ	ਣਾਣਾ	nhaanhaa	nh
ਤ	ਤੱਤਾ	<u>t</u>a<u>tt</u>aa	<u>t</u>
ਥ	ਥੱਥਾ	<u>thaththaa</u>	<u>th</u>
ਦ	ਦੱਦਾ	<u>daddaa</u>	<u>d</u>
ਧ	ਧੱਦਾ	<u>dhaddaa</u>	<u>dh</u>
ਨ	ਨੱਨਾ	nannaa	n
ਪ	ਪੱਪਾ	pappaa	p

ਫ	ਫੱਫਾ	phaphphaa	ph
ਬ	ਬੱਬਾ	babbaa	b
ਭ	ਭੱਬਾ	bhabbaa	bh
ਮ	ਮੱਮਾ	mammaa	m
ਯ	ਯੱਯਾ	yayyaa	y
ਰ	ਰਾਰਾ	raaraa	r
ਲ	ਲੱਲਾ	lallaa	l
ਵ	ਵੱਵਾ	vavvaa	v
ੜ	ੜਾੜਾ	rhaarhaa	rh
ਸ਼	ਸ਼ੱਸ਼ਾ	shashshaa	sh
ਖ਼	ਖ਼ੱਖ਼ਾ	<u>kh</u>a<u>kh</u><u>kh</u>aa	<u>kh</u>
ਗ਼	ਗ਼ੱਗ਼ਾ	<u>gh</u>a<u>gh</u><u>gh</u>aa	<u>gh</u>
ਜ਼	ਜ਼ੱਜ਼ਾ	zazzaa	z
ਫ਼	ਫ਼ੱਫ਼ਾ	faffaa	f

Relationship between independent and dependent vowels:

Independent	ਅ	ਆ	ਇ	ਈ	ਉ	ਊ	ਏ	ਐ	ਓ	ਔ
Dependent	–	ਾ	ਿ	ੀ	ੁ	ੂ	ੇ	ੈ	ੋ	ੌ
Transliteration	a	aa	i	ee	u	oo	e	ai	o	au

Sample reading and writing lessons

1 ਮੁਕਤਾ ਅ muk<u>t</u>aa a

The vowel **muk<u>t</u>aa** has no visible symbol in the Gurmukhi script. For transliteration purposes it is represented by the letter *a*.

Reading 1 ਕਰਮ, ਕਪ, ਕਮਰ
karam, kap, kamar
Karam, cup, Kamar

2 ਕਮਲ, ਮਗ ਭਰ
kamal, mag bhar
Kamal, fill the mug

3 ਅਮਰ, ਚਰਚ ਚਲ
amar, charach chal
Amar, go to the church

4 ਮਲਕ, ਜਗ ਭਰ
malak, jag bhar
Malik, fill the jug

Writing Pattern

ਅ ੨ ੨ੴ ਅਅ ਅਅ ਕ ‾ ਤ ਕ

ਗ ‾ ੮ ਗ ਅ ਚ ‾ ੮ ੮ ੮

ਜ ‾ ੭ ੜ ਜ ਪ ੮ ੮ ਪ

ਠ ‾ ੮ ਠ ਠ ਮ ੮ ੮ ੮ ਮ

ਤ ‾ ੮ ਤ ਲ ‾ ੮ ੮ ਲ

Exercises

1. Read the following sentences out loud and check your pronunciation with the audio recording.

a. ਕਪ ਭਰ ਕਰਮ   b. ਮਗ ਭਰ ਕਮਲ

c. ਭਰ ਜਗ ਮਲਕ   d. ਚਰਚ ਚਲ ਕਮਰ

2. Write out the following words:

a. ਕਮਲ   b. ਚਰਚ   c. ਜਗ

2 ਕੰਨਾ ਆ ' kannaa aa

The dependent form of the **kannaa** vowel is placed to the right of the letter that is affected. For transliteration purposes it is represented by the symbol *aa*.

Reading

1. ਸ਼ਾਮ, ਨਾਨਾ, ਵਾਲ ਵਾਹ
 shaam, naanaa, vaal vaah
 sham, grandfather, comb hair

2. ਰਾਮ, ਬਸ ਫੜ
 raam, bas pharh
 ram, catch the bus

3. ਚਾਚਾ, ਘਰ ਆ
 chaachaa, ghar aa
 uncle, come home

4. ਕਾਕਾ, ਅਨਾਰ ਖਾ
 kaakaa, anaar khaa
 baby, eat the pomegranate

Writing Pattern

ਸ → ੧ ੜ ਸ਼   ਹ → ੨ ੩ ਹ

ਅ ੧ ੩ ਅ ਅ   ਨ → ੨ ੨ ਨ

ੲ → ੨ ੲ ੲ   ਬ → ੨ ੩ ਬ

ੜ → ੨ ੬ ੜ   ੜ → ੨ ੬ ੜ

ਸ → ੧ ਸ ਸ   ਖ → ੮ ੮ ਖ ਖ

Exercises

1. Read the following sentences out loud and check your pronunciation with the audio recording.

a. ਨਾਨਾ ਬਸ ਫੜ   b. ਸ਼ਾਮ ਵਾਲ ਵਾਹ

c. ਕਾਕਾ ਘਰ ਆ   d. ਚਾਚਾ ਅਨਾਰ ਖਾ

2. Write out the following words

a. ਬਸ   b. ਸ਼ਾਮ   c. ਨਾਨਾ

3 ਅਧਕ <u>adh</u>ak ੱ

The ਅਧਕ <u>adh</u>ak ੱ should be placed above the preceding letter that is to be read twice, in practice, however, it is placed in between the two letters. Therefore, when the **adhak** occurs between two letters it is the second letter of the two that is to be repeated. For transliteration purposes the **adhak** has the effect of doubling the consonant effected.

Reading   1. ਅੱਖ, ਪੱਟ, ਲੱਤ
akhkh, patt, la<u>tt</u>
eye, thigh, leg

2. ਰੱਖ, ਪੱਗ ਸ਼ਾਮ
rakhkh, pagg shaam
sham, put on the turban

3. ਅੱਠ ਹੱਥ
aththh ha<u>thth</u>
eight hands

4. ਸੱਤ ਨੱਕ
satt nakk
seven noses

Writing pattern

Exercises

1. Read the following words out loud and check your pronunciation with the audio recording.

a. ਸ਼ਾਮ ਪੱਗ ਰੱਖ　　　　　b. ਅੱਠ ਨੱਕ
c. ਸੱਤ ਹੱਥ　　　　　　　d. ਅੱਖ, ਲੱਤ, ਪੱਟ

2. Write out the following words:

a. ਪੱਟ　　　　b. ਅੱਠ　　　　c. ਹੱਥ

4　ਸਿਹਾਰੀ ਇ f　sihaaree i

The dependent form of the sihaaree vowel is placed to the left of the letter being affected. For transliteration purposes it is represented by the letter *i*.

Reading　1. ਕਿਰਨ, ਇੱਟ, ਇੱਕ, ਕਿੱਲ　　　2. ਜਿੱਲ, ਸਿੱਧਾ ਲਿਖ
　　　　　　　kiran, itt, ikk, kill　　　　　jill, si<u>dh-dh</u>aa likh
　　　　　　　Kiran, brick, one, nail　　　　*Jill, write straight*

　　　　　　3. ਦਿਲਬਰ, ਰਿੱਛ ਗਿਣ　　　　4. ਇਹ ਚਾਰ ਹਿਰਨ ਹਨ
　　　　　　　<u>d</u>ilbar, ri<u>chch</u> ginh　　　ih chaar hiran han
　　　　　　　Dilbar, count the bears　　　*these are four deers*

Writing pattern

Exercises

1. Read the following sentences out loud and check your pronunciation with the audio recording.

a. ਇੱਕ ਇੱਟ   b. ਕਿਰਨ ਸਿੱਧਾ ਲਿਖ   c. ਦਿਲਬਰ ਕਿੱਲ ਗਿਣ   d. ਇਹ ਚਾਰ ਰਿੱਛ ਹਨ

2. Write the names in Gurmukhi of the items in the pictures.

a) richch   b) kill   c) hiran

5 ਬਿਹਾਰੀ ਦੀ ੀ **bihaaree ee**

The dependent form of the **bihaaree** vowel is placed to the right of the letter that is being affected. For transliteration purposes it is represented by the letter *ee*.

Reading

1. ਸੀਟੀ, ਡੱਬੀ, ਵਾਲੀ, ਸੀਤਾ
   seetee, dabbee, vaalee, seetaa
   whistle, small box, earring, Sita

3. ਚਾਚੀ ਖਤਾਈ ਲਿਆਈ
   chaachee khataaee liaaee
   Aunty has bought a biscuit

2. ਰੀਟਾ, ਗਲੀਚਾ ਸਾਫ਼ ਕਰ
   reetaa, ghaleechaa saaf kar
   Rita, clean the rug

4. ਈਸ਼ਰ ਦੀ ਬਿੱਲੀ ਕਾਲੀ ਸੀ
   eeshar dee billee kaalee see
   Ishar's cat was black

Writing pattern

Exercises

1. Read the following sentences out loud and check your pronunciation with the audio recording.

a. ਰੀਟਾ ਬਿੱਲੀ ਲਿਆਈ   b. ਸੀਤਾ ਖ਼ਤਾਈ ਲਿਆਈ
c. ਚਾਚੀ ਗਲੀਚਾ ਲਿਆਈ   d. ਈਸ਼ਰ ਸੀਟੀ ਲਿਆਈ

2. Write the names in Gurmukhi of the items in the pictures.

    a. seetee   b. billee   c. vaalee

6 ਔਂਕੜ ੁ _ au<u>n</u>karh u

The dependent form of the vowel **au<u>n</u>karh** is placed under the letter to be affected. For transliteration purposes it is represented by the letter *u*.

Reading
1. ਦੁੱਧ, ਢਕੱਣ, ਸੁਖ, ਪੀ
   du<u>dh</u> <u>dh</u>, dhakkanh, sukh, pee
   milk, lid, Sukh, drink
3. ਯੁਵਕ, ਜ਼ਬਾਨ ਨਾ ਕੱਢ
   yuvak zabaan naa kadh<u>dh</u>
   *Young boy! Do not stick
   out your tongue.*

2. ਉਪਕਾਰ, ਉੱਨ ਲਿਆ
   upkaar, unn liaa
   Upkar, bring the wool
4. ਗੁਲਾਬ, ਚੁੱਪ ਕਰ
   gulaab, chupp kar
   Gulab, keep quiet

Writing pattern

Exercises

1. Read the following sentences out loud and check your pronunciation with the audio recording.

a. ਸੁਖ ਚੱਕਣ ਲਿਆ   b. ਗੁਲਾਬ ਉੱਨ ਲਿਆ

c. ਯੁਵਕ ਦੁੱਧ ਪੀ   d. ਉਪਕਾਰ ਚੁੱਪ ਕਰ

2. Write the name of the following pictures in Gurmukhi:

a. dhakkanh   b. zabaan   c. unn

7 ਦੁਲੈਂਕੜੇ ਉ ੂ _dulainkarhe_   oo

The dependent form of the vowel **dulainkarhe** appears under the letter being affected. For purposes of transliteration the symbol *oo* is used to represent the **dulainkarhe**.

Reading   1. ਸੂਰ, ਫੜ, ਝਾੜੂ, ਭੂਪ

           soor, pharh, jhaarhoo, bhoop

           pig, hold, broom, Bhup

2. ਰੂਪ, ਆਰੂ ਖਾ

    roop, aarhoo khaa

    Rup, eat the peach

        3. ਸਰੂਪ ਦਾ ਊਠ

           Saroop _daa_ ooth

           Sarup's camel

4. ਅਨੂਪ, ਮੂਰਤ ਬਣਾ

    Anoop, moora_t_ banhaa

    Anup, draw a picture

Writing pattern

Exercises

1. Read the following sentences out loud and check your pronunciation with the audio recording.

a. ਸਰੂਪ ਦਾ ਊਠ   b. ਰੂਪ ਮੂਰਤ ਬਣਾ

c. ਅਨੂਪ ਆਰੂ ਖਾ   d. ਭੂਪ ਝਾੜੂ ਫੜ

2. Write the Gurmukhi of the items in the pictures.

a. ooth   b. soor   c. jhaarhoo

8 ਲਾਂਵ ਏ ` laanv e

The dependent form of the vowel **laanv** is placed on top of the affected letter. For transliteration purposes the letter e will be used to symbolise the **laanv**.

Reading 1. ਲੇਲੇ, ਪਿਆਰੇ, ਭੇਡ, ਮੇਰਾ   2. ਇਹ ਛੇ ਮੇਜ਼ ਹਨ
            lele, piaare, bhed, meraa   ih <u>ch</u>e mez han
            lambs, beloved, sheep, my   *These are six tables*

      3. ਉਹ ਜੇਨ ਦਾ ਸੇਬ ਏ   4. ਡੇਵਿਡ, ਸ਼ੇਰ ਦੇਖ
             uh jen <u>d</u>aa seb e   devid, sher <u>d</u>ekh
             That is Jane's apple   *David, look at the lion*

Exercises

1. Read the following sentences out loud and check your pronunciation with the audio recording.

a. ਇਹ ਛੇ ਲੇਲੇ ਹਨ   b ਲੇਲੇ ਪਿਆਰੇ ਹਨ
c. ਇਹ ਮੇਰਾ ਸੇਬ ਏ   d. ਉਹ ਭੇਡ ਏ

2. Fill in the blanks by writing the correct words in Gurmukhi:

a. _____ lele   b. _____ bhed   c. _____ seb

9 ਦੁਲਾਂਵਾਂ ਐ ` dulaanvaan ai

The dependent form of the vowel **dulaanvaan** is written on top of the affected letter. For transliteration purposes the symbol *ai* is used to represent **dulaanvaan**.

Reading

1. ਸਵੈਟਰ, ਬੈਗ, ਜਰਨੈਲ, ਪੈਰ
svaitar, baig, jarnail, pair
sweater, bag, Jarnail, foot

2. ਇਹ ਐਨਕ ਲੈ
ih ainak lai
Have these spectacles

3. ਅੱਜ ਐਤਵਾਰ ਹੈ
ajj aitvaar hai
Today is Sunday

4. ਇਹ ਕੈਮਰਾ ਮੇਰੀ ਭੈਣ ਦਾ ਹੈ
ih kaimraa meree bhainh daa hai
This is my sister's camera

Exercises

1. Read the following sentences out loud and check your pronunciation with the audio recording.

a. ਇਹ ਕੈਮਰਾ ਜਰਨੈਲ ਦਾ ਹੈ b ਇਹ ਮੇਰਾ ਸਵੈਟਰ ਹੈ

c. ਇਹ ਬੈਗ ਮੇਰੀ ਭੈਣ ਦਾ ਹੈ d. ਇਹ ਐਨਕ ਲੈ

2. Fill in the blanks by writing the correct words in Gurmukhi:

a. _____ bhainh   b. _____ aitvaar   c. _____ ainak

10 ਹੋੜਾ ੳ ੈ horhaa o

The dependent form of the vowel **horhaa** appears above the affected letter. For transliteration purposes the letter *o* is used to represent **horhaa**.

Reading 1. ਖੋਤਾ, ਮੋਟਾ, ਘੋੜਾ, ਸੋਟੀ
khotaa, motaa, ghorhaa, sotee
donkey, fat, horse, stick

2. ਸੋਹਣ ਕੋਲ ਤੋਤਾ ਹੈ
sohanh kol totaa hai
Sohan has a parrot.

3. ਰੋਟੀ ਖਾ ਮੋਹਨ
rotee khaa mohan
Eat your food Mohan.

4. ਆਓ ਬੱਚਿਓ ਮੋਰ ਦੇਖੋ
aao bachchio mor dekho
*Come on children look at
the peacock.*

Exercises

1. Read the following sentences out loud and check your pronunciation with the audio recording.

a. ਸੋਹਣ ਰੋਟੀ ਖਾ b ਖੋਤਾ ਮੋਟਾ ਹੈ

c. ਮੋਹਨ ਕੋਲ ਘੋੜਾ ਹੈ d. ਆਓ ਬੱਚਿਓ ਤੋਤਾ ਦੇਖੋ

2. Fill in the missing letters in Gurmukhi:

a. — ੪ khoṭaa   b. — ੴ motaa   c. — ੜ ghorhaa

11 ਕਨੌੜਾ ਔ ˆ kanaurhaa au

The dependent form of the **kanaurhaa** vowel appears above the affected letter. For transliteration purposes the symbol *au* is used to represent **kanaurhaa**.

Reading

1. ਫੌਜੀ, ਪੌੜੀ, ਬਲੌਰ, ਦੌੜ
   faujee, paurhee, balaur, ḏaurh
   soldier, ladder, playing marbles, run

2. ਸ਼ਰਨ ਕੌਰ, ਚੌਲ ਉਬਾਲ
   sharan kaur, chaul ubaal
   Sharan Kaur, boil the rice

3. ਉਹ ਔਰਤ ਕੌਣ ਹੈ ?
   uh auraṯ kaunh hai?
   Who is that woman?

4. ਇਹ ਮੇਰੇ ਖਿਡੌਣੇ ਹਨ
   ih mere khidaunhe han
   These are my toys.

Exercises

1. Read the following sentences out loud and check your pronunciation with the audio recording.

a. ਚੌਲ ਉਬਾਲ   b ਉਹ ਕੌਣ ਹੈ ?
c. ਉਹ ਫੌਜੀ ਹੈ   d. ਇਹ ਮੇਰੇ ਬਲੌਰ ਹਨ

2. Fill in the missing letters and vowels in Gurmukhi:

a. — ਲ chaul   b. ਿ — ਣੇ khidaunhe   c. — ਜੀ faujee

12 ਬਿੰਦੀ **bindee** •   and ਟਿੱਪੀ **tippee** ˘ **n**

The bindee and the tippee both serve to add a nasal sound to a particular vowel. For transliteration purposes, the letter **n** is used for both the *tippee* and bindee.

Reading

1. ਸਿੰਘ, ਚੁੰਜ, ਮੂੰਹ
   singh, chunj, moonh
   lion, beak, mouth

2. ਅੰਬ, ਜੰਞ, ਲੰਙਾ
   anb, jannj, lanngaa
   mango, marriage party, lame person

3. ਕਾਂ, ਗੇਂਦ, ਕੈਂਚੀ, ਮੀਂਹ
   kaan, gend, kainchee, meenh
   crow, ball, scissors, rain

4. ਹੋਂਠ, ਪੌਂਡ, ਉਂਗਲੀ, ਵਤਾਊਂ
   honth, paund, unglee, vataaoon
   lips, pound, finger, aubergine

Writing pattern

ਦ → ਦੁ ਦ੍ ਦ ੜ → ਝ ੜ ਝ

Exercises

1. Read the following words out loud and check your pronunciation with
the audio recording.

a. ਸਿੰਧ, ਜੰਦ, ਕੈਂਚੀ   b ਚੁੰਜ, ਲੰਝਾ, ਉਂਗਲੀ

c. ਮੂੰਹ, ਅੰਬ, ਮੀਂਹ   d. ਕਾਂ, ਗੋਂਦ, ਵਤਾਊਂ

2. Fill in the missing letters and vowels in Gurmukhi:

a. ਜ— jannj   b. ਲ— lanngaa   c. ਵ— vataaoon

1 ਤੁਹਾਡਾ ਕੀ ਹਾਲ ਹੈ?

tuhaadaa kee haal hai?

How are you?

In this unit you will learn:

- how to use simple greetings
- how to introduce yourself
- how to ask how people are

1 What is your name?

ਗੱਲ ਬਾਤ ੧ ਤੁਹਾਡਾ ਕੀ ਨਾਮ ਹੈ?

gall baat 1 tuhaadaa kee naam hai?

It is the first day of the new Panjabi class at Heywood College. Mr Charan Singh is the teacher and Jane, Henry and David are students.

ਚਰਨ ਸਿੰਘ **Charan Singh**	ਸਤਿ ਸ੍ਰੀ ਅਕਾਲ ਜੀ! sat sree akaal jee! *Hello!* (see Commentary section)
ਜੇਨ **Jane**	ਸਤਿ ਸ੍ਰੀ ਅਕਾਲ ਜੀ! sat sree akaal jee! *Hello!*
ਚਰਨ ਸਿੰਘ **Charan Singh**	ਮੇਰਾ ਨਾਮ ਚਰਨ ਸਿੰਘ ਹੈ। ਤੁਹਾਡਾ ਕੀ ਨਾਮ ਹੈ? meraa naam charan singh hai. tuhaadaa kee naam hai? *My name is Charan Singh. What's your name?* (to Jane)
ਜੇਨ **Jane**	ਜੀ ਮੇਰਾ ਨਾਮ ਜੇਨ ਹੈ। jee meraa naam jen hai. *My name is Jane.*

ਚਰਨ ਸਿੰਘ **Charan Singh**	ਅੱਛਾ ! ਤੁਹਾਡਾ ਕੀ ਨਾਮ ਹੈ ? ach<u>ch</u>aa. <u>t</u>uhaadaa kee naam hai? *OK! What's your name?* (to Henry)	
ਹੈਨਰੀ **Henry**	ਜੀ ਮੇਰਾ ਨਾਮ ਹੈਨਰੀ ਹੈ। jee meraa naam hainree hai. *My name is Henry.*	
ਚਰਨ ਸਿੰਘ **Charan Singh**	ਸ਼ਾਬਾਸ਼ ! shaabaash! *Well done!*	

David and Jane exchange greetings in an informal manner.

ਜੇਨ **Jane**	ਸਤਿ ਸ੍ਰੀ ਅਕਾਲ। ਮੇਰਾ ਨਾਂ ਜੇਨ ਏ। ਤੇਰਾ ਕੀ ਨਾਂ ਏ ? sa<u>t</u> sree akaal. meraa naa<u>n</u> jen e. <u>t</u>eraa kee naa<u>n</u> e? *Hello. My name is Jane. What's your name?*
ਡੇਵਿਡ **David**	ਸਤਿ ਸ੍ਰੀ ਅਕਾਲ। ਮੇਰਾ ਨਾਂ ਡੇਵਿਡ ਏ। sa<u>t</u> sree akaal. meraa naa<u>n</u> devid e. *Hello. My name is David.*

ਸ਼ਬਦਾਵਲੀ   **shab<u>d</u>aavalee   Vocabulary**

ਤੁਹਾਡਾ	<u>t</u>uhaadaa	*your* (formal)
ਕੀ	kee	*what*
ਨਾਮ	naam	*name* (m.) (formal)
ਹੈ	hai	*is* (formal)*
ਸਤਿ ਸ੍ਰੀ ਅਕਾਲ	sa<u>t</u> sree akaal	Sikh greeting (literal meaning: God is truth)
ਜੀ	jee	honorific particle signifying respect (see Commentary)
ਮੇਰਾ	meraa	*my*
ਅੱਛਾ	ach <u>ch</u>aa	*OK, alright*
ਸ਼ਾਬਾਸ਼	shaabaash	*well done*
ਤੇਰਾ	<u>t</u>eraa	*your* (informal)
ਨਾਂ	naa<u>n</u>	*name* (m.) (informal)
ਏ	e	*is* (informal)*

* The ways in which is, am and are are formed in Panjabi will be referred to in Unit 2

☑ ਅਭਿਆਸ   abhiaas   **Exercises**

After reading the dialogue and/or listening to the audio tape, try to do the
following exercises.

🖳 **1. True or false?**

a) ਤੁਹਾਡਾ	<u>t</u>uhaadaa	means *your*	True/ False
b) ਮੇਰਾ	meraa	means *my*	True/ False
c) ਅੱਛਾ	a<u>chchh</u>aa	means *well done*	True/ False

2. Arrange in correct word order

a) ਮੇਰਾ ਹੈ ਡੇਵਿਡ ਨਾਂ   meraa-hai-devid-naa<u>n</u>   *My name is David.*

b) ਤੁਹਾਡਾ ਹੈ ਨਾਮ ਕੀ?   <u>t</u>uhaadaa-hai-naam-kee?   *What is your name?*

c) ਨਾਂ ਏ ਕੀ ਤੇਰਾ?   naa<u>n</u>-e-kee-<u>t</u>eraa?   *What is your name?*

🎧 2 How are you?

🖳 ਗੱਲ ਬਾਤ ੨ ਤੁਹਾਡਾ ਕੀ ਹਾਲ ਹੈ?

gall baa<u>t</u> 2 <u>t</u>uhaadaa kee haal hai?

Parveen and Talat meet each other in the city centre. Parveen is with her
brother Rahim and sister Salma.

ਪਰਵੀਨ **Parveen**	ਅੱਸਲਾਮ ਅਲੈਕਮ. ਤੁਹਾਡਾ ਕੀ ਹਾਲ ਹੈ? asslaam alaikam. <u>t</u>uhaadaa kee haal hai? *Hello. How are you?*
ਤਲਤ **Talat**	ਵਾਲੈਕਮ ਅੱਸਲਾਮ. ਮੇਰਾ ਹਾਲ ਠੀਕ ਹੈ। vaalaikam asslaam. meraa haal theek hai. *Hello. I'm fine.*
ਪਰਵੀਨ **Parveen**	ਇਹ ਮੇਰਾ ਭਰਾ ਹੈ ਅਤੇ ਇਹ ਮੇਰੀ ਭੈਣ ਹੈ। ih meraa bharaa hai a<u>t</u>e ih meree bhainh hai. *This is my brother and this is my sister.*
ਤਲਤ **Talat**	ਕੀ ਤੁਹਾਡਾ ਪਰਵਾਰ ਠੀਕ ਹੈ? kee <u>t</u>uhaadaa parvaar theek hai? *Is your family alright?*

ਸਲਮਾ ਤੇ ਰਹੀਮ	ਸ਼ੁਕਰੀਆ। ਸਾਡਾ ਪਰਵਾਰ ਠੀਕ ਹੈ।
Salma and Rahim	shukreeaa. saadaa parvaar theek hai.
	Thank you. Our family is fine.

ਤਲਤ	ਖ਼ੁਦਾ ਹਾਫ਼ਿਜ਼।
Talat	<u>kh</u>u<u>d</u>aa haafiz.
	Goodbye.

ਰਹੀਮ, ਸਲਮਾ ਤੇ ਪਰਵੀਨ	ਖ਼ੁਦਾ ਹਾਫ਼ਿਜ਼।
Rahim, Salma	<u>kh</u>u<u>d</u>aa haafiz.
and Parveen	*Goodbye.*

🔑 ਸ਼ਬਦਾਵਲੀ   shab<u>d</u>aavalee   Vocabulary

ਹਾਲ	haal	*condition* (lit.) (m.)
ਹੈ	hai	*is*
ਤੁਹਾਡਾ ਕੀ ਹਾਲ ਹੈ ?	<u>t</u>uhaadaa kee haal hai?	*How are you?* (see Commentary)
ਅੱਸਲਾਮ ਅਲੈਕਮ	asslaam alaikam	Muslim greeting
ਵਾਲੈਕਮ ਅੱਸਲਾਮ	vaalaikam asslaam	response to Muslim greeting
ਠੀਕ	theek	*fine/OK/alright*
ਇਹ	ih	*this*
ਭਰਾ	bharaa	*brother* (m.)
ਅਤੇ	a<u>t</u>e	*and*
ਭੈਣ	bhainh	*sister* (f.)
ਪਰਵਾਰ	parvaar	*family* (m.)
ਸ਼ੁਕਰੀਆ	shukreeaa	*thank you* (m.)
ਸਾਡਾ	saadaa	*our*
ਖ਼ੁਦਾ ਹਾਫ਼ਿਜ਼	<u>kh</u>u<u>d</u>aa haafiz	Muslim departing phrase

◢ ਅਭਿਆਸ   abhiaas   Exercises

After reading the dialogue and/or listening to the audio tape, try to do the following exercises.

1. Begin the conversation

a) **ਵਾਲੈਕਮ ਅੱਸਲਾਮ**
   vaalaikam asslaam
   Hello.

b) **ਮੇਰਾ ਹਾਲ ਠੀਕ ਏ**
   meraa haal theek e
   I am fine.

c) **ਜੀ, ਪਰਵਾਰ ਠੀਕ ਹੈ**
   Jee, parvaar theek hai
   The family is fine.

2. Match the expressions

a) **ਮੇਰਾ ਭਰਾ** meraa bharaa   1. *our family*
b) **ਮੇਰੀ ਭੈਣ** meree bhainh   2. *my brother*
c) **ਸਾਡਾ ਪਰਵਾਰ** saadaa parvaar   3. *my sister*

ਬੋਲੀ ਬਾਰੇ   bolee baare   Language points

Possessive adjectives

1. Adjectives are words which describe people, places and objects. The words my, your and his/her are possessive adjectives. Unlike in English, the possessive adjective in Panjabi changes according to what is being possessed. In Dialogues 1 and 2 the word **ਹਾਲ haal** (*condition*) is grammatically masculine and therefore requires a masculine possessive adjective. Similarly, a woman talking about her children will use two forms of the word *my*, distinguishing between her son and daughter. ਮੇਰਾ **meraa** would apply to the male and ਮੇਰੀ **meree** for the female. Note that it is the ending which changes. This distinction is the same even if the father were talking about his son and daughter.

Examples:

Mother talking about her children:

ਮੇਰਾ ਲੜਕਾ ਠੀਕ ਹੈ।	meraa larhkaa theek hai.	*My son is fine.*
ਮੇਰੀ ਲੜਕੀ ਠੀਕ ਹੈ।	meree larhkee theek hai.	*My daughter is fine.*

Father talking about his children:

ਮੇਰਾ ਲੜਕਾ ਠੀਕ ਹੈ।	meraa larhkaa theek hai.	*My son is fine.*
ਮੇਰੀ ਲੜਕੀ ਠੀਕ ਹੈ।	meree larhkee theek hai.	*My daughter is fine.*

You will have noticed that there is no difference between the sentences spoken by the mother and the father. The form of the possessive adjective does not depend on the gender of the possessor (i.e. whether male or female) but on the gender of what is being possessed. In addition to gender, possessive adjectives also change according to whether the possessed object is singular or plural. As both parents are talking about one person, the possessive adjective is in the *singular* form.

There are, therefore, three factors which need to be taken into account when selecting the appropriate possessive adjective:

- whether the object is masculine or feminine
- whether the object is singular or plural
- whether the situation is formal or informal

2. In addition to describing objects, possessive adjectives are also used to describe different states of being, i.e. how you are, how you are feeling or other personal descriptions such as your name. You will remember from Dialogue 2 that Parveen uses the possessive adjective *your* when asking her friend Talat *How are you?* The literal meaning of this question in Panjabi is *How is your condition?*. Talat responds by saying *I'm fine*, literally *My condition is fine* with the possessive adjective *my*.

The following tables illustrate the way in which possessive adjectives are formed with singular, masculine and feminine objects. Note that the plural forms given here (their, our) refer only to the nature of the possessor, not of the object being possessed.

Possessive adjectives with singular masculine objects

1st person

ਮੇਰਾ	meraa	*my*
ਸਾਡਾ	saadaa	*our*

2nd person

ਤੇਰਾ	<u>t</u>eraa	*your* (informal)
ਤੁਹਾਡਾ	<u>t</u>uhaadaa	*your* (formal)

3rd person

ਇਹ ਦਾ/ਇਸ ਦਾ	ih <u>d</u>aa/is <u>d</u>aa	*his/her*
ਇਹਨਾਂ ਦਾ	ihnaa<u>n</u>daa	*his/her* (formal) *their*
ਉਹ ਦਾ/ਉਸ ਦਾ	uh <u>d</u>aa/us <u>d</u>aa	*his/her*
ਉਹਨਾਂ ਦਾ	uhnaa<u>n</u> <u>d</u>aa	*his/her* (formal) *their*

Possessive adjectives with singular feminine objects

1st person

ਮੇਰੀ	meree	*my*
ਸਾਡੀ	saadee	*our*

2nd person

ਤੇਰੀ	<u>t</u>eree	*your* (informal)
ਤੁਹਾਡੀ	<u>t</u>uhaadee	*your* (formal)

3rd person

ਇਹ ਦੀ/ਇਸ ਦੀ	ih dee/is dee	*his/her*
ਇਹਨਾਂ ਦੀ	ihnaan dee	*his/her* (formal) *their*
ਉਹ ਦੀ/ਉਸ ਦੀ	uh dee/us dee	*his/her*
ਉਹਨਾਂ ਦੀ	uhnaan dee	*his/her* (formal) *their*

Further examples of possessive adjectives with plural objects will be illustrated in Unit 3.

Formal and informal speech

There is a clear distinction between formal and informal speech in Panjabi. For instance, two sisters talking over the phone will use significantly different speech from two strangers meeting for the first time. Let us consider the example of a telephone conversation between Surinder and Mohinder who are sisters.

Surinder ਕਿੱਦਾਂ ਮੋਹਿੰਦਰ ? kiddaan Mohinder? *How are you, Mohinder?*
Mohinder ਠੀਕ ਹਾਂ। ਤੇਰਾ ਕੀ ਹਾਲ ਏ ? theek haan. teraa kee haal e? *I'm fine. How are you?*

Now let's contrast this situation with two strangers meeting in an office.

Mr Sandhu ਤੁਹਾਡਾ ਕੀ ਹਾਲ ਹੈ ਜੀ ? tuhaadaa kee haal hai jee? *How are you?*
Mr Johal ਧੰਨਵਾਦ। ਮੇਰਾ ਹਾਲ ਠੀਕ ਹੈ। dhannvaad meraa haal theek hai. *Thank you. I am fine.*

If you compare these two example situations, you will notice that there are two Panjabi words for the same English word *your*. In the first meeting between Mr Singh and the Panjabi class at Heywood College, the words ਤੇਰਾ **teraa** and ਤੁਹਾਡਾ **tuhaadaa** are used for your. Either word is used depending on who is being addressed. The word ਤੁਹਾਡਾ **tuhaadaa** is used normally when addressing more than one person (plural) or when addressing one person, male or female, formally as a sign of respect. Therefore, the word ਤੁਹਾਡਾ **tuhaadaa** serves two purposes:

■ to address a singular male/female in a formal manner
■ to address more than one person, male or female, in an informal or formal manner

Conversely, the word ਤੇਰਾ ṯeraa is used only in an informal manner to address a single person, male or female.

Here are two common examples of the formal and informal:

ਤੁਹਾਡਾ ਕੀ ਨਾਮ ਹੈ ? ṯuhaadaa kee naam hai? *What is your name?* (formal)

ਤੇਰਾ ਕੀ ਨਾਂ ਹੈ/ਏ ? ṯeraa kee naan hai/e? *What is your name?* (informal)

Asking questions in Panjabi

In Dialogue 1 the word ਕੀ **kee** is used to turn a statement into a question. For example:

Statement–ਤੁਹਾਡਾ ਪਰਵਾਰ ਠੀਕ ਹੈ। ṯuhaadaa parvaar   *Your family is*
                                                theek hai.   *fine.*
Question–ਕੀ ਤੁਹਾਡਾ ਪਰਵਾਰ ਠੀਕ ਹੈ ? kee ṯuhaadaa   *Is your family*
                                                parvaar theek hai?   *fine?*

However, you do not always need to use a question word, or *interrogative*, to turn a statement into a question. The use of intonation (rise and fall of the voice in speech) and emphasis can serve the same purpose. Raising your voice at the end of a sentence or using a questioning tone are equally effective. To ask the question *What is your name?* you can simply say:

ਜੀ ਤੁਹਾਡਾ ਨਾਮ ? jee ṯuhaadaa naam?   *Your name, please?*

The use of any question depends on the context of the conversation, the relationship between the speakers, and the number of people involved. You may have noted that the question *How are you?* is given as ਤੁਹਾਡਾ ਕੀ ਹਾਲ ਹੈ ? **ṯuhaadaa kee haal hai?** There are three literal meanings of this sentence: *What is your condition?*, *How are you getting on?* and *How are you feeling?* The various forms of *How are you?* will be used throughout the rest of the book. So look out for them!

There are many ways of asking and responding to the question *How are you?* in Panjabi. Some of the possibilities are listed in the Commentary section. You do not have to learn all of these, but they are useful to know when trying to understand the speech of other Panjabi speakers.

ਵਿਆਖਿਆ   **viaakhiaa**   **Commentary**

1. How are you?

There are various ways of saying *How are you?* in Panjabi. Here are some examples:

- ਤੂੰ ਕਿਵੇਂ ਹੈਂ ?   <u>t</u>oo<u>n</u> kive<u>n</u> hai<u>n</u>? (informal)
- ਤੇਰਾ ਕੀ ਹਾਲ ਹੈ ?   <u>t</u>eraa kee haal hai? (informal)
- ਕਿੱਦਾਂ ?   ki<u>dd</u>aa<u>n</u>? (colloquial)

Now let's have a look at the variety of responses to the question *How are you?*

- ਠੀਕ ਏ   theek e   *Fine.* (informal)
- ਤੁਹਾਡੀ ਕਿਰਪਾ ਹੈ   <u>t</u>uhaadee kirpaa   *By your blessings.*
                      hai   *(I am fine)* (formal)
- ਵਾਹਿਗੁਰੂ ਦਾ ਸ਼ੁਕਰ ਹੈ vaahiguroo <u>d</u>aa   *By the grace of God.*
                      shukar hai   *(I am fine)* (formal)

It is common for Panjabi speakers to respond to *How are you?* reciprocally by asking the same of the enquirer:

- ਤੂੰ ਸੁਣਾ   <u>t</u>oo<u>n</u> sunhaa   *You tell (how you are).* (informal)
- ਤੁਸੀਂ ਸੁਣਾਓ   <u>t</u>usee<u>n</u> sunhaao   *You tell (how you are).* (formal)

As in English when asked the question *How are you?* many people say *thank you* after replying with such responses as *I'm fine*. There are a few common ways of expressing *thank you* in Panjabi:

- ਧੰਨਵਾਦ   <u>d</u>ha<u>nn</u>vaa<u>d</u>
- ਸ਼ੁਕਰੀਆ   shukreeaa
- ਮਿਹਰਬਾਨੀ   miharbaanee
- ਤੁਹਾਡੀ ਕਿਰਪਾ ਹੈ।   <u>t</u>uhaadee kirpaa hai.

2. Panjabi greetings

Panjabi greetings are chosen, not according to the time of day – as in cases such as *Good morning* or *Good evening* – but according to the religion of the speakers. All the world's main faiths are represented in Panjab. However, after the partition of the region, the main religious group in West Panjab (Pakistan) is Muslim, with a sizeable Christian minority, and in East Panjab there is a mixture of Sikhs and Hindus with a Christian and

Buddhist minority. Throughout the remainder of the book, we have focused on the Hindu, Sikh and Muslim religious groupings.

Sikhs greet each other by saying: ਸਤਿ ਸ੍ਰੀ ਅਕਾਲ ਜੀ **sat sree akaal jee**, or simply ਸਤਿ ਸ੍ਰੀ ਅਕਾਲ **sat sree akaal**. There is an associated body language with each greeting. When saying ਸਤਿ ਸ੍ਰੀ ਅਕਾਲ **sat sree akaal** the hands are, usually, joined together in front of the chest, with the head slightly bowed. In formal and respectful circumstances the suffix ਜੀ **jee** is added. The reply to the greeting is the same, ਸਤਿ ਸ੍ਰੀ ਅਕਾਲ **sat sree akaal**. This is also used on departure, and may be combined with other sayings such as ਫਿਰ ਮਿਲਾਂ ਗੇ **phir milaan ge** (*see you again*) or ਰੱਬ ਰਾਖਾ **rabb raakhaa** (*May God protect you*).

The Muslim greeting is ਅੱਸਲਾਮ ਅਲੈਕਮ **asslaam alaikam**, which is taken from Arabic and means *Peace be upon you*. The reply to this is ਵਾਲੈਕਮ ਅੱਸਲਾਮ **vaalaikam asslaam**, which means *Peace be upon you also*. On departing a Muslim may say ਖ਼ੁਦਾ ਹਾਫ਼ਿਜ਼ **khudaa haafiz**, which means *May God protect you*. Men will greet each other by a shake of the hand and an embrace or by the raising of the right hand. Women would greet one another with an embrace or a clasping of the hand.

ਨਮਸਤੇ **namaste**, ਨਮਸਤੇ ਜੀ **namaste jee**, or ਨਮਸਕਾਰ, **namaskaar** are different forms of Hindu greetings. The greeting is from Sanskrit and literally means *I greet you respectfully*. The reply to ਨਮਸਤੇ **namaste** is ਨਮਸਤੇ, **namaste**. Men may shake hands in greeting. However, to and among women the folding of hands and a slight bowing of the head is considered a mark of respect. There is no specific departing phrase.

It is considered good practice to use the greeting of the other person's religion on first meeting. Therefore if Mr Singh, who is a Sikh teacher, had a Muslim student in his class, he would greet him by saying ਅੱਸਲਾਮ ਅਲੈਕਮ **asslaam alaikam**. The student could equally reply ਵਾਲੈਕਮ ਅੱਸਲਾਮ, **vaalaikam asslaam** or say ਸਤਿ ਸ੍ਰੀ ਅਕਾਲ **sat sree akaal** as a sign of respect. However, if you are not certain of the other person's religious background, it is advisable to use the westernised, secular greeting *hello* or *hello jee*.

ਜੀ **jee** is an extra added word known as an honorific particle, signifying respect. The use of the word ਜੀ **jee** is very common in the Panjabi language. It can be added to the end (and sometimes before) almost any sentence as a sign of respect in a formal context. To some extent **jee** is the equivalent of *please* and also of *sir/madam* in English.

✅ ਅਭਿਆਸ   abhiaas   Exercises

1. Word search

Three words are hidden in the box. These words are ਅੱਛਾ a<u>ch</u>chaa, OK, ਸ਼ਾਬਾਸ਼ **shaabaash**, *well done*, and ਰੱਬ ਰਾਖਾ **rabb raakhaa**, *goodbye*. Find them by looking horizontally across each of the rows.

ਉ	ਰੱ	ਬ	ਰਾ	ਖਾ
ਮਾ	ਪਾ	ਰ	ਗ	ਚ
ਸ਼ਾ	ਬਾ	ਸ਼	ਕਾ	ਜ
ਜ	ਜ਼	ਖ	ਸ਼	ਬਾ
ਕੱ	ਲ	ਹਿ	ਅੱ	ਛਾ

2. Greeting response

How would you respond to someone who greets you with the following expressions?

a) ਨਮਸਤੇ   namas<u>t</u>e   b) ਅੱਸਲਾਮ ਅਲੈਕਮ   asslaam alaikam
c) ਸਤਿ ਸ੍ਰੀ ਅਕਾਲ   sa<u>t</u> sree akaal

3. Use the appropriate formal and informal possessive adjectives in the following sentences.

a) _____ ਕੀ ਨਾਮ ਹੈ ? _____ kee naam hai? *What is your name?* (formal)

b) _____ ਕੀ ਹਾਲ ਹੈ ? _____ kee haal hai? *How are you?* (informal)

c) _____ ਕੀ ਨਾਂ ਏ ? _____ kee naa<u>n</u> e? *What is your name?* (informal)

⊟ 4. Complete the conversation

You have just met Kiran, a new student in the Panjabi class. Following the English prompts complete the following conversation in Panjabi.

Kiran   ਸਤਿ ਸ੍ਰੀ ਅਕਾਲ ਜੀ। ਤੁਹਾਡਾ ਕੀ ਨਾਮ ਹੈ ?   sa<u>t</u> sree akaal jee. <u>t</u>uhaadaa
        kee naam hai?
        Hello. What is your name?

You   Say hello, tell her your name and ask what her name is.

_____

Kiran   ਮੇਰਾ ਨਾਮ ਕਿਰਨ ਹੈ। ਤੁਹਾਡਾ ਕੀ ਹਾਲ ਹੈ ?   meraa naam Kiran hai.
              ṭuhaadaa kee haal hai?
              My name is Kiran. How are you?

You   Tell her you are fine and then ask her how she is.

_____

Kiran   ਮੇਰਾ ਹਾਲ ਵੀ ਠੀਕ ਹੈ।   meraa haal vee theek hai.
              I am fine too.

You   Say goodbye.

_____

2 ਮੈਂ ਕਿਰਨ ਹਾਂ
mai<u>n</u> kiran haa<u>n</u>
I'm Kiran

In this unit you will learn:
- how to say who you are
- how to ask about and describe ethnicity or nationality
- about Panjabi sentence word order

1 Are you English too?

ਗੱਲ ਬਾਤ ੧ ਕੀ ਤੁਸੀਂ ਵੀ ਅੰਗਰੇਜ਼ ਹੋ ?

gall baa<u>t</u> 1 kee <u>t</u>usee<u>n</u> vee a<u>n</u>grez ho?

It is the second day of the Panjabi class at Heywood College. Mr Singh is the teacher and Henry, Jane, Ashok, Kiran and David are students attending the class.

ਚਰਨ ਸਿੰਘ **Charan Singh**	ਜੇਨ, ਕੀ ਤੂੰ ਜਰਮਨ ਹੈਂ ? jen, kee <u>t</u>oo<u>n</u> jarman hai<u>n</u>? *Jane, are you German?*
ਜੇਨ **Jane**	ਨਹੀਂ ਜੀ, ਮੈਂ ਜਰਮਨ ਨਹੀਂ ਹਾਂ। ਮੈਂ ਅੰਗਰੇਜ਼ ਹਾਂ। nahee<u>n</u> jee, mai<u>n</u> jarman nahee<u>n</u> haa<u>n</u>. mai<u>n</u> a<u>n</u>grez haa<u>n</u>. *No, I'm not German. I'm English.*
ਡੇਵਿਡ **David**	ਮੈਂ ਵੀ ਅੰਗਰੇਜ਼ ਹਾਂ ਅਤੇ ਮੈਂ ਵਿਦਿਆਰਥੀ ਹਾਂ। mai<u>n</u> vee a<u>n</u>grez haa<u>n</u> a<u>t</u>e mai<u>n</u> vidiaar<u>th</u>ee haa<u>n</u>. *I'm also English and I am a student.*
ਚਰਨ ਸਿੰਘ **Charan Singh**	ਬਹੁਤ ਅੱਛਾ। ਅਸ਼ੋਕ, ਕੀ ਤੁਸੀਂ ਭਾਰਤੀ ਹੋ ? bahu<u>t</u> a<u>chch</u>aa. ashok, kee <u>t</u>usee<u>n</u> bhaar<u>t</u>ee ho? *Very good. Ashok, are you Indian?*

ਅਸ਼ੋਕ	ਮੇਰਾ ਦੇਸ਼ ਭਾਰਤ ਹੈ ਅਤੇ ਮੇਰੀ ਬੋਲੀ ਗੁਜਰਾਤੀ ਹੈ।
Ashok	meraa <u>d</u>esh bhaara<u>t</u> hai a<u>t</u>e meree bolee gujraa<u>t</u>ee hai.
	My country is India and my language is Gujarati.

ਚਰਨ ਸਿੰਘ	ਸ਼ਾਬਾਸ਼ ! ਹੈਨਰੀ, ਕੀ ਕਿਰਨ ਗੁਜਰਾਤੀ ਹੈ ?
Charan Singh	shaabaash! hainree, kee kiran gujraa<u>t</u>ee hai?
	Well done! Henry, is Kiran Gujarati?

ਹੈਨਰੀ	ਨਹੀਂ, ਉਹ ਪੰਜਾਬੀ ਹੈ ਅਤੇ ਹਿੰਦੂ ਹੈ।
Henry	naheen, uh pa<u>n</u>jaabee hai a<u>t</u>e hin<u>d</u>oo hai.
	No, she is Panjabi and Hindu.

ਚਰਨ ਸਿੰਘ	ਧੰਨਵਾਦ।
Charan Singh	<u>dh</u>a<u>nn</u>vaad.
	Thank you.

✎ ਸ਼ਬਦਾਵਲੀ   **shab<u>d</u>aavalee   Vocabulary**

ਤੂੰ	<u>t</u>oo<u>n</u>	*you (informal)*
ਜਰਮਨ	jarman	*German (m./f.)*
ਅੰਗਰੇਜ਼	a<u>n</u>grez	*English (m./f.)*
ਵਿਦਿਆਰਥੀ	vi<u>d</u>iaar<u>th</u>ee	*student (m./f.)*
ਤੁਸੀਂ	<u>t</u>usee<u>n</u>	*you (formal)*
ਭਾਰਤੀ	bhaar<u>t</u>ee	*Indian (m./f.)*
ਦੇਸ਼	<u>d</u>esh	*country (m.)*
ਭਾਰਤ	bhaara<u>t</u>	*India (m.)*
ਬਹੁਤ ਅੱਛਾ	bahu<u>t</u> a<u>chch</u>aa	*very good*
ਬੋਲੀ	bolee	*language (f.)*
ਗੁਜਰਾਤੀ	gujraa<u>t</u>ee	*a person from Gujarat or of Gujarati origin (m./f.)*
ਵੀ	vee	*also*
ਹੋਣਾ	honhaa	*to be*
ਮੈਂ	mai<u>n</u>	*I*
ਤੇ	<u>t</u>e	*and*
ਨਹੀਂ	nahee<u>n</u>	*no*
ਪੰਜਾਬੀ	pa<u>n</u>jaabee	*a person from Panjab or of Panjabi origin (m./f.)*
ਅਤੇ	a<u>t</u>e	*and*
ਹਿੰਦੂ	hin<u>d</u>oo	*Hindu (m./f.)*

☑ ਅਭਿਆਸ   abhiaas   Exercises

After reading the dialogue and/or listening to the audio tape, try to do the following exercises.

1. True or false?

Say whether these statements about the students' ethnicities and nationalities are true or false.

a) ਕਿਰਨ ਗੁਜਰਾਤੀ ਹੈ	kiran gujraatee hai	True / False
b) ਜੇਨ ਜਰਮਨ ਹੈ	jen jarman hai	True / False
c) ਅਸ਼ੋਕ ਭਾਰਤੀ ਹੈ	ashok bhaartee hai	True / False

▣ 2. Listen to the tape and tick the correct box

	Panjabi	English	Gujarati
Jeevan			
John			
Ram			

☺ 2 I'm Kiran

▣ ਗੱਲ ਬਾਤ ੨ ਮੈਂ ਕਿਰਨ ਹਾਂ

gall baat 2 main kiran haan

Kiran and Ashok meet at the Hindu temple. They have only met once in the Panjabi class and are still unacquainted with one another.

ਕਿਰਨ	ਨਮਸਤੇ। ਮੈਂ ਕਿਰਨ ਹਾਂ। ਕੀ ਤੁਸੀਂ ਅਸ਼ੋਕ ਹੋ ?
Kiran	namaste. main kiran haan. kee tuseen ashok ho?
	Hello. I'm Kiran. Are you Ashok?
ਅਸ਼ੋਕ	ਨਮਸਤੇ। ਹਾਂ ਜੀ, ਮੈਂ ਅਸ਼ੋਕ ਹਾਂ। ਇਹ ਮੇਰੇ ਮਾਤਾ ਜੀ ਹਨ, ਮਿਸਜ਼ ਸ਼ਰਮਾ।
Ashok	namaste. haan jee, main ashok haan. ih mere maataa jee han, misaz sharmaa.
	Hello. Yes, I'm Ashok. This is my mother, Mrs Sharma.

ਕਿਰਨ	ਨਮਸਤੇ ਮਿਸਜ਼ ਸ਼ਰਮਾ। ਤੁਹਾਡਾ ਕੀ ਹਾਲ ਹੈ ?
Kiran	namaste misaz sharmaa. tuhaadaa kee haal hai?
	Hello Mrs Sharma. How are you?

ਮਿਸਜ਼ ਸ਼ਰਮਾ	ਮੈਂ ਠੀਕ ਹਾਂ। ਕੀ ਤੇਰੇ ਮਾਤਾ ਜੀ ਇੱਥੇ ਹਨ? ਅਸੀਂ ਦੋਨੋ ਸਹੇਲੀਆਂ ਹਾਂ।
Mrs Sharma	main theek haan. kee tere maataa jee iththe han? aseen donon saheleeaan haan.
	I'm fine. Is your mother here? We are both friends.

ਕਿਰਨ	ਨਹੀਂ ਜੀ, ਉਹ ਇੱਥੇ ਨਹੀਂ ਹਨ, ਉਹ ਘਰ ਹਨ।
Kiran	naheen jee, uh iththe naheen han, uh ghar han.
	No, she's not here. She's at home.

ਅਸ਼ੋਕ	ਮਾਤਾ ਜੀ, ਕਿਰਨ ਤੇ ਮੈਂ ਦੋਨੋ ਇੱਕੋ ਕਲਾਸ ਵਿਚ ਹਾਂ।
Ashok	maataa jee, kiran te main donon ikko kalaas vich haan.
	Mother, Kiran and I are both in the same class.

ਸ਼ਬਦਾਵਲੀ   shabdaavalee   Vocabulary

ਇਹ	ih	*he, she, it*
ਮਾਤਾ ਜੀ	maataa jee	*mother* (f.)
ਮੈਂ	main	*I*
ਇੱਥੇ	iththe	*here*
ਅਸੀਂ	aseen	*we*
ਦੋਨੋ	donon	*both*
ਸਹੇਲੀ	sahelee	*friend* (f.)
ਉਹ	uh	*he, she, that, they*
ਨਹੀਂ	naheen	*no*
ਘਰ	ghar	*house, home* (m.)
ਅਸੀਂ ਦੋਨੋ	aseen donon	*both of us*
ਇੱਕੋ	ikko	*same*
ਕਲਾਸ	kalaas	*class* (f.)
ਵਿਚ	vich	*in*

ਅਭਿਆਸ   abhiaas   Exercises

After reading the dialogue and/or listening to the audio tape, try to do the following exercises.

1. Listen and give appropriate responses

Kiran ਕੀ ਤੁਸੀਂ ਅਸ਼ੋਕ ਹੋ ? kee <u>t</u>useen ashok ho?	Ashok
Kiran ਤੁਹਾਡਾ ਕੀ ਹਾਲ ਹੈ ? <u>t</u>uhaadaa kee haal hai?	Mrs Sharma
Mrs Sharma ਕੀ ਤੇਰੇ ਮਾਤਾ ਜੀ ਇੱਥੇ ਹਨ ? kee <u>t</u>ere maa<u>t</u>aa jee iththe han?	Kiran

2. Arrange in correct word order

a. ਹਾਂ ਮੈਂ ਕਿਰਨ   haa<u>n</u>-main-kiran   *I am Kiran.*
b. ਹੋ ਅਸ਼ੋਕ ਕੀ ਤੁਸੀਂ ?   ho-ashok-kee-<u>t</u>useen?   *Are you Ashok?*
c. ਨਹੀਂ ਇੱਥੇ ਉਹ ਹਨ   naheen-iththe-uh-han   *She is not here.*

3. Crossword

Complete the crossword in English using clues taken from Dialogues 1 and 2.

1) ਕਿਰਨ _____ ਹੈ   kiran _____ hai

2) ਜੇਨ _____ ਹੈ   jen _____ hai

3) ਕਿਰਨ ਤੇ ਅਸ਼ੋਕ ਦੋਨੋਂ ਇੱਕੋ _____ ਵਿਚ ਹਨ   kiran <u>t</u>e ashok <u>d</u>onon ikko _____ vich han

4) ਅਸ਼ੋਕ ਦੇ ਮਾਤਾ ਜੀ ਦਾ ਨਾਮ _____ ਹੈ   ashok <u>d</u>e maa<u>t</u>aa jee <u>d</u>aa naam _____ hai

5) ਕਿਰਨ ਦੇ ਮਾਤਾ ਜੀ _____ ਹਨ   kiran <u>d</u>e maa<u>t</u>aa jee _____han

ਬੋਲੀ ਬਾਰੇ   **bolee baare**   **Language points**

Subject pronouns

Pronouns are words used in the place of nouns, or naming words, which are used to refer to persons, places or objects. In English the words *I, you, he, she, it, they* and *we* are called subject pronouns. In Panjabi they are very important as the endings of verbs change according to which subject pronoun is being used, as will be seen in subsequent units.

Singular subject pronouns

First person	ਮੈਂ	main	*I*
Second person	ਤੂੰ	<u>t</u>oo<u>n</u>	*you* (informal)
	ਤੁਸੀਂ	<u>t</u>usee<u>n</u>	*you* (formal)
Third person	ਇਹ	ih	*he/she/it*
	ਉਹ	uh	*he/she/it*

Plural subject pronouns

First person	ਅਸੀਂ	asee<u>n</u>	*we*
Second person	ਤੁਸੀਂ	<u>t</u>usee<u>n</u>	*you*
Third person	ਇਹ	ih	*they* (near)
	ਉਹ	uh	*they* (far)

Unlike in English, but as in all the Latin-based languages, persons, places and objects (nouns) are grammatically either male or female in Panjabi. Even though some objects have ambiguous status in the sense that some people may refer to them as masculine and others as feminine, generally all nouns, even those with ambiguous status, belong to either the masculine or feminine gender. Some nouns can be used for both male and female, such as doctor. You will note in the vocabulary sections that we have given (m.), (f.) and (m./f.) to represent the gender of a noun.

There is no gender distinction in the actual forms of subject pronouns, only in the verb endings that refer to the subject pronoun. For example, ਉਹ uh can refer to one man or woman or a group of either men or women. There is no way of distinguishing, by looking only at the subject pronoun, between he, she or they as the third person singular and plural forms are interchangeable. It is the *verb ending* which will enable you to recognise whether it is he, she or they being referred to. In Panjabi there is no equivalent to the word *it* which implies gender neutrality in English.

Use of subject pronouns

1. ਇਹ **ih** and ਉਹ **uh** literally mean *he/she/it* in the singular and *they* in the plural. There is however a recognisable distinction between the use of ਉਹ **uh** and ਇਹ **ih**. ਉਹ **uh** refers to a person or persons absent or at a distance, whereas ਇਹ **ih** is used when the person or persons are present or in close proximity.

2. In English the words these and those are called demonstrative pronouns. In Panjabi there are no specific equivalents. ਉਹ **uh** and ਇਹ **ih**, however, often translate into those and these, respectively, in many situations.

3. When talking about a singular person who is deserving of respect, such as Kiran's mother in Dialogue 2, it is grammatically correct always to use the plural form:

ਉਹ ਇੱਥੇ ਨਹੀਂ ਹਨ, ਉਹ ਘਰ ਹਨ। uh iththe naheen han, uh ghar han. *She's not here, she's at home.*

ਉਹ **uh** and ਇਹ **ih** are used in the plural, in this case, which is reflected in the use of the plural form of ਹੋਣਾ (ਹਨ) **honhaa** (**han**) instead of the singular ਹੈ **hai**, even though only one mother (she) is being talked about.

4. In a similar way, the word ਤੂੰ **t̤oon** you is used informally and ਤੁਸੀਂ **t̤useen** is used in both formal speech as well as in the plural form. These two forms of you require discretion in their application. ਤੂੰ **t̤oon** is used between family members and close friends as well as when speaking to younger people. It is also used in public speech where a degree of informality is expected, such as when bargaining in the market or fixing the price of a taxi fare. ਤੁਸੀਂ **t̤useen** is a more formal and polite form which is used between people of equal status and age as well as to people deserving respect due to age or social standing. However, when the distinction between the formal and informal use is not obvious, it is always safest to use the formal. Formal and informal speech is a crucial distinction in Panjabi and will crop up many times as you progress through the course. If you have some knowledge of French or Spanish, you will note the similarity here between the singular, informal use of *you*, *tú* and the plural and singular formal, forms of *you*, *vous* (French) and *usted* (Spanish).

The present tense of ਹੋਣਾ honhaa *is, am* and *are*

Subject pronouns are assigned appropriate forms of the verb *to be*. This can similarly be compared with English: *I am*, *you are*, *we are*, *he is*, *they are*. In Panjabi *to be* is expressed in the verb ਹੋਣਾ **honhaa** which denotes states of being, conditions and existence. Note the following pairings of subject pronouns with their assigned forms of ਹੋਣਾ **honhaa**:

Singular

First person	ਮੈਂ ਹਾਂ	main haan	*I am*
Second person	ਤੂੰ ਹੈਂ ਤੁਸੀਂ ਹੋ	toon hain tuseen ho	*you are* (informal) *you are* (formal)
Third person	ਇਹ ਹੈ ਉਹ ਹੈ	ih hai uh hai	*he/she/it is* *he/she/it is*

Plural

First person	ਅਸੀਂ ਹਾਂ	aseen haan	*we are*
Second person	ਤੁਸੀਂ ਹੋ	tuseen ho	*you are*
Third person	ਇਹ ਹਨ ਉਹ ਹਨ	ih han uh han	*they/these are* *they/those are*

Formal uses of possessive adjectives

The formal uses of subject pronouns in Panjabi also extend to possessive adjectives. In Unit 1 we saw how possessive adjectives are formed with singular masculine and feminine objects. Possessive adjectives used to describe people with respect or in a formal situation always take the formal form, even when the person being described is in the singular. Note the following examples where the possessive adjectives and forms of ਹੋਣਾ **honhaa**, *to be* change according to the formal and informal contexts in which they are used to describe singular people. In the following examples, note how ਮੇਰੀ **meree** (*my*) and ਤੇਰੀ **teree** (*your*) change into ਮੇਰੇ **mere** and ਤੁਹਾਡੇ **tuhaade**.

Formal	ਇਹ ਮੇਰੇ ਮਾਤਾ ਜੀ ਹਨ ih mere maataa jee han	*This is my mother.*
Informal	ਇਹ ਮੇਰੀ ਮਾਤਾ ਹੈ ih meree maataa hai	*This is my mother.*
Formal	ਕੀ ਤੁਹਾਡੇ ਮਾਤਾ ਜੀ ਇੱਥੇ ਹਨ ? kee ṯuhaade maataa jee iṯhṯhe han?	*Is your mother here?*
Informal	ਕੀ ਤੇਰੀ ਮਾਤਾ ਇੱਥੇ ਹੈ ? kee ṯeree maataa iṯhṯhe hai?	*Is your mother here?*

These examples illustrate how the plural in Panjabi can be used to make speech more formal. However, this is only one aspect of plural possessive adjectives. In these examples the object here is itself not in the plural (and the form of the adjective is being used in a formal situation). Unit 3 illustrates possessive adjectives with plural objects.

Word order

Note the word order of a simple Panjabi sentence – subject (person carrying out the action) first, verb (the action) last and the rest in between. The sentence *I am fine* is written in Panjabi as *I fine am*, where *I* is the subject and *am* is the verb. For example: ਮੈਂ ਠੀਕ ਹਾਂ   main theek haan   *I am fine*

ਮੈਂ	ਠੀਕ	ਹਾਂ
main	theek	haan
I	*fine*	*am*
subject		**verb**

Word order in Panjabi is generally more flexible than it is in English. Note how the meaning does not change though the word order does in the following sentences:

ਤੁਹਾਡਾ ਨਾਮ ਕੀ ਹੈ ?   ṯuhaadaa naam kee hai?

ਤੁਹਾਡਾ ਕੀ ਨਾਮ ਹੈ ?   ṯuhaadaa kee naam hai?

Both examples mean *What is your name?* However, this does not mean that any word order is allowed. The form of the verb ਹੋਣਾ **honhaa (ਹੈ hai)** is still at the end of the sentence in both examples.

ਵਿਆਖਿਆ   **viaakhiaa**   **Commentary**

1. Where are you from?

The question of where someone comes from depends on who is doing the asking and where the conversation is taking place. For example, a person born in Panjab living in London will respond that they are from India if the questioner is an English person. However, if the questioner is a fellow Panjabi they may say the district or the village they are from. This apparently simple question becomes even more complicated when asked to diaspora South Asians. The response to the question *Where are you from?* can give rise to replies such as *Birmingham* or *New Jersey* which are quite legitimate responses. Increasingly, the use of a religious identity tagged onto a national identity is a form of self-identification used in the diaspora. Therefore, a young person responding to the question *Who are you?* may reply a *British Muslim* or *Canadian Sikh*. It is important to remember that Panjabi speakers come from a huge variety of national, religious and social contexts and this is reflected in the many possibilities that the questions *Where do you come from?* and *Who are you?* can evoke.

If you meet a Panjabi in England or North America, they are likely to live, or at least have relatives, in three areas which are known as centres of Panjabi settlement: Southall in England, Yuba City in California and Vancouver in Canada. Each of these areas is often called *Little Panjab*. Early Panjabi immigrants settled here and these places are still icons on the global map of Panjabi travels, serving as temporary embarkation ports to would-be emigrants. These areas are distinctive for the range of shops selling South Asian goods such as groceries, sweets, music, jewellery, clothing and food. Apart from being a central shopping area they are the focus of social, religious, political and cultural activities.

2. Names

South Asian names can provide many clues about a person's sex, background, country of origin and religious affiliation. These are often very important pieces of information, particularly when engaging in formal conversation.

Sikh names

Most Sikhs have three names: a personal name, a second name and a surname. The second name, 'Singh' for men and 'Kaur' for women is in fact a religious name and its addition is one of the main ways of distinguishing men from women. Otherwise first names can be the same for men and women. Surnames vary from representing someone's caste or the name of their village.

Hindu names

The Hindu naming system is similar to the English naming system, in that most individuals have one or two personal names followed by a common surname. First names are generally male and female specific. A middle name of Kumar or Chand is quite popular in North India and is a way of distinguishing a Hindu Panjabi from a Sikh.

Muslim names

Muslim names tend to be less fixed in the order of first and second name. There is also a tendency for women not to have the surnames of their husbands, but just to have the word **bibi** or **begum** attached, which means lady or woman. Muslim names tend to be a composite of Koranic names with some local flavour. Male and female names are distinguished.

Throughout the book you will come across a range of Sikh, Hindu and Muslim names. Try and see if you can distinguish them. It is worth remembering, however, that some names transcend religious boundaries, and also that you may come across a lot of nicknames.

☑ ਅਭਿਆਸ   abhiaas   Exercises

1. Complete the box

ਹਨ	han	
ਹੈ		*is*
	ho	*are*

2. Say the sentences in Panjabi

a) Are you Ashok?;   b) Are you Kiran?;   c) I am Kiran.;   d) He is Ashok.

3. Refer to the dialogue and choose the correct forms of *to be* from the options given

a) ਕੀ ਤੂੰ ਜਰਮਨ _____ (ਹੋ , ਹੈਂ) ?   kee toon jarman _____ (ho, hain)?
   Are you German?

b) ਮੈਂ ਵੀ ਅੰਗਰੇਜ਼ _____ (ਹਾਂ, ਹੈ)   main vee angrez _____ (haan, hai).
   I'm also English.

c) ਕੀ ਅਸ਼ੋਕ ਤੇ ਕਿਰਨ ਪੰਜਾਬੀ _____ (ਹੈਂ, ਹਨ) ?   kee ashok te kiran
   panjaabee _____ (hain, han)?   *Are Ashok and Kiran Panjabi?*

4. Word search

Three words are hiddens in the box. These words are ਜਰਮਨ **jarman**
German, ਪੰਜਾਬੀ **panjaabee** *Panjabi* and ਅੰਗਰੇਜ਼ **angrez** *English*. Find them
by looking horizontally across each of the rows.

ਉ	ਜ	ਰ	ਮ	ਨ
ਕ	ਖ	ਪ	ਰ	ਲ
ਪੰ	ਜਾ	ਬੀ	ਸੀ	ਸਿ
ਟ	ਅੰ	ਗ	ਰੇ	ਜ਼
ਕੋ	ਕਾ	ਕਿ	ਕੀ	ਕੋ

3 | ਇਸ ਦਾ ਸੁਆਦ ਕੀ ਹੈ ?

is daa suaad kee hai?

What does it taste like?

In this unit you will learn:
- the names of vegetables and Panjabi food
- how to ask questions
- how to describe people and things

🔊 1 What is this?

📼 ਗੱਲ ਬਾਤ ੧ ਇਹ ਕੀ ਹੈ ?

gall baat 1 ih kee hai?

Mr Singh has taken the Panjabi class to Southall in order to give the students an opportunity to hear and speak Panjabi in a real situation. They are in a grocery shop.

ਹੈਨਰੀ	ਇਹ ਕੀ ਹੈ ?
Henry	ih kee hai?
	What is this?
ਦੁਕਾਨਦਾਰ	ਇਹ ਕਰੇਲਾ ਹੈ।
<u>d</u>ukaan<u>d</u>aar	ih karelaa hai.
Shopkeeper	*It (this) is a bitter gourd.*
ਹੈਨਰੀ	ਇਸ ਦਾ ਸੁਆਦ ਕੀ ਹੈ ?
Henry	is <u>d</u>aa suaa<u>d</u> kee hai?
	What does it taste like?
ਦੁਕਾਨਦਾਰ	ਇਸ ਦਾ ਸੁਆਦ ਕੌੜਾ ਹੈ।
Shopkeeper	is <u>d</u>aa suaa<u>d</u> kaurhaa hai.
	It has a bitter taste.
ਜੇਨ	ਉਸ ਸਬਜ਼ੀ ਦਾ ਕੀ ਨਾਮ ਹੈ ?
Jane	us sabzee <u>d</u>aa kee naam hai?
	What is the name of that vegetable?

ਦੁਕਾਨਦਾਰ	ਛੋਟੀ ਸਬਜ਼ੀ ਭਿੰਡੀ ਹੈ ਤੇ ਵੱਡੇ ਸ਼ਲਗਮ ਹਨ।
Shopkeeper	chotee sabzee bhindee hai te vadde shalgam han.
	The small vegetable is okra and the large ones are turnips.
ਜੇਨ	ਕੀ ਸ਼ਲਗਮ ਮਿੱਠਾ ਹੈ ਜਾਂ ਕਸੈਲਾ ?
Jane	kee shalgam miththaa hai jaan kasailaa?
	Are turnips sweet or bitter?
ਦੁਕਾਨਦਾਰ	ਉਹ ਮਿੱਠੇ ਹਨ ਤੇ ਬਹੁਤ ਸਸਤੇ ਵੀ ਹਨ।
Shopkeeper	uh miththe han te bahut saste vee han.
	They are sweet and also very cheap.

ਸ਼ਬਦਾਵਲੀ   shabdaavalee   Vocabulary

ਕਰੇਲਾ	karelaa	*bitter gourd* (type of vegetable) (m.)
ਇਸ	is	*it, this*
ਦਾ	daa	*of*
ਸੁਆਦ	suaad	*taste* (m.)
ਕੌੜਾ/ ਕਸੈਲਾ	kaurhaa/ kasailaa	*bitter* (v.)
ਉਸ	us	*that*
ਸਬਜ਼ੀ	sabzee	*vegetable* (f.)
ਛੋਟਾ	chotaa	*small* (v.)
ਭਿੰਡੀ	bhindee	*okra* (type of vegetable) (f.)
ਵੱਡਾ	vaddaa	*big, large* (v.)
ਸ਼ਲਗਮ	shalgam	*turnip* (m.)
ਸਸਤਾ	sastaa	*cheap* (v.)
ਮਿੱਠਾ	miththaa	*sweet* (v.)
ਜਾਂ	jaan	*or*
ਬਹੁਤ	bahut	*very*

ਅਭਿਆਸ   abhiaas   Exercises

After reading the dialogue and/or listening to the audio tape, try to do the following exercises.

1. True or false?

a. ਭਿੰਡੀ	bhindee means *bitter*	True / False
b. ਕਰੇਲਾ	karelaa means *okra*	True / False
c. ਸ਼ਲਗਮ	shalgam means *turnip*	True / False
d. ਸਸਤਾ	sastaa means *expensive*	True / False
e. ਸੁਆਦ	suaad means *taste*	True / False

▣ 2. Mr Khan's shopping list

Mr Khan is at the local grocery shop buying vegetables. Listen to the tape to hear which items he has purchased from the shopping list that Mrs Khan has given him. As the items are spoken on the tape, tick them off the list. Don't worry if you can't recognise all the words.

ਕਰੇਲਾ	karelaa	*bitter gourd*
ਸ਼ਲਗਮ	shalgam	*turnip*
ਭਿੰਡੀ	bhindee	*okra*
ਗਾਜਰ	gaajar	*carrots*
ਆਲੂ	aaloo	*potatoes*
ਗੋਭੀ	gobhee	*cauliflower*
ਟਮਾਟਰ	tamaatar	*tomatoes*
ਮਟਰ	matar	*peas*

▣ 2 Which sweets are good?

▣ ਗੱਲ ਬਾਤ ੨ ਕਿਹੜੀਆਂ ਮਿਠਿਆਈਆਂ ਚੰਗੀਆਂ ਹਨ ?

gall baat 2 kihrheeaan mithiaaeeaan changeeaan han?

After visiting the grocery shop, Mr Singh takes Jane and Henry to the Panjabi sweet shop (ਮਿਠਿਆਈ ਦੀ ਦੁਕਾਨ **mithiaaee dee dukaan**). Panjabi sweet shops are not like confectionery shops, because although they are most famous for the sweet dishes that they sell, they also provide a range of other dishes.

ਮਿਸਟਰ ਸਿੰਘ **Mr Singh**	ਇਹ ਬਹੁਤ ਚੰਗੀ ਮਿਠਿਆਈ ਦੀ ਦੁਕਾਨ ਹੈ।
	ih bahut changee mithiaaee dee dukaan hai.
	This is a very good sweet shop.
ਜੇਨ **Jane**	ਇੱਥੇ ਕਿਹੜੀਆਂ ਮਿਠਿਆਈਆਂ ਚੰਗੀਆਂ ਹਨ ?
	iththe kihrheeaan mithiaaeeaan changeeaan han?
	Which sweets are good here?
ਮਿਸਟਰ ਸਿੰਘ **Mr Singh**	ਸਾਰੀਆਂ ਮਿਠਿਆਈਆਂ ਚੰਗੀਆਂ ਹਨ ਪਰ ਲੱਡੂ ਖ਼ਾਸ ਸੁਆਦੀ ਹਨ।
	saareeaan mithiaaeeaan changeeaan han par laddoo khaas suaadee han.
	All of them are good, but ladoos *are especially tasty.*

ਹੈਨਰੀ	ਪਰ ਲੱਡੂ ਮਹਿੰਗੇ ਹਨ।	
Henry	par laddoo mahinge han.	
	But ladoos *are expensive.*	
ਜੇਨ	ਕੀ ਕੋਈ ਨਮਕੀਨ ਚੀਜ਼ ਹੈ ?	
Jane	kee koee namkeen cheez hai?	
	Is there anything salty?	
ਦੁਕਾਨਦਾਰ	ਹਾਂ ਜੀ, ਪਕੌੜੇ ਤੇ ਸਮੋਸੇ ਹਨ।	
Shopkeeper	haan jee, pakaurhe te samose han.	
	Yes, there are pakoras and samosas.	
ਜੇਨ	ਕੀ ਸਮੋਸੇ ਕਰਾਰੇ ਹਨ ?	
Jane	kee samose karaare han?	
	Are the samosas *spicy?*	
ਦੁਕਾਨਦਾਰ	ਹਾਂ ਜੀ, ਸਮੋਸੇ ਬਹੁਤ ਕਰਾਰੇ ਹਨ।	
Shopkeeper	haan jee, samose bahut karaare han.	
	Yes, the samosas *are very spicy.*	

ਸ਼ਬਦਾਵਲੀ   **shabdaavalee   Vocabulary**

ਕਿਹੜੀ	kihrhee	*which, which one* (v.)
ਮਿਠਿਆਈ	mithiaaee	*Panjabi sweet* (f.)
ਚੰਗੀ	changee	*good* (v.)
ਦੁਕਾਨ	dukaan	*shop* (f.)
ਇੱਥੇ	iththe	*here*
ਲੱਡੂ	laddoo	*a type of Panjabi sweet* (m.)
ਖ਼ਾਸ	khaas	*especially*
ਸੁਆਦੀ	suaadee	*tasty*
ਪਰ	par	*but*
ਮਹਿੰਗਾ	mahingaa	*expensive, costly* (v.)
ਕੋਈ	koee	*any*
ਚੀਜ਼	cheez	*thing* (f.)
ਨਮਕੀਨ	namkeen	*salty*
ਹਾਂ ਜੀ	haan jee	*yes* (polite)
ਪਕੌੜਾ	pakaurhaa	*a type of deep-fried pastry similar to fritters* (m.)
ਸਮੋਸਾ	samosaa	*triangular stuffed pastry* (m.)
ਕਰਾਰਾ	karaaraa	*spicy* (v.)

✓ ਅਭਿਆਸ   abhiaas   Exercises

After reading the dialogue and/or listening to the audio tape, try to do the following exercises.

1. Complete the table

ਮਿੱਠਾ		sweet
ਕੌੜਾ	kaurhaa	
	suaa<u>d</u>	taste

2. Arrange in correct word order

a) ਹੈ ਦੁਕਾਨ ਇਹ   hai-<u>d</u>ukaan-ih   *This is a shop.*

b) ਹੈ ਚੰਗੀ ਦੁਕਾਨ ਇਹ   hai-changee-<u>d</u>ukaan-ih   *This is a good shop.*

c) ਇਹ ਦੀ ਮਿਠਿਆਈ ਹੈ ਦੁਕਾਨ   ih-<u>d</u>ee-mithiaaee-hai-<u>d</u>ukaan   *This is a sweet shop.*

d) ਹੈ ਦੁਕਾਨ ਦੀ ਮਿਠਿਆਈ ਚੰਗੀ ਇਹ   hai-<u>d</u>ukaan-<u>d</u>ee-mithiaaee-cha<u>n</u>gee-ih   *This is a good sweet shop.*

🔊 3 This is our sitting room

🖾 ਗੱਲ ਬਾਤ 3 ਇਹ ਸਾਡੀ ਬੈਠਕ ਹੈ

gall baa<u>t</u> 3 ih saadee baithak hai

Mr Singh has taken his students to visit his house and is showing them around.

ਚਰਨ ਸਿੰਘ **Charan Singh**	ਇਹ ਸਾਡੀ ਬੈਠਕ ਹੈ। ਮਾਫ਼ ਕਰਨਾ, ਹਰ ਪਾਸੇ ਮੇਰੀਆਂ ਕਿਤਾਬਾਂ ਹਨ ih saadee baithak hai. maaf karnaa, har paase mereeaa<u>n</u> ki<u>t</u>aabaan han. *This is our sitting room. Sorry, my books are everywhere.*
ਹੈਨਰੀ **Henry**	ਤੁਹਾਡਾ ਘਰ ਵੱਡਾ ਹੈ। ਪੌੜੀਆਂ ਚੌੜੀਆਂ ਹਨ। <u>t</u>uhaadaa ghar vaddaa hai. paurheeaa<u>n</u> chaurheeaa<u>n</u> han. *Your house is big. The stairs are wide.*
ਜੇਨ **Jane**	ਕਿੰਨੇ ਕਮਰੇ ਹਨ ? ki<u>nn</u>e kamre han? *How many rooms are there?*

ਚਰਨ ਸਿੰਘ **Charan Singh**	ਚਾਰ ਕਮਰੇ ਹਨ ਅਤੇ ਦੋ ਗੁਸਲਖ਼ਾਨੇ ਹਨ। chaar kamre han a<u>t</u>e <u>d</u>o <u>gh</u>usal <u>kh</u>aane han. *There are four rooms and two bathrooms.*
ਅਸ਼ੋਕ **Ashok**	ਬਗ਼ੀਚਾ ਲੰਬਾ ਹੈ ਪਰ ਰਸੋਈ ਛੋਟੀ ਹੈ। ba<u>gh</u>eechaa la<u>n</u>baa hai par rasoee <u>ch</u>otee hai. *The garden is long but the kitchen is small.*
ਚਰਨ ਸਿੰਘ **Charan Singh**	ਇਹ ਸੱਚ ਹੈ, ਪਰ ਮੇਰੇ ਬੱਚੇ ਅਤੇ ਮੇਰੀ ਪਤਨੀ ਇੱਥੇ ਖ਼ੁਸ਼ ਹਨ। ih sachch hai, par mere bachche a<u>t</u>e meree pa<u>t</u>nee i<u>thth</u>e <u>kh</u>ush han. *That's true, but my children and my wife are happy here.*

ਸ਼ਬਦਾਵਲੀ shab<u>d</u>aavalee Vocabulary

ਬੈਠਕ	baithak	*sitting room* (f.)
ਮਾਫ਼ ਕਰਨਾ	maaf karnaa	*sorry*
ਹਰ ਪਾਸੇ	har paase	*everywhere*
ਪੌੜੀਆਂ	paurheeaa<u>n</u>	*stairs* (f.)
ਚੌੜਾ	chaurhaa	*wide* (v.)
ਕਮਰਾ	kamraa	*room* (m.)
ਕਿੰਨੇ	ki<u>n</u>ne	*how many*
ਗੁਸਲਖ਼ਾਨਾ	<u>gh</u>usal <u>kh</u>aanaa	*bathroom* (m.)
ਬਗ਼ੀਚਾ	ba<u>gh</u>eechaa	*garden* (m.)
ਲੰਬਾ	la<u>n</u>baa	*long* (v.)
ਰਸੋਈ	rasoee	*kitchen* (f.)

ਸੱਚ	sachch	*true, truth* (v.)
ਬੱਚੇ	bachche	*children* (m.)
ਪਤਨੀ	pa<u>t</u>nee	*wife* (f.)
ਖ਼ੁਸ਼	<u>kh</u>ush	*happy*

◖◗ ਬੋਲੀ ਬਾਰੇ   bolee baare   Language points

Interrogative words

Interrogative words change sentences into questions. In Panjabi interrogative words generally begin with the letter ਕ **k** and may appear at the beginning of the sentence or within the sentence.

ਕੌਣ	kaunh	*who*
ਕੀ	kee	*what*
ਕਿੱਥੇ	ki<u>th</u>the	*where*
ਕਿਉਂ	kiu<u>n</u>	*why*
ਕਿਵੇਂ	kive<u>n</u>	*how*
ਕਦੋਂ	ka<u>d</u>on	*when*
ਕਿਹੜਾ	kihrhaa	*which**
ਕਿਹੜੀ	kihrhee	*which**

*Note that these two examples of which only apply to singular objects.

The endings of ਕਿਹੜਾ **kihrhaa** and ਕਿਹੜੀ **kihrhee** change according to the nature of the noun to which it is referring: whether it is singular or plural, or masculine or feminine.

Examples:

ਉਹ ਕੌਣ ਹੈ ?	uh kaunh hai?	*Who is he/she?*
ਉਹ ਕੀ ਹੈ ?	uh kee hai?	*What is that?*
ਉਹ ਕਿੱਥੇ ਹੈ ?	uh ki<u>th</u>the hai?	*Where is she/he?*
ਉਹ ਇੱਥੇ ਕਿਉਂ ਹੈ ?	uh i<u>th</u>the kiu<u>n</u> hai?	*Why is he/she here?*
ਉਹ ਕਿਵੇਂ ਹੈ ?	uh kive<u>n</u> hai?	*How is she/he?*

ਕਲਾਸ ਕਦੋਂ ਹੈ ?	kalaas ka<u>d</u>o<u>n</u> hai?	*When is the class?*
ਕਿਹੜਾ ਫਲ ? (m.)	kihrhaa phal? (m.)	*Which fruit?*
ਕਿਹੜੀ ਸਬਜ਼ੀ ? (f.)	kihrhee sabzee? (f.)	*Which vegetable?*

Nouns

In Panjabi, nouns are affected by gender, either masculine or feminine, and number, either singular or plural. Every noun in Panjabi, even an inanimate object, is assigned a masculine or feminine gender and has a singular or plural numerical character. The process of assignment of gender to nouns is quite arbitrary. There are no obvious reasons, for example, why ਕੁਰਸੀ **kursee** *chair* is feminine and ਮੇਜ਼ **mez** *table* is masculine. However, in logical terms, all nouns which represent males are masculine and those which represent females are feminine. For example, ਮੁੰਡਾ **mu<u>n</u>daa** *boy* is masculine and ਕੁੜੀ **kurhee** *girl* is feminine.

There are no steadfast rules about the distinction of the gender of inanimate objects. In Panjabi this is a matter of convention, whereby the gender of a noun is often simply understood. There is a general code that nouns ending in ਈ (ee) are feminine and nouns ending in ਆ (aa) are masculine, such as ਲੜਕਾ **larhkaa** *boy* and ਲੜਕੀ **larhkee** *girl*. Exceptions to this, however, are plentiful, with words such as ਹਾਥੀ, haa<u>th</u>ee (*elephant*) masculine, ਮਾਂ, **maa<u>n</u>** (*mother*) feminine and ਮਾਲਾ, **maalaa** (*necklace*) feminine all having endings which counter this general code. So be careful! You will learn more about nouns as you go along.

Type 1: Variable nouns

Variable nouns are those which change from the singular form when they are plural.

Masculine

Singular	ਮੁੰਡਾ	mu<u>n</u>daa	*boy*
Plural	ਮੁੰਡੇ	mu<u>n</u>de	*boys*
Singular	ਚਾਚਾ	chaachaa	*uncle*
Plural	ਚਾਚੇ	chaache	*uncles*

Feminine

Singular	ਕੁੜੀ	kurhee	*girl*
Plural	ਕੁੜੀਆਂ	kurheeaa<u>n</u>	*girls*
Singular	ਦੁਕਾਨ	<u>d</u>ukaan	*shop*
Plural	ਦੁਕਾਨਾਂ	<u>d</u>ukaanaa<u>n</u>	*shops*

Type 2: Invariable nouns

Invariable nouns are those which do not change forms from the singular to the plural.

Masculine

Singular	ਆਦਮੀ	aa<u>d</u>mee	*man*
Plural	ਆਦਮੀ	aa<u>d</u>mee	*men*
Singular	ਹੱਥ	hath<u>th</u>	*hand*
Plural	ਹੱਥ	hath<u>th</u>	*hands*

Some other examples of invariable nouns:

ਮੋਤੀ	mo<u>t</u>ee	*pearl*
ਹਾਰ	haar	*necklace*
ਨੱਕ	nakk	*nose*
ਦਰਿਆ	<u>d</u>ariaa	*river*

Note that generally all feminine nouns are variable, that is feminine nouns change from the singular to the plural form.

Adjustable nouns

In Panjabi the same noun can often be used to represent both genders by simply changing the ending to express their femininity or masculinity. These types of nouns are irregular, though the pattern of endings that they take can be distinctly identified.

Masculine			**Feminine**		
ਚਾਚਾ	chaachaa	*uncle*	= ਚਾਚੀ	chaachee	*paternal aunt*
ਪੁੱਤਰ	puttar	*son*	= ਪੁੱਤਰੀ	puttaree	*daughter*
ਊਠ	ooth	*male camel*	= ਊਠਨੀ	oothnhee	*female camel*
ਨੌਕਰ	naukar	*male servant*	= ਨੌਕਰਾਣੀ	naukaraanhee	*maid*
ਬਾਲ	baal	*male child*	= ਬਾਲੜੀ	baalrhee	*female child*
ਰਾਜਾ	raajaa	*king*	= ਰਾਣੀ	raanhee	*queen*
ਮੋਚੀ	mochee	*male cobbler*	= ਮੋਚਣ	mochanh	*female cobbler*

Some nouns are significantly different from their masculine/feminine counterparts:

ਭਰਾ	bharaa	*brother*	=	ਭੈਣ	bhainh	*sister*
ਮੁੰਡਾ	mundaa	*boy*	=	ਕੁੜੀ	kurhee	*girl*
ਬੰਦਾ	ba<u>n</u>daa	*man*	=	ਜਨਾਨੀ	janaanee	*woman*

Nouns borrowed from English

Words borrowed from English are also classified in terms of gender and are pluralised according to the pattern of Panjabi nouns. For example:

Masculine

singular   plural

ਕੈਮਰਾ	kaimraa	*camera*	ਕੈਮਰੇ	kaimre	*cameras*
ਟੈਲੀਫ਼ੋਨ	taileefon	*telephone*	ਟੈਲੀਫ਼ੋਨ	taileefon	*telephones*

Feminine

singular   plural

ਪਲੇਟ	palet	*plate*	ਪਲੇਟਾਂ	paletaa<u>n</u>	*plates*
ਪੈਂਸਲ	pai<u>n</u>sal	*pencil*	ਪੈਂਸਲਾਂ	pai<u>n</u>salaa<u>n</u>	*pencils*

Similarly, the plural of ਸਮੋਸਾ **samosaa** (*samosa*) is ਸਮੋਸੇ **samose** in Panjabi and *samosas* in English.

Adjectives

An adjective is a word that gives descriptive information about a noun, pronoun or another adjective. Generally, adjectives come before the noun and after the pronoun. Similar to nouns, adjectives are also either masculine or feminine and are used in singular and plural forms, reflecting the gender and numerical traits of the nouns that they are describing. There are two types of simple adjectives, variable and invariable.

Variable adjectives

Variable adjectives end in ਆ **aa** for the masculine and ਈ **ee** for the feminine such as ਵੱਡਾ **vaddaa** (masculine) and ਵੱਡੀ **vaddee** (feminine) *big*. They inflect (i.e. change their endings) with the number and the gender of the noun.

Masculine singular	ਵੱਡਾ ਲੜਕਾ	vaddaa larhkaa	*big boy*
Masculine plural	ਵੱਡੇ ਲੜਕੇ	vadde larhke	*big boys*
Feminine singular	ਵੱਡੀ ਲੜਕੀ	vaddee larhkee	*big girl*
Feminine plural	ਵੱਡੀਆਂ ਲੜਕੀਆਂ	vaddeeaa<u>n</u> larhkeeaa<u>n</u>	*big girls*

When the noun is the same for both genders and singular/plural forms, it is the variable adjective and/or the verb which will indicate the numerical and gender characteristics of the noun.

Examples:

| Singular | ਇਹ ਵੱਡਾ ਮਕਾਨ ਹੈ | ih vaddaa makaan hai | *This is a big house.* |
| Plural | ਇਹ ਵੱਡੇ ਮਕਾਨ ਹਨ | ih vadde makaan han | *These are big houses.* |

Variable adjectives also indicate the gender characteristic of the noun.

| ਇਹ ਵੱਡਾ ਮੇਜ਼ ਹੈ | ih vaddaa mez (m.) hai | *This is a big table.* (m.) |
| ਇਹ ਵੱਡੀ ਕੁਰਸੀ ਹੈ | ih vaddee kursee (f.) hai | *This is a big chair.* (f.) |

There are some exceptions regarding adjectives of this type. Some adjectives do not change their form according to the noun's gender and number associations, despite the fact that they end in ਈ **ee** or ਆ **aa** such as:

ਵਧੀਆ   va<u>dh</u>iaa   *superior*   ਗੁਲਾਬੀ   gulaabee   *pink*

You need to learn such exceptions as you go along.

Invariable adjectives

Invariable adjectives do not change according to the nouns that they specify and do not end with ਆ **aa** or ਈ **ee**, such as:

ਲਾਲ	laal	*red*
ਖ਼ੁਸ਼	<u>kh</u>ush	*happy*
ਸਾਫ਼	saaf	*clean*

ਖ਼ੁਸ਼ ਲੜਕਾ	<u>kh</u>ush larhkaa	*happy boy*
ਖ਼ੁਸ਼ ਲੜਕੇ	<u>kh</u>ush larhke	*happy boys*
ਖ਼ੁਸ਼ ਲੜਕੀ	<u>kh</u>ush larhkee	*happy girl*
ਖ਼ੁਸ਼ ਲੜਕੀਆਂ	<u>kh</u>ush larhkee<u>aan</u>	*happy girls*

The simple verb

Verbs indicate activity and are also called action words. Throughout the book the Panjabi verb is referred to in the infinitive form (i.e. the form *to*). The root of the verb plus the ending -ਣਾ **nhaa** or the ending -ਨਾ **naa** form the infinitive. Here are some common examples of verbs in the infinitive, or simple form:

Infinitive form (= 'to _____')				Root		Ending	
ਲਿਖਣਾ	likhnhaa	*to write*	-	ਲਿਖ	likh	-ਣਾ	nhaa
ਦੇਣਾ	<u>d</u>enhaa	*to give*	-	ਦੇ	<u>d</u>e	-ਣਾ	nhaa
ਖਾਣਾ	khaanhaa	*to eat*	-	ਖਾ	khaa	-ਣਾ	nhaa
ਆਉਣਾ	aaunhaa	*to come*	-	ਆਉ	aau	-ਣਾ	nhaa
ਬੋਲਣਾ	bolnhaa	*to speak*	-	ਬੋਲ	bol	-ਣਾ	nhaa
ਕਹਿਣਾ	kahinhaa	*to say*	-	ਕਹਿ	kahi	-ਣਾ	nhaa
ਰਹਿਣਾ	rahinhaa	*to live, stay*	-	ਰਹਿ	rahi	-ਣਾ	nhaa
ਕਰਨਾ	karnaa	*to do*	-	ਕਰ	kar	-ਨਾ	naa

The simple verb is also used as a form of command particularly related to actions in the near future.

Examples:

ਜਲਦੀ ਆਉਣਾ	jal<u>d</u>ee aaunhaa	*come back quickly*
ਹੌਲੀ ਬੋਲਣਾ	haulee bolnhaa	*speak softly*
ਚਿੱਠੀ ਲਿਖਣਾ	chiththee likhnhaa	*write a letter*

The possessive particle ਦਾ <u>d</u>aa *of*

In Panjabi, possession is expressed through the particle ਦਾ. In English possession is not usually expressed using the word *of*, for example, *the pencil of the girl.* would usually be written *the girl's pencil.* The particle ਦਾ <u>d</u>aa is therefore similar to the apostrophe *s* in English as it establishes the relationship between possessions. The particle ਦਾ <u>d</u>aa *of* should agree with the gender and number of the object being possessed. Generally, it takes the following forms:

ਦਾ	<u>d</u>aa	masculine singular
ਦੇ	<u>d</u>e	masculine plural
ਦੀ	<u>d</u>ee	feminine singular
ਦੀਆਂ	<u>d</u>eeaa<u>n</u>	feminine plural

Words such as *of, in, to* or *from* are called prepositions in English and signify place or position. These words come before the noun and are therefore called prepositions.

In Panjabi these kinds of words come after the noun and are therefore called postpositions. This is also the second function of ਦਾ <u>d</u>aa in that it dictates word order and acts as a grammatical point determining the endings of the nouns and adjectives associated with the possession.

Examples:

ਕੁੜੀ ਦੀਆਂ ਪੈੱਨਸਲਾਂ	kurhee <u>d</u>eeaa<u>n</u> pai<u>n</u>salaa<u>n</u>	*the girl's pencils*
ਆਦਮੀ ਦੀ ਦੁਕਾਨ	aa<u>d</u>mee <u>d</u>ee <u>d</u>ukaan	*the man's shop*
ਮੇਰੀ ਭੈਣ ਦਾ ਕਮਰਾ	meree bhain<u>h</u> <u>d</u>aa kamraa	*my sister's room*

Possessive adjectives with plural objects

In Unit 1 you learned about possessive adjectives with singular objects. When objects being possessed are plural, the endings of possessive adjectives change accordingly. The following tables illustrate the use of the possessive adjective with plural objects.

Possessive adjectives with plural masculine objects

1st person

ਮੇਰੇ	mere	*my*
ਸਾਡੇ	saade	*our*

2nd person

ਤੇਰੇ	tere	*your* (informal)
ਤੁਹਾਡੇ	tuhaade	*your* (formal)

3rd person

ਇਹ ਦੇ/ਇਸ ਦੇ	ih de/is de	*his/her*
ਇਹਨਾਂ ਦੇ	ihnaan de	*his/her* (formal) *their*
ਉਹ ਦੇ/ਉਸ ਦੇ	uh de/us de	*his/her*
ਉਹਨਾਂ ਦੇ	uhnaan de	*his/her* (formal) *their*

Possessive adjectives with plural feminine objects

1st person

ਮੇਰੀਆਂ	mereeaan	*my*
ਸਾਡੀਆਂ	saadeeaan	*our*

2nd person

ਤੇਰੀਆਂ	tereeaan	*your* (informal)
ਤੁਹਾਡੀਆਂ	tuhaadeeaan	*your* (formal)

3rd person

ਇਹ ਦੀਆਂ / ਇਸ ਦੀਆਂ	ih deeaan /is deeaan	*his/her*
ਇਹਨਾਂ ਦੀਆਂ	ihnaan deeaan	*his/her* (formal) *their*
ਉਹ ਦੀਆਂ/ ਉਸ ਦੀਆਂ	uh deeaan/ us deeaan	*his/her*
ਉਹਨਾਂ ਦੀਆਂ	uhnaan deeaan	*his/her* (formal) *their*

ਮੇਰੇ ਬੱਚੇ	mere bachche	*my children*
ਤੁਹਾਡੀਆਂ ਕਿਤਾਬਾਂ	tuhaadeeaan kitaabaan	*your books*
ਉਹਨਾਂ ਦੀਆਂ ਮਿਠਿਆਈਆਂ	uhnaan deeaan mithiaaeeaan	*their sweets*
ਸਾਡੇ ਲੜਕੇ	saade larhke	*our sons*

Numbers

In Dialogue 3, you were introduced to the numbers ਚਾਰ **chaar** and ਦੋ <u>do</u>. The following is the list of numbers from 1–20. The topic vocabulary list at the end of the book gives the remaining numbers up to 100.

੧	1	ਇੱਕ	ikk	੧੧	11	ਗਿਆਰਾਂ	gi<u>aa</u>raa<u>n</u>
੨	2	ਦੋ	<u>do</u>	੧੨	12	ਬਾਰਾਂ	baar-haa<u>n</u>
੩	3	ਤਿੰਨ	<u>ti</u>nn	੧੩	13	ਤੇਰਾਂ	ter-haa<u>n</u>
੪	4	ਚਾਰ	chaar	੧੪	14	ਚੌਦਾਂ	chau<u>d</u>-haa<u>n</u>
੫	5	ਪੰਜ	pa<u>n</u>j	੧੫	15	ਪੰਦਰਾਂ	pa<u>n</u>daraa<u>n</u>
੬	6	ਛੇ	<u>che</u>	੧੬	16	ਸੋਲਾਂ	solhaa<u>n</u>
੭	7	ਸੱਤ	sa<u>tt</u>	੧੭	17	ਸਤਾਰਾਂ	sataar-haa<u>n</u>
੮	8	ਅੱਠ	a<u>thth</u>	੧੮	18	ਅਠਾਰਾਂ	athaar-haa<u>n</u>
੯	9	ਨੌਂ	nau<u>n</u>	੧੯	19	ਉੱਨੀ	unnee
੧੦	10	ਦਸ	<u>d</u>as	੨੦	20	ਵੀਹ	veeh

ਵਿਆਖਿਆ   viaakhiaa   Commentary

1. The vegetable seller ਸਬਜ਼ੀ ਵਾਲਾ sabzee vaalaa

In Panjab, fresh seasonal vegetables are available in abundance. The land is rich and the climate is tropical. Vegetables can generally be bought from a variety of sources. A street hawker carrying vegetables in his hand-pulled cart will make his daily rounds in the streets, shouting the names of vegetables at the top of his lungs in a manner that signals his presence more than does the content of his wares. Vegetables can also be bought from the market (often called a ਮੰਡੀ **ma<u>n</u>dee** or even ਮਾਰਕੇਟ **maarket**) where dozens of greengrocery stalls and shops are situated next to each other. These stalls offer a wide variety of fresh vegetables (ਸਬਜ਼ੀਆਂ **sabzeeaa<u>n</u>**) according to the season. In Panjab, visiting the market, especially in the evenings, is more than just for shopping; it is also a social and entertaining experience. Prices are not displayed so that customers have to make enquiries to shopkeepers, comparing prices of different stalls and bargaining as they go along. An accepted and often time-consuming part of shopping in Panjab is bargaining. Once a bargain has been made, the shopkeeper uses his age-old technique of weighing the goods between two pans on his scale. Most shopkeepers are efficient in mentally calculating the price of the weighed goods and are keen to chat, pointing out the low prices of other vegetables on offer and generally to praise their goods. This is a contrast to shopping for vegetables in western countries which is usually impersonal and mechanical.

2. The Panjabi sweet shop ਮਿਠਿਆਈ ਦੀ ਦੁਕਾਨ mithiaaee <u>d</u>ee <u>d</u>ukaan

Sweet shops are an integral part of shopping areas catering for South Asian communities in England, America, Canada and other parts of the world. These sweet shops are not like confectionery shops or bakeries, as they are often attached to take-away restaurants and also offer a range of spicy snacks and nibbles. It is customary for most South Asians to exchange boxes of sweets among friends and family on happy occasions. These can range from weddings and birthdays to festivals. Sweet shops, therefore, remain busy throughout the year. There is an enormous variety of sweets from different regions of the Indian sub-continent. Most sweet shops in the diaspora offer about fifty of the more common types of sweets and savoury dishes. Here is a list of some of the more popular items.

Sweets

ਲੱਡੂ	a sweet round ball, generally orange in colour,
laddoo	consisting of tiny particles made of gram flour

ਗੁਲਾਬ ਜਾਮਣ gulaab jaamanh	a round soft brown ball made of milk powder soaked in a sweet syrup
ਬਰਫ਼ੀ barfee	a bar of milk powder, similar to fudge, which is cut into diamond and rectangular shapes and is also found in a variety of colours such as white, pink and green
ਜਲੇਬੀਆਂ jalebeeaa<u>n</u>	whirls of batter, yellow-orange in colour, which are soaked in a sweet syrup
ਰਸ ਗੁੱਲੇ ras gulle	sweet round balls made of cheese soaked in a clear sweet syrup
ਰਸ ਮਲਾਈ ras malaaee	sweet round balls made of cheese soaked in thick, sweet milk
ਗਜਰੇਲਾ gajrelaa	a sweet dish made from grated carrots
ਪਿੰਨੀਆਂ pi<u>n</u>neeaa<u>n</u>	sweet round balls made from ground lentils and gram flour

Savouries

There are about a dozen salty dishes which are available from sweet shops. These are the most common ones:

ਪਕੌੜੇ pakaurhe	seasoned and spiced vegetables covered in a gram flour batter which are deep fried in oil
ਸਮੋਸੇ samose	deep-fried triangular pastries filled with boiled peas, potatoes and sometimes minced meat

✅ **ਅਭਿਆਸ**   **abhiaas**   **Exercises**

1. Choose the appropriate adjectives

Bitter gourd and turnip are masculine and okra is feminine.

small

ਛੋਟਾ	<u>chotaa</u>	ਛੋਟੀ	<u>chotee</u>

big

ਵੱਡਾ	**vaddaa**	ਵੱਡੀ	**vaddee**

a) ਇਹ ਕਰੇਲਾ _____ ਹੈ।   ih karelaa _____ hai.   *This bitter gourd is small.*

b) ਇਹ ਕਰੇਲਾ _____ ਹੈ।   ih karelaa _____ hai.   *This bitter gourd is large.*

c) ਇਹ ਭਿੰਡੀ _____ ਹੈ।   ih bhindee _____ hai.   *This okra is small.*

d) ਇਹ ਭਿੰਡੀ _____ ਹੈ।   ih bhindee_____ hai.   *This okra is large.*

e) ਇਹ ਸ਼ਲਗਮ _____ ਹੈ।   ih shalgam _____ hai.   *This turnip is small.*

f) ਇਹ ਸ਼ਲਗਮ _____ ਹੈ।   ih shalgam _____ hai.   *This turnip is large.*

ਕਰੇਲਾ   ਭਿੰਡੀ   ਸ਼ਲਗਮ

2. Who has ordered what?

Mr Singh, Jane and Henry have each ordered several food items. Listen to the tape and tick the box to show who has ordered what.

	ਸਮੋਸਾ samosaa	ਲੱਡੂ laddoo	ਪਕੌੜੇ pakaurhe	ਰਸ ਮਲਾਈ ras malaaee	ਭਿੰਡੀ bhindee	ਗੋਭੀ gobhee
Mr Singh						
Jane						
Henry						

3. Who am I?

After reading the commentary section, try to guess who I am from the descriptions given below.

a) I am sweet, full of syrup, round and dark brown in colour.

b) I am sweet like fudge, in diamond and rectangular shapes and come in a variety of different colours such as white, pink and green.

c) I am a very popular savoury snack, triangular in shape, covered in pastry, filled with potatoes and peas, and deep fried.

d) I am like a fritter, dipped in a batter of gram flour mixture, and deep fried. My core ingredients are usually cauliflower, potatoes and aubergine.

4. Insert the correct possessive adjectives

(Remember that the forms of possessive adjectives change not only in terms of who is in possession of the object, but also by the gender and number of the object being possessed.)

a. —— ਸਮੋਸੇ ਸੁਆਦੀ ਹਨ   samose suaadee han.   *Their samosas are tasty.*

b. —— ਲੜਕੇ ਕਿੱਥੇ ਹਨ?   larhke kiththe han?   *Where are my sons?*

c. —— ਕਿਤਾਬਾਂ ਹਰ ਪਾਸੇ ਹਨ   kitaabaan har paase han.   *Our books are everywhere.*

d. —— ਮਿਠਿਆਈਆਂ ਸਭ ਤੋਂ ਚੰਗੀਆਂ ਹਨ!   mithiaaeeaan sabh ton changeeaan han.   *Your (formal) sweets are the best!*

4 | ਬੜੀ ਖ਼ੁਸ਼ੀ ਦੀ ਗੱਲ ਹੈ !
barhee khushee dee gall hai!

That's very good news!

In this unit you will learn:

■ how to introduce yourself and others
■ how to ask and answer questions about work
■ how to ask and respond to questions about place of origin
■ how to talk about your family
■ how to describe actions and objects in the present

1 What do you do?

ਗੱਲ ਬਾਤ ੧ ਤੁਸੀਂ ਕੀ ਕਰਦੇ ਹੋ ?

gall baat 1 tuseen kee karde ho?

Dr Singh and Mrs Sharma are travelling on a train going from Birmingham to London. They are meeting for the first time.

ਮਿਸਜ਼ ਸ਼ਰਮਾ	ਸਤਿ ਸ੍ਰੀ ਅਕਾਲ। ਕੀ ਇਹ ਸੀਟ ਖ਼ਾਲੀ ਹੈ ?
Mrs Sharma	sat sree akaal. kee ih seet khaalee hai?
	Hello. Is this seat vacant?
ਡਾਕਟਰ ਸਿੰਘ	ਸਤਿ ਸ੍ਰੀ ਅਕਾਲ। ਹਾਂ ਜੀ ਖ਼ਾਲੀ ਹੈ। ਬੈਠੋ ਜੀ।
Dr Singh	sat sree akaal. haan jee, khaalee hai. baitho jee.
	Hello. Yes, it's vacant. Please sit down.
ਮਿਸਜ਼ ਸ਼ਰਮਾ	ਧੰਨਵਾਦ। ਮੇਰਾ ਨਾਮ ਮਿਸਜ਼ ਸ਼ਰਮਾ ਹੈ। ਸਰਦਾਰ ਸਾਹਿਬ, ਤੁਹਾਡਾ ਕੀ ਨਾਮ ਹੈ।
Mrs Sharma	dhannvaad. meraa naam misaz sharmaa hai. sardaar saahib tuhaadaa kee naam hai?
	Thank you. My name is Mrs Sharma. Sardar Sahib, what is your name?

ਡਾਕਟਰ ਸਿੰਘ	ਮੇਰਾ ਨਾਮ ਅਜੀਤ ਸਿੰਘ ਹੈ। ਮੈਂ ਡਾਕਟਰ ਹਾਂ। ਤੁਸੀਂ ਕੀ ਕਰਦੇ ਹੋ, ਮਿਸਜ਼ ਸ਼ਰਮਾ ?
Dr Singh	meraa naam ajeet singh hai. main daaktar haan. tuseen kee karde ho, misaz sharmaa ?
	My name is Ajeet Singh. I'm a doctor. What do you do, Mrs Sharma?
ਮਿਸਜ਼ ਸ਼ਰਮਾ	ਮੈਂ ਅਧਿਆਪਕਾ ਹਾਂ ਅਤੇ ਮੈਂ ਬਰਮਿੰਘਮ ਵਿਚ ਰਹਿੰਦੀ ਹਾਂ। ਤੁਸੀਂ ਕਿੱਥੇ ਰਹਿੰਦੇ ਹੋ ?
Mrs Sharma	main adhiaapkaa haan ate main barmingham vich rahindee haan. tuseen kiththe rahin de ho?
	I am a teacher and I live in Birmingham. Where do you live?
ਡਾਕਟਰ ਸਿੰਘ	ਮੈਂ ਵੀ ਬਰਮਿੰਘਮ ਵਿਚ ਰਹਿੰਦਾ ਹਾਂ। ਮੈਂ ਕੀਨੀਆ ਤੋਂ ਹਾਂ। ਕੀ ਤੁਸੀਂ ਪੰਜਾਬ ਤੋਂ ਹੋ ?
Dr Singh	main vee barmingham vich rahindaa haan. main kee-neeaa ton haan. kee tuseen panjaab ton ho?
	I live in Birmingham too. I am from Kenya. Are you from Panjab?
ਮਿਸਜ਼ ਸ਼ਰਮਾ	ਨਹੀਂ ਜੀ। ਮੈਂ ਦਿੱਲੀ ਤੋਂ ਹਾਂ।
Mrs Sharma	naheen jee. main dillee ton haan.
	No. I'm from Delhi.

🔑 ਸ਼ਬਦਾਵਲੀ   shabdaavalee   Vocabulary

ਸੀਟ	seet	*seat* (f.)
ਖ਼ਾਲੀ	khaalee	*empty, vacant*
ਬੈਠਣਾ	baithnhaa	*to sit*
ਬੈਠੋ ਜੀ	baitho jee	*please sit down* (formal)
ਸਰਦਾਰ ਸਾਹਿਬ	sardaar saahib	*Mr* (see Commentary)
ਡਾਕਟਰ	daaktar	*doctor* (m./f.)
ਅਧਿਆਪਕਾ	adhiaapkaa	*teacher* (f.)
ਬਰਮਿੰਘਮ	barmingham	*Birmingham* (m.)
ਰਹਿਣਾ	rahinhaa	*to stay, to live*
ਕੀਨੀਆ	keeneeaa	*Kenya* (m.)
ਤੋਂ	ton	*from*
ਪੰਜਾਬ	panjaab	*Panjab* (m.)
ਦਿੱਲੀ	dillee	*Delhi* (f.)

☑ ਅਭਿਆਸ   **abhiaas   Exercises**

After reading the dialogue and/or listening to the audio tape, try to do the following exercises

1. Fill in the blanks

Following the first example, fill in the blanks with the Panjabi phrases according to the English ones given to you. You may borrow phrases from the dialogue.

a) ਮੈਂ ਡਾਕਟਰ ਹਾਂ   main daaktar haan   *I am a doctor.*

b) _____   *Is this seat vacant?*   _____   *Yes, it is.*

c) _____   *I'm a teacher.*

d) _____   *What do you (formal) do?*

2. Arrange in correct word order

a) *I live in Birmingham too.*
   ਵੀ ਮੈਂ ਬਰਮਿੰਘਮ ਰਹਿੰਦਾ ਹਾਂ
   vee main barmingham rahindaa haan

b) *I am from Delhi.*   ਦਿੱਲੀ ਤੋਂ ਮੈਂ ਹਾਂ   dillee ton main haan

c) *What do you do?*   ਤੁਸੀਂ ਹੋ ਕਰਦੇ ਕੀ ?   tuseen ho karde kee ?

3. Remarks and responses

The following conversation is between two unacquainted passengers on a train. Put the responses of Passenger B into order according to Passenger A's remarks by using the correct corresponding number.

Passenger A		Passenger B
1 ਕੀ ਇਹ ਟਰੇਨ ਲੰਡਨ ਜਾਂਦੀ ਹੈ ? kee ih taren landan jaandee hai?	a	ਮੈਂ ਲੀਡਜ਼ ਰਹਿੰਦਾ ਹਾਂ main leedz rahindaa haan
2 ਤੁਸੀਂ ਕਿੱਥੇ ਰਹਿੰਦੇ ਹੋ ? tuseen kiththe rahinde ho?	b	ਮੈਂ ਅਧਿਆਪਕਾ ਹਾਂ main adhiaapkaa haan
3 ਤੁਸੀਂ ਕੀ ਕੰਮ ਕਰਦੇ ਹੋ ? tuseen kee kanm karde ho?	c	ਹਾਂ, ਇਹ ਟਰੇਨ ਲੰਡਨ ਜਾਂਦੀ ਹੈ haan, ih taren landan jaandee hai
4 ਕੀ ਤੁਸੀਂ ਹਿੰਦੀ ਬੋਲਦੇ ਹੋ ? kee tuseen hindee bolde ho?	d	ਮੈਂ ਪੰਜਾਬ ਤੋਂ ਹਾਂ main panjaab ton haan
5 ਕੀ ਤੁਸੀਂ ਪੰਜਾਬ ਤੋਂ ਹੋ ਜਾਂ ਦਿੱਲੀ ਤੋਂ ਹੋ ? kee tuseen panjaab ton ho jaan dillee ton ho?	e	ਮੈਂ ਹਿੰਦੀ ਅਤੇ ਪੰਜਾਬੀ ਬੋਲਦਾ ਹਾਂ main hindee ate panjaabee boldaa haan

▣ 2 That's very good news!
▣ ਗੱਲ ਬਾਤ ੨ ਬੜੀ ਖ਼ੁਸ਼ੀ ਦੀ ਗੱਲ ਹੈ !
gall baat 2 barhee khushee dee gall hai!

While Dr Singh and Mrs Sharma chat on the train going from Birmingham to London, Fatima Khan boards the train at Coventry. Mrs Sharma and Fatima Khan know each other. Fatima Khan addresses Mrs Sharma by her first name, Sita.

ਫ਼ਾਤਿਮਾ ਖ਼ਾਨ	ਨਮਸਤੇ ਸੀਤਾ। ਤੇਰੀ ਸਿਹਤ ਕਿਵੇਂ ਹੈ ?
	namaste seetaa. teree sihat kiven hai?
Fatima Khan	*Hello Sita. How's your health?*
ਸੀਤਾ ਸ਼ਰਮਾ	ਨਮਸਤੇ ! ਮੇਰੀ ਸਿਹਤ ਹੁਣ ਬਿਲਕੁਲ ਠੀਕ ਹੈ। ਮਿਹਰਬਾਨੀ।
	namaste! meree sihat hunh bilkul theek hai.
	miharbaanee.
Sita Sharma	*Hello! My health is perfectly fine now. Thank you.*
ਫ਼ਾਤਿਮਾ ਖ਼ਾਨ	ਬੜੀ ਖ਼ੁਸ਼ੀ ਦੀ ਗੱਲ ਹੈ !
	barhee khushee dee gall hai!
Fatima Khan	*That's very good news!*
ਸੀਤਾ ਸ਼ਰਮਾ	ਤੇਰੇ ਪਰਵਾਰ ਦਾ ਕੀ ਹਾਲ ਹੈ ?
	tere parvaar daa kee haal hai?
Sita Sharma	*How is your family?*
ਫ਼ਾਤਿਮਾ ਖ਼ਾਨ	ਸਾਰੇ ਠੀਕ ਹਨ। ਮਿਸਟਰ ਖ਼ਾਨ ਮੌਜਾਂ ਕਰਦੇ ਹਨ। ਸਾਡਾ ਬੇਟਾ ਅਤੇ ਬੇਟੀ ਕਾਲਜ ਵਿਚ ਪੜ੍ਹਦੇ ਹਨ।
	saare theek han. mistar khaan maujaan karde han.
	saadaa betaa ate betee kaalaj vich parhhde han.
Fatima Khan	*Everyone is fine. Mr Khan is enjoying life. Our son and daughter are studying at college.*

(Sita Sharma introduces Dr Singh and Fatima Khan to one another.)

ਮਿਸਜ਼ ਸ਼ਰਮਾ	ਡਾਕਟਰ ਸਿੰਘ, ਇਹ ਮੇਰੀ ਸਹੇਲੀ ਫ਼ਾਤਿਮਾ ਖ਼ਾਨ ਹੈ। ਫ਼ਾਤਿਮਾ, ਇਹ ਡਾਕਟਰ ਸਿੰਘ ਹਨ।
	daaktar singh, ih meree sahelee faatimaa khaan hai.
	faatimaa, ih daaktar singh han.
Sita Sharma	*Dr Singh, this is my friend Fatima Khan. Fatima, this is Dr Singh.*

ਡਾਕਟਰ ਸਿੰਘ	ਅਸੱਲਾਮ ਅਲੈਕਮ
	asslaam alaikam.
Dr Singh	*Hello.*
ਫ਼ਾਤਿਮਾ ਖ਼ਾਨ	ਵਲੈਕਮ ਅਸੱਲਾਮ।
	vaalaikam asslaam.
Fatima Khan	*Hello.*

(Sita addresses Fatima.)

ਸੀਤਾ ਸ਼ਰਮਾ	ਫ਼ਾਤਿਮਾ, ਅਗਲੇ ਹਫ਼ਤੇ ਨੂੰ ਸਕੂਲ ਦੀਆਂ ਛੁੱਟੀਆਂ ਸ਼ੁਰੂ ਹੁੰਦੀਆਂ ਹਨ। ਬੱਚਿਆਂ ਨਾਲ ਬਰਮਿੰਘਮ ਆਉਣਾ।
	faatimaa, agle hafte noon sakool deeaan chutteeaan shuroo hundeeaan han. bachchiaan naal barmingham aaunhaa.
Sita Sharma	*School holidays start next week. Come with the children to Birmingham.*
ਫ਼ਾਤਿਮਾ ਖ਼ਾਨ	ਇਨਸ਼ਾ ਅੱਲਾ।
	inshaa allaa.
Fatima Khan	*We'll try.* [literally: If God wishes]

ਸ਼ਬਦਾਵਲੀ   **shabdaavalee**   **Vocabulary**

ਬੜੀ	barhee	*very (v.)*
ਖ਼ੁਸ਼ੀ	khushee	*good (f.) (lit. happiness)*
ਗੱਲ	gall	*matter, news (f.)*
ਸਿਹਤ	sihat	*health (f.)*
ਹੁਣ	hunh	*now*
ਬਿਲਕੁਲ	bilkul	*absolutely, perfectly*
ਸਾਰੇ	saare	*everyone, all (v.)*
ਮੌਜਾਂ ਕਰਨਾ	maujaan karnaa	*to enjoy*
ਬੇਟਾ	betaa	*son (m.)*
ਬੇਟੀ	betee	*daughter (f.)*
ਕਾਲਜ	kaalaj	*college (m.)*
ਪੜ੍ਹਨਾ	parhhnaa	*to read, to study*
ਸਹੇਲੀ	sahelee	*friend (f.)*
ਅਗਲਾ	aglaa	*next*
ਹਫ਼ਤਾ	haftaa	*week (m.)*
ਸ਼ੁਰੂ ਹੋਣਾ	shuroo honhaa	*to start, to begin*
ਸਕੂਲ	sakool	*school (m.)*
ਛੁੱਟੀਆਂ	chutteeaan	*holidays (f.)*

☑ ਅਭਿਆਸ abhiaas Exercises

After reading the dialogue and/or listening to the audio tape, try to do the following exercises.

1. True or false?

a) ਮਿਸਜ਼ ਸ਼ਰਮਾ ਬਰਮਿੰਘਮ ਰਹਿੰਦੀ ਹੈ।   misaz sharmaa barmingham rahindee hai.   True / False

b) ਮਿਸਜ਼ ਸ਼ਰਮਾ ਅਧਿਆਪਕਾ ਹੈ।   misaz sharmaa adhiaapkaa hai.   True / False

c) ਮਿਸਜ਼ ਸ਼ਰਮਾ ਡਾਕਟਰ ਹੈ।   misaz sharmaa daaktar hai.   True / False

▤ 2. Talking about yourself

You have just met someone for the first time. Listen to their questions on the audio tape and/or read them from the following list and respond with information about yourself.

a) ਤੁਹਾਡਾ ਨਾਮ ਕੀ ਹੈ ?   tuhaadaa naam kee hai?   _____

b) ਤੁਸੀਂ ਕੀ ਕਰਦੇ ਹੋ ?   tuseen kee karde ho?   _____

c) ਕੀ ਤੁਸੀਂ ਇੰਗਲੈਂਡ ਤੋਂ ਹੋ ? kee tuseen inglaind ton ho? _____

d) ਤੁਸੀਂ ਕਿੱਥੇ ਰਹਿੰਦੇ ਹੋ ?   tuseen kiththe rahinde ho?   _____

▣ ਬੋਲੀ ਬਾਰੇ bolee baare Language points

The present tense

The simple present tense is used to describe either actions which are habitual (i.e. done on a regular basis) or objects which have permanent or fixed qualities. It is formed by adding the appropriate endings to the root of the main verb followed by a corresponding auxiliary verb. The 'ingredients' for constructing the present tense are, therefore, as follows:

   subject + main verb (simple present) + auxiliary verb = present tense

ਦਾ **daa**, ਦੀ **dee**, ਦੇ **de** and ਦੀਆਂ **deeaan** are the endings which are added to the root of the main verb to reflect the gender, person and number of the subject.

The auxiliary is formed by use of the simple present of the verb ਹੋਣਾ **honhaa** *to be* (see Unit 2 where it is used for *is*, *am* and *are*). The auxiliary verb operates at three levels:

1) helping the main verb

ਮੈਂ ਕਰਦੀ ਹਾਂ   main kar<u>d</u>ee haa<u>n</u>   *I do*

2) functioning independently

ਮੈਂ ਠੀਕ ਹਾਂ   mai<u>n</u> theek haa<u>n</u>   *I'm fine*

3) showing the existence of the object or situation being described

ਕੀ ਕੋਈ ਕਿਤਾਬਾਂ ਹਨ ?   kee koee ki<u>t</u>aabaa<u>n</u> han   *Are there any books?*

Now we can look at examples of the simple present tense. The verb ਕਰਨਾ **karnaa** (*to do*) is used here as an illustration. Verb root ਕਰ- kar:

ਮੈਂ **mai<u>n</u>** *I* (1st person singular masculine) + ਕਰਦਾ **kar<u>d</u>aa** *do* (present form of *to do*) + ਹਾਂ **haa<u>n</u>** am (auxiliary, 1st person singular) = ਮੈਂ ਕਰਦਾ ਹਾਂ **mai<u>n</u> kar<u>d</u>aa haa<u>n</u>** *I do*

Singular

Masculine	Feminine	
ਮੈਂ ਕਰਦਾ ਹਾਂ mai<u>n</u> kar<u>d</u>aa haa<u>n</u>	ਮੈਂ ਕਰਦੀ ਹਾਂ mai<u>n</u> kar<u>d</u>ee haa<u>n</u>	*I do*
ਤੂੰ ਕਰਦਾ ਹੈਂ <u>t</u>oon kar<u>d</u>aa hai<u>n</u>	ਤੂੰ ਕਰਦੀ ਹੈਂ <u>t</u>oon kar<u>d</u>ee hai<u>n</u>	*you do*
ਇਹ/ਉਹ ਕਰਦਾ ਹੈ ih/uh kar<u>d</u>aa hai	ਇਹ/ਉਹ ਕਰਦੀ ਹੈ ih/uh kar<u>d</u>ee hai	*he, she, it does*

Plural

Masculine	Feminine	
ਅਸੀਂ ਕਰਦੇ ਹਾਂ asee<u>n</u> kar<u>d</u>e haa<u>n</u>	ਅਸੀਂ ਕਰਦੀਆਂ ਹਾਂ asee<u>n</u> kar<u>d</u>eeaa<u>n</u> haa<u>n</u>	*we do*
ਤੁਸੀਂ ਕਰਦੇ ਹੋ <u>t</u>usee<u>n</u> kar<u>d</u>e ho	ਤੁਸੀਂ ਕਰਦੀਆਂ ਹੋ <u>t</u>usee<u>n</u> kar<u>d</u>eeaa<u>n</u> ho	*you do*
ਇਹ/ਉਹ ਕਰਦੇ ਹਨ ih/uh kar<u>d</u>e han	ਇਹ/ਉਹ ਕਰਦੀਆਂ ਹਨ ih/uh kar<u>d</u>eeaa<u>n</u> han	*they/these/those do*

The example of ਕਰਨਾ shows the manner in which verb roots ending with consonants are formed in the simple present tense. However, those roots which end in vowels follow a slightly different pattern. The nasal consonant is placed between the root and the present tense endings. Here, the verb ਪੀਣਾ **peenhaa** (*to drink*) is used to illustrate. Note that the **bindee** ˙ follows the **bihaaree** ੀ **ee** of ਪੀਣਾ **peenhaa.**

Simple verb: ਪੀਣਾ **peenhaa** *to drink.* Verb root: ਪੀ **pee:**

subject + (object, where appropriate) + simple present + auxiliary = present tense

ਮੈਂ **main** *I* (subject) (1st person, singular feminine) + ਪਾਣੀ **paanhee** water (object) + ਪੀਂਦੀ **peendee** *drink* (present of *to drink*) + ਹਾਂ **haan** *am* (auxiliary) (1st person singular) = ਮੈਂ ਪਾਣੀ ਪੀਂਦੀ ਹਾਂ **main paanhee peendee haan** *I drink water.*

Singular

Masculine	Feminine	

ਮੈਂ ਪਾਣੀ ਪੀਂਦਾ ਹਾਂ
main paanhee peendaa
  haan
	ਮੈਂ ਪਾਣੀ ਪੀਂਦੀ ਹਾਂ
	main paanhee peendee
	  haan
		I drink water

ਤੂੰ ਪਾਣੀ ਪੀਂਦਾ ਹੈਂ toon paanhee peendaa hain	ਤੂੰ ਪਾਣੀ ਪੀਂਦੀ ਹੈਂ toon paanhee peendee hain	*you drink water*

ਇਹ/ਉਹ ਪਾਣੀ ਪੀਂਦਾ ਹੈ
ih/uh paanhee peendaa hai
	ਇਹ/ਉਹ ਪਾਣੀ ਪੀਂਦੀ ਹੈ
	ih/uh paanhee peendee
	  hai
		*he, she, it
		  drinks water*

Plural

Masculine	Feminine	
ਅਸੀਂ ਪਾਣੀ ਪੀਂਦੇ ਹਾਂ asee<u>n</u> paanhee pee<u>nde</u> haa<u>n</u>	ਅਸੀਂ ਪਾਣੀ ਪੀਂਦੀਆਂ ਹਾਂ asee<u>n</u> paanhee pee<u>nde</u>eaa<u>n</u> haa<u>n</u>	*we drink water*
ਤੁਸੀਂ ਪਾਣੀ ਪੀਂਦੇ ਹੋ <u>t</u>usee<u>n</u> paanhee pee<u>nde</u> ho	ਤੁਸੀਂ ਪਾਣੀ ਪੀਂਦੀਆਂ ਹੋ <u>t</u>usee<u>n</u> paanhee pee<u>nde</u>eaa<u>n</u> ho	*you drink water*
ਇਹ/ਉਹ ਪਾਣੀ ਪੀਂਦੇ ਹਨ ih/uh paanhee pee<u>nde</u> han	ਇਹ/ਉਹ ਪਾਣੀ ਪੀਂਦੀਆਂ ਹਨ ih/uh paanhee pee<u>nde</u>eaa<u>n</u> han	*they drink water*

Here are a few more examples of other verbs in the simple present:

ਮੈਂ ਸੋਚਦੀ ਹਾਂ	mai<u>n</u> sochdee haa<u>n</u>	*I think*
ਬੱਚੇ ਖੇਡਦੇ ਹਨ	bachche khed<u>de</u> han	*the children play*
ਅਸੀਂ ਉਰਦੂ ਬੋਲਦੀਆਂ ਹਾਂ	asee<u>n</u> urdoo bol<u>de</u>eaa<u>n</u> haa<u>n</u>	*we speak Urdu*

Subject–verb agreement

The verb in a sentence must agree with the gender and number of its subject (with a few exceptions in the past tense which will be discussed in Unit 10). If the subject is feminine and singular, then the verb must also be feminine and singular. As you should have noticed in the previous section on the simple present tense, there are two verbs: one is the main verb which indicates the action and the other is the auxiliary verb (a form of ਹੋਣਾ *to be*). The main verb changes according to the gender and number of the subject, and the auxiliary verb must also agree with the subject but only changes according to the person (1st – *I*, 2nd – *you*, 3rd – *they*) of the subject.

In the following examples note how the verbs (main and auxiliary) are in agreement with the subject.

ਮੈਂ	ਜਾਂਦੀ	ਹਾਂ		mai<u>n</u>	jaa<u>n</u>dee	haa<u>n</u>
ਉਹ	ਜਾਂਦੇ	ਹਨ		uh	jaa<u>n</u>de	han
ਤੁਸੀਂ	ਜਾਂਦੇ	ਹੋ		<u>t</u>usee<u>n</u>	jaa<u>n</u>de	ho
ਮੁੰਡੇ	ਜਾਂਦੇ	ਹਨ		mu<u>n</u>de	jaa<u>n</u>de	han

Notice that the main verb and the auxiliary verb agree with one another in the singular and plural aspect of the subject. This is an essential element of forming sentences in Panjabi, and it should therefore be understood how verbs change accordingly.

Simple postpositions

You will recall from Unit 3 that the particle ਦਾ **daa**, in addition to showing possession, can be used as a postposition. Simple postpositions can be used to denote a number of different senses. In Panjabi the most common simple postpositions are as follows:

ਵਿਚ, ਦੇ ਵਿਚ	vich, de vich	*in, inside*
ਤੋਂ	ton	*from*
ਤੇ	te	*on*
ਤਕ	tak	*until, up to*
ਨਾਲ, ਦੇ ਨਾਲ	naal, de naal	*with*
ਨੂੰ	noon	*to*

Here are some simple examples of the uses of postpositions:

ਬਾਗ਼ ਵਿਚ	baagh vich	*in the garden*
ਪੰਜਾਬ ਤੋਂ	panjaab ton	*from Panjab*
ਮੇਜ਼ ਤੇ	mez te	*on the table*
ਅੱਜ ਤਕ	ajj tak	*until today*
ਇੱਥੇ ਤਕ	iththe tak	*up to here*
ਪਰਵਾਰ ਨਾਲ	parvaar naal	*with the family*
ਕਲਮ ਨਾਲ	kalam naal	*with a pen*
ਅਮਰੀਕਾ ਨੂੰ	amreekaa noon	*to America*
ਸ਼ਾਮ ਨੂੰ	shaam noon	*in the evening*

Nouns in the oblique

Panjabi nouns can be used in three different cases (modes of expression): the vocative, direct, and oblique. Each has its own corresponding way of formation. The vocative case reflects direct speech and will be dealt with in Unit 8. Direct nouns only change according to gender and number, as has been explained in Unit 3, and are not affected by any postposition. In contrast, the oblique case refers to the changes that some nouns undergo when affected by postpositions. In the examples of nouns with postpositions, all of the nouns are in the oblique case, though their forms do not reveal this because they are either invariable or are feminine in gender (see Unit 3). All nouns before a postposition, whether or not in a changed form, take on the oblique case. Generally, proper nouns such as names of people and places are not inflected by the postposition which follows them. In addition, masculine and feminine nouns have noticeably different formations in the oblique. You will note that feminine nouns in the singular and plural do not change in the oblique. Only masculine nouns change form when followed by postpositions.

Masculine singular

direct			oblique		
ਮੁੰਡਾ	mundaa	*boy*	ਮੁੰਡੇ ਨੂੰ	munde noon	*to the boy*
ਘੋੜਾ	ghorhaa	*horse*	ਘੋੜੇ ਤੇ	ghorhe te	*on the horse*
ਕਮਰਾ	kamraa	*room*	ਕਮਰੇ ਵਿਚ	kamre vich	*in the room*

Masculine plural

direct			oblique		
ਮੁੰਡੇ	munde	*boys*	ਮੁੰਡਿਆਂ ਨੂੰ	mundiaan noon	*to the boys*
ਘੋੜੇ	ghorhe	*horses*	ਘੋੜਿਆਂ ਤੇ	ghorhiaan te	*on the horses*
ਕਮਰੇ	kamre	*rooms*	ਕਮਰਿਆਂ ਵਿਚ	kamriaan vich	*in the rooms*

Feminine singular

direct			oblique		
ਤਸਵੀਰ	tasveer	*picture*	ਤਸਵੀਰ ਵਿਚ	tasveer vich	*in the picture*
ਕੁੜੀ	kurhee	*girl*	ਕੁੜੀ ਨੂੰ	kurhee noon	*to the girl*
ਜਨਾਨੀ	janaanee	*lady*	ਜਨਾਨੀ ਤੋਂ	janaanee ton	*from the lady*

Feminine plural

direct			oblique		
ਤਸਵੀਰਾਂ	tasveeraan	*pictures*	ਤਸਵੀਰਾਂ ਵਿਚ	tasveeraan vich	*in the pictures*
ਕੁੜੀਆਂ	kurheeaan	*girls*	ਕੁੜੀਆਂ ਨੂੰ	kurheeaan noon	*to the girls*
ਜਨਾਨੀਆਂ	janaaneeaan	*ladies*	ਜਨਾਨੀਆਂ ਤੋਂ	janaaneeaan ton	*from the ladies*

Adjectives in the oblique

Adjectives must agree with the nouns they describe. Therefore, it is only
logical that adjectives should also change form when attached to a noun
followed by a postposition. In a similar manner to the oblique forms of
nouns, adjectives are inflected in the oblique case, in addition to carrying
the feminine or masculine, singular or plural nature of the nouns which
they qualify. When adjectives are attached to oblique nouns, they also
become oblique. Invariable adjectives, however, do not change. Notice the
pattern of inflection of the adjectives in the following examples:

Direct		Oblique	
ਵੱਡਾ ਬੇਟਾ vaddaa betaa	*elder son*	ਵੱਡੇ ਬੇਟੇ ਨੂੰ vadde bete noon	*to the elder son*
ਵੱਡੇ ਬੇਟੇ vadde bete	*elder sons*	ਵੱਡਿਆਂ ਬੇਟਿਆਂ ਨੂੰ vaddiaan betiaan noon	*to the elder sons*
ਵੱਡੀ ਬੇਟੀ vaddee betee	*elder daughter*	ਵੱਡੀ ਬੇਟੀ ਨਾਲ vaddee betee naal	*with the elder daughter*

ਵੱਡੀਆਂ ਬੇਟੀਆਂ
vaddeeaan
  beteeaan
	elder daughters	ਵੱਡੀਆਂ ਬੇਟੀਆਂ ਨਾਲ
		vaddeeaan beteeaan
		  naal
			*with the elder
			daughters*

ਲਾਲ ਗੱਡੀ laal gaddee	*red car*	ਲਾਲ ਗੱਡੀ ਵਿਚ laal gaddee vich	*in the red car*
ਲਾਲ ਗੱਡੀਆਂ laal gaddeeaan	*red cars*	ਲਾਲ ਗੱਡੀਆਂ ਵਿਚ laal gaddeeaan vich	*in the red cars*

ਵਿਆਖਿਆ   viaakhiaa   Commentary

Employment and the Panjabi diaspora

There has been a long history of labour migration from Panjab to all parts
of the world. The descendants of officers in the British Indian police force
formed the core of the community in Malaysia and the Philippines, while
political migrants at the beginning of the twentieth century formed the
core of the old community in Vancouver, Canada. In Britain, migration
occurred after World War II and was primarily into the old industrial
heartlands of the Midlands and the North, with a sizeable group also
working in London. From a predominantly rural background to urban
Britain, Panjabi men went from tilling the land to toiling on factory floors.

In the 1960s in Britain a Panjabi man would almost definitely be working in a factory or foundry in labouring or semi-skilled occupations. This is in contrast to migration to America in the 1960s where, due to the operation of quotas, only professionals such as doctors and engineers were allowed entry from the Indian sub-continent.

As communities have settled and the old industrial manufacturing sector has gone into decline, Panjabis are now found in all walks of life in Britain and North America. However, there is a concentration in certain parts of the economy, particularly in traditional professions such as law, medicine and engineering as well as self-employment. A large number of Panjabis are also involved in business ventures in textiles, food processing and retailing, the most popular niche markets. At the same time there is an increasing diversity of occupational and class profiles of Panjabis, from the long-term unemployed to multimillionaires.

ਅਭਿਆਸ   abhiaas   Exercises

1. True or false?

a. ਸਿਹਤ	sihat	means *health*	True / False
b. ਬਿਲਕੁਲ	bilkul	means *alright*	True / False
c. ਅਧਿਆਪਕਾ	adhiaapakaa	means *doctor*	True / False
d. ਖ਼ੁਸ਼ੀ	khushee	means *fine*	True / False

2. Who made the statements?

Reread the dialogues, then look at the following:

a) ਇਹ ਡਾਕਟਰ ਸਿੰਘ ਹਨ।   ih daaktar singh han.   *This is Doctor Singh.*

b) ਮਿਸਟਰ ਖ਼ਾਨ ਮੌਜਾਂ ਕਰਦੇ ਹਨ।   mistar khaan maujaan karde han.
Mr Khan is enjoying life.

c) ਮੈਂ ਵੀ ਬਰਮਿੰਘਮ ਰਹਿੰਦਾ ਹਾਂ।   main vee barmingham rahindaa haan.
I live in Birmingham too.

3. Oblique or direct?

The following sentences contain adjectives and nouns which have been underlined. Identify which ones are direct and which ones are oblique.

a) ਕੀ ਇਹ ਤੁਹਾਡੀ ਬੇਟੀ ਹੈ ?   kee ih tuhaadee betee hai?   *Is this your
                                                        daughter?*

b) ਤੁਹਾਡੇ ਬੇਟੇ ਦਾ ਨਾਮ ਕੀ ਹੈ ?   <u>t</u>uhaade bete <u>d</u>aa naam kee hai?   *What is your son's name?*

c) ਕਮਰਾ ਸਾਫ ਹੈ।   <u>kamraa</u> saaf hai.   *The room is clean.*

d) ਕੁੜੀਆਂ ਕਮਰੇ ਵਿਚ ਹਨ।   kurheeaa<u>n</u> <u>kamre</u> <u>vich</u> han.   *There are girls in the room.*

e) ਅਗਲੇ ਹਫਤੇ ਨੂੰ ਆਉਣਾ।   <u>agle hafte</u> noo<u>n</u> aaunhaa.   *Come next week.*

▦ 4. Subjects and verbs into plural forms

Listen to the following sentences and/or read them in the following list. The sentences are in the present tense. Change the subjects and verbs from the singular to the plural. Remember that the verbs (both main and auxiliary) must agree with the subject. The first one has been done for you.

a) ਮੈਂ ਲੰਡਨ ਵਿਚ ਕੰਮ ਕਰਦੀ ਹਾਂ   main la<u>n</u>dan vich ka<u>n</u>m kar<u>d</u>ee haa<u>n</u>
I work in London.

ਅਸੀਂ ਲੰਡਨ ਵਿਚ ਕੰਮ ਕਰਦੀਆਂ ਹਾਂ   asee<u>n</u> la<u>n</u>dan vich ka<u>n</u>m kar<u>d</u>eeaa<u>n</u> haa<u>n</u>
We work in London.

b) ਮੇਰੀ ਬੇਟੀ ਸਕੂਲ ਵਿਚ ਪੜ੍ਹਦੀ ਹੈ   meree betee sakool vich parhh<u>d</u>ee hai

c) ਤੁਹਾਡਾ ਲੜਕਾ ਕਿੱਥੇ ਰਹਿੰਦਾ ਹੈ ?   <u>t</u>uhaadaa larhkaa ki<u>thth</u>e rahi<u>nd</u>aa hai?

d) ਕੀ ਉਹ ਮੁੰਡਾ ਪੰਜਾਬੀ ਬੋਲਦਾ ਹੈ ?   kee uh mu<u>nd</u>aa pa<u>n</u>jaabee bol<u>d</u>aa hai?

5 | ਕੀ ਗੱਲ ਸੀ ?
kee gall see?
What was the matter?

In this unit you will learn:

- ■ how to describe continuous actions in the present and past
- ■ how to form commands and requests
- ■ how to express *was* and *were*

1 What are you doing?
ਗੱਲ ਬਾਤ ੧ ਤੂੰ ਕੀ ਕਰ ਰਹੀ ਹੈਂ ?
gall baat 1 toon kee kar rahee hain?

Geeta and Sita are two women working in a garments factory. They are sitting next to one another as they are sewing and have the following conversation.

ਗੀਤਾ	ਨਮਸਤੇ ! ਤੂੰ ਕੀ ਕਰ ਰਹੀ ਹੈਂ ?
Geeta	namaste! toon kee kar rahee hain?
	Hello! What are you doing?
ਸੀਤਾ	ਨਮਸਤੇ। ਮੈਂ ਜੇਬਾਂ ਲਗਾ ਰਹੀ ਹਾਂ। ਮੇਰੀ ਮਸ਼ੀਨ ਕੰਮ ਨਹੀਂ ਕਰ ਰਹੀ। ਮੈਂ ਸੂਈ ਵਰਤ ਰਹੀ ਹਾਂ।
Sita	namaste. main jebaan lagaa rahee haan. meree masheen kanm naheen kar rahee. main sooee vart rahee haan.
	Hello. I am stitching pockets. My machine is not working so I am using a needle.
ਗੀਤਾ	ਤੂੰ ਸਮਾਂ ਜ਼ਾਇਆ ਕਰ ਰਹੀ ਹੈਂ। ਸੁਣ! ਮੈਂ ਕੰਮ ਛੱਡ ਰਹੀ ਹਾਂ।
Geeta	toon samaan zaaiaa kar rahee hain. sunh! main kanm chadd rahee haan.
	You are wasting your time. Listen! I am leaving work.
ਸੀਤਾ	ਤੂੰ ਕੰਮ ਕਿਉਂ ਛੱਡ ਰਹੀ ਹੈਂ ?
Sita	toon kanm kiun chadd rahee hain?
	Why are you leaving work?

ਗੀਤਾ	ਮੈਨੇਜਰ ਸਾਡੀ ਤਨਖ਼ਾਹ ਨਹੀਂ ਵਧਾ ਰਿਹਾ। ਉਹ ਸਾਡੀਆਂ ਮੰਗਾ ਪੂਰੀਆਂ ਨਹੀਂ ਕਰ
	ਰਿਹਾ ਹੈ।
Geeta	mainejar saadee tankhaah naheen vadhaa rihaa. uh
	saadeeaan mangaan pooreeaan naheen kar rihaa hai.
	The manager is not increasing our pay. He is not fulfilling
	our demands.
ਸੀਤਾ	ਤੂੰ ਠੀਕ ਕਹਿ ਰਹੀ ਹੈਂ !
Sita	toon theek kahi rahee hain!
	You're right! (literally: *You are saying it right*).

🔑 ਸ਼ਬਦਾਵਲੀ   **shabdaavalee   Vocabulary**

ਕਰਨਾ	karnaa	*to do*
ਜੇਬਾਂ	jebaan	*pockets* (m./f.)
ਲਗਾਉਣਾ	lagaaunhaa	*to stitch, to apply, to put on*
ਮਸ਼ੀਨ	masheen	*machine* (f.)
ਕੰਮ ਕਰਨਾ	kanm karnaa	*to work*
ਸੂਈ	sooee	*needle* (f.)
ਵਰਤਨਾ	varatnhaa	*to use*
ਸਮਾਂ	samaan	*time* (m.)
ਜ਼ਾਇਆ ਕਰਨਾ	zaaiaa karnaa	*to waste time*
ਸੁਣਨਾ	sunhnaa	*to listen*
ਕੰਮ	kanm	*work* (m.)
ਛੱਡਣਾ	chaddnhaa	*to leave, to quit*
ਮੈਨੇਜਰ	mainejar	*manager* (m./f.)
ਤਨਖ਼ਾਹ	tankhaah	*pay, salary* (f.)
ਵਧਾਉਣਾ	vadhaaunhaa	*to increase*
ਮੰਗਾਂ	mangaan	*demands* (f.)
ਪੂਰੀਆਂ	pooreeaan	*fulfilling*
ਠੀਕ	theek	*right, correct*
ਕਹਿਨਾ	kahinhaa	*to speak*

✅ ਅਭਿਆਸ   **abhiaas   Exercises**

After reading the dialogue and/or listening to the audio tape, try to do the
following exercises.

1. Arrange in correct word order

a) ਨਮਸਤੇ ਹੈਂ ਰਹੀ ਕਰ ਕੀ ਤੂੰ ? namaste-hain-rahee-kar-kee-toon? *Hello.*
What are you doing?

b) ਮੈਂ ਜੇਬਾਂ ਹਾਂ ਰਹੀ ਲਗਾ main-jebaan-haan-rahee-lagaa   *I am stitching pockets.*

c) ਨਹੀਂ ਵਧਾ ਰਿਹਾ ਤਨਖ਼ਾਹ ਮੈਨੇਜਰ ਸਾਡੀ naheen-vadhaa-rihaa tankhaah-mainejar-saadee   *The manager is not increasing our pay.*

2. Crossword

Using the words given to you in Panjabi, complete the crossword with the English translations.

1. ਮਸ਼ੀਨ   masheen
2. ਕੰਮ   kanm
3. ਤਨਖ਼ਾਹ   tankhaah
4. ਜੇਬਾਂ   jebaan
5. ਸਮਾਂ   samaan
6. ਸੂਈ   sooee

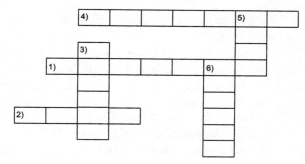

2 What was the matter?

ਗੱਲ ਬਾਤ ੨ ਕੀ ਗੱਲ ਸੀ ?

gall baat 2 kee gall see?

Preet and Sumeet are close friends. They are meeting each other after the weekend.

ਪ੍ਰੀਤ	ਤੁਸੀਂ ਕੱਲ੍ਹ ਕਿੱਥੇ ਸੀ ?
Preet	tuseen kallh kiththe see?
	Where were you yesterday?
ਸੁਮੀਤ	ਅਸੀਂ ਘਰ ਸੀ।
Sumeet	aseen ghar see.
	We were at home.

ਪ੍ਰੀਤ	ਤੁਸੀਂ ਸਵੇਰੇ ਕੀ ਕਰ ਰਹੇ ਸੀ ?
Preet	<u>t</u>usee<u>n</u> savere kee kar rahe see?
	What were you doing in the morning?
ਸੁਮੀਤ	ਮੈਂ ਫ਼ਿਲਮ ਦੇਖ ਰਹੀ ਸੀ। ਬੱਚੇ ਖੇਡ ਰਹੇ ਸਨ।
Sumeet	mai<u>n</u> filam <u>d</u>ekh rahee see. bachche khed rahe san.
	I was watching a film. The children were playing.
ਪ੍ਰੀਤ	ਤੁਹਾਡੇ ਪਤੀ ਜੀ ਕੀ ਕਰ ਰਹੇ ਸਨ ?
Preet	<u>t</u>uhaade pa<u>t</u>ee jee kee kar rahe san?
	What was your husband doing?
ਸੁਮੀਤ	ਉਹ ਕਾਰ ਧੋ ਰਹੇ ਸਨ।
Sumeet	uh kaar <u>dh</u>o rahe san.
	He was washing the car.
ਪ੍ਰੀਤ	ਤੁਸੀਂ ਕਿਉਂ ਪੁੱਛ ਰਹੇ ਹੋ? ਕੀ ਗੱਲ ਸੀ ?
Preet	<u>t</u>usee<u>n</u> kiu<u>n</u> pu<u>chch</u> rahe ho? kee gall see?
	Why are you asking? What was the matter?
ਸੁਮੀਤ	ਮੈਂ ਬੋਰ ਹੋ ਰਹੀ ਸੀ ਤੇ ਮੈਂ ਸਭ ਪਾਸੇ ਟੈਲੀਫ਼ੋਨ ਕਰ ਰਹੀ ਸੀ। ਮੈਂ ਤੁਹਾਡੇ ਬਾਰੇ ਸੋਚ ਰਹੀ ਸੀ।
Sumeet	mai<u>n</u> bor ho rahee see <u>t</u>e mai<u>n</u> sabh paase taileefon kar rahee see. mai<u>n</u> <u>t</u>uhaade baare soch rahee see.
	I was feeling bored and I called [was calling] everywhere. I was thinking of you.
ਪ੍ਰੀਤ	ਪਰ ਸਾਡਾ ਟੈਲੀਫ਼ੋਨ ਕੰਮ ਨਹੀਂ ਕਰ ਰਿਹਾ ਸੀ।
Preet	par saadaa taileefon ka<u>n</u>m nahee<u>n</u> kar rihaa see.
	But our telephone was not working.

☑ ਸ਼ਬਦਾਵਲੀ   **shab<u>d</u>aavalee**   **Vocabulary**

ਗੱਲ	gall	*matter* (f.) (literal meaning: talk)
ਕੱਲ੍ਹ	kallh	*yesterday*
ਸਵੇਰੇ	savere	*morning*
ਫ਼ਿਲਮ	filam	*film* (f.)
ਦੇਖਣਾ	<u>d</u>ekhnhaa	*to watch*
ਖੇਡਣਾ	khednhaa	*to play*
ਪਤੀ	pa<u>t</u>ee	*husband* (m.)
ਕਾਰ	kaar	*car* (f.)
ਧੋਣਾ	<u>dh</u>onhaa	*to wash*
ਪੁੱਛਣਾ	pu<u>chch</u>nhaa	*to ask*
ਬੋਰ ਹੋਣਾ	bor honhaa	*to be bored, to feel bored*

ਸਭ	sabh	*all, every*
ਸਭ ਪਾਸੇ	sabh paase	*everywhere*
ਪਾਸੇ	paase	*direction, way*
ਟੈਲੀਫ਼ੋਨ ਕਰਨਾ	taileefon karnaa	*to call by telephone*
ਤੁਹਾਡੇ ਬਾਰੇ	ṯuhaade baare	*about you*
ਸੋਚਣਾ	sochnhaa	*to think*

☑ ਅਭਿਆਸ   **abhiaas**   **Exercises**

After reading the dialogue and/or listening to the audio tape, try to do the following exercises.

1. Word search

Four Panjabi words are hidden in the box. These words are **kaar**, **sumeeṯ**, **kallh** and **ghar**. Find them by looking horizontally across each of the rows.

ੳ	ਸੁ	ਮੀ	ਤ
ਕੱ	ਲ੍ਹ	ਟ	ਤ
ਬ	ਭ	ਅ	ਰ
ਸ	ਕਾ	ਰ	ਮ

2. Answer in Panjabi questions about the dialogue

a) ਸੁਮੀਤ ਕੀ ਕਰ ਰਹੀ ਸੀ ?   sumeeṯ kee kar rahee see?
b) ਬੱਚੇ ਕੀ ਕਰ ਰਹੇ ਸਨ ?   bachche kee kar rahe san?
c) ਸੁਮੀਤ ਦਾ ਪਤੀ ਕੀ ਕਰ ਰਿਹਾ ਸੀ ?   sumeeṯ daa paṯee kee kar rihaa see?

◈ ਬੋਲੀ ਬਾਰੇ   **bolee baare**   **Language points**

The present continuous tense (-ing)

The present continuous tense is generally used when an action is in progress. In English it is often signified by adding *-ing* to the end of a verb. In Panjabi, the stem, also known as the root, of the verb does not change its form. But the auxiliary verb and the progressive marker must agree with the subject. The progressive aspect of the verb, comparable with *-ing* in English, is expressed through ਰਹਿ **rahi** *the stem of* ਰਹਿਣਾ

rahinhaa. It stands on its own as a separate word and should not be attached to either the main verb (*to . . .*) or the auxiliary verb. The progressive marker changes according to the gender and number of the subject.

For example: ਮੈਂ ਖਾ ਰਿਹਾ ਹਾਂ   main khaa rihaa haan   *I am eating*

ਮੈਂ **main** *I* (subject) (1st person singular, masculine) + ਖਾ **khaa** (stem of the verb ਖਾਣਾ (*to eat*)) + ਰਿਹਾ **rihaa** (= *-ing*) (progressive marker) (masculine/singular) + ਹਾਂ **haan** (auxiliary verb (*am*))

The forms of ਰਹਿ rahi are as follows:

Masculine singular	Masculine plural	Feminine singular	Feminine plural
ਰਿਹਾ	ਰਹੇ	ਰਹੀ	ਰਹੀਆਂ
rihaa	rahe	rahee	raheeaan

The auxiliary verb also reflects the person, number and gender of the subject and takes on the present tense forms of ਹੋਣਾ **honhaa** as discussed in Unit 2.

1st person

Masculine singular	ਮੈਂ ਖਾ ਰਿਹਾ ਹਾਂ main khaa rihaa haan	*I am eating*
Feminine singular	ਮੈਂ ਖਾ ਰਹੀ ਹਾਂ main khaa rahee haan	*I am eating*
Masculine plural	ਅਸੀਂ ਖਾ ਰਹੇ ਹਾਂ aseen khaa rahe haan	*we are eating*
Feminine plural	ਅਸੀਂ ਖਾ ਰਹੀਆਂ ਹਾਂ aseen khaa raheeaan haan	*we are eating*

2nd person´

Masculine singular	ਤੂੰ ਖਾ ਰਿਹਾ ਹੈਂ toon khaa rihaa hain	*you are eating*
Feminine singular	ਤੂੰ ਖਾ ਰਹੀ ਹੈਂ toon khaa rahee hain	*you are eating*

| Masculine plural | ਤੁਸੀਂ ਖਾ ਰਹੇ ਹੋ
<u>t</u>usee<u>n</u> khaa rahe ho | *you are eating* |
| Feminine plural | ਤੁਸੀਂ ਖਾ ਰਹੀਆਂ ਹੋ
<u>t</u>usee<u>n</u> khaa raheeaa<u>n</u> ho | *you are eating* |

3rd person

Masculine singular	ਉਹ/ਇਹ ਖਾ ਰਿਹਾ ਹੈ uh/ih khaa rihaa hai	*he is eating*
Feminine singular	ਉਹ/ਇਹ ਖਾ ਰਹੀ ਹੈ uh/ih khaa rahee hai	*she is eating*
Masculine plural	ਉਹ/ਇਹ ਖਾ ਰਹੇ ਹਨ uh/ih khaa rahe han	*they are eating*
Feminine plural	ਉਹ/ਇਹ ਖਾ ਰਹੀਆਂ ਹਨ uh/ih khaa raheeaa<u>n</u> han	*they are eating*

Uses of present continuous

Sometimes the simple present (see Unit 4) and present continuous tenses become interchangeable with one another when the action is on going and habitual.

Simple present

ਮੈਂ ਸਕੂਲ ਵਿਚ ਕੰਮ ਕਰਦਾ ਹਾਂ mai<u>n</u> sakool vich ka<u>n</u>m   *I work in a school.*
kar<u>d</u>aa haa<u>n</u>

Present continuous

ਮੈਂ ਸਕੂਲ ਵਿਚ ਕੰਮ ਕਰ   mai<u>n</u> sakool vich   *I am working in a*
ਰਿਹਾ ਹਾਂ   ka<u>n</u>m kar rihaa haa<u>n</u>   *school.*

The present continuous tense may also be used in instances where an action in the immediate future is being denoted, though it may not be happening at the present time:

ਉਹ ਸ਼ਾਮ ਨੂੰ ਆ ਰਿਹਾ ਹੈ   uh shaam noo<u>n</u> aa   *He is coming in the*
rihaa hai   *evening.*

A less formal but more common manner of this use of the present continuous occurs if we drop the auxiliary verb. The meaning of the sentence does not change. However, because the sense becomes slightly less formal a change of ਰਿਹਾ **rihaa** to ਰਿਹਾਂ **rihaa<u>n</u>** by nasalising the ending is required.

Examples:

| ਉਹ ਜਾ ਰਿਹਾਂ | uh jaa rihaan | *He's going* |
| ਮੈਂ ਪੜ੍ਹ ਰਿਹਾਂ | main parhh rihaan | *I'm reading* |

The imperative

The imperative is a form of the verb which expresses request, command or suggestion. The imperative has two forms: formal and informal. The formal imperative adds the vowel sound 'o' to the stem of the verb and the informal uses the stem on its own. Here are two examples which illustrate the formal and informal aspects of the imperative using the verb ਸੁਣਨਾ **sunhnaa**, *to listen*:

| (ਤੂੰ) ਸੁਣ | (toon) sunh | *Listen!* (you, informal) |
| (ਤੁਸੀਂ) ਸੁਣੋ | (tuseen) sunho | *Listen!* (you, formal) |

ਤੂੰ **toon** (*you*) is generally used with children, close relatives, equals and intimate relations while ਤੁਸੀਂ **tuseen** (*you*) is used as a respectful address with elders or formal acquaintances or in references to more than one person. The person and the tone of voice used to express imperative situations determine the nature of the order or request. For example, an imperative form in the 2nd person ਤੁਸੀਂ **tuseen** would denote a more polite, formal request while an imperative using the 2nd person ਤੂੰ **toon** would reflect a more informal although authoritative order.

Was and *were*

The past tense of the verb *to be* ਹੋਣਾ **honhaa** is *was* and *were*. You have already learned that the auxiliary verb is formed with the verb *to be*. Just as the present tense of *to be* becomes *is*, *am* and *are*, the past tense of *to be* becomes *was* and *were*.

Here is the past tense of the verb **honhaa** ਹੋਣਾ *to be*:

Singular   Plural

ਮੈਂ ਸੀ	main see	*I was*	ਅਸੀਂ ਸੀ	aseen see	*we were*
ਤੂੰ ਸੀ	toon see	*you were*	ਤੁਸੀਂ ਸੀ	tuseen see	*you were*
ਇਹ ਸੀ	ih see	*he/ she/ it was*	ਇਹ ਸਨ/ਸੀ	ih san/see	*they were*
ਉਹ ਸੀ	uh see	*he/she/that was*	ਉਹ ਸਨ/ਸੀ	uh san/see	*they were*

Note that ਸੀ **see** can be used with any number, person or gender.

The past continuous tense

The past continuous tense describes actions which had continued to happen before and after a particular time (in English *was ...-ing* and *were ...-ing*). The past continuous tense follows the same pattern as the present continuous except that the auxiliary verb takes the past form. The progressive marker (*-ing*) is followed by the appropriate forms of *was* and *were*. ਸੀ **see** is the most commonly used past auxiliary, although ਸਨ **san** is also used for the plural. Both are neutral of gender and number.

Masculine singular	Masculine plural	Feminine singular	Feminine plural
ਰਿਹਾ ਸੀ rihaa see	ਰਹੇ ਸਨ rahe san	ਰਹੀ ਸੀ rahee see	ਰਹੀਆਂ ਸਨ raheeaan san

ਮੈਂ **main** *I* (subject) (1st person singular, masculine) + ਖਾ **khaa** (stem of the verb ਖਾਣਾ (*to eat*)) + ਰਿਹਾ **rihaa** (= *-ing*) (progressive marker) (masculine singular) + ਸੀ **see** (auxiliary verb) (*was*) =

ਮੈਂ ਖਾ ਰਿਹਾ ਸੀ   main khaa rihaa see   *I was eating*

1st person

Masculine singular	ਮੈਂ ਜਾ ਰਿਹਾ ਸੀ	main jaa rihaa see	*I was going*
Feminine singular	ਮੈਂ ਜਾ ਰਹੀ ਸੀ	main jaa rahee see	*I was going*
Masculine plural	ਅਸੀਂ ਜਾ ਰਹੇ ਸੀ	aseen jaa rahe see	*we were going*
Feminine plural	ਅਸੀਂ ਜਾ ਰਹੀਆਂ ਸੀ	aseen jaa raheeaan see	*we were going*

2rd person

Masculine singular	ਤੂੰ ਜਾ ਰਿਹਾ ਸੀ	toon jaa rihaa see	*you were going*
Feminine singular	ਤੂੰ ਜਾ ਰਹੀ ਸੀ	toon jaa rahee see	*you were going*
Masculine plural	ਤੁਸੀਂ ਜਾ ਰਹੇ ਸੀ	tuseen jaa rahe see	*you were going*
Feminine plural	ਤੁਸੀਂ ਜਾ ਰਹੀਆਂ ਸੀ	tuseen jaa raheeaan see	*you were going*

3rd person

Masculine singular	ਉਹ/ਇਹ ਜਾ ਰਿਹਾ ਸੀ	uh/ih jaa rihaa see	*he was going*
Feminine singular	ਉਹ/ਇਹ ਜਾ ਰਹੀ ਸੀ	uh/ih jaa rahee see	*she was going*
Masculine plural	ਉਜ/ਇਹ ਜਾ ਰਹੇ ਸਨ/ਸੀ	uh/ih jaa rahe san/see	*they were going*
Feminine plural	ਉਹ/ਇਹ ਜਾ ਰਹੀਆਂ ਸਨ/ਸੀ	uh/ih jaa raheeaan san/see	*they were going*

Negative sentences

Generally, sentences are made negative by inserting ਨਹੀਂ nahee<u>n</u> (*not*) between the verb stem and the progressive marker.

| Statement | ਮੈਂ ਖਾ ਰਿਹਾ ਹਾਂ | mai<u>n</u> khaa rihaa haa<u>n</u> | *I am eating* |
| Negative | ਮੈਂ ਖਾ ਨਹੀਂ ਰਿਹਾ ਹਾਂ | mai<u>n</u> khaa nahee<u>n</u> rihaa haa<u>n</u> | *I am not eating* |

In colloquial speech the auxiliary verb is often dropped in positive and negative statements. A native Panjabi speaker may instead say: ਮੈਂ ਖਾ ਨਹੀਂ ਰਿਹਾ। mai<u>n</u> khaa nahee<u>n</u> rihaa.

Making interrogative sentences

An interrogative sentence is made simply by adding ਕੀ kee at the beginning of the sentence. The literal definition of ਕੀ kee is 'what' which can turn a statement into a question.

| Statement | ਤੂੰ ਖਾ ਰਿਹਾ ਹੈਂ | <u>too</u>n khaa rihaa hai<u>n</u> | *you are eating* |
| Interrogative | ਕੀ ਤੂੰ ਖਾ ਰਿਹਾ ਹੈਂ ? | kee <u>too</u>n khaa rihaa hai<u>n</u>? | *Are you eating?* |

If ਕੀ kee is inserted between the subject and the verb, the meaning of the sentence will change. Note and compare the following sentences:

ਤੂੰ ਖਾ ਰਿਹਾ ਹੈਂ	toon khaa rihaa hain	*you are eating*
ਕੀ ਤੂੰ ਖਾ ਰਿਹਾ ਹੈਂ ?	kee toon khaa rihaa hain?	*Are you eating?*
ਤੂੰ ਕੀ ਖਾ ਰਿਹਾ ਹੈਂ ?	toon kee khaa rihaa hain?	*What are you eating?*

Similarly, other interrogative pronouns can be used in turning statements into questions such as ਕਿਉਂ **kiun** (*why*), ਕਿਵੇਂ **kiven** (*how*) and ਕਿੱਥੇ **kiththe** (*where*).

ਵਿਆਖਿਆ   viaakhiaa   Commentary

1. ਕੱਲ੍ਹ kallh (*yesterday* and *tomorrow*)

In Panjabi there is one word which means both *yesterday* and *tomorrow* ਕੱਲ੍ਹ **kallh**. This may at first seem quite confusing, but the sense in which ਕੱਲ੍ਹ **kallh** is used in a conversation can be gauged from the tense of the verbs and the sense of the context. For example:

| ਮੈਂ ਕੱਲ੍ਹ ਘਰ ਸੀ | main kallh ghar see | *I was (at) home yesterday.* |
| ਮੈਂ ਕੱਲ੍ਹ ਆ ਰਹੀ ਹਾਂ | main kallh aa rahee haan | *I am coming tomorrow.* |

There is, however, a specific word for tomorrow – ਭਲਕ **bhalak** – but it is rarely used. The most common forms of signifying time are:

ਅੱਜ	ajj	*today*
ਕੱਲ੍ਹ	kallh	*yesterday/tomorrow*
ਭਲਕ/ਭਲਕੇ	bhalak/ bhalke	*tomorrow*
ਪਰਸੋਂ	parson	*day before yesterday/ day after tomorrow*

You will see all of these forms used in later units.

2. Panjabi women at work

In rural Panjab, women play a significant part in the contribution to the household economy. From helping in the fields to animal husbandry, women play a central role in the rural economy. This has continued in the diaspora, where Panjabi women have worked in factories in a similar way to their male counterparts. The factories of the Midlands in Britain and more recently Silicon Valley in California have employed Panjabi women. In Britain these women have been at the forefront of industrial struggles, the most well known being 'Imperial Typewriters' and the more recent 'Burnsalls' Strike'. The contemporary concentration of Panjabi women in the textiles sector in sewing and stitching of garments is a continuity with the jobs they had on arrival. The daughters of these migrants are now forging new paths in a wide variety of occupations and businesses, a selection of which can be found in the book, *The Golden Thread,* by Zerbanoo Gifford.

☑ ਅਭਿਆਸ   abhiaas   Exercises

1. Change the informal sentences into formal sentences

Complete this exercise by replacing the subject pronoun ਤੂੰ (**<u>t</u>oo<u>n</u>**) with ਤੁਸੀਂ (**<u>t</u>usee<u>n</u>**).

a) ਤੂੰ ਸਮਾਂ ਜ਼ਾਇਆ ਕਰ ਰਹੀ ਹੈਂ   <u>t</u>oo<u>n</u> samaan zaaiaa kar rahee hai<u>n</u>   *You are wasting your time*

b) ਤੂੰ ਕੰਮ ਕਿਉਂ ਛੱਡ ਰਹੀ ਹੈਂ ?   <u>t</u>oo<u>n</u> ka<u>n</u>m kiu<u>n</u> <u>ch</u>add rahee hai<u>n</u>?   *Why are you leaving work?*

c) ਤੂੰ ਠੀਕ ਕਹਿ ਰਹੀ ਹੈਂ   <u>t</u>oo<u>n</u> theek kahi rahee hai<u>n</u>   *You are (saying) right.*

2. Complete the table

ਪਤੀ		husband
ਘਰ	ghar	
	kallh	yesterday

▦ 3. Change present continuous to past continuous

Listen to the tape. Phrases have been given to you in the present continuous (i.e. am/is/are ___ -ing). Change them to the past continuous (i.e. was/were ___-ing). The first one has been done for you.

a. ਮੈਂ ਕੰਮ ਕਰ ਰਹੀ ਹਾਂ   mai<u>n</u> ka<u>n</u>m kar rahee haan   *I am working*
   ਮੈਂ ਕੰਮ ਕਰ ਰਹੀ ਸੀ   mai<u>n</u> ka<u>n</u>m kar rahee see   *I was working*

b. ਤੁਸੀਂ ਕੀ ਪੁੱਛ ਰਹੇ ਹੋ? <u>t</u>usee<u>n</u> kee pu<u>chch</u> rahe ho? *What are you asking?*

c. ਉਹ ਕੀ ਕਰ ਰਹੇ ਹਨ ?uh kee kar rahe han?   *What are they doing?*

d. ਉਹ ਕਾਰ ਧੋ ਰਿਹਾ ਹੈ   uh kaar <u>dh</u>o rihaa hai   *He is washing the car.*

4. Fill in the blanks

Using the pictorial clues given, fill in the blanks with the main verb stem
of the continuous actions being done.

a. ਗੀਤਾ ਟੈਨਸ _____

   geetaa tainas (tennis)_____

b. ਅਵਤਾਰ ਖਾਣਾ _____

   avtaar khaanhaa _____

c. ਸੀਤਾ ਤੇ ਗੀਤਾ ਪੰਜਾਬੀ _____

   seetaa te geetaa panjaabee

   _____

d. ਮੁੰਡਾ ਕਿਤਾਬ _____

   mundaa kitaab _____

6 | ਕੀ ਤੁਸੀਂ ਜਲੰਧਰ ਪੜ੍ਹੇ ਸੀ?

kee ṯuseen jalandhar parhhe see?

Did you study in Jalandhar?

In this unit you will learn:

- ■ how to express actions in the immediate past
- ■ how to express habitual actions in the past
- ■ about Sikh wedding customs
- ■ about kinship and relations

1 We went to London

ਗੱਲ ਬਾਤ ੧ ਅਸੀਂ ਲੰਡਨ ਗਏ ਸੀ

gall baaṯ 1 aseen laṇdan gae see

Surjit Singh and Pavan Singh are friends and both belong to the Sikh religion. They are having a conversation on the phone.

ਸੁਰਜੀਤ ਸਿੰਘ **Surjit Singh**	ਸਤਿ ਸ੍ਰੀ ਅਕਾਲ। ਤੁਸੀਂ ਐਤਵਾਰ ਕਿੱਥੇ ਸੀ? ਮੈਂ ਤੁਹਾਡੇ ਘਰ ਆਇਆ ਸੀ।
	saṯ sree akaal. ṯuseen aiṯvaar kiṯhṯhe see? main ṯuhaade ghar aaiaa see.
	Hello. Where were you on Sunday? I came to your house.
ਪਵਨ ਸਿੰਘ **Pavan Singh**	ਅਸੀਂ ਇੱਥੇ ਨਹੀਂ ਸੀ। .ਅਸੀਂ ਹਫ਼ਤੇ ਦੇ ਅਖੀਰ ਲੰਡਨ ਗਏ ਸੀ।
	aseen iṯhṯhe naheen see. aseen hafṯe de akheer laṇdan gae see.
	We were not here. We went to London over the weekend.
ਸੁਰਜੀਤ ਸਿੰਘ **Surjit Singh**	ਕੀ ਕੋਈ ਖ਼ਾਸ ਮੌਕਾ ਸੀ?
	kee koee khaas maukaa see?
	Was there any special occasion?

ਪਵਨ ਸਿੰਘ	ਹਾਂ ! ਮੇਰੀ ਭਤੀਜੀ ਦਾ ਵਿਆਹ ਸੀ।
Pavan Singh	haan! meree bhaṯeejee ḏaa viaah see.
	Yes! It was my niece's wedding.

ਸੁਰਜੀਤ ਸਿੰਘ	ਵਧਾਈਆਂ। ਕਿਹੜੇ ਸ਼ਹਿਰ ਤੋਂ ਬਰਾਤ ਆਈ ਸੀ ?
Surjit Singh	vadhaaeeaan. kihrhe shahir ṯon baraaṯ aaee see?
	Congratulations. Which city did the marriage party come from?

ਪਵਨ ਸਿੰਘ	ਉਹ ਮਾਨਚੈਸਟਰ ਤੋਂ ਆਈ ਸੀ। ਤਕਰੀਬਨ ੧੦੦ ਬੰਦੇ ਸਨ।
Pavan Singh	uh maanchaistar ṯon aaee see. ṯakreeban 100 banḏe san.
	They came from Manchester. There were about 100 people.

ਸੁਰਜੀਤ ਸਿੰਘ	ਵਿਆਹ ਕਿਵੇਂ ਰਿਹਾ ?
Surjit Singh	viaah kiven rihaa?
	How did the wedding go?

ਪਵਨ ਸਿੰਘ	ਬਹੁਤ ਸੁਹਣਾ। ਤੁਸੀਂ ਕਦੀ ਆਓ ਤੇ ਵਿਆਹ ਦੀਆਂ ਫ਼ੋਟੋ ਦੇਖੋ।
Pavan Singh	bahuṯ suhnhaa. ṯuseen kadee aao ṯe viaah ḏeeaan foto dekho.
	Excellent. Come over sometime and see the wedding photographs.

ਸ਼ਬਦਾਵਲੀ shabḏaavalee Vocabulary

ਲੰਡਨ	laṉdan	*London* (m.)
ਐਤਵਾਰ	aiṯvaar	*Sunday* (m.)
ਹਫ਼ਤੇ	hafṯe	*week* (m.)
ਅਖ਼ੀਰ	akheer	*end*
ਹਫ਼ਤੇ ਦੇ ਅਖ਼ੀਰ	hafṯe ḏe akheer	*weekend* (m.)
ਕੋਈ	koee	*any*
ਖ਼ਾਸ	khaas	*special*
ਮੌਕਾ	maukaa	*occasion* (m.)
ਭਤੀਜੀ	bhaṯeejee	*niece* (f.)
ਵਿਆਹ	viaah	*wedding* (m.)
ਵਧਾਈਆਂ	vadhaaeeaan	*congratulations*
ਸ਼ਹਿਰ	shahir	*city* (m.)
ਮਾਨਚੈਸਟਰ	maanchaistar	*Manchester* (m.)
ਤਕਰੀਬਨ	ṯakreeban	*about, approximately*

ਬੰਦੇ	bande	*people* (m.)
ਕਿਵੇਂ ਰਿਹਾ	kiven rihaa	*how did it go?*
ਬਹੁਤ ਸੁਹਣਾ	bahut suhnhaa	*very nice, excellent* (v.)
ਫੋਟੋ	foto	*photograph* (f.)
ਕਦੀ	kadee	*sometime*
ਆਓ	aao	*come* (formal)

☑ ਅਭਿਆਸ   abhiaas   Exercises

After reading the dialogue and/or listening to the audio tape, try to do the following exercises.

1. Answer the following questions about Dialogue 1 in either short or long form

a) ਪਵਨ ਹਫ਼ਤੇ ਦੇ ਅਖ਼ੀਰ ਕਿੱਥੇ ਸੀ ?   pavan hafte de akheer kiththe see?

b) ਖ਼ਾਸ ਮੌਕਾ ਕੀ ਸੀ ?   khaas maukaa kee see?

c) ਕਿਹੜੇ ਸ਼ਹਿਰ ਤੋਂ ਬਰਾਤ ਆਈ ਸੀ ?   kihrhe shahir ton baraat aaee see?

d) ਵਿਆਹ ਤੇ ਤਕਰੀਬਨ ਕਿੰਨੇ ਬੰਦੇ ਸਨ ?   viaah te takreeban kinne bande san?

2. Translate the following into formal Panjabi

a) Where were you on Sunday?
b) Where were you yesterday?
c) Where were you over the weekend?

☷ 2 Did you study in Jalandhar?

🖾 ਗੱਲ ਬਾਤ ੨ ਕੀ ਤੁਸੀਂ ਜਲੰਧਰ ਪੜ੍ਹੇ ਸੀ ?

gall baat 2 kee tuseen jalandhar parhhe see?

Surjit Singh visits Pavan Singh in order to see the photographs of Pavan's niece's wedding.

ਸੁਰਜੀਤ ਸਿੰਘ	ਸਤਿ ਸ੍ਰੀ ਅਕਾਲ ਜੀ। ਕੀ ਹਾਲ ਹੈ ?
Surjit Singh	sat sree akaal jee. kee haal hai?
	Hello. How are you?

ਪਵਨ ਸਿੰਘ **Pavan Singh**	ਸਤਿ ਸ੍ਰੀ ਅਕਾਲ। ਵਾਹਿਗੁਰੂ ਦੀ ਕਿਰਪਾ ਨਾਲ ਸਭ ਕੁਝ ਠੀਕ ਠਾਕ ਹੈ। sat sree akaal. vaahiguroo dee kirpaa naal sabh kujh theek thaak hai. *Hello. By the grace of God, everything is fine.*

(Pavan hands the wedding album over to Surjit)

ਸੁਰਜੀਤ ਸਿੰਘ **Surjit Singh**	(pointing to one of the photographs) ਇਹ ਪੁਰਸ਼ ਤੇ ਇਸਤਰੀ ਕੋਣ ਹਨ ? ih pursh te istaree kaunh han? *Who are this gentleman and lady?*
ਪਵਨ ਸਿੰਘ **Pavan Singh**	ਇਹ ਮੇਰਾ ਭਰਾ ਹੈ ਅਤੇ ਇਹ ਮੇਰੀ ਭਾਬੀ ਹੈ। ਅਸੀਂ ਇੱਕੋ ਮਕਾਨ ਵਿਚ ਰਹਿੰਦੇ ਸੀ। ih meraa bharaa hai ate ih meree bhaabee hai. aseen ikko makaan vich rahinde see. *He is my brother, and she is my sister-in-law. We used to live in one house.*
ਸੁਰਜੀਤ ਸਿੰਘ **Surjit Singh**	(looking at another photograph) ਕੀ ਇਹ ਤੁਹਾਡੇ ਚਾਚਾ ਜੀ ਹਨ ? kee ih tuhaade chaachaa jee han? *Is this your uncle?*
ਪਵਨ ਸਿੰਘ **Pavan Singh**	ਹਾਂ ਜੀ। ਅਸੀਂ ਕਾਲਜ ਵਿਚ ਹਾਕੀ ਇਕੱਠੇ ਖੇਡਦੇ ਸੀ। haan jee. aseen kaalaj vich haakee ikaththe khedde see. *Yes. We used to play hockey together in college.*
ਸੁਰਜੀਤ ਸਿੰਘ **Surjit Singh**	ਕੀ ਤੁਸੀਂ ਜਲੰਧਰ ਪੜ੍ਹੇ ਸੀ ? kee tuseen jalandhar parhhe see? *Did you study in Jalandhar?*
ਪਵਨ ਸਿੰਘ **Pavan Singh**	ਨਹੀਂ ਜੀ ਮੈਂ ਹੁਸ਼ਿਆਰਪੁਰ ਪੜ੍ਹਦਾ ਸੀ। naheen jee. main hushiaarpur parhhdaa see. *No. I used to study in Hoshiarpur.*
ਸੁਰਜੀਤ ਸਿੰਘ **Surjit Singh**	ਕੀ ਵਿਆਹ ਵਿਚ ਬਹੁਤ ਪ੍ਰਾਹੁਣੇ ਸਨ ? kee viaah vich bahut praahunhe san? *Were there a lot of guests at the wedding?*
ਪਵਨ ਸਿੰਘ **Pavan Singh**	ਹਾਂ, ਇਹ ਇੱਕ ਚੰਗਾ ਇਕੱਠ ਸੀ। haan, ih ikk changaa ikathth see. *Yes, it was a good gathering.*

ਸ਼ਬਦਾਵਲੀ   shabdaavalee   Vocabulary

ਰਹਿਣਾ	rahinhaa	*to live, to stay*
ਕਿਰਪਾ	kirpaa	*blessings* (f.)
ਸਭ ਕੁਝ	sabh kujh	*everything*
ਠੀਕ ਠਾਕ	theek thaak	*OK, fine*
ਪੁਰਸ਼	purash	*gentleman* (m.)
ਇਸਤਰੀ	istaree	*lady* (f.)
ਭਾਬੀ	bhabee	*sister-in-law* (f.) (brother's wife)
ਚਾਚਾ ਜੀ	chaachaa jee	*uncle* (m.) (father's brother)
ਕਾਲਜ	kaalaj	*college* (m.)
ਖੇਡਣਾ	khednhaa	*to play*
ਪ੍ਰਾਹੁਣੇ	praahunhe	*guests* (m.)
ਇੱਕ	ikk	*one, a*
ਇਕੱਠ	ikathth	*gathering* (m.)

ਅਭਿਆਸ   abhiaas   Exercises

After reading the dialogue and/or listening to the audio tape, try to do the following exercises.

1. Complete the table

The first one has been done for you.

ਪੁਰਸ਼	purash	man
	istaree	
ਇਕੱਠ		
		guests
	kaalaj	
		sister-in-law

2. Identify whether the statements are formal or informal

Tick the appropriate box.

	Formal	Informal

a) ਇਹ ਮੇਰਾ ਭਰਾ ਹੈ   ih meraa bharaa hai
   This is my brother.

		Formal	Informal
b) ਇਹ ਮੇਰੀ ਭਾਬੀ ਹੈ ih meree bhabee hai *This is my sister-in-law.*		☐	☐
c) ਇਹ ਮੇਰੇ ਚਾਚਾ ਜੀ ਹਨ ih mere chaachaa jee han *This is my uncle.*		☐	☐

🔊 ਬੋਲੀ ਬਾਰੇ   bolee baare   Language points

The past tense

The past tense in Panjabi describes actions or states of condition which have taken place at a particular time before the present one. Here we will discuss three different constructions of the past tense: the simple past, the remote past and the past habitual. As was shown in Unit 5, was and were in Panjabi are expressed through the past tense of the auxiliary verb *to be* ਹੋਣਾ **honhaa**. The more common forms for the past tense, however, are ਸੀ **see** and ਸਨ **san**. The appropriate form of the past of *to be* is determined by person, number and mode of address (formal or informal). Here are some examples to refresh your memory:

ਮੁੰਡਾ ਚੰਗਾ ਸੀ   mundaa changaa see   *The boy was good.*
ਮੁੰਡੇ ਚੰਗੇ ਸਨ   munde change san   *The boys were good.*

The simple past tense

The simple past tense is used when expressing actions or conditions completed in the past. The simple past is formed by adding appropriate endings to the stem of the main verb. The endings added to the stem reflect the gender and number of the subject. To determine if the subject is 1st/ 2nd or 3rd person, you need to refer to the subject pronoun. Here, the verb 'to speak' ਬੋਲਣਾ **bolnhaa**, will be used to illustrate the various past tenses:

Verb	Stem
ਬੋਲਣਾ bolnhaa (to speak)	ਬੋਲ - bol

Now note the endings added to the stem:

ਮੈਂ	main	I (subject) (1st person masculine)
ਬੋਲਿਆ	boliaa	spoke (simple past form of the verb 'to speak' ਬੋਲਣਾ)

1st person

Masculine singular	ਮੈਂ ਬੋਲਿਆ	main boliaa	*I spoke*
Feminine singular	ਮੈਂ ਬੋਲੀ	main bolee	*I spoke*
Masculine plural	ਅਸੀਂ ਬੋਲੇ	aseen bole	*we spoke*
Feminine plural	ਅਸੀਂ ਬੋਲੀਆਂ	aseen boleeaan	*we spoke*

2nd person

Masculine singular informal	ਤੂੰ ਬੋਲਿਆ	toon boliaa	*you spoke*
Feminine singular informal	ਤੂੰ ਬੋਲੀ	toon bolee	*you spoke*
Masculine plural formal	ਤੁਸੀਂ ਬੋਲੇ	tuseen bole	*you spoke*
Feminine plural	ਤੁਸੀਂ ਬੋਲੀਆਂ	tuseen boleeaan	*you spoke*

3rd person

Masculine singular	ਉਹ/ਇਹ ਬੋਲਿਆ	uh/ih boliaa	*he spoke*
Feminine singular	ਉਹ/ਇਹ ਬੋਲੀ	uh/ih bolee	*she spoke*
Masc. plural f.	ਉਹ/ਇਹ ਬੋਲੇ	uh/ih bole	*they spoke*
Feminine plural	ਉਹ/ਇਹ ਬੋਲੀਆਂ	uh/ih boleeaan	*they spoke*

Some verbs change in a more irregular manner in the past tense. You will have to learn and watch out for them. Verbs such as ਜਾਣਾ **jaanhaa** *to go* ਕਰਨਾ **karnaa** *to do* and ਦੇਣਾ **denhaa** *to give* take on irregular forms in the past tense which do not derive from the root. Here we give the example of how ਜਾਣਾ **jaanhaa** *to go* is formed in the simple past tense. Note that the forms are not affected by person, only by gender and number.

ਜਾਣਾ **jaanhaa** – *to go* (went)

Masculine singular	Feminine singular	Masculine plural	Feminine plural
ਗਿਆ	ਗਈ	ਗਏ	ਗਈਆਂ
giaa	gaee	gae	gaeeaan

The remote past

The remote past in Panjabi expresses actions which occurred prior to the present or the immediate past. The main verb used in the simple past is combined with the auxiliary verb in the past to form the remote past. The remote past tense is used when one is:

- being definitive in a statement
- emphasising a particular point
- conveying the completion of an action
- referring to the remote past

The form of the main verb follows the pattern of the simple past just shown while the auxiliary verb reflects the appropriate forms of *was* and *were*. For example:

1st person

Masculine singular	ਮੈਂ ਬੋਲਿਆ ਸੀ	mai<u>n</u> boliaa see	*I spoke, had spoken*
Feminine singular	ਮੈਂ ਬੋਲੀ ਸੀ	mai<u>n</u> bolee see	*I spoke, had spoken*
Masculine plural	ਅਸੀਂ ਬੋਲੇ ਸੀ	asee<u>n</u> bole see	*we spoke, had spoken*
Feminine plural	ਅਸੀਂ ਬੋਲੀਆਂ ਸੀ	asee<u>n</u> boleeaa<u>n</u> see	*we spoke, had spoken*

2nd person

Masculine singular informal	ਤੂੰ ਬੋਲਿਆ ਸੀ	<u>t</u>oo<u>n</u> boliaa see	*you spoke, had spoken*
Feminine singular informal	ਤੂੰ ਬੋਲੀ ਸੀ	<u>t</u>oo<u>n</u> bolee see	*you spoke, had spoken*
Masculine plural formal	ਤੁਸੀਂ ਬੋਲੇ ਸੀ	<u>t</u>usee<u>n</u> bole see	*you spoke, had spoken*
Feminine plural	ਤੁਸੀਂ ਬੋਲੀਆਂ ਸੀ	<u>t</u>usee<u>n</u> boleeaa<u>n</u> see	*you spoke, had spoken*

3rd person

Masculine singular	ਇਹ/ਉਹ ਬੋਲਿਆ ਸੀ	ih/uh boliaa see	*he spoke, had spoken*
Feminine singular	ਇਹ/ਉਹ ਬੋਲੀ ਸੀ	ih/uh bolee see	*she spoke, had spoken*
Masculine plural formal	ਇਹ/ਉਹ ਬੋਲੇ ਸਨ/ ਸੀ	ih/uh bole san/see	*they spoke, had spoken*
Feminine plural	ਇਹ/ਉਹ ਬੋਲੀਆਂ ਸਨ/ਸੀ	ih/uh boleeaan san/see	*they spoke, had spoken*

The remote past of ਜਾਣਾ **jaanhaa** *to go* follows the same pattern using the simple past form with the appropriate form of was and were.

ਜਾਣਾ jaanhaa – to go

Masculine singular	Feminine singular	Masculine plural	Feminine plural
ਗਿਆ ਸੀ	ਗਈ ਸੀ	ਗਏ ਸੀ/ਸਨ	ਗਈਆਂ ਸੀ/ਸਨ
giaa see	gaee see	gae see/san	gaeeaan see/san

Past habitual tense – *used to*

In English *used to* expresses actions which occurred regularly in the past but which no longer exist in the present. In Panjabi the past habitual tense is used in the same manner. For example:

ਮੈਂ ਬੋਲਦਾ ਸੀ	main boldaa see	*I used to speak*

The components of this example can be broken down as follows:

ਮੈਂ	main	*I* (subject) (1st person masculine)
ਬੋਲਦਾ	boldaa	*speak* (simple present form of *to speak* ਬੋਲਣਾ **bolnhaa**)
ਸੀ	see	*was* (simple past of *to be* ਹੋਣਾ **honhaa**)

Note from the example that the past habitual tense is formed with the main verb, which takes on the same form as in the simple present tense, and the past tense of *to be* ਹੋਣਾ **honhaa**. Some examples follow.

1st person

Masculine singular	ਮੈਂ ਬੋਲਦਾ ਸੀ	main boldaa see	*I used to speak*
Feminine singular	ਮੈਂ ਬੋਲਦੀ ਸੀ	main boldee see	*I used to speak*
Masculine plural	ਅਸੀਂ ਬੋਲਦੇ ਸੀ	aseen bolde see	*we used to speak*
Feminine plural	ਅਸੀਂ ਬੋਲਦੀਆਂ ਸੀ	aseen boldeeaan see	*we used to speak*

2nd person

Masculine singular informal	ਤੂੰ ਬੋਲਦਾ ਸੀ	toon boldaa see	*you used to speak*
Feminine singular informal	ਤੂੰ ਬੋਲਦੀ ਸੀ	toon boldee see	*you used to speak*
Masculine plural formal	ਤੁਸੀਂ ਬੋਲਦੇ ਸੀ	tuseen bolde see	*you used to speak*
Feminine plural	ਤੁਸੀਂ ਬੋਲਦੀਆਂ ਸੀ	tuseen boldeeaan see	*you used to speak*

3rd person

Masculine singular	ਇਹ/ਉਹ ਬੋਲਦਾ ਸੀ	ih/uh boldaa see	*he used to speak*
Feminine singular	ਇਹ/ਉਹ ਬੋਲਦੀ ਸੀ	ih/uh boldee see	*she used to speak*
Masculine plural formal	ਇਹ/ਉਹ ਬੋਲਦੇ ਸਨ/ਸੀ	ih/uh bolde san/see	*they used to speak*
Feminine plural	ਇਹ/ਉਹ ਬੋਲਦੀਆਂ ਸਨ/ਸੀ	ih/uh boldeeaan san/see	*they used to speak*

Another form of the past habitual uses the verb expressing the action in the habitual and the habitual forms of ਹੋਣਾ **honhaa** with the past auxiliary. *I used to go* in this form is expressed in the following ways:

1st person

ਮੈਂ ਜਾਂਦਾ ਹੁੰਦਾ ਸੀ	main jaandaa hundaa see	*I used to go*
ਮੈਂ ਜਾਂਦੀ ਹੁੰਦੀ ਸੀ	main jaandee hundee see	*I used to go*
ਅਸੀਂ ਜਾਂਦੇ ਹੁੰਦੇ ਸੀ	aseen jaande hunde see	*we used to go*
ਅਸੀਂ ਜਾਂਦੀਆਂ ਹੁੰਦੀਆਂ ਸੀ	aseen jaandeeaan hundeeaan see	*we used to go*

2nd person

ਤੂੰ ਜਾਂਦਾ ਹੁੰਦਾ ਸੀ	toon jaandaa hun daa see	*you used to go*
ਤੂੰ ਜਾਂਦੀ ਹੁੰਦੀ ਸੀ	toon jaandee hun dee see	*you used to go*
ਤੁਸੀਂ ਜਾਂਦੇ ਹੁੰਦੇ ਸੀ	tuseen jaande hun de see	*you used to go*
ਤੁਸੀਂ ਜਾਂਦੀਆਂ ਹੁੰਦੀਆਂ ਸੀ	tuseen jaandeeaan hundee aan see	*you used to go*

3rd person

ਇਹ/ਉਹ ਜਾਂਦਾ ਹੁੰਦਾ ਸੀ	ih/uh jaandaa hundaa see	*he used to go*
ਇਹ/ਉਹ ਜਾਂਦੀ ਹੁੰਦੀ ਸੀ	ih/uh jaandee hundee see	*she used to go*
ਇਹ/ਉਹ ਜਾਂਦੇ ਹੁੰਦੇ ਸਨ	ih/uh jaande hunde san	*he/she/they used to go*
ਇਹ/ਉਹ ਜਾਂਦੀਆਂ ਹੁੰਦੀਆਂ ਸਨ	ih/uh jaandeeaan hundeeaan san	*they used to go*

You will come across these various forms of the past tense in subsequent units and there will therefore be plenty of opportunity to practice all of these constructions.

Negative sentences

Negative sentences in the various past tenses are formed by adding ਨਹੀਂ **naheen** either before or after the main verb.

Simple past

ਮੈਂ ਬੋਲਿਆ	ਮੈਂ ਨਹੀਂ ਬੋਲਿਆ	ਮੈਂ ਬੋਲਿਆ ਨਹੀਂ
main boliaa	main naheen boliaa	main boliaa naheen
I spoke	*I did not speak*	*I did not speak*

Remote past

ਮੈਂ ਬੋਲਿਆ ਸੀ	ਮੈਂ ਨਹੀਂ ਬੋਲਿਆ ਸੀ	ਮੈਂ ਬੋਲਿਆ ਨਹੀਂ ਸੀ
main boliaa see	main naheen boliaa see	main boliaa naheen see
I spoke/had spoken	*I did not speak/had not spoken*	*I did not speak/had not spoken*

Habitual past

ਮੈਂ ਬੋਲਦਾ ਸੀ	ਮੈਂ ਨਹੀਂ ਬੋਲਦਾ ਸੀ	ਮੈਂ ਬੋਲਦਾ ਨਹੀਂ ਸੀ
main boldaa see	main naheen boldaa see	main boldaa naheen see
I used to speak	*I did not use to speak*	*I did not use to speak*

Interrogative sentences

As with the other verb tenses in Panjabi, interrogative sentences are formed in the past by adding the question word ਕੀ **kee** at the beginning of the sentence. Here are some examples of how questions are made out of statements in the past:

Simple past

Statement	Question
ਮੈਂ ਬੋਲਿਆ main boliaa	ਕੀ ਮੈਂ ਬੋਲਿਆ ? kee main boliaa?
I spoke	*Did I speak?*

Remote past

Statement	Question
ਮੈਂ ਬੋਲਿਆ ਸੀ main boliaa see	ਕੀ ਮੈਂ ਬੋਲਿਆ ਸੀ ? kee main boliaa see
I spoke/ had spoken	*Did I speak/ Had I spoken?*

Habitual past

Statement	Question
ਮੈਂ ਬੋਲਦਾ ਸੀ main boldaa see	ਕੀ ਮੈਂ ਬੋਲਦਾ ਸੀ ? kee main boldaa see?
I used to speak	*Did I use to speak?*

ਵਿਆਖਿਆ viaakhiaa Commentary

Panjabi families

Panjabi weddings are seen as social occasions and signify the coming together of two families rather than of two individuals, as is traditionally the case in modern western marriages. Kinship relations form a central part of Panjabi society. Often families live in extended units with three or more generations all living under one roof. In contrast to English-speaking cultures, Panjabi has very specific terms for members of the nuclear and extended family. Most kinship terms are determined by the paternal and maternal nature of the relationship and whether or not it is a relationship by marriage. Beware ... these are only half of the possible kin names you may come across in conversation with Panjabis!

Paternal		Maternal	
ਦਾਦਾ	daadaa *father's father*	ਨਾਨਾ	naanaa *mother's father*
ਦਾਦੀ	daadee *father's mother*	ਨਾਨੀ	naanee *mother's mother*
ਪਿਤਾ	pitaa *father*	ਮਾਤਾ	maataa *mother*
ਅੱਬਾ	abbaa *papa (father)*	ਅੱਮੀ	ammee *mother*
ਪਤੀ	patee *husband*	ਪਤਨੀ	patnee *wife*
ਭਰਾ	bharaa *brother*	ਭੈਣ	bhainh *sister*
ਜੀਜਾ	jeejaa *sister's husband*	ਭਾਬੀ	bhaabee *brother's wife*
ਚਾਚਾ	chaachaa *father's younger brother*	ਮਾਸੀ	maasee *mother's sister*
ਚਾਚੀ	chaachee *father's younger brother's wife*	ਮਾਸੜ	maasarh *mother's sister's husband*
ਤਾਇਆ	taaiaa *father's elder brother*	ਮਾਮਾ	maamaa *mother's brother*

ਤਾਈ	ṯaaee *father's elder brother's wife*	ਮਾਮੀ	maamee *mother's brother's wife*
ਭੂਆ	bhooaa *father's sister*	ਪੁੱਤਰੀ	puṯṯaree *daughter*
ਫੁਫੜ	phupharh *father's sister's husband*	ਭਾਂਜਾ	bhaanjaa *nephew (sister's son)*
ਪੁੱਤਰ	puṯṯar *son*		
ਭਤੀਜਾ	bhaṯeejaa *nephew (brother's son)*	ਭਾਂਜੀ	bhaanjee *niece (sister's daughter)*
ਭਤੀਜੀ	bhaṯeejee *niece (brother's daughter)*		

✅ ਅਭਿਆਸ   abhiaas   Exercises

After reading the dialogue and/or listening to the audio tape, try to do the following exercises.

1. The family tree

Pavan is showing his family photos to Surjit. Read and/or listen to the following passage on the audio tape. Then try to complete Pavan's family tree.(ਕੁਰਸੀ ਨਾਮਾ kursee naamaa.)

ਇਹ ਹੈ ਮੇਰਾ ਕੁਰਸੀ ਨਾਮਾ:

ਮੇਰੇ ਪਿਤਾ ਜੀ ਦਾ ਨਾਮ ਜੋਗਿੰਦਰ ਸਿੰਘ ਹੈ ਅਤੇ ਮੇਰੇ ਮਾਤਾ ਜੀ ਦਾ ਨਾਮ ਗੁਰਮੀਤ ਕੌਰ ਹੈ। ਉਹਨਾਂ ਦੇ ਤਿੰਨ ਬੱਚੇ ਹਨ। ਮੈਂ, ਮੇਰਾ ਭਰਾ ਸੁਖਜੀਤ ਸਿੰਘ ਤੇ ਮੇਰੀ ਭੈਣ ਕੁਲਦੀਪ ਕੌਰ। ਮੇਰੀ ਭਾਬੀ ਦਾ ਨਾਮ ਜਗਜੀਤ ਕੌਰ ਹੈ ਤੇ ਮੇਰੇ ਭਤੀਜੇ ਦਾ ਨਾਮ ਗੁਰਤੇਜ ਸਿੰਘ ਹੈ। ਮੇਰੀ ਪਤਨੀ ਦਾ ਨਾਮ ਹਰਲੀਨ ਕੌਰ ਹੈ ਅਤੇ ਸਾਡੇ ਦੋ ਬੱਚੇ ਹਨ, ਇੱਕ ਪੁੱਤਰ, ਮਨਜੀਤ ਸਿੰਘ ਤੇ ਇੱਕ ਪੁੱਤਰੀ, ਬਲਦੇਵ ਕੌਰ।

ih hai meraa kursee naamaa:

mere piṯaa jee ḏaa naam jogindar singh hai aṯe mere maaṯaa jee ḏaa naam gurmeeṯ kaur hai. uhnaan ḏe ṯinn bachche han. main, meraa bharaa sukhjeeṯ singh ṯe meree bhainh kulḏeep kaur. meree bhabee ḏaa naam jagjeeṯ kaur hai ṯe mere bhaṯeeje ḏaa naam gurṯej singh hai. meree paṯnee ḏaa naam harleen kaur hai aṯe saade ḏo bachche han, ikk puṯṯar, manjeeṯ singh ṯe ikk puṯṯree, balḏev kaur.

2. Matching

Match the questions with their correct responses.

a) ਮੈਂ ਹਫ਼ਤੇ ਦੇ ਅਖੀਰ
   ਮਾਨਚੈਸਟਰ ਸੀ
   main hafṯe ḏe akheer
   maanchaistar see

i) ਤੁਸੀਂ ਕੱਲ੍ਹ ਕਿੱਥੇ ਸੀ ?
   tuseen kallh kiththe see?

b) ਮੈਂ ਐਤਵਾਰ ਘਰ ਸੀ
   main aiṯvaar ghar see

ii) ਤੁਸੀਂ ਹਫ਼ਤੇ ਦੇ ਅਖੀਰ
    ਕਿੱਥੇ ਸੀ ?
    tuseen hafṯe ḏe akheer
    kiththe see?

c) ਮੈਂ ਕੱਲ੍ਹ ਲੰਡਨ ਸੀ
   main kallh landan see

iii) ਤੁਸੀਂ ਐਤਵਾਰ ਕਿੱਥੇ ਸੀ ?
     tuseen aiṯvaar kiththe see?

3. True or false?

Indicate whether the following statements from the dialogues in the unit are true or false.

a) ਪਵਨ ਸਿੰਘ ਹਾਕੀ ਖੇਡਦਾ ਸੀ। pavan singh haakee kheddaa see.   True/ False

b) ਪਵਨ ਸਿੰਘ ਜਲੰਧਰ ਪੜ੍ਹਦਾ ਸੀ। pavan singh jalandhar parhhdaa see.
True / False

c) ਵਿਆਹ ਵਿਚ ਬਹੁਤ ਪ੍ਰਾਹੁਣੇ ਸਨ। viaah vich bahut praahunhe san. True / False

4. Construct negative and interrogative sentences

The first example is given.

1. ਰਾਮ ਲੰਡਨ ਰਹਿੰਦਾ ਸੀ ।
   Raam landan rahindaa see.
   Ram used to live in London.

Negative: ਰਾਮ ਲੰਡਨ ਨਹੀਂ ਰਹਿੰਦਾ ਸੀ ।
                  raam landan naheen rahindaa see.
                  Ram did not use to live in London.

Interrogative: ਕੀ   ਰਾਮ ਲੰਡਨ ਰਹਿੰਦਾ ਸੀ ?
                  kee raam landan rahindaa see ?
                  Did Ram use to live in London?

2. ਉਹ ਹਫ਼ਤੇ ਦੇ ਅਖੀਰ ਲੰਡਨ ਗਏ ਸਨ। uh hafte de akheer landan gae san.
   They went to London over the weekend.

3. ਅਸੀਂ ਇਕੱਠੇ ਟੈਨਸ ਖੇਡਦੇ ਸੀ ।   aseen ikaththe tainas khedde see.
   We used to play tennis together.

4. ਉਹ ਪੰਜਾਬੀ ਬੋਲਦੀ ਹੁੰਦੀ ਸੀ ।   uh panjaabee boldee hundee see.
   She used to speak Panjabi.

7 | ਤੁਸੀਂ ਕੀ ਪੀਓ ਗੇ ?
| <u>t</u>usee<u>n</u> kee peeo ge?

What will you (have to) drink?

In this unit you will learn:

- how to express actions in the future
- days of the week
- how to tell the time
- about repetitive and rhyming words

1 I'll wait

ਗੱਲ ਬਾਤ ੧ ਮੈਂ ਉਡੀਕਾਂ ਗਾ

gall baa<u>t</u> 1 mai<u>n</u> udeekaa<u>n</u> gaa

Mr Ali and Mr Malik are old friends. Mr Ali is standing outside his house as Mr Malik happens to pass by.

ਮਿਸਟਰ ਅਲੀ	ਅੱਸਲਾਮ ਅਲੈਕਮ। ਕੀ ਹਾਲ ਚਾਲ ਏ ?
Mr Ali	asslaam alaikam. kee haal chaal e?
ਮਿਸਟਰ ਮਲਿਕ	ਵਲੈਕਮ ਅੱਸਲਾਮ। ਮੈਂ ਠੀਕ ਠਾਕ ਹਾਂ।
Mr Malik	vaalaikam asslaam. mai<u>n</u> theek thaak haa<u>n</u>.
ਮਿਸਟਰ ਅਲੀ	ਅੰਦਰ ਆ ਜਾ। ਚਾਹ ਚੁ ਪੀ।
Mr Ali	a<u>n</u>dar aa jaa. chaah choo pee.
ਮਿਸਟਰ ਮਲਿਕ	ਅੱਜ ਮੈਂ ਨਹੀਂ ਠਹਿਰਾਂ ਗਾ। ਮੈਂ ਕਾਹਲ ਵਿਚ ਹਾਂ।
Mr Malik	ajj mai<u>n</u> nahee<u>n</u> thahiraa<u>n</u> gaa. mai<u>n</u> kaahal vich haa<u>n</u>.
ਮਿਸਟਰ ਅਲੀ	ਕੀ ਤੂੰ ਕੱਲ੍ਹ ਆਵੇਂ ਗਾ ?
Mr Ali	kee <u>t</u>oon kallh aave<u>n</u> gaa?
ਮਿਸਟਰ ਮਲਿਕ	ਇਨਸ਼ਾ ਅੱਲਾ। ਮੈਂ ਜ਼ਰੂਰ ਆਵਾਂ ਗਾ। ਕੱਲ੍ਹ ਐਤਵਾਰ ਹੈ। ਵਕਤ ਖੁੱਲ੍ਹਾ ਹੋਵੇ ਗਾ।
Mr Malik	inshaa alla. mai<u>n</u> zaroor aavaa<u>n</u> gaa. kallh ai<u>t</u>vaar hai. vaka<u>t</u> khullhaa hove gaa.

ਮਿਸਟਰ ਅਲੀ	ਸੁਣ ! ਤੂੰ ਕਿੰਨੇ ਵਜੇ ਆਵੇਂ ਗਾ ?
Mr Ali	sunh! toon kinne vaje aaven gaa?
ਮਿਸਟਰ ਮਲਿਕ	ਅਸੀਂ ਸਾਰੇ ਕੱਲ੍ਹ ਪੰਜ ਵਜੇ ਆਵਾਂ ਗੇ।
Mr Malik	aseen saare kallh panj vaje aavaan ge.
ਮਿਸਟਰ ਅਲੀ	ਚੰਗਾ ਫਿਰ। ਮੈਂ ਉਡੀਕਾਂ ਗਾ।
Mr Ali	changaa phir. main udeekaan gaa.

Mr Ali	*Hello! How are you?*
Mr Malik	*Hello! I'm fine.*
Mr Ali	*Come inside. Have some tea.*
Mr Malik	*I'm sorry. I won't stop today. I'm in a hurry.*
Mr Ali	*Will you come tomorrow?*
Mr Malik	*Hopefully [lit. If God wishes]. I'll definitely come.*
	Tomorrow is Sunday. There will be plenty of time.
Mr Ali	*Listen! What time will you come round?*
Mr Malik	*We'll all come tomorrow, at 5 o'clock.*
Mr Ali	*Fine then. I'll wait.*

ਸ਼ਬਦਾਵਲੀ   shabdaavalee   Vocabulary

ਉਡੀਕਣਾ	udeeknhaa	*to wait*
ਅੰਦਰ	andar	*inside*
ਆ ਜਾ	aa jaa	*come* (informal request)
ਅੱਜ	ajj	*today*
ਠਹਿਰਨਾ	thahirnaa	*to stay*
ਕਾਹਲ ਵਿਚ	kaahal vich	*in a hurry*
ਇਨਸ਼ਾ ਅੱਲਾ	inshaa allaa	*hopefully* [lit. *If God wishes*]
ਜ਼ਰੂਰ	zaroor	*definitely*
ਵਕਤ	vakat	*time* (m.)
ਖੁੱਲ੍ਹ	khullhaa	*open, plenty* (v.)
ਕਿੰਨੇ ਵਜੇ	kinne vaje	*what time*
ਅਸੀਂ ਸਾਰੇ	aseen saare	*all of us, we all*
ਪੰਜ ਵਜੇ	panj vaje	*five o' clock*

✔ ਅਭਿਆਸ   abhiaas   Exercises

After reading the dialogue and/or listening to the audio tape, try to do the
following exercises.

1. Fill in the blanks

Complete the sentences by filling in the blank with the correct Panjabi word.

a. ਮੈਂ _____ ਆਵਾਂ ਗਾ   I'll definitely come.
b. ਕੀ ਤੂੰ _____ ਆਵੇਂ ਗਾ ?   Will you come tomorrow?
c. ਤੂੰ _____ ਆਵੇਂ ਗਾ ?   What time will you come?

2. Arrange the sentences in the correct order

The order of the following sentences from the dialogue is mixed up. Can
you unscramble them by numbering them in the correct order?

ਮਿਸਟਰ ਮਲਿਕ:	ਅਸੀਂ ਸਾਰੇ ਕੱਲ੍ਹ ਪੰਜ ਵਜੇ ਆਵਾਂ ਗੇ।
Mr Malik:	aseen saare kallh panj vaje aavaan ge.
ਮਿਸਟਰ ਮਲਿਕ:	ਵਲੈਕਮ ਅੱਸਲਾਮ, ਮੈਂ ਠੀਕ ਠਾਕ ਹਾਂ।
Mr Malik:	vaalaikam asslaam, main theek thaak haan.
ਮਿਸਟਰ ਅਲੀ:	ਸੁਣ! ਤੂੰ ਕਿੰਨੇ ਵਜੇ ਆਵੇਂ ਗਾ ?
Mr Ali:	sunh! toon kinne vaje aaven gaa?
ਮਿਸਟਰ ਅਲੀ:	ਅੱਸਲਾਮ ਅਲੈਕਮ। ਕੀ ਹਾਲ ਚਾਲ ਏ ?
Mr Ali:	asslaam alaikam. kee haal chaal e?

▶ 2 What will you (have to) drink?

📼 ਗੱਲ ਬਾਤ ੨ ਤੁਸੀਂ ਕੀ ਪੀਓ ਗੇ ?

gall baat 2 tuseen kee peeo ge?

Mr and Mrs Malik visit Mr Ali's home. Mr Malik knocks on the door
and Mr Ali opens it.

ਮਿਸਟਰ ਅਲੀ	ਜੀ ਆਇਆਂ ਨੂੰ ਭਾਈ ਸਾਹਿਬ ਤੇ ਭਾਬੀ ਜੀ।
Mr Ali	jee aaiaan noon bhaaee saahib te bhaabee jee.

(Mr and Mrs Ali exchange greetings with Mr and Mrs Malik)

ਮਿਸਜ਼ ਅਲੀ	ਤਸ਼ਰੀਫ਼ ਰੱਖੋ ਜੀ। ਤੁਸੀਂ ਕੀ ਪੀਓ ਗੇ ?
Mrs Ali	tashreef rakhkho jee. tuseen kee peeo ge?
ਮਿਸਟਰ ਮਲਿਕ	ਸ਼ੁਕਰੀਆ। ਮੈਂ ਚਾਹ ਪੀਵਾਂ ਗਾ।
Mr Malik	shukreeaa. main chaah peevaan gaa.
ਮਿਸਜ਼ ਮਲਿਕ	ਮੈਂ ਰਸ ਲਵਾਂ ਗੀ।
Mrs Malik	main ras lavaan gee.

(Mrs Ali serves the drinks and then begins talking to Mrs Malik)

ਮਿਸਜ਼ ਅਲੀ	ਬੱਚੇ ਕਦੋਂ ਆਉਣ ਗੇ ?
Mrs Ali	bachche ka<u>d</u>on aaunh ge?
ਮਿਸਜ਼ ਮਲਿਕ	ਉਹ ੧੫ ਮਿੰਟਾਂ ਵਿਚ ਆਉਣ ਗੇ।
Mrs Malik	uh 15 mi<u>nt</u>aan vich aaunh ge.
ਮਿਸਜ਼ ਅਲੀ	ਕੀ ਤੂੰ ਮੇਰੇ ਨਾਲ ਉਰਦੂ ਫ਼ਿਲਮ ਦੇਖੇਂ ਗੀ ?
Mrs Ali	kee <u>too</u>n mere naal ur<u>doo</u> filam <u>d</u>ekhe<u>n</u> gee?
ਮਿਸਜ਼ ਮਲਿਕ	ਕਿਹੜੀ ਫ਼ਿਲਮ ?
Mrs Malik	kirhhee filam?
ਮਿਸਜ਼ ਅਲੀ	'ਅਨਾਰਕਲੀ' ੮ ਵਜੇ ਟੀ ਵੀ ਤੇ ਆ ਰਹੀ ਹੈ।
Mrs Ali	'anaarkalee' 8 vaje tee vee <u>t</u>e aa rahee hai.
ਮਿਸਜ਼ ਮਲਿਕ	ਹਾਂ ਜੀ। ਮੈਂ ਜ਼ਰੂਰ ਦੇਖਾਂ ਗੀ !
Mrs Malik	haan jee. main zaroor <u>d</u>ekhaa<u>n</u> gee!

Mr Ali	*Welcome brother and sister-in-law.*

     (Mr and Mrs Ali exchange greetings with Mr and Mrs Malik)

Mr Ali	*Please have a seat. What will you drink?*
Mr Malik	*I'll have [drink] tea.*
Mrs Malik	*I'll have juice.*

(Mrs Ali serves the drinks and then begins talking to Mrs Malik)

Mrs Ali	*When will the children arrive?*
Mrs Malik	*They'll be here in 15 minutes.*
Mrs Ali	*Will you [would you like to] watch an Urdu film with me?*
Mrs Malik	*Which film?*
Mrs Ali	*Anarkali [name of a film] is on television at 8 o'clock.*
Mrs Malik	*Yes. I'll definitely watch it!*

ਸ਼ਬਦਾਵਲੀ   **shab<u>d</u>aavalee**   **Vocabulary**

ਜੀ ਆਇਆਂ ਨੂੰ	jee aaiaa<u>n</u> noo<u>n</u>	*welcome*
ਭਾਈ ਸਾਹਿਬ	bhaaee saahib	*brother* (m.)
ਭਾਬੀ ਜੀ	bhaabee jee	*sister-in-law* (f.)
ਤਸ਼ਰੀਫ਼ ਰੱਖੋ ਜੀ	<u>t</u>ashreef rakhkho jee	*Please have a seat.*
ਪੀਣਾ	peenhaa	*to drink*
ਰਸ	ras	*(fruit) juice* (m.)
ਲੈਣਾ	lainhaa	*to take, to have*
ਕਦੋਂ	ka<u>d</u>on	*when*
ਮਿੰਟਾਂ	mi<u>nt</u>aan	*minutes* (m.)
ਮੇਰੇ ਨਾਲ	mere naal	*with me*

ਦੇਖਣਾ	dekhnhaa	to see, to watch
ਉਰਦੂ	urdoo	Urdu (m./f.)
ਅਨਾਰਕਲੀ	anaarkalee	name of a classic Urdu film (f.)
੮ ਵਜੇ	8 vaje	8 o'clock
ਟੀ ਵੀ	tee vee	TV (television) (m.)

☑ ਅਭਿਆਸ   abhiaas   Exercises

After reading the dialogue and/or listening to the audio tape, try to do the following exercises.

📼 1. Questions to ask guests

Two guests, Mr and Mrs Malik, have come to your house for tea. Ask them the following questions.

a) What will you have to drink?
b) Would you like to watch television?
c) Would you like to have juice or tea?

2. Word search

Three words *children, Urdu* and *sister-in-law* are hidden in Panjabi in the box. Find them by reading horizontally across each of the rows.

ਬੱ	ਚੇ	ਓ	ਪ	ੲ
ਸਾ	ਸ	ਕ	ਨ	ਹੀਂ
ਕਾ	ਕਿ	ਉ	ਰ	ਦੂ
ਸੌ	ਸਿ	ਕੁ	ਚ	ਨ
ਇ	ਭਾ	ਬੀ	ਹਾ	ਕੈ

🔊 ਬੋਲੀ ਬਾਰੇ   bolee baare   language points

The future tense

In Panjabi, as in English, the future tense is used when one is making predictions about the future or referring to intentions, offers, or promises in the future. The Panjabi ending -ਗਾ **gaa** is used to denote actions or

conditions in the future and means *will, shall* or *would*. As has been
explained with other verb tenses in Panjabi, the form of the future tense
varies according to the number and gender of the subject. Here are the
ways in which -ਗਾ **gaa** is formed (notice that the forms of -ਗਾ **gaa** do not
change according to the person of the subject):

-ਗਾ	gaa	masculine singular
-ਗੀ	gee	feminine singular
-ਗੇ	ge	masculine plural
-ਗੀਆਂ	geeaa<u>n</u>	feminine plural

The future tense therefore, as is also the case with the present tenses, is
constructed by combining the main verb with the auxiliary ending, -ਗਾ
gaa. The main verb in the future tense, however, does vary according to
the person as well as the number of the subject. In the first dialogue in this
unit, the verb ਉਡੀਕਣਾ, **udeeknhaa** *to wait* was used in the future tense ਮੈਂ
ਉਡੀਕਾਂ ਗਾ **mai<u>n</u> udeekaa<u>n</u> gaa**, *I will wait*. The example of ਕਰਨਾ **karnaa**,
to do is now illustrated to show how verbs with stems ending in consonants are formed in the future.

ਕਰਨਾ – infinitive form of *to do* ਕਰ – stem

1st person

Masc. sing.	ਮੈਂ ਕਰਾਂ ਗਾ	mai<u>n</u> karaa<u>n</u> gaa	*I shall/will do*
Fem. sing.	ਮੈਂ ਕਰਾਂ ਗੀ	mai<u>n</u> karaa<u>n</u> gee	*I shall/will do*
Masc. pl.	ਅਸੀਂ ਕਰਾਂ ਗੇ	asee<u>n</u> karaa<u>n</u> ge	*we shall/will do*
Fem. pl.	ਅਸੀਂ ਕਰਾਂ ਗੀਆਂ	asee<u>n</u> karaa<u>n</u> geeaa<u>n</u>	*we shall/will do*

2nd person

Masc. sing. informal	ਤੂੰ ਕਰੇਂ ਗਾ	<u>t</u>oo<u>n</u> kare<u>n</u> gaa	*you will do*
Fem. sing. informal	ਤੂੰ ਕਰੇਂ ਗੀ	<u>t</u>oo<u>n</u> kare<u>n</u> gee	*you will do*
Masc. pl. formal	ਤੁਸੀਂ ਕਰੋ ਗੇ	<u>t</u>usee<u>n</u> karo ge	*you will do*
Fem. pl.	ਤੁਸੀਂ ਕਰੋ ਗੀਆਂ	<u>t</u>usee<u>n</u> karo geeaa<u>n</u>	*you will do*

3rd person

Masc. sing.	ਉਹ/ਇਹ ਕਰੇ ਗਾ	uh/ih kare gaa	*he will do*
Fem. sing.	ਉਹ/ਇਹ ਕਰੇ ਗੀ	uh/ih kare gee	*she will do*
Masc. pl. formal	ਉਹ/ਇਹ ਕਰਨ ਗੇ	uh/ih karan ge	*they will do*
Fem. pl.	ਉਹ/ਇਹ ਕਰਨ ਗੀਆਂ	uh/ih karan geeaa<u>n</u>	*they will do*

Another construction of the future tense occurs when the stem of the main verb ends in a vowel such as ਜਾ-ਣਾ **jaa-nhaa** *to go*, ਆਉ-ਣਾ **aau-nhaa** *to come*, ਪੀ-ਣਾ **pee-nhaa** *to drink*, and ਲੈ-ਣਾ **lai-nhaa** *to have*. There are generally two acceptable ways of forming the future tense with such vowel-ending stems. The first manner follows the pattern as given for consonant-ending verb stems. The second manner in which the future tense is often formed is by inserting ਵ **vavvaa** after the vowel. There is no significant difference between the two, although the ਵ **vavvaa** forms often have a slightly more formal tone. Note these examples of the two commonly used main verb formations in the future tense:

ਮੈਂ mai<u>n</u> *I* ਅਸੀਂ aseen, *we*	ਤੂੰ <u>toon</u> *you* (informal)	ਤੁਸੀਂ <u>tuseen</u>, *you* (formal)	ਇਹ ih *he/she/it* ਉਹ uh (sing/informal)	ਇਹ ih *he/she/they* ਉਹ uh (plural/formal)

ਜਾਣਾ **jaanhaa** – *to go*, ਜਾ – *stem*

(1)				
ਜਾਵਾਂ jaavaa<u>n</u>	ਜਾਏਂ jaae<u>n</u>	ਜਾਓ jaao	ਜਾਏ jaae	ਜਾਣ jaanh
(2)				
ਜਾਵਾਂ jaavaa<u>n</u>	ਜਾਵੇਂ jaave<u>n</u>	ਜਾਵੋ jaavo	ਜਾਵੇ jaave	ਜਾਵਣ jaavanh

ਆਉਣਾ **aaunhaa** *aaunhaa* – *to come*, ਆ – *stem*

(1)				
ਆਵਾਂ aavaa<u>n</u>	ਆਏ aae	ਆਓ aao	ਆਏ aae	ਆਉਣ aaunh

(2)				
ਆਵਾਂ	ਆਵੇਂ	ਆਵੋ	ਆਵੇ	ਆਵਣ
aavaan	aaven	aavo	aave	aavanh

ਪੀਣਾ peenhaa – *to drink*, ਪੀ – stem

(1)				
ਪੀਆਂ	ਪੀਏਂ	ਪੀਓ	ਪੀਏ	ਪੀਣ
peeaan	peeen	peeo	peee	peenh
(2)				
ਪੀਵਾਂ	ਪੀਵੇਂ	ਪੀਵੋ	ਪੀਵੇ	ਪੀਵਣ
peevaan	peeven	peevo	peeve	peevanh

ਲੈਣਾ lainhaa – t*o have, to take*, ਲੈ – stem

(1)				
ਲਵਾਂ	ਲਏਂ	ਲੋ	ਲਏ	ਲੈਣ
lavaan	laen	lo	lae	lainh
(2)				
ਲਵਾਂ	ਲਵੇਂ	ਲਵੋ	ਲਵੇ	ਲਵਣ
lavaan	laven	lavo	lave	lavanh

More forms of the imperative

In Unit 5 the imperative was briefly introduced as a means of expressing a request, order or command. The formal and informal uses of the imperative were illustrated through the verb ਸੁਣਨਾ **sunhnaa** *to listen*:

ਤੂੰ ਸੁਣ   <u>t</u>oon <u>s</u>unh   *listen* (you, informal)

ਤੁਸੀਂ ਸੁਣੋ   <u>t</u>usee<u>n</u> sunho   *listen* (you, formal/plural)

The plural form of the imperative is used to denote a respectful tone when addressed to a single person. To make the request yet more formal and respectful, the English equivalent of *please* can also be added by use of the honorific particle ਜੀ **jee**.

ਸੁਣੋ ਜੀ   sunho jee   *please listen* (you, formal)

Please in Panjabi is expressed in the phrase ਕਿਰਪਾ ਕਰ ਕੇ **kirpaa kar ke**. By using this phrase, a formal request can be made more polite:

| ਅੰਦਰ ਆਓ | andar aao | *come in* |
| ਕਿਰਪਾ ਕਰ ਕੇ ਅੰਦਰ ਆਓ | kirpaa kar ke andar aao | *please come in* |

Politeness is also expressed by forming the imperative in the future tense.

| ਕੀ ਤੁਸੀਂ ਸੁਣੋ ਗੇ ਜੀ ? | kee tuseen sunho ge jee? | *will you please listen?* |

The tone of the request can be softened with the word ਜ਼ਰਾ **zaraa**, *just a little* used in combination with the infinitive form of the verb. The infinitive specifies the action of what is being requested. The colloquial sense of the earlier request becomes ਜ਼ਰਾ ਸੁਣਨਾ **zaraa sunhnaa**, *have a listen*. With ਦੇਖਣਾ **dekhnhaa**, *to look* the request becomes:

| ਜ਼ਰਾ ਦੇਖਣਾ | zaraa dekhnhaa | *have a look* |

Ordinal numbers

In Unit 3 you learned the cardinal numbers from 1 to 20. To expand your knowledge of numbers further here are the ordinal numbers.

ਪਹਿਲਾ	pahilaa	*first*
ਦੂਸਰਾ/ਦੂਜਾ	doosraa/doojaa	*second*
ਤੀਸਰਾ/ਤੀਜਾ	teesraa/teejaa	*third*
ਚੌਥਾ	chauthaa	*fourth*
ਪੰਜਵਾਂ	panjvaan	*fifth*
ਛੇਵਾਂ	chevaan	*sixth*
ਸੱਤਵਾਂ	sattvaan	*seventh*
ਅੱਠਵਾਂ	aththvaan	*eighth*

As you can see, from *fifth* onwards ordinal numbers are formed with the ending -ਵਾਂ **vaan**. Since ordinals are adjectives, they follow the same rules of agreement as other adjectives. The endings of ordinals will therefore agree with the nouns that they are describing.

| ਪਹਿਲੀ ਵਾਰੀ | pahilee vaaree | *first time* |
| ਦੂਜਾ ਦਿਨ | doojaa din | *second day* |

What time is it?

In English, time is expressed by the use of *o'clock* which refers specifically to the position of the hands on the clock when telling the time. Similarly in Panjabi, time is most commonly expressed through the use of the verb ਵੱਜਣਾ **vajjnhaa** which means *to chime, to strike*. When asking someone the time, the same rules apply as when transforming statements into interrogative sentences as shown in Unit 5. The word ਕੀ **kee** is simply placed at the beginning of the sentence. However, other words for time are also appropriate when asking someone the time in Panjabi. Here are a few commonly used phrases:

ਕੀ ਵਕਤ ਹੈ ?	kee vakaṯ hai?	*What time is it?*
ਕਿੰਨੇ ਵਜੇ ਹਨ ?	kinne vaje han?	*What time is it?*
		(literally: how many times
		has the clock struck?)
ਕੀ ਟਾਇਮ ਹੈ ?	kee taaim hai?	*What is the time?*

Therefore, when someone says that it is one o'clock, the expression in Panjabi would be:

| ਇੱਕ ਵਜਿਆ ਹੈ | ikk vajiaa hai | *It is one o'clock* |

The verb ਵੱਜਣਾ **vajjnhaa** is formed in the present perfect tense here, literally meaning that *the clock has struck one*. Note that ਵਜਿਆ **vajiaa** is the singular form as it agrees with the number one. All other times which relate to the number one (such as quarter to one, quarter past one, half past one) also take on the singular form.

ਡੇਢ ਵਜਿਆ ਹੈ	dedh vajiaa hai	*It is half past one.*
ਪੌਣਾ ਇੱਕ ਵਜਿਆ ਹੈ	paunhaa ikk vajiaa hai	*It is a quarter to one.*
ਸਵਾ ਇੱਕ ਵਜਿਆ ਹੈ	savaa ikk vajiaa hai	*It is a quarter past one.*

As you will have noticed in the earlier examples there are terms in Panjabi for each 15-minute sequence of time on the clock. One thirty and two thirty, however, have specific names while all other times use ਸਵਾ **savaa**, ਸਾਢੇ **saadhe** and ਪੌਣੇ **paunhe**.

half past one = ਡੇਢ dedh
half past two = ਢਾਈ dhaaee
quarter past the hour = ਸਵਾ savaa
thirty minutes past the hour = ਸਾਢੇ saadhe
quarter to the hour = ਪੌਣਾ paunhaa, ਪੌਣੇ paunhe

All times relating to numbers greater than one use the plural form of ਵਜਣਾ. Here are some examples:

ਦੋ ਵਜੇ ਹਨ	do vaje han	*It is two o'clock.*
ਪੌਣੇ ਦੋ ਵਜੇ ਹਨ	paunhe do vaje han	*It is a quarter to two.*
ਤਿੰਨ ਵਜੇ ਹਨ	tinn vaje han	*It is three o'clock.*
ਸਾਢੇ ਤਿੰਨ ਵਜੇ ਹਨ	saadhe tinn vaje han	*It is three thirty.*
ਚਾਰ ਵਜੇ ਹਨ	chaar vaje han	*It is four o'clock.*
ਸਵਾ ਚਾਰ ਵਜੇ ਹਨ	savaa chaar vaje han	*It is a quarter past four.*
ਪੰਜ ਵਜੇ ਹਨ	panj vaje han	*It is five o'clock.*
ਛੇ ਵਜੇ ਹਨ	che vaje han	*It is six o'clock.*
ਪੌਣੇ ਛੇ ਵਜੇ ਹਨ	paunhe che vaje han	*It is a quarter to six.*
ਸੱਤ ਵਜੇ ਹਨ	satt vaje han	*It is seven o'clock.*
ਅੱਠ ਵਜੇ ਹਨ	athth vaje han	*It is eight o'clock.*
ਨੌਂ ਵਜੇ ਹਨ	naun vaje han	*It is nine o'clock.*
ਦਸ ਵਜੇ ਹਨ	das vaje han	*It is ten o'clock.*
ਸਾਢੇ ਗਿਆਰਾਂ ਵਜੇ ਹਨ	saadhe giaaraan vaje han	*It is eleven thirty.*
ਬਾਰ੍ਹਾਂ ਵਜੇ ਹਨ	baar-h-aan vaje han	*It is twelve o'clock.*

When the exact nature of the time is being expressed, it is also possible to use other forms of expression. Here are a few examples:

ਕਲਾਸ ਇੱਕ ਵਜੇ ਤੋਂ ਸ਼ੁਰੂ ਹੁੰਦੀ ਹੈ	kalaas ikk vaje ton shuroo hundee hai	The class starts at one o'clock
ਤਿੰਨ ਵਜ ਰਹੇ ਹਨ	tinn vaj rahe han	It is just three o'clock
ਨੌਂ ਵਜਣ ਵਾਲੇ ਹਨ	naun vajanh vaale han	It is nearly nine o'clock

When the time of day needs to be specified, morning (ਸਵੇਰ saver), afternoon (ਦੁਪਹਿਰ dupahir), day (ਦਿਨ din), evening (ਸ਼ਾਮ shaam) and night (ਰਾਤ raat) can also be used:

ਛੇ ਵਜੇ ਸ਼ਾਮ ਨੂੰ	che vaje shaam noon	at six o'clock in the evening
ਸਵੇਰ ਦੇ ਅੱਠ ਵਜੇ	saver de athth vaje	at eight o'clock in the morning
ਦੁਪਹਿਰ ਦੇ ਡੇਢ ਵਜੇ	dupahir de dedh vaje	at one thirty in the afternoon
ਦਿਨ ਦੇ ਦੋ ਵਜੇ	din de do vaje	at two o'clock in the afternoon (day)
ਬਾਰ੍ਹਾਂ ਵਜੇ ਰਾਤ ਨੂੰ	baar-h-aan vaje raat noon	at twelve o'clock at night

Further usages and expressions of time will be explained in subsequent units.

ਵਿਆਖਿਆ   **viaakhiaa   Commentary**

1. Repetitive and echo/rhyming words

The habitual use of repetitive and echo words is one of the many special characteristics of Panjabi which make it such an expressive language. Many words in Panjabi are repeated in the written and spoken forms to add emphasis. Repetition occurs when the same word is repeated while the echoing and rhyming of words occur through the use of two words which sound similar. Here are some examples:

ਹੌਲੀ ਹੌਲੀ ਚਲੋ	haulee haulee chalo	*walk slowly* (emphasising slowly)
ਹਟ ਹਟ	hat hat	*get away* (showing intensity)
ਦੇਸ ਦੇਸ ਤੋਂ ਲੋਕ ਆਏ	<u>d</u>es <u>d</u>es <u>t</u>on lok aae	*people came from different countries* (emphasis on countries to signify the many different countries)
ਚਾਹ ਚੂ	chaah choo	*tea* [here the echo word ਚੂ has no specific meaning other than for emphasis]
ਦੁੱਖ ਸੁੱਖ	<u>d</u>ukhkh sukhkh	*miseries and comforts*
ਦਿਨ ਰਾਤ	<u>d</u>in raa<u>t</u>	*day and night* (all the time) [these words technically neither rhyme nor are echo words. However, their opposite meanings uttered together gives the idea of continuity.]
ਸੱਚ ਸੱਚ	sachch sachch	*the whole truth*
ਚੁੱਪ ਚਾਪ	chupp chaap	*(absolutely) quiet*

2. Days of the week

There are two words for day in Panjabi which are used to designate the days of the week: ਦਿਨ **din** and ਵਾਰ **vaar**. If you want to ask someone what the day of the week is today, there are two ways to ask:

ਅੱਜ ਕੀ ਦਿਨ ਹੈ ?	ajj kee <u>d</u>in hai?	*What day is it today?*
ਅੱਜ ਕੀ ਵਾਰ ਹੈ ?	ajj kee vaar hai?	*What day is it today?*

The names of the days of the week are all masculine nouns. Some of the days of the week are different in West Panjab due to the influence of the Islamic calendar in Pakistan. The days of the week in Panjabi are as follows (*shows the Islamic calendar days):

Monday	ਸੋਮਵਾਰ	somvaar
	ਪੀਰ *	peer
Tuesday	ਮੰਗਲਵਾਰ	mangalvaar
Wednesday	ਬੁੱਧਵਾਰ	budhdhvaar
Thursday	ਵੀਰਵਾਰ	veervaar
	ਜੁਮੇਰਾਤ *	jumeraat
Friday	ਸ਼ੁੱਕਰਵਾਰ	shukkarvaar
	ਜੁਮਾ *	jumaa
Saturday	ਸਨਿਚਰਵਾਰ	sanicharvaar
	ਹਫ਼ਤਾ *	haftaa
Sunday	ਐਤਵਾਰ	aitvaar

Other useful calendar terms are:

ਹਫ਼ਤਾ	haftaa	*week* (m.)
ਸਪਤਾਹ	saptaah	*week* (m.)
ਮਹੀਨਾ	maheenaa	*month* (m.)
ਦਿਨ	din	*day* (m.)
ਸਾਲ	saal	*year* (m.)

3. Expressions of friendship

You will have noticed in Dialogue 2 that Mr Ali greets Mr Malik as ਭਾਈ ਸਾਹਿਬ **bhaaee saahib** (*brother*) and Mrs Malik as ਭਾਬੀ ਜੀ **bhaabee jee** (*sister-in-law*). It is not uncommon to address people with whom you wish to express closeness or affection with such terms ordinarily associated with kinship. In this example, it is quite clear that Mr Ali and Mr Malik are not brothers, but their friendship is the basis for Mr Ali referring to Mr Malik as *brother*. Since the relationship is primarily based upon the two men, Mrs Malik is referred to as ਭਾਬੀ ਜੀ **bhaabee jee** (as Mr Malik's wife) and not *sister*.

☑ ਅਭਿਆਸ   abhiaas   Exercises

After reading the dialogue and/or listening to the audio tape, try to do the following exercises.

1. The imperative

You are trying to convey to someone that he or she should listen to you. How would you form the imperative of ਸੁਣਨਾ **sunhnaa**, *to listen* in the following circumstances?

a) to someone who is younger than you (informal)
b) to someone who is older than you (formal)
c) to someone to whom you wish to show respect (formal, polite)
d) to someone with whom you wish to use a mild tone of request

2. What time is it?

Write the answers in Panjabi.

3. The future tense

After reviewing the future tense section in the unit, express the fact that you will have tea in the following gender and number situations:

a) You are a singular male.   c) You are a plural male.
b) You are a singular female.   d) You are a plural female.

4. Conversation

Suppose you have been asked to go to someone's house. Express the following conversational phrases in Panjabi.

a) Yes, thank you.   b) Yes, I'll come tomorrow.
c) No, I'm in a hurry.   d) Fine then. I'll wait.

8 ਮੈਨੂੰ ਸਿਤਾਰ ਵਜਾਉਣ ਦਾ ਸ਼ੌਕ ਹੈ

mainoon siṭaar vajaaunh ḏaa shauk hai

I enjoy playing the sitar

In this unit you will learn:

- ■ how to express your likes and dislikes
- ■ how to express need, want, should, ought
- ■ how to discuss visas
- ■ how to negotiate a taxi ride

1 I enjoy playing the sitar

ਗੱਲ ਬਾਤ ੧ ਮੈਨੂੰ ਸਿਤਾਰ ਵਜਾਉਣ ਦਾ ਸ਼ੌਕ ਹੈ।

gall baaṯ 1 mainoon siṭaar vajaaunh ḏaa shauk hai

Jaspreet and Simran are two sisters living in Yuba City, California. They are planning a trip to India and are having a conversation with their father, Mr Sandhu.

ਮਿਸਟਰ ਸੰਧੂ	ਤੁਹਾਨੂੰ ਭਾਰਤ ਜਾਣ ਲਈ ਕਿੰਨੇ ਪੈਸੇ ਚਾਹੀਦੇ ਹਨ ?
Mr Sandhu	ṯuhaanoon bhaaraṯ jaanh laee kinne paise chaaheeḏe han?
ਜਸਪ੍ਰੀਤ ਤੇ ਸਿਮਰਨ	ਸਾਨੂੰ ਘੱਟੋ ਘੱਟ (੨੦੦੦) ਦੋ ਹਜ਼ਾਰ ਡਾਲਰ ਚਾਹੀਦੇ ਹਨ।
Jaspreet and Simran	saanoon ghatto ghatt (2000) ḏo hazaar ḏaalar chaaheeḏe han.
ਮਿਸਟਰ ਸੰਧੂ	ਐਨੇ ਸਾਰੇ ਪੈਸੇ ? ਤੁਹਾਡਾ ਖ਼ਰਚਾ ਇੰਨਾ ਕਿਵੇਂ ਹੋਵੇ ਗਾ ?
Mr Sandhu	aine saare paise? ṯuhaaḏaa kharchaa innaa kiven hove gaa?
ਜਸਪ੍ਰੀਤ	ਪਿਤਾ ਜੀ ! ਤੁਹਾਨੂੰ ਪਤਾ ਹੈ ਕਿ ਮੈਨੂੰ ਸਿਤਾਰ ਵਜਾਉਣ ਦਾ ਸ਼ੌਕ ਹੈ। ਮੈਂ ਉੱਥੋਂ ਵਧੀਆ ਸਿਤਾਰ ਲਿਆਵਾਂ ਗੀ।
Jaspreet	piṭaa jee! ṯuhaanoon paṭaa hai ki mainoon siṭaar

	vajaaunh daa shauk hai. main uththon vadheeaa sitaar liaavaan gee.
ਸਿਮਰਨ	... ਤੇ ਮੈਨੂੰ ਘੁੰਮਣਾ ਫਿਰਨਾ ਪਸੰਦ ਹੈ।
Simran	... te mainoon ghunmnhaa phirnaa pasand hai.
ਮਿਸਟਰ ਸੰਧੂ	ਮੇਰੀਓ ਧੀਓ, ਮੈਨੂੰ ਅਫਸੋਸ ਹੈ ਕਿ ਤੁਹਾਨੂੰ ਦੇਣ ਲਈ ਮੇਰੇ ਕੋਲ ਐਨੇ ਪੈਸੇ ਨਹੀਂ ਹਨ।
Mr Sandhu	mereeo dheeo, mainoon afsos hai ki tuhaanoon denh laee mere kol aine paise naheen han.
ਜਸਪ੍ਰੀਤ ਤੇ ਸਿਮਰਨ	ਤੁਸੀਂ ਫਿਕਰ ਨਾ ਕਰੋ, ਪਿਤਾ ਜੀ। ਮਾਤਾ ਜੀ ਕੋਲ ਪੈਸੇ ਬਹੁਤ ਹਨ !
Jaspreet and Simran	tuseen fikar naa karo, pitaa jee. maataa jee kol paise bahut han!

Mr Sandhu	*How much money do you need for going to India?*
Jaspreet and Simran	*We need at least $2000.*
Mr Sandhu	*So much money? Why will your expenses be so high?*
Jaspreet	*Father, you know that I am fond of playing the sitar. I'm going to bring a good quality sitar from there.*
Simran	*... and I like travelling around.*
Mr Sandhu	*My daughters, I am sorry that I don't have that much money to give you.*
Jaspreet and Simran	*Don't worry, Father. Mother has plenty of money!*

ਸ਼ਬਦਾਵਲੀ shabdaavalee Vocabulary

ਲਈ	laee	*for, in order to*
ਕਿੰਨੇ	kinne	*how much, how many*
ਚਾਹੁਣਾ	chaahunhaa	*to need, to want*
ਖ਼ਰਚਾ	kharchaa	*expense, expenses* (m.)
ਘੱਟੋ ਘੱਟ	ghatto ghatt	*at least*
ਡਾਲਰ	daalar	*dollar* (m.)
ਐਨੇ ਸਾਰੇ	aine saare	*so much*
ਪਤਾ	pataa	*to know*
ਸਿਤਾਰ	sitaar	*sitar* (f.) (a stringed classical musical instrument)
ਵਜਾਉਣਾ	vajaaunhaa	*to play* (music)
ਸ਼ੌਕ	shauk	*fondness, enjoyment*

ਵਜਾਉਣ ਦਾ ਸ਼ੌਕ	vajaaunh <u>d</u>aa shauk	*fond of playing, enjoy playing*
ਉੱਥੋਂ	u<u>ththon</u>	*from there*
ਵਧੀਆ	vadheeaa	*good quality*
ਲਿਆਉਣਾ	liaaunhaa	*to bring*
ਘੁੰਮਣਾ	ghu<u>n</u>mnhaa	*to go around*
ਫਿਰਨਾ	phirnaa	*to travel*
ਘੁੰਮਣਾ ਫਿਰਨਾ	ghu<u>n</u>mnhaa phirnaa	*to travel around*
ਪਸੰਦ	pas<u>and</u>	*like*
ਅਫ਼ਸੋਸ	afsos	*regret, sorry*
ਕੋਲ	kol	*with, next to, in possession*
ਮੇਰੇ ਕੋਲ ਨਹੀਂ	mere kol nahee<u>n</u>	*not with me, not in my possession*
ਫ਼ਿਕਰ	fikar	*worry* (m.)
ਧੀਏ	<u>d</u>heeo	*daughters* (f.) (vocative case: see language points)

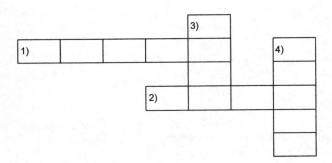

✅ ਅਭਿਆਸ **abhiaas** **Exercises**

After reading the dialogue and/or listening to the audio tape, try to do the following exercises.

1 Crossword

Complete the crossword in Gurmukhi script using the clues given.

1) a stringed classical instrument 2) US currency
3) expense 4) to travel

2. Match the statements

a. ਫ਼ਿਕਰ ਨਾ ਕਰੋ
b. ਐਨੇ ਸਾਰੇ ਪੈਸੇ ?
c. ਮੈਂ ਵਧੀਆ ਸਿਤਾਰ ਲਿਆਵਾਂ ਗੀ

i) *I will bring a good quality sitar.*
ii) *Don't worry.*
iii) *So much money?*

🔊 2 We want to go to Connaught Place

🔲 ਗੱਲ ਬਾਤ ੨ ਅਸੀਂ ਕਨਾਟ ਪਲੇਸ ਜਾਣਾ ਚਾਹੁੰਦੀਆਂ ਹਾਂ

gall baat 2 aseen kanaat pales jaanhaa chaahundeeaan haan

Simran and Jaspreet have just arrived at the airport in Delhi. They have approached the immigration counter where they show their passports to the officer with whom they are having a conversation.

ਇਮੀਗ੍ਰੇਸ਼ਨ ਅਫ਼ਸਰ	ਤੁਸੀਂ ਅਮਰੀਕਾ ਕਿੰਨਾ ਚਿਰ ਤੋਂ ਰਹਿ ਰਹੀਆਂ ਹੋ ?
Immigration Officer	tuseen amreekaa kinnaa chir ton rahi raheeaan ho?
ਸਿਮਰਨ	ਅਸੀਂ ਅਮਰੀਕਾ ਵਿਚ ਜੰਮੀਆਂ ਸੀ।
Simran	aseen amreekaa vich janmeeaan see.
ਇਮੀਗ੍ਰੇਸ਼ਨ ਅਫ਼ਸਰ	ਤੁਹਾਨੂੰ ਐਨੀ ਚੰਗੀ ਪੰਜਾਬੀ ਕਿਵੇਂ ਆਉਂਦੀ ਹੈ ?
Immigration Officer	tuhaanoon ainee changee panjaabee kiven aaundee hai?
ਜਸਪ੍ਰੀਤ	ਸਾਨੂੰ ਸਿਰਫ਼ ਥੋੜੀ ਬਹੁਤੀ ਆਉਂਦੀ ਹੈ।
Jaspreet	saanoon siraf thorhee bahutee aaundee hai.
ਸਿਮਰਨ	ਇੱਕ ਬੇਨਤੀ ਹੈ, ਅਫ਼ਸਰ ਸਾਹਿਬ...
Simran	ikk bentee hai, afsar saahib...
ਇਮੀਗ੍ਰੇਸ਼ਨ ਅਫ਼ਸਰ	ਉਹ ਕੀ ਹੈ ?
Immigration Officer	uh kee hai?
ਸਿਮਰਨ	ਸਾਡੇ ਕੋਲ ਕੇਵਲ ਇੱਕ ਮਹੀਨੇ ਦਾ ਵੀਜ਼ਾ ਹੈ। ਜੀ ਕੀ ਤੁਸੀਂ ਸਾਨੂੰ ਦੋ ਮਹੀਨੇ ਰਹਿਣ ਦੀ ਆਗਿਆ ਦੇਵੋ ਗੇ ?
Simran	saade kol keval ikk maheene daa veezaa hai. jee kee tuseen saanoon do maheene rahinh dee aagiaa devo ge?
ਇਮੀਗ੍ਰੇਸ਼ਨ ਅਫ਼ਸਰ	ਇਹ ਮੇਰੇ ਵੱਸ ਵਿਚ ਨਹੀਂ ਹੈ। ਤੁਹਾਨੂੰ ਵੀਜ਼ਾ ਅਮਰੀਕਾ ਤੋਂ ਲੈਣਾ ਚਾਹੀਦਾ ਸੀ।
Immigration Officer	ih mere vass vich naheen hai. tuhaanoon veezaa amreekaa ton lainhaa chaaheedaa see.

ਸਿਮਰਨ ਤੇ ਜਸਪ੍ਰੀਤ   ਫਿਰ ਸਾਨੂੰ ਇੱਕ ਮਹੀਨੇ ਵਿਚ ਸਾਰਾ ਕੁਝ ਦੇਖਣਾ ਪੈਣਾ।
Simran and Jaspreet phir saanoon ikk maheene vich saara kujh dekhn haa
                       painhaa.
ਇਮੀਗ੍ਰੇਸ਼ਨ ਅਫਸਰ   ਦਿੱਲੀ ਦੇ ਆਸ ਪਾਸ ਕਾਫੀ ਕੁਝ ਦੇਖਣ ਵਾਲਾ ਹੈ। ਅਨੰਦ ਮਾਣੋ !
Immigration Officer dillee de aas paas kaafee kujh dekhanh vaalaa hai.
                        anand maanho !

Immigration Officer	*How long have you been living in America?*
Simran	*We were born in America.*
Immigration Officer	*How do you know Panjabi so well?*
Jaspreet	*We only know a little.*
Simran	*Officer, one request...*
Immigration Officer	*What is it?*
Simran	*We only have a one-month visa. Could you please give us permission to stay for two months?*
Immigration Officer	*This is not within my authority. You should have obtained the visa from America.*
Simran and Jaspreet	*In that case, we'll have to see everything in a month.*
Immigration Officer	*There are plenty of things to see around Delhi. Enjoy yourselves!*

Jaspreet and Simran have cleared customs with their luggage and exit
from the airport. They approach a taxi driver about travelling into the
centre of Delhi.

ਜਸਪ੍ਰੀਤ   ਅਸੀਂ ਕਨਾਟ ਪਲੇਸ ਜਾਣਾ ਚਾਹੁੰਦੀਆਂ ਹਾਂ। ਤੂੰ ਕਿੰਨੇ ਪੈਸੇ ਲਵੇਂ ਗਾ ?
Jaspreet aseen kanaat pales jaanhaa chaahundeeaan haan. toon
              kinne paise laven gaa?
ਟੈਕਸੀਵਾਲਾ   ਸਿਰਫ ਸੌ ਰੁਪਇਆ ।
Taxi driver siraf sau rupaiaa.
ਸਿਮਰਨ   ਕਨਾਟ ਪਲੇਸ ਹਵਾਈ ਅੱਡੇ ਤੋਂ ਕਿੰਨੀ ਦੂਰ ਹੈ ?
Simran   kanaat pales havaaee adde ton kinnee door hai?
ਟੈਕਸੀਵਾਲਾ   ਤਕਰੀਬਨ ਵੀਹ ਮੀਲ ਦੂਰ ਹੈ। ਤੁਸੀਂ ਠੀਕ ਕਿਹੜੀ ਜਗ੍ਹਾ ਜਾਣਾ ਹੈ ?
Taxi driver takreeban veeh meel door hai. tuseen theek kihrhee
              jag-h-aa jaanhaa hai?
ਸਿਮਰਨ   ਅਸੀਂ ਅੰਤਰ ਰਾਸ਼ਟਰੀ ਯੁਵਕ ਹੋਸਟਲ ਜਾਣਾ ਹੈ ਪਰ ਤੂੰ ਜ਼ਿਆਦਾ ਪੈਸੇ
              ਮੰਗ ਰਿਹਾ ਹੈਂ।
Simran   aseen antar raashtaree yuvak hostal jaanhaa hai par toon
              ziaadaa paise mang rihaa hain.

ਟੈਕਸੀਵਾਲਾ	ਨਹੀਂ ਨਹੀਂ। ਮੈਂ ਕਿਰਾਇਆ ਵਾਜਬੀ ਦੱਸਿਆ ਹੈ। ਤੁਸੀਂ ਦੋ ਸਵਾਰੀਆਂ ਹੋ ਤੇ ਸਮਾਨ ਵੀ ਬਹੁਤ ਹੈ। ਤੁਸੀਂ ਜਾਣਾ ਏ ਕਿ ਨਹੀਂ ?
Taxi driver	naheen naheen. main kiraaiaa vaajbee dassiaa hai. tuseen do savaareeaan ho te samaan vee bahut hai. tuseen jaanhaa e ki naheen?
ਜਸਪ੍ਰੀਤ	ਅੱਛਾ, ਕਾਹਲਾ ਨ ਪਓ । ਸਮਾਨ ਰੱਖ ਗੱਡੀ ਵਿਚ।
Jaspreet	achchaa, kaahalaa na pao. samaan rakhkh gaddee vich.

Jaspreet	*We want to go to Connaught Place. How much will you charge?**
Taxi driver	*Only one hundred rupees.*
Simran	*How far is Connaught Place from the airport?*
Taxi driver	*It's about 20 miles away. Exactly where are you going?*
Simran	*Take us [we want to go] to the International Youth Hostel, but you're asking for too much money.*
Taxi driver	*No, no. I've told you the reasonable fare. There are two of you travelling and there is a lot of luggage. Are you going or not?*
Jaspreet	*OK. Don't be impatient. Put the luggage in the car.*

* The language used in this dialogue with the taxi driver may seem a little informal (or even rude) in the English translation. This is because informal speech is generally used when haggling over the fare with taxi drivers in India and Pakistan (see Unit 2: Language points: Subject pronouns).

ਸ਼ਬਦਾਵਲੀ   shabdaavalee   Vocabulary

ਅਮਰੀਕਾ	amreekaa	*America* (m.)
ਚਿਰ	chir	*length of time*
ਕਿੰਨਾ ਚਿਰ ਤੋਂ	kinnaa chir ton	*since when, for how long*
ਜੰਮਣਾ	janmnhaa	*to be born*

ਥੋੜੀ ਬਹੁਤੀ	thorhee bahutee	more or less, to some extent
ਬੇਨਤੀ	bentee	request (f.)
ਕੇਵਲ	keval	only
ਵੀਜ਼ਾ	veezaa	visa (m.)
ਆਗਿਆ	aagiaa	permission (f.)
ਵੱਸ	vass	authority, jurisdiction (m.)
ਪਾਸਪੋਰਟ	paasport	passport (m.)
ਅਫਸਰ	afsar	officer (m./f.)
ਸਾਹਿਬ	saahib	sir (m.)
ਆਸ ਪਾਸ	aas paas	around, around and about
ਕਾਫੀ ਕੁਝ	kaafee kujh	quite a lot, plenty
ਅਨੰਦ ਮਾਣੋ	anand maanho	enjoy yourselves
ਚਾਹੁਣਾ	chaahunhaa	to want, to need
ਸੌ (੧੦੦)	sau	one hundred
ਰੁਪਇਆ	rupaiaa	rupees (m.)
ਹਵਾਈ ਅੱਡਾ	havaaee addaa	airport (m.)
ਕਿੰਨੀ ਦੂਰ	kinnee door	how far
ਦੂਰ	door	far, distant
ਵੀਹ (੨੦)	veeh	twenty
ਮੀਲ	meel	mile, miles (m.)
ਜਗ੍ਹਾ	jag-h-aa	place, location (f.)
ਅੰਤਰ ਰਾਸ਼ਟਰੀ	antar raashatree	international
ਯੁਵਕ	yuvak	youth (m.)
ਹੋਸਟਲ	hostal	hostel (m.)
ਜ਼ਿਆਦਾ	ziaadaa	too much
ਮੰਗਣਾ	mangnhaa	to request, to ask, to charge
ਕਿਰਾਇਆ	kiraaiaa	rate, fare, rent (m.)
ਵਾਜਬੀ	vaajbee	reasonable, fair, right
ਸਵਾਰੀਆਂ	savaareeaan	passengers, travellers (f.)
ਸਮਾਨ	samaan	luggage, things (m.)
ਕਾਹਲਾ	kaahalaa	impatient, hasty (v.)
ਪੈਣਾ	painhaa	to act (to fall)
ਰੱਖਣਾ	rakhkhnhaa	to put
ਗੱਡੀ	gaddee	car, vehicle (f.)

☑ ਅਭਿਆਸ   abhiaas   **Exercises**

After reading the dialogue and/or listening to the audio tape, try to do the following exercises.

1. Write in the correct word order

a. ਹੈ ਪੰਜਾਬੀ ਬਹੁਤੀ ਆਉਂਦੀ ਥੋੜੀ ਸਾਨੂੰ
   hai-panjaabee-bahutee-aundee-thorhee-saanoon
   We only know a little Panjabi.

b. ਪਲੇਸ ਅਸੀਂ ਹਾਂ ਜਾਣਾ ਚਾਹੁੰਦੀਆਂ ਕਨਾਟ
   pales-aseen-haan-jaanhaa-chaahundeeaan-kanaat
   We want to go to Connaught Place.

c. ਤੁਸੀਂ ਜੀ ਦੋ ਦੀ ਦੇਵੋ ਗੇ ਮਹੀਨੇ ਰਹਿਣ ਕੀ ਆਗਿਆ
   tuseen-jee-do-dee-devo-ge-maheene-rahinh-kee-aagiaa
   Could you please give us permission to stay for two months?

2. Translate into Panjabi

a. There are two of you travelling and there is a lot of luggage.
b. We only have a one-month visa.
c. Enjoy yourselves!

🔊 ਬੋਲੀ ਬਾਰੇ   bolee baare   **Language points**

Pronouns in the oblique

In Unit 2 personal pronouns were introduced representing the English equivalents of *I*, *we*, *you*, *he*, *she* and *they*. As with nouns, personal pronouns also take on the oblique form when followed by postpositions. The most commonly used postposition with pronouns is ਨੂੰ **noon** *to* as is illustrated. Note that interrogative pronouns such as ਕੌਣ **kaunh**, *who* and ਕੀ **kee** *what* are also affected by postpositions.

Singular

Direct			Oblique		
I	ਮੈਂ	main	*to me*	ਮੈਨੂੰ	mainoon
you (inf.)	ਤੂੰ	toon	*to you* (inf.)	ਤੈਨੂੰ	tainoon
you (form.)	ਤੁਸੀਂ	tuseen	*to you* (form.)	ਤੁਹਾਨੂੰ	tuhaanoon
he/she/it (near)	ਇਹ	ih	*to he/she/it*	ਇਹ ਨੂੰ,	ih noon
				ਇਸ ਨੂੰ	is noon
he/she/it (far)	ਉਹ	uh	to he/she/it	ਉਹ ਨੂੰ,	uh noon
				ਉਸ ਨੂੰ	us noon

Interrogative pronouns					
who	ਕੌਣ	kaunh	*to whom*	ਕਿਸ ਨੂੰ	kis noo<u>n</u>
what	ਕੀ	kee	*to what*	ਕਿਹਨੂੰ	kihnoo<u>n</u>

Plural

Direct   Oblique

we	ਅਸੀਂ	asee<u>n</u>	*to us*	ਸਾਨੂੰ	saanoo<u>n</u>
you	ਤੁਸੀਂ	<u>t</u>usee<u>n</u>	*to you*	ਤੁਹਾਨੂੰ	<u>t</u>uhaanoo<u>n</u>
they (near)	ਇਹ	ih	*to them*	ਇਹਨਾਂ ਨੂੰ	ihnaa<u>n</u> noo<u>n</u>
they (far)	ਉਹ	uh	*to them*	ਉਹਨਾਂ ਨੂੰ	uhnaa<u>n</u> noo<u>n</u>
Interrogative pronouns					
who	ਕੌਣ	kaunh	*to whom*	ਕਿਹਨਾਂ ਨੂੰ	kihnaa<u>n</u> noo<u>n</u>
what	ਕੀ	kee	*to what*	ਕਿਹਨਾਂ ਨੂੰ	kihnaa<u>n</u> noo<u>n</u>

The postposition ਨੂੰ **noo<u>n</u>** is used in a number of ways. Generally, it directs an action, state or object towards the pronoun or noun after which it follows. Here are a few examples of how ਨੂੰ **noo<u>n</u>** can be used with pronouns.

ਪੰਜਾਬੀ ਮੈਨੂੰ ਥੋੜੀ ਬਹੁਤੀ ਆਉਂਦੀ ਹੈ	pa<u>n</u>jaabee mainoo<u>n</u> <u>th</u>orhee bahu<u>t</u>ee aau<u>nd</u>ee hai	*I know Panjabi to some extent.*
ਸਾਨੂੰ ਮਿਠਿਆਈ ਪਸੰਦ ਹੈ	saanoo<u>n</u> mithiaaee pasa<u>nd</u> hai	*We like sweets.* (literally: sweets are liked by us)
ਤੂੰ ਕਿਹਨਾਂ ਨੂੰ ਦੱਸਿਆ ਸੀ ?	<u>t</u>oo<u>n</u> kihnaa<u>n</u> noo<u>n</u> <u>d</u>assiaa see?	*Whom did you tell?*

There are many other postpositions which are also used with pronouns. ਤੋਂ **<u>t</u>o<u>n</u>**, ਨਾਲ **naal**, ਵਾਸਤੇ **vaas<u>t</u>e**, ਕੋਲ **kol** and ਲਈ **laee** are some commonly used ones which were introduced in Unit 4. The manner in which the oblique is formed with these postpositions is noticeably different from pronouns followed by ਨੂੰ **noon**. The first and second person pronouns are changed to the appropriate possessive adjectives while the third person pronouns follow the same pattern of ਨੂੰ **noon** as already shown. Here are some examples using the postposition ਤੋਂ **ton** (*from*).

1st person

Direct			Oblique		
I	ਮੈਂ	main	*from me*	ਮੇਰੇ ਤੋਂ	mere ton
we	ਅਸੀਂ	aseen	*from us*	ਸਾਡੇ ਤੋਂ	saade ton

2nd person

Direct			Oblique		
you (inf.)	ਤੂੰ	toon	*from you* (inf.)	ਤੇਰੇ ਤੋਂ	tere ton
you (form.)	ਤੁਸੀਂ	tuseen	*from you* (form.)	ਤੁਹਾਡੇ ਤੋਂ	tuhaade ton

3rd person

Direct			Oblique		
he/she/it (singular, near)	ਇਹ	ih	*from him/her/it*	ਇਸ ਤੋਂ	is ton
he/she/it (singular, far)	ਉਹ	uh	*from him/her/it*	ਉਸ ਤੋਂ	us ton
they (plural, near)	ਇਹ	ih	*from them*	ਇਹਨਾਂ ਤੋਂ	ihnaan ton
they (plural, far)	ਉਹ	uh	*from them*	ਉਹਨਾਂ ਤੋਂ	uhnaan ton

ਮੇਰੇ ਕੋਲ ਐਨੇ ਪੈਸੇ ਨਹੀਂ ਹਨ	mere kol aine paise naheen han	*I don't have that much money.*
ਉਹਨਾਂ ਵਾਸਤੇ ਵੀ ਚਾਹ ਬਣਾਓ	uhnaan vaaste vee chaah banhaao	*Make tea for them too.*
ਕੀ ਤੁਸੀਂ ਸਾਡੇ ਨਾਲ ਆਵੋ ਗੇ ?	kee tuseen saade naal aavo ge?	*Will you come with us?*
ਅਸੀਂ ਕਪੜੇ ਇਹਨਾਂ ਤੋਂ ਖ਼ਰੀਦਾਂ ਗੇ	aseen kaprhe ihnaan ton khareedaan ge	*We will buy the clothes from them.*

Must, have to

In Panjabi, expressions of compulsion come in three forms: an intention to do something, a certainty about doing something and a strong sense of compulsion about doing something. In each of these cases, it is usually the infinitive of the verb which directs the action related to the situation. Often ਹੋਣਾ **honhaa** is used to give a sense of the present or past condition, depending on which tense of *to be* is used. The direct form of the pronoun is used in these cases.

ਮੈਂ ਜਾਣਾ ਹੈ   main jaanhaa hai *I am to go/ I intend to go*
ਮੈਂ ਜਾਣਾ ਸੀ   main jaanhaa see *I should have gone/ I was to go/ I had to go*

Strong compulsion is indicated by the use of the verb ਪੈਣਾ **painhaa** (*to fall*). This gives a sense of habitual compulsion and is positioned after the infinitive. Note that the infinitive behaves as the subject in many of these expressions, and therefore the form of ਪੈਣਾ **painhaa** generally takes the singular masculine form (in agreement with the infinitive). For example:

ਮੈਨੂੰ ਹਰ ਰੋਜ਼ ਜਾਣਾ ਪੈਂਦਾ ਹੈ   mainoon har roz jaanhaa   I *have to go*
                            paindaa hai   *every day.*

Use of the verb ਚਾਹੁਣਾ chaahunhaa

In Panjabi, expressions such as *should/ought* and *need/want* are generally formed with the verb ਚਾਹੁਣਾ **chaahunhaa** (*to want, to need*). These expressions use the infinitive followed by ਚਾਹੀਦਾ **chaaheedaa**, which is the passive form of the verb ਚਾਹੁਣਾ **chaahunhaa**. (The passive voice will be explained in a later unit.) ਚਾਹੀਦਾ **chaaheedaa** in the sentence ਮੈਨੂੰ ਚਾਹੀਦਾ ਹੈ **mainoon chaaheedaa hai** literally means *it is wanted by me*. However, the use of ਚਾਹੀਦਾ **chaaheedaa** can have two different meanings:

■ should/ought   ■ need/want

Should, ought ਚਾਹੀਦਾ **chaaheedaa** as with all other verb formations, changes according to the subject. In the case of expressions of *should* and *ought*, pronouns followed by postpositions behave like objects (*to me, for me, with them*). Therefore, in the case of someone who has to go somewhere, the form of ਚਾਹੀਦਾ **chaaheedaa** must be in the singular masculine form in agreement with the infinitive. Similarly, if the object is feminine and/or plural, then the form of ਚਾਹੁਣਾ **chaahunhaa**, as well as the infinitive would reflect this:

ਮੈਨੂੰ ਜਾਣਾ ਚਾਹੀਦਾ ਹੈ mainoo_n jaanhaa chaaheedaa hai *I should go*

ਮੈਨੂੰ ਜਾਣਾ ਚਾਹੀਦਾ ਸੀ mainoo_n jaanhaa chaaheedaa see *I should have gone*

Care must be taken to identify the object in expressions of *ought* and *should*. In our earlier example, the pronoun served as the object, however in the following examples the infinitive and the form of ਚਾਹੀਦਾ **chaaheedaa** follow the gender and numerical nature of the *subject of obligation* which now becomes the object, in the first case tea and in the second books.

ਮੈਨੂੰ ਚਾਹ ਨਹੀਂ ਪੀਣੀ ਚਾਹੀਦੀ	mainoo_n chaah nahee_n peenhee chaaheedee	*I should not drink tea.*
ਤੁਹਾਨੂੰ ਹੋਰ ਕਿਤਾਬਾਂ ਪੜ੍ਹਨੀਆਂ ਚਾਹੀਦੀਆਂ ਹਨ	tuhaanoo_n hor kitaabaa_n parhhneeaa_n chaaheedeeaa_n han	*You should read more books.*

To want, to need   Expressions of desire or necessity are also formed with ਚਾਹੁਣਾ **chaahunhaa**. However, the verb is formed according to the subject of the sentence. For example, in Dialogue 2 Jaspreet and Simran say to the taxi driver, *We want to go to Connaught Place*. This is expressed as:

ਅਸੀਂ ਕਨਾਟ ਪਲੇਸ ਜਾਣਾ ਚਾਹੁੰਦੀਆਂ ਹਾਂ	asee_n kanaat pales jaanhaa chaahu_ndeeaa_n haa_n	*We want to go to Connaught Place.*

Notice in this example that ਅਸੀਂ **asee_n** and ਚਾਹੁੰਦੀਆਂ ਹਾਂ **chaahu_ndeeaan haa_n** are in agreement with each other. Therefore, the subject *we* dictates the form of *to want*. Here are some more examples of expressions of desire and necessity:

ਕੀ ਤੁਸੀਂ ਅਮਰੀਕਾ ਜਾਣਾ ਚਾਹੁੰਦੇ ਹੋ ?	kee tusee_n amreekaa jaanhaa chaahu_nde ho?	*Do you want to go to America?*
ਮੇਰਾ ਭਰਾ ਪੜ੍ਹਨਾ ਚਾਹੁੰਦਾ ਹੈ	meraa bharaa parhhnaa chaahu_ndaa hai	*My brother wants to study.*

As with constructions of *should* and *ought* the oblique form of pronouns with the postposition ਨੂੰ **noon** are also used in expressing *need* and *want* with the passive of ਚਾਹੁਣਾ **chaahunhaa**. This may seem confusing but you will be able to tell from the context of the sentence whether the speaker means that they need or want something, or that they should or ought to do something.

ਮੈਨੂੰ ਇੱਕ ਕਮੀਜ਼ ਚਾਹੀਦੀ ਹੈ	mainoo<u>n</u> ikk kameez chaahee<u>dee</u> hai	*I need a shirt.*
ਮੈਨੂੰ ਦੋ ਕਮੀਜ਼ਾਂ ਚਾਹੀਦੀਆਂ ਹਨ	mainoo<u>n</u> <u>d</u>o kameezaa<u>n</u> chaahee<u>dee</u>aa<u>n</u> han	*I need two shirts.*
ਉਹਨਾਂ ਨੂੰ ਪੈਸੇ ਚਾਹੀਦੇ ਹਨ	uhnaa<u>n</u> noo<u>n</u> paise chaahee<u>de</u> han	*They need money.*

Infinitives in the oblique

The presence of postpositions after nouns, adjectives and pronouns has been discussed in previous units. You know by now that the forms of direct nouns, adjectives and pronouns are changed to the oblique when they are followed by a postposition. The same is true for infinitives. In the first dialogue, Mr Sandhu asks his daughters, 'How much money do you need to go to India?' In this sentence 'to go to India' is a phrase which contains an infinitive followed by a postposition:

ਭਾਰਤ ਜਾਣ ਲਈ   bhaara<u>t</u> jaanh laee   *to go to India*

The infinitive of the verb *to go* ਜਾਣਾ **jaanhaa** preceeds the postposition ਲਈ **laee** requiring the infinitive to be in the oblique. The oblique of the infinitive is a shortened form which merely omits the vowel ending ਆ **aa**. Therefore, ਜਾਣਾ **jaanhaa** in the oblique becomes ਜਾਣ **jaanh**. The example given of ਜਾਣਾ **jaanhaa** is that of an infinitive with a vowel-ending stem. Other verbs such as ਖਰੀਦਣਾ <u>kh</u>areednhaa, ਲਿਖਣਾ **likhnhaa** and ਬੋਲਣਾ **bolnhaa** all have stems which end in consonants. These types of infinitives also have shortened forms which omit the ਆ **aa** ending making them ਖਰੀਦਣ <u>kh</u>areedanh, ਲਿਖਣ **likhanh** and ਬੋਲਣ **bolanh**. Here are some examples of infinitives in the oblique and how they are formed:

ਉਹ ਸਾਨੂੰ ਪੈਸੇ ਦੇਣ ਨੂੰ ਤਿਆਰ ਨਹੀਂ	uh saanoo<u>n</u> paise denh noo<u>n</u> <u>t</u>iaar naheen	*He isn't ready* [willing] *to give us money.*
ਘੁੰਮਣ ਲਈ ਸਮਾਂ ਚਾਹੀਦਾ ਹੈ	ghu<u>n</u>manh laee samaa<u>n</u> chaahee<u>d</u>aa hai	*Time is needed for travelling.*
ਮੈਂ ਦੋਸਤ ਨੂੰ ਮਿਲਣ ਲਈ ਆਈ ਹਾਂ	main <u>d</u>ost noo<u>n</u> milanh laee aaee haa<u>n</u>	*I have come to meet a friend.*

Vocative case

The vocative case is used when addressing somebody directly or as an exclamation to someone. It can be used in both formal and informal situations. For example, in Dialogue 1, Mr Sandhu says ਧੀਓ ! **dheeo!** which means *daughters!*. Another more formal setting might be in a meeting in which you wish to address the audience: ਭੈਣੋ ਤੇ ਭਰਾਵੋ **bhainho ṭe bharaavo** (*brothers and sisters*). The manner in which the vocative case is formed is quite similar to the plural oblique forms of nouns as shown in Unit 4, though the vocative case ends with ਓ o and not ਆਂ aaṇ. When the vocative case is used in reference to singular people, the noun takes on the ending ਏ e for feminine people and the ending ਆ aa for masculine people:

ਮੁੰਡਿਆ !	muṇdiaa!	*boy!*
ਮੁੰਡਿਓ !	muṇdio!	*boys!*
ਬੱਚਿਓ !	bachchio!	*children!*
ਕੁੜੀਏ !	kurhee-e!	*girl!*
ਕੁੜੀਓ !	kurheeo!	*girls!*
ਦੋਸਤੋ !	ḍosto!	*friends!*

The ending -ਵਾਲਾ vaalaa

ਵਾਲਾ **vaalaa** is added to nouns and verbs to give two main senses: *the one or ones* or *about to*. The use of -ਵਾਲਾ **vaalaa** with nouns expresses a relationship between the noun and the object or person being referred to. You will recall in the commentary in Unit 3 that the vegetable seller was called ਸਬਜ਼ੀਵਾਲਾ **sabzeevaalaa** and that earlier in this unit the taxi driver was referred to as ਟੈਕਸੀਵਾਲਾ **taikseevaalaa**. The ending -ਵਾਲਾ **vaalaa** in these examples has changed the role of the noun through the following pattern:

ਸਬਜ਼ੀ	+	-ਵਾਲਾ	=	ਸਬਜ਼ੀਵਾਲਾ
sabzee		-vaalaa		sabzeevaalaa
vegetable		*the one*		*vegetable seller*
ਟੈਕਸੀ	+	-ਵਾਲਾ	=	ਟੈਕਸੀਵਾਲਾ
taiksee		-vaalaa		taikseevaalaa
taxi		*the one*		*taxi driver*

Here are some more examples of this type of use of the ending -ਵਾਲਾ **vaalaa** with nouns:

ਲਾਹੌਰਵਾਲੀ ਔਰਤ	laahaurvaalee auraṭ	*the woman from Lahore*
ਪਿੰਡਵਾਲਾ	piṇdvaalaa	*villager*
ਪੈਸੇਵਾਲੇ	paisevaale	*wealthy people*
ਸਾੜ੍ਹੀਵਾਲੀ	saarhheevaalee	*the one wearing the sari*
ਘਰਵਾਲਾ	gharvaalaa	*husband*

Note that like other endings or adjectives, the ending -ਵਾਲਾ **vaalaa** changes according to the gender and number of the persons or objects being referred to.

The second meaning produced by the ending -ਵਾਲਾ **vaalaa** is *about to* or *on the point of doing*. This is created when -ਵਾਲਾ **vaalaa** is used with the oblique of the infinitive. The form resembles that of the oblique infinitive (or shortened form) used with postpositions presented earlier in this unit. Here are some examples of how this meaning is constructed:

ਉਹ ਭਾਰਤ ਜਾਣ ਵਾਲੇ ਹਨ	uh bhaara<u>t</u> jaanh vaale han	*They are about to go to India.*
ਮੈਂ ਤੁਹਾਨੂੰ ਚਿੱਠੀ ਲਿਖਣ ਵਾਲੀ ਸੀ	main <u>t</u>uhaanoo<u>n</u> chiththee likhanh vaalee see	*I was about to write you a letter.*
ਕੁੜੀਆਂ ਆਉਣ ਵਾਲੀਆਂ ਸਨ	kurheeaa<u>n</u> aaunh vaaleeaa<u>n</u> san	*The girls were about to come.*
ਮੈਂ ਕਿਤਾਬ ਪੜ੍ਹਨ ਵਾਲਾ ਹਾਂ	main <u>k</u>itaab parhhanh vaalaa haa<u>n</u>	*I am about to read the book.*

The ending -ਵਾਲਾ **vaalaa** used with oblique infinitives can also have the same meaning as that when used with nouns such as ਇੱਥੇ ਰਹਿਣ ਵਾਲਾ **iththe rahinh vaalaa** *the one who lives here* or ਕੰਮ ਕਰਨ ਵਾਲੇ **ka<u>n</u>m karan vaale** *the ones who work* or *working people*. Once you understand how to use the ending -ਵਾਲਾ **vaalaa** , you will find it a very useful tool when referring to people and objects as well as to actions that are about to happen.

ਵਿਆਖਿਆ   viaakhiaa   Commentary

1. I like it!

Fondness is shown in Panjabi in a number of ways. Depending upon the degree of liking and context, fondness can be expressed through:

ਪਸੰਦ **pasa<u>nd</u>** means *pleasing* or *like*
ਸ਼ੌਕ **shauk** means *fondness* or *enjoyment*
ਲੱਗਣਾ **laggnhaa** means *seems* (e.g. *it seems nice/bad*)

Therefore, expressions of fondness generally require the use of ਨੂੰ **noo<u>n</u>** in order to direct the feelings or emotions towards the person. A sentence such as *I like bananas* would translate directly into Panjabi as *Bananas are liked by me*. ਮੈਨੂੰ ਕੇਲੇ ਪਸੰਦ ਹਨ **mainoo<u>n</u> kele pasa<u>nd</u> han**, thereby making *bananas* the subject and *me* the object. Another way of using ਪਸੰਦ **pasand** is in combination with ਕਰਨਾ **karnaa**. The use of ਕਰਨਾ **karnaa** gives an added sense of habituality, such as *I generally like bananas* or *I always like bananas* in ਮੈਂ ਕੇਲਿਆਂ ਨੂੰ ਪਸੰਦ ਕਰਦਾ ਹਾਂ **main keliaan noon pasand kardaa haan**. ਲੱਗਣਾ **laggnhaa** (*to seem*) is a less specific word which requires the use of a qualifying adjective such as good, bad, tasty or ugly, in order to express how something seems. If you were to say *this food is good* one way in Panjabi to express this would be ਇਹ ਖਾਣਾ ਮੈਨੂੰ ਚੰਗਾ ਲੱਗਦਾ ਹੈ **ih khaanhaa mainoon changaa laggdaa hai** (literally, *this food seems good to me*). Here are a few more examples:

ਮੈਨੂੰ ਸਿਤਾਰ ਵਜਾਉਣ ਦਾ ਸੌਕ ਹੈ	mainoon sitaar vajaaunh daa shauk hai	*I enjoy playing the sitar.*
ਅਸੀਂ ਮਿਠਿਆਈ (ਨੂੰ) ਪਸੰਦ ਕਰਦੇ ਹਾਂ	aseen mithiaaee noon pasand karde haan	*We like sweets.*
ਤਸਵੀਰਾਂ ਉਹਨਾਂ ਨੂੰ ਚੰਗੀਆਂ ਲੱਗਦੀਆਂ ਹਨ	tasveeraan uhnaan noon changeeaan laggdeeaan han	*They like the pictures.*

2. Usefulness of Panjabi in South Asia

Despite the fact that Hindi and Urdu are the national languages of India and Pakistan respectively, in practice once you leave the urban centres regional languages come to the fore. Panjabi has a unique position in the languages of North India and Pakistan, in that it has a large usage in the urban centres. In Lahore and throughout much of Pakistan, Panjabi is the language of the people and is spoken widely and understood almost universally. Furthermore, in Delhi many taxi drivers, rickshaw **vaalaas** and bus drivers tend to speak Panjabi (sometimes a few words may save the passenger from being overcharged!).

Taxi drivers are notorious in the sub-continent for overcharging and haggling with customers. Even though many main tourist resorts and public transport centres such as railway stations and airports now operate a prepayment system, there are still many occasions where unsuspecting travellers will be caught unaware. This has to be accepted as one of the many facets of travel to the sub-continent and should not cause frustration or anguish. On a more positive front, the fun of haggling, as you will see in the next unit, is a must when shopping.

3. Music in Panjab

Panjab is well known for folk music (as we shall see in Unit 16), however, there is a long tradition of classical music in Panjab. The world-renowned tabla player, Zakheer Hussain comes from the tradition of the Panjabi gharana, which reflects a particular type of musical style and a particular rhythmic form known as ਕੈਰਵਾ **kairvaa**, which is an eight-beat cycle. One other musical form which crosses over the classical and popular is the Qawaali, made popular internationally by the late Nusrat Fateh Ali Khan. The Panjabi Qawaals sung by Khan are some of the most popular tunes throughout Panjab, and the elegant, poetic language is quite easy to understand.

☑ ਅਭਿਆਸ   **abhiaas**   **Exercises**

After reading the dialogue and/or listening to the audio tape, try to do the following excercises.

1. Fill in the blanks

a) ਮੈਨੂੰ ਕਿਤਾਬ _____ ਹੈ। mainoon kitaab _____ hai. *I want a book.*

b) ਮੈਨੂੰ ਜਾਣਾ _____ ਹੈ। mainoon jaanhaa _____ hai. *I should go.*

c) ਮੈਨੂੰ ਸਿਤਾਰ _____ ਦਾ ਸ਼ੌਕ ਹੈ। mainoon sitaar _____ daa shauk hai.

   I like playing the sitar.

2. Translation

Say the following English sentences in Panjabi.

a) What does he want?
b) Daughters! What do you want?
c) Whom did you tell?
d) Should we go?

3. Use of vaalaa

From the following equations work out what the words using the ending
–ਵਾਲਾ are.

a)   + ਵਾਲਾ   =   [husband]

b)   + ਵਾਲਾ   =   [taxi driver]

c)   + ਵਾਲਾ   =   [vegetable vendor]

4. Listening comprehension

You are having a conversation with a taxi driver. Listen to the recording
on the audio tape and then answer the following questions.

How many passengers?
Where are you travelling to?
How much is the fare?
How far is the hotel?
How much luggage?
Do you accept the taxi ride?

9 ਸਾਡਾ ਕਪੜਾ ਸਭ ਤੋਂ ਵਧੀਆ ਹੈ !

saadaa kaprhaa sabh ton vadheeaa hai!

Our cloth is the best!

In this unit you will learn:

- how to compare things
- how to talk about your health
- how to express actions which you can and cannot do
- how to express actions which have already occurred

1 Our cloth is the best!

ਗੱਲ ਬਾਤ ੧ ਸਾਡਾ ਕਪੜਾ ਸਭ ਤੋਂ ਵਧੀਆ ਹੈ !

gall baat 1 saadaa kaprhaa sabh ton vadheeaa hai!

Jaspreet and Simran have arrived in Delhi and are shopping in Karol Bagh, a popular place in Delhi to buy ready-made clothing as well as unstitched cloth. They are just entering a material shop where the shopkeeper greets them.

ਦੁਕਾਨਦਾਰ	ਅੰਦਰ ਆਓ, ਭੈਣ ਜੀ। ਸਾਰੀ ਦਿੱਲੀ ਵਿਚ ਸਾਡਾ ਕਪੜਾ ਸਭ ਤੋਂ ਵਧੀਆ ਹੈ!
Shopkeeper	<u>an</u>dar aao, bhainh jee. saaree <u>d</u>illee vich saadaa kaprhaa sabh <u>ton</u> va<u>dh</u>eeaa hai!
ਜਸਪ੍ਰੀਤ	ਸਾਨੂੰ ਛਪਾਈਵਾਲਾ ਕਪੜਾ ਚਾਹੀਦਾ ਹੈ ਜਿਸ ਦਾ ਅੱਜ ਕੱਲ੍ਹ ਰਵਾਜ ਹੈ।
Jaspreet	saanoon <u>ch</u>apaaeevaalaa kaprhaa chaahee<u>d</u>aa hai jis <u>d</u>aa ajj kallh ravaaj hai.
ਦੁਕਾਨਦਾਰ	ਫ਼ਿਕਰ ਨਾ ਕਰੋ ! ਮੈਂ ਤੁਹਾਨੂੰ ਉਹ ਕਪੜਾ ਦਿਖਾ ਰਿਹਾ ਹਾਂ ਜਿਹੜਾ ਵਧੇਰੇ ਹੰਢਣਸਾਰ ਹੈ ਅਤੇ ਸਭ ਤੋਂ ਵੱਧ ਵਿਕਦਾ ਹੈ।
Shopkeeper	fikar naa karo! main <u>t</u>uhaanoon uh kaprhaa <u>d</u>ikhaa rihaa haan jihrhaa va<u>dh</u>ere ha<u>ndh</u>anhsaar hai a<u>t</u>e sabh <u>ton</u> va<u>dhdh</u> vik<u>d</u>aa hai.

(The shopkeeper shows the girls some cloth pieces)

ਸਿਮਰਨ	ਮੈਨੂੰ ਇਸ ਕਪੜੇ ਦਾ ਰੰਗ ਪਸੰਦ ਹੈ ਪਰ ਕਪੜਾ ਇਸ ਤੋਂ ਮੋਟਾ ਹੋਣਾ ਚਾਹੀਦਾ ਹੈ।
Simran	mainoon is kaprhe daa rang pasand hai par kaprhaa is ton motaa honhaa chaaheedaa hai.
ਦੁਕਾਨਦਾਰ	ਸਾਡੇ ਕੋਲ ਇਸ ਤੋਂ ਪਤਲਾ ਵੀ ਹੈ ਤੇ ਮੋਟਾ ਵੀ। ਤੁਸੀਂ ਛਾਪੇ ਦੀ ਚੋਣ ਕਰੋ।
Shopkeeper	saade kol is ton patlaa vee hai te motaa vee. tuseen chaape dee chonh karo.
ਸਿਮਰਨ	ਜਸਪ੍ਰੀਤ, ਤੈਨੂੰ ਕਿਹੜਾ ਵਧੇਰੇ ਚੰਗਾ ਲੱਗਦਾ ਹੈ, ਲਾਲ ਜਾਂ ਨੀਲਾ ?
Simran	jaspreet, tainoon kihrhaa vadhere changaa laggdaa hai, laal jaan neelaa?
ਜਸਪ੍ਰੀਤ	ਨੀਲਾ ਕਪੜਾ ਲਾਲ ਕਪੜੇ ਤੋਂ ਪਤਲਾ ਹੈ, ਪਰ ਫਿੱਕੇ ਰੰਗ ਵਾਲਾ ਸਭ ਤੋਂ ਸੁਹਣਾ ਹੈ।
Jaspreet	neelaa kaprhaa laal kaprhe ton patlaa hai, par phikke rang vaalaa sabh ton suhnhaa hai.
ਸਿਮਰਨ	ਇਹ ਕਪੜਾ ਕਿੰਨੇ ਦਾ ਮੀਟਰ ਹੈ ?
Simran	ih kaprhaa kinne daa meetar hai?
ਦੁਕਾਨਦਾਰ	ਇੱਕ ਸੌ ਵੀਹ ਰੁਪਏ ਦਾ ਮੀਟਰ ।
Shopkeeper	ikk sau veeh rupae daa meetar.
ਸਿਮਰਨ	ਇਹ ਕੀਮਤ ਬਹੁਤ ਜ਼ਿਆਦਾ ਹੈ। ਅਸੀਂ ਹੋਰ ਵੀ ਕਈ ਦੁਕਾਨਾਂ ਤੇ ਜਾ ਚੁਕੀਆਂ ਹਾਂ ਅਤੇ ਉਹਨਾਂ ਦੇ ਮੁਕਾਬਲੇ ਵਿਚ ਤੁਹਾਡੀਆਂ ਕੀਮਤਾਂ ਬਹੁਤ ਜ਼ਿਆਦਾ ਹਨ।
Simran	ih keemat bahut ziaadaa hai. aseen hor vee kaee dukaanaan te jaa chukeeaan haan ate uhnaan de mukaable vich tuhaadeeaan keemataan bahut ziaadaa han.
ਦੁਕਾਨਦਾਰ	ਮੈਨੂੰ ਅਫ਼ਸੋਸ ਹੈ ਕਿ ਮੈਂ ਕੀਮਤ ਹੋਰ ਘੱਟ ਨਹੀਂ ਕਰ ਸਕਦਾ।
Shopkeeper	mainoon afsos hai ki main keemat hor ghatt naheen kar sakdaa.

Shopkeeper	*Come in, sisters! Our cloth is the best in all of Delhi!*
Jaspreet	*We want printed cloth that's in fashion these days.*
Shopkeeper	*Don't worry. What I'm showing you is cloth that is durable and sells a lot.*
Simran	*I like the colour, but the material should be thicker than this.*
Shopkeeper	*We have thinner and also thicker than this. Choose whatever print you like.*
Simran	*Jaspreet, which do you like better, red or blue?*
Jaspreet	*The blue is thinner than the red, but the light-coloured one is the nicest.*

Simran	*How much is this cloth per metre?*
Shopkeeper	*One hundred and twenty rupees per metre.*
Simran	*The price is too high. We've been to several other shops and in comparison with them, your prices are very high.*
Shopkeeper	*I'm sorry but (that) I can't lower the price any more.*

ਸ਼ਬਦਾਵਲੀ   **shabdaavalee**   **Vocabulary**

ਦੁਕਾਨਦਾਰ	dukaandaar	*shopkeeper* (m.)
ਕਪੜਾ	kaprhaa	*cloth* (m.)
ਸਭ ਤੋਂ ਵਧੀਆ	sabh ton vadheeaa	*the best*
ਛਪਾਈਵਾਲਾ	chapaaeevaalaa	*the printed one* (m.)
ਜਿਸ	jis	*which* (oblique)
ਰਵਾਜ	ravaaj	*fashion* (m.)
ਅੱਜ ਕੱਲ੍ਹ	ajj kallh	*these days*
ਦਿਖਾਉਣਾ	dikhaaunhaa	*to show*
ਜਿਹੜਾ	jihrhaa	*that, which*
ਹੰਢਣਸਾਰ	handhanhsaar	*durable, hardwearing*
ਚਲਣਾ	chalnhaa	*to go*
ਵਿਕਣਾ	viknhaa	*to be sold*
ਰੰਗ	rang	*colour* (m.)
ਮੋਟਾ	motaa	*fat, thick* (v.)
ਪਤਲਾ	patlaa	*thin* (v.)
ਛਾਪੇ	chaape	*print* (m.)
ਚੋਣ	chonh	*choice, selection* (f.)
ਕਿਹੜਾ	kihrhaa	*which*
ਵਧੇਰੇ	vadhere	*more*
ਲਾਲ	laal	*red*
ਨੀਲਾ	neelaa	*blue* (v.)
ਜਾਂ	jaan	*or*
ਫਿੱਕਾ	phikkaa	*light, pale* (v.)
ਸੁਹਣਾ	suhnhaa	*nice, pretty* (v.)
ਕਿੰਨੇ ਦਾ ਮੀਟਰ ?	kinne daa meetar?	*how much per metre?*
ਇੱਕ ਸੌ ਵੀਹ	ikk sau veeh	*one hundred and twenty*
ਕੀਮਤ	keemat	*price* (f.)
ਬਹੁਤ ਜ਼ਿਆਦਾ	bahut ziaadaa	*far too much*
ਕਈ	kaee	*several*
ਚੁਕਣਾ	chuknhaa	*to be settled, finished*

ਜਾ ਚੁਕਣਾ	jaa chuknhaa	*have (already) been*
ਮੁਕਾਬਲਾ	mukaablaa	*competition*
ਵੱਧ	vadhdh	*high*
ਘੱਟ	ghatt	*less, lower*
ਸਕਣਾ	saknhaa	*can, to be able to*

☑ ਅਭਿਆਸ   **abhiaas**   **Exercises**

After reading the dialogue and/or listening to the audio tape, try to do the following exercises.

1. In the cloth shop

You are in a cloth shop telling the sales person exactly what you are looking for. Express the following in Panjabi:

a) *I want light-coloured cloth.*
b) *I want material that is thick and also durable.*
c) *The print should be in fashion.*
d) *The price should not be too high.*

2. Complete the table

ਵਧੀਆ		
		better
	keemat	
ਮੁਕਾਬਲਾ		
	sabh ton vadheeaa	

▶ 2 What's the problem?
📺 ਗੱਲ ਬਾਤ ੨ ਕੀ ਤਕਲੀਫ਼ ਹੈ ?

gall baat 2 kee takleef hai?

On their way back from the market place in Delhi, Simran and Jaspreet had some snacks at a roadside restaurant, commonly known as a 'dhaba'. On their way back to their hotel Simran begins to feel ill and has gone to visit the doctor.

ਡਾਕਟਰ	ਬੇਟੀ, ਕੀ ਤਕਲੀਫ਼ ਹੈ ?
daaktar	betee, kee takleef hai?
ਸਿਮਰਨ	ਮੇਰੀ ਤਬੀਅਤ ਖ਼ਰਾਬ ਹੈ।
simran	meree tabeeat kharaab hai.
ਡਾਕਟਰ	ਕੀ ਤੈਨੂੰ ਬੁਖ਼ਾਰ ਹੈ ?
daaktar	kee tainoon bukhaar hai?
ਸਿਮਰਨ	ਹਾਂ ਜੀ। ਮੈਨੂੰ ਠੰਡ ਲੱਗ ਰਹੀ ਹੈ, ਪੇਟ ਵਿਚ ਦਰਦ ਹੈ ਅਤੇ ਮੈਨੂੰ ਕਮਜ਼ੋਰੀ ਵੀ ਹੈ।
simran	haan jee. mainoon thand lagg rahee hai, pet vich dard hai ate mainoon kamzoree vee hai.
ਡਾਕਟਰ	ਬਿਮਰ ਹੋਣ ਤੋਂ ਪਹਿਲੇ ਤੂੰ ਕੀ ਕੁਝ ਖਾਧਾ ਸੀ ?
daaktar	bimaar honh ton pahile toon kee kujh khaadhaa see?
ਸਿਮਰਨ	ਮੈਨੂੰ ਯਾਦ ਨਹੀਂ ਪਰ ਮੈਨੂੰ ਇੱਥੋਂ ਦੀਆਂ ਛੱਲੀਆਂ ਬਹੁਤ ਪਸੰਦ ਹਨ।
simran	mainoon yaad naheen par mainoon iththon deeaan challeeaan bahut pasand han.
ਡਾਕਟਰ	ਹੁਣ ਮੈਂ ਸਮਝਿਆ। ਜਿਹੜੇ ਲੋਕ ਬਾਹਰੋਂ ਆਉਂਦੇ ਹਨ, ਉਹਨਾਂ ਨੂੰ ਦੇਸੀ ਖਾਣਾ ਹਜ਼ਮ ਨਹੀਂ ਹੁੰਦਾ। ਇਹ ਲਵੋ ਦਵਾਈ, ਅਰਾਮ ਕਰੋ ਤੇ ਛੱਲੀਆਂ ਤੋਂ ਦੂਰ ਰਵੋ !
daaktar	hunh main samajhiaa. jihrhe lok baahron aaunde han, uhnaan noon desee khaanhaa hazam naheen hundaa. ih lavo davaaee, araam karo, te challeeaan ton door ravo!
ਸਿਮਰਨ	ਧੰਨਵਾਦ।
simran	dhannvaad.

Doctor	*Dear (daughter), what's the problem?*
Simran	*I'm not feeling well (literally: my health is bad).*
Doctor	*Do you have a fever?*
Simran	*Yes. I feel cold, I have a stomach ache and I'm also weak.*
Doctor	*Before falling ill, what did you eat?*
Simran	*I don't remember, but I like the corn on the cob here a lot.*
Doctor	*Now I understand. People who come from abroad can't digest the food here. Take this medicine, rest, and stay away from corn on the cob!*
Simran	*Thank you.*

🔑 ਸ਼ਬਦਾਵਲੀ   **shabdaavalee**   **Vocabulary**

ਤਕਲੀਫ਼	takleef	*trouble, irritation, bother* (f.)
ਤਬੀਅਤ	tabeeat	*state of health, condition* (f.)
ਬੁਖ਼ਾਰ	bukhaar	*fever/temperature* (m.)

ਠੰਡ	tha<u>n</u>d	*cold* (f.)
ਲੱਗਣਾ	laggnhaa	*to feel*
ਪੇਟ	pet	*stomach, belly* (m.)
ਦਰਦ	<u>d</u>ar<u>d</u>	*pain, hurt* (f.)
ਕਮਜ਼ੋਰੀ	kamzoree	*weakness* (f.)
ਬਿਮਾਰ	bimaar	*ill, sick*
ਬਿਮਾਰ ਹੋਣ	bimaar honh	*before falling ill*
ਤੋਂ ਪਹਿਲੇ	<u>t</u>on pahile	
ਯਾਦ	yaa<u>d</u>	*memory, remember* (f.)
ਛੱਲੀ	<u>ch</u>allee	*corn on the cob* (f.)
ਸਮਝਣਾ	samajhnhaa	*to understand/* *comprehend*
ਬਾਹਰੋਂ	baahro<u>n</u>	*from outside/ from abroad*
ਦੇਸੀ	<u>d</u>esi	*Indian, Panjabi, home*
ਹਜ਼ਮ	hazam	*digest*
ਦੂਰ	<u>d</u>oor	*far/away*
ਅਰਾਮ	araam	*rest* (m.)
ਦਵਾਈ	<u>d</u>avaaee	*medicine* (f.)

✅ ਅਭਿਆਸ   **abhiaas**   **Exercises**

After reading the dialogue and/or listening to the audio tape, try to do the following exercises.

1. Write in the correct word order

a. ਹੈ ਤਕਲੀਫ਼ ਕੀ ?   hai <u>t</u>akleef kee?
b. ਹੈ ਤੈਨੂੰ ਕੀ ਬੁਖ਼ਾਰ ?   hai <u>t</u>ainoo<u>n</u> kee bu<u>kh</u>aar?
c. ਸਮਝਿਆ ਹੁਣ ਮੈਂ   samajhiaa hunh mai<u>n</u>

2. Fill in the blanks

Fill in the blanks with the correct terms from the dialogue. The English has been given in brackets, although not necessarily in the correct order.

You: ਮੇਰੀ ____ ਖ਼ਰਾਬ ਹੈ। (health)
        meree ____ kharab hai.
Dr: ਕੀ ____ ਹੈ ? (problem)
        kee ____ hai ?

You: ਮੇਰੇ _____ ਵਿਚ _____ ਹੈ ਤੇ ਮੈਨੂੰ _____ ਵੀ ਹੈ ।
(pain, fever, stomach)
mere _____ vich _____ hai ate mainoon _____ vee hai.

Dr: ਤੈਨੂੰ _____ ਹੈ ਤੇ _____ ਲੱਗ ਰਹੀ ਹੈ ? (fever, cold)
tainoon _____ hai te _____ lagg rahee hai ?

You: ਹਾਂ ਜੀ   haan jee

Dr: ਇਹ _____ ਲਵੋ ਤੇ _____ ਕਰੋ। (rest, medicine)
ih _____ lavo te _____ karo.

ਬੋਲੀ ਬਾਰੇ   bolee baare   Language points

Comparison of adjectives

When people or things are compared in Panjabi in terms of quality,
size, number and price, there are no direct translations of the English
expressions 'good better best' or 'big bigger biggest'. Instead the
postpositions ਨਾਲੋਂ **naalon** (than) and ਤੋਂ **ton** (from) are commonly used to
express comparison such as '*more* _____' or '_____ *than*'. For example:

ਇਸ ਤੋਂ/ ਨਾਲੋਂ ਮੋਟਾ **is ton/ naalon motaa**   *thicker than this*
ਉਸ ਤੋਂ/ ਨਾਲੋਂ ਪਤਲਾ **us ton/ naalon patlaa**   *thinner that that*
ਰਾਮ ਸ਼ਾਮ ਤੋਂ ਲੰਬਾ ਹੈ **raam shaam ton lanbaa hai** *Ram is taller than Sham.*

ਵਧੇਰੇ **vadhere** and ਜ਼ਿਆਦਾ **ziaadaa**, which mean *much* or *more* are also
used when making comparisons, especially when the object or objects
being referred to are absent. The literal translations in Panjabi of *better*
ਚੰਗੇਰਾ **changeraa** and *taller/longer* ਲੰਬੇਰਾ **lanberaa** are also occasionally
used in a similar manner. Note in the following examples how adjectives
such as *tall* are changed to comparisons such as *taller*:

ਰਾਮ ਲੰਬਾ ਹੈ	raam lanbaa hai	*Ram is tall.*
ਰਾਮ ਜ਼ਿਆਦਾ ਲੰਬਾ ਹੈ	raam ziaadaa lanbaa hai	*Ram is taller.*
ਰਾਮ ਵਧੇਰੇ ਲੰਬਾ ਹੈ	raam vadhere lanbaa hai	*Ram is taller.*
ਇਹ ਕਪੜਾ ਚੰਗਾ ਹੈ	ih kaprhaa changaa hai	*this cloth is good*
ਇਹ ਕਪੜਾ ਚੰਗੇਰਾ ਹੈ	ih kaprhaa changeraa hai	*this cloth is better*
ਉਹ ਕਮਰਾ ਲੰਬਾ ਹੈ	uh kamraa lanbaa hai	*that room is long*
ਉਹ ਕਮਰਾ ਲੰਬੇਰਾ ਹੈ	uh kamraa lanberaa hai	*that room is longer*

In English the superlative degree is generally expressed with the ending
–est, such as *tallest, biggest* and *nicest*. In Panjabi the superlative degree
uses the words ਸਭ **sabh**, ਸਭਨਾਂ **sabhnaan**, and ਸਾਰੇ **saare** which mean *all*

or *whole* with the postpositions ਨਾਲੋਂ **naalon** and ਤੋਂ **ton**, to give the overall sense *out of all* or *of all*.

The superlative '*the best*' in Panjabi would literally translate as *out of all the best* in English:

ਸਭ ਤੋਂ ਚੰਗਾ ਕਪੜਾ   **sabh ton changaa kaprhaa**   *the best cloth*

To say that something is even better or even taller, ਹੋਰ ਵੀ **hor vee**, meaning *more* and *also*, is used. Here are some examples of a variety of different uses of comparison and superlative degrees:

ਉਹ ਕੁੜੀ ਸਭ ਨਾਲੋਂ ਛੋਟੀ ਹੈ	uh kurhee sabh naalon chotee hai	*This girl is the smallest.*
ਰਮੇਸ਼ ਸਾਰੇ ਭਰਾਵਾਂ ਨਾਲੋਂ ਲੰਬਾ ਹੈ	ramesh saare bharaavaan naalon lanbaa hai	*Ramesh is the tallest of the brothers.*
ਉਹਨਾਂ ਦਾ ਖਾਣਾ ਸਭ ਤੋਂ ਸੁਆਦ ਹੁੰਦਾ ਹੈ	uhnaan daa khaanhaa sabh ton suaad hundaa hai	*Their food is the tastiest.*
ਉਹਨਾਂ ਦਾ ਖਾਣਾ ਹੋਰ ਵੀ ਸੁਆਦ ਹੁੰਦਾ ਹੈ	uhnaan daa khaanhaa hor vee suaad hundaa hai	*Their food is even tastier.*

ਸਕਣਾ **saknhaa,** 'can and can't'

You will recall in the first dialogue that during the bargaining over the price of the cloth, the shopkeeper said to Simran and Jaspreet:

ਮੈਂ ਕੀਮਤ ਹੋਰ ਘੱਟ ਨਹੀਂ ਕਰ ਸਕਦਾ	main keemat hor ghatt naheen kar sakdaa	*I can't lower the price any further.*

He expressed his inability (or unwillingness!) to lower the price by saying *I can't*. In Panjabi ਸਕਣਾ **saknhaa** is used in combination with the stem of the verb portraying the action which can or cannot be done. In this example, the shopkeeper is saying that he can't (i.e. is not able to) lower the price. Therefore, the stem of ਘਟਣਾ **ghatnhaa** (to decrease, to lower) is used with the negative ਨਹੀਂ **naheen** to give the expression *can't lower*. Alternatively, if he had wanted to say *I can lower the price*, the negative ਨਹੀਂ **naheen** would simply have been omitted. The form of ਸਕਣਾ **saknhaa** is always in agreement with the subject. Here are some more examples to illustrate how this construction is formed:

ਅਸੀਂ ਪੰਜਾਬੀ ਬੋਲ ਸਕਦੀਆਂ ਹਾਂ	aseen panjaabee bol sakdeeaan haan	*We can speak Panjabi.*

| ਕੀ ਤੁਸੀਂ ਕੱਲ੍ਹ ਨੂੰ ਆ ਸਕੋ ਗੇ ? | kee tuseen kallh noon aa sako ge? | *Will you be able to come tomorrow?* |
| ਮੈਂ ਗਾ ਨਹੀਂ ਸਕਦੀ | main gaa naheen sakdee | *I cannot sing.* |

You should remember that ਸਕਣਾ **saknhaa** never stands on its own and therefore always requires the stem, even when giving a reply to a question:

| *Question* – ਕੀ ਤੁਸੀਂ ਕੱਲ੍ਹ ਨੂੰ ਆ ਸਕਦੇ ਹੋ ? | kee tuseen kallh noon aa sakde ho? | *Can you come tomorrow?* |
| *Reply* – ਹਾਂ ਜੀ, ਮੈਂ ਆ ਸਕਦੀ/ਸਕਦਾ ਹਾਂ | haan jee, main aa sakdee/sakdaa haan | *Yes, I can (come).* |

ਚੁਕਣਾ chuknhaa, 'already completed'

The stem of a verb followed by ਚੁਕਣਾ **chuknhaa** means *to have already done* or *to have finished doing*. This type of construction with ਚੁਕਣਾ **chuknhaa** is formed in a fashion similar to that of ਸਕਣਾ **saknhaa** as just described. ਚੁਕਣਾ **chuknhaa** also cannot stand alone and requires a preceding stem to indicate the action that has already occurred.

ਮੈਂ ਖਾ ਚੁਕਾ ਹਾਂ	main khaa chukaa haan	*I have (already) eaten.*
ਜਸਬੀਰ ਜਾ ਚੁਕਾ ਸੀ	jasbeer jaa chukaa see	*Jasbir had (already) gone.*
ਕੁੜੀਆਂ ਸਾਰੀਆਂ ਕਿਤਾਬਾਂ ਪੜ੍ਹ ਚੁਕੀਆਂ ਹਨ	kurheeaan saareeaan kitaabaan parhh chukeeaan han	*The girls have (already) read all of the books.*
ਅਸੀਂ ਉੱਥੇ ਜਾ ਚੁਕੇ ਹਾਂ	aseen uththe jaa chuke haan	*We have (already) been there.*

The relative pronouns ਜਿਹੜਾ jihrhaa and ਜੋ jo

The English relative pronouns *that* and *which* are used to form relative clauses following a pattern which relates the relative pronouns back to the subject, such as *The woman who came today teaches Urdu*. In Panjabi this sentence would be constructed in a rather different manner: ***That** woman who came today, **she** teaches Urdu*. In this example, ***that*** is the relative pronoun and ***she*** is the correlative pronoun. Another example of an English relative clause translated into Panjabi would be: *Go to the shop which (**that**) is closest*. In Panjabi this sentence would be expressed as: ***Which** shop is closest, go to **that one***. In this example, ***which*** is the relative pronoun and ***that one*** is the correlative pronoun.

In Panjabi, the relative pronoun and adjective ਜਿਹੜਾ **jihrhaa** is used to represent words such as *that*, *which*, *those*, *he*, *she* and *who* and changes according to the gender and number of the objects being referred to. The relative pronoun ਜੋ **jo** means whatever or whoever and is used when referring to more abstract people and things. Often, the presence of the relative pronoun in the English translation is simply understood. Here are some examples of the ways in which relative clauses are formed with ਜਿਹੜਾ **jihrhaa** and ਜੋ **jo**:

ਜੋ ਕੁਝ ਤੁਸੀਂ ਕੀਤਾ ਹੈ ਮੈਨੂੰ ਠੀਕ ਲੱਗਦਾ ਹੈ	jo kujh tuseen keetaa hai, mainoon theek laggdaa hai	*Whatever you've done looks fine to me.*
ਜਿਹੜੇ ਲੋਕ ਬਾਹਰੋਂ ਆਉਂਦੇ ਹਨ, ਉਹਨਾਂ ਨੂੰ ਖਾਣਾ ਹਜ਼ਮ ਨਹੀਂ ਹੁੰਦਾ	jihrhe lok baahron aaunde han, uhnaan noon khaanhaa hazam naheen hundaa	*[Those] people who come from abroad can't digest the food.*
ਜਿਹੜਾ ਆਦਮੀ ਅੱਜ ਆਇਆ ਸੀ, ਉਹ ਕੱਲ੍ਹ ਨਹੀਂ ਆ ਸਕੇਗਾ	jihrhaa aadmee ajj aaiaa see, uh kallh naheen aa sakegaa	*That man who came today will not be able to come tomorrow.*

Like other adjectives and pronouns in Panjabi, relative pronouns change their form in the oblique. In the singular ਜਿਹੜਾ jihrhaa takes the oblique form ਜਿਸ jis and in the plural it becomes ਜਿਹਨਾਂ jihnaan followed by the appropriate postposition. Here are some examples of the oblique forms of the relative pronoun ਜਿਹੜਾ jihrhaa:

ਅਸੀਂ ਜਿਨ੍ਹਾਂ ਦੇ ਘਰ ਗਏ ਸੀ, ਉਹ ਰਾਵਲਪਿੰਡੀ ਦੇ ਹਨ	aseen jinnaan de ghar ge see, uh raavalpindee de han	*(The people) whose house we went to are from Rawalpindi.*
ਜਿਸ ਜਨਨੀ ਨੂੰ ਪੰਜਾਬੀ ਆਉਂਦੀ ਹੈ, ਉਹ ਨੂੰ ਪੁੱਛੋ	jis janaanee noon panjaabee aaundee hai, uh noon puchcho	*Ask the lady who knows Panjabi.*
ਜਿਸ ਨੂੰ ਪਤਾ ਸੀ ਉਹ ਦਾ ਕਸੂਰ ਹੈ	jis noon pataa see uh daa kasoor hai	*He [who knew] was aware; it's his fault.*

More uses of ਨੂੰ **noon**

By now you should be beginning to feel acquainted with the significance of postpositions in Panjabi. In Unit 4 simple postpositions were introduced as they affect nouns and adjectives in the oblique. In Unit 8 the two sisters Simran and Jaspreet illustrated in the dialogues some further uses of the postposition ਨੂੰ **noon** in expressing likes and dislikes, want, need, should and ought. In this unit more uses of ਨੂੰ **noon** have already been exemplified in the second dialogue, in which Simran and the doctor discuss health conditions. ਨੂੰ **noon** literally means *to* and directs the condition or state towards the person or pronoun it governs. It is used in a number of different senses ranging from awareness and health to feelings. Therefore, when the doctor asks Simran ਕੀ ਤੈਨੂੰ ਬੁਖਾਰ ਹੈ? **kee tainoon bukhaar hai?** he is literally asking *Is there a fever to you?* Here are some more examples of how ਨੂੰ **noon** can be used in this sense:

ਮੈਨੂੰ ਬੁਖਾਰ ਹੈ	mainoon bukhaar hai	*I have a fever.*
ਸਾਨੂੰ ਠੰਡ ਲੱਗ ਰਹੀ ਹੈ	saanoon thand lagg rahee hai	*We are feeling cold.*
ਮੈਨੂੰ ਅਫਸੋਸ ਹੈ	mainoon afsos hai	*I am sorry.*
ਉਹ ਨੂੰ ਉਮੀਦ ਹੈ	uh noon umeed hai	*He/she hopes.*
ਉਹਨਾਂ ਨੂੰ ਪਤਾ ਨਹੀਂ	uhnaan noon pataa naheen	*They do not know.*
ਮੈਨੂੰ ਜ਼ੁਕਾਮ ਹੈ	mainoon zukaam hai	*I have a cold.*
ਤੁਹਾਨੂੰ ਕੋਈ ਪਤਾ ਹੈ ਕਿ ਇਕਬਾਲ ਕਿੱਥੇ ਹੈ?	tuhaanoon koee pataa hai ki ikbaal kiththe hai?	*Do you have any idea where Iqbal is?*
ਸਾਨੂੰ ਬਹੁਤ ਖ਼ੁਸ਼ੀ ਹੈ	sanoon bahut khushee hai	*We are very happy.*

ਵਿਆਖਿਆ viaakhiaa Commentary

1. Parts of the body

a	–	ਅੱਖ
b	–	ਨੱਕ
c	–	ਸੁੰਹ
d	–	ਕੰਨ
e	–	ਸਿਰ
f	–	ਹੱਥ
g	–	ਗਰਦਨ
h	–	ਉਂਗਲ
i	–	ਬਾਂਹ
j	–	ਛਾਤੀ
k	–	ਪੇਟ
l	–	ਲੱਤ
m	–	ਗੋਡਾ
n	–	ਪੈਰ
o	–	ਪੱਬ

2. Clothes people wear

There are various forms of dress worn by Panjabis. Perhaps the most
popular form is the **salwaar kameez (shalwaar kameez in** West Panjab).
This form of dress is now ubiquitous in almost all of South Asia, but it is
most popular in Pakistan Panjab, where both men and women wear it.
Traditionally, women in rural Panjab would wear a flowing skirt – **ghagra**
– and a blouse, although this is a rare sight in contemporary Panjab.
Women may wear a sari for special occasions and Christian women often
wear dresses as a way of distinguishing themselves. Male dress was traditionally a turban with a flowing top shirt and a wrap called a lungi or
dhoti around the legs. However, western dress is increasingly popular. The
following pictures illustrate the various forms of dress.

ਅਭਿਆਸ   **abhiaas   Exercises**

After reading the dialogue and/or listening to the audio tape, try to do the
following exercises.

1. Word search

The following words are hidden in the 'word search' boxes below. In the first box they are hidden horizontally and in the second they are hidden vertically.

ਬੁਖ਼ਾਰ, ਭੈਣਜੀ, ਕਪੜਾ, ਦੁਕਾਨਦਾਰ, ਬਿਮਾਰ, ਛਾਪੇ, ਦਰਦ, ਕਮਜ਼ੋਰੀ, ਕੀਮਤ, ਹੰਢਣਸਾਰ

ਭੈ	ਣ	ਜੀ	ਜਾ	ਭ
ਜੋ	ਕ	ਪ	ੜਾ	ਕੀ
ਦੁ	ਕਾ	ਨ	ਦਾ	ਰ
ਉ	ਉ	ਛਾ	ਪੇ	ਸ਼
ਤਾ	ਕੀ	ਮ	ਤ	ਭ

ਨ	ਮੈ	ਰ	ਕ	ਹੰ
ਮਾ	ਬਿ	ਬੁ	ਮ	ਢ
ਦ	ਮਾ	.ਖ਼ਾ	ਜ਼ੋ	ਣ
ਰ	ਰ	ਰ	ਰੀ	ਸਾ
ਦ	ਦ	ਰੀ	ਗੋ	ਰ

2. Talking to the doctor

Look at the pictures and tell how each person would respond in Panjabi to the doctor's question: ਕੀ ਤਕਲੀਫ਼ ਹੈ ? What's the problem?

a.

I feel cold.

b.

I have a headache.

c.

I have a stomach ache.

d.

I have a fever.

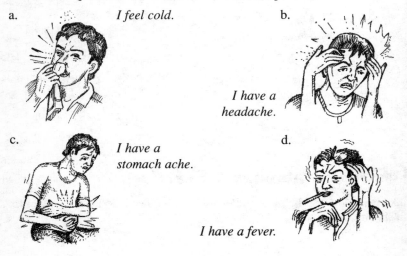

3. Write sentences in Panjabi

Express the following sentences in Panjabi using either ਚੁਕਣਾ **chuknhaa** or ਸਕਣਾ **saknhaa**:

a) *I can't come tomorrow.*
b) *Can you speak Panjabi?*
c) *We've already been there.*
d) *They have already eaten.*

4. Relative pronouns

Insert the correct forms of the relative pronouns ਜੋ jo, ਜਿਹੜਾ jihrhaa and ਜਿਸ jis:

a) ——————— ਆਦਮੀ ਅੱਜ ਪਾਕਿਸਤਾਨ ਗਿਆ ਹੈ, ਉਹ ਮੇਰਾ ਚਾਚਾ ਹੈ।
——————— aadmee ajj paakistaan giaa hai, uh meraa chaachaa hai.
The man who went to Pakistan today is my uncle.

b) ——————— ਨੂੰ ਪਤਾ ਹੈ, ਉਹ ਨੂੰ ਪੁੱਛੋ।
——————— noon pataa hai, uh noon puchcho.
Ask the person who knows.

c) ——————— ਲੋਕ ਪਿੰਡ ਵਿਚ ਰਹਿੰਦੇ ਹਨ ਉਹਨਾਂ ਨੂੰ ਸ਼ਹਿਰ ਪਸੰਦ ਨਹੀਂ।
——————— lok pind vich rahinde han uhnaan noon
shahir pasand naheen.
People who live in the village don't like the city.

d) ——————— ਕੁਝ ਤੁਸੀਂ ਚਾਹੁੰਦੇ ਹੋ ਉਹ ਮੇਰੇ ਲਈ ਠੀਕ ਹੈ।
——————— kujh tuseen chaahunde ho uh mere laee theek hai.
Whatever you want is fine with me.

10 | ੲੱਕ ਦਿਨ ਪਿੰਡ ਵਿਚ
ikk din pind vich
A day in the village

In this unit you will learn:

■ about Panjabi village life
■ how to talk about things you've done and seen

What else did you buy?

ਗੱਲ ਬਾਤ ਤੂੰ ਹੋਰ ਕੀ ਕੁਝ ਖ਼ਰੀਦਿਆ ?

gall baat toon hor kee kujh khareediaa?

Jaspreet and Simran have arrived at their relatives' house in Jalandhar after their tour of Delhi. Their aunt is asking them about their stay in Delhi.

ਚਾਚੀ	ਤੁਹਾਡੀ ਦਿੱਲੀ ਦੀ ਸੈਰ ਕਿਵੇਂ ਰਹੀ ?
Aunt (chaachee)	tuhaadee dillee dee sair kiven rahee?
ਜਸਪ੍ਰੀਤ	ਬਹੁਤ ਸੁਹਣੀ ਰਹੀ। ੲੱਕ ਦਿਨ ਮੈਂ ਪੁਰਾਣੀ ਦਿੱਲੀ ਵਿਚ ਘੁੰਮੀ। ਲਾਲ ਕਿਲ੍ਹਾ ਅਤੇ ਸੀਸ ਗੰਜ ਗੁਰਦਵਾਰਾ ਦੇਖਿਆ। ਉਹ ਦਿਨ ਸਭ ਤੋਂ ਚੰਗਾ ਗੁਜ਼ਰਿਆ। ਮੈਂ ਚਾਂਦਨੀ ਚੌਕ ਬਜ਼ਾਰ ਤੋਂ ਸਿਤਾਰ ਵੀ ਖ਼ਰੀਦੀ।
Jaspreet	bahut suhnhee rahee. ikk din main puraanhee dillee vich ghunmee. laal kilhaa ate sees ganj gurdavaaraa dekhiaa. uh din sabh ton changaa guzriaa. main chaandnee chaunk bazaar ton sitaar vee khareedee.
ਚਾਚੀ	ਤੂੰ ਹੋਰ ਕੀ ਕੁਝ ਖ਼ਰੀਦਿਆ ?
Aunt	toon hor kee kujh khareediaa?
ਜਸਪ੍ਰੀਤ	ਚਾਚੀ ਜੀ, ਮੈਂ ਕਪੜੇ ਖ਼ਰੀਦੇ ਤੇ ਜੁੱਤੀ ਵੀ ਖ਼ਰੀਦੀ।
Jaspreet	chaachee jee, main kaprhe khareede te juttee vee khareedee.
ਚਾਚੀ	ਸਿਮਰਨ, ਤੂੰ ਕੀ ਕੀਤਾ ?
Aunt	simran, toon kee keetaa?

ਸਿਮਰਨ	ਮੈਂ ਹਰ ਕਿਸਮ ਦੇ ਖਾਣੇ ਖਾਧੇ, ਪਰ ਮੈਂ ਬਿਮਾਰ ਹੋ ਗਈ ਸੀ।
	ਫਿਰ ਮੈਂ ਡਾਕਟਰ ਕੋਲ ਗਈ ਅਤੇ ਉਸ ਨੇ ਮੈਨੂੰ ਦਵਾਈ ਦਿੱਤੀ।
Simran	main har kisam de khaanhe khaadhe par main bimaar ho gaee see. phir main daaktar kol gaee ate us ne mainoon davaaee dittee.
ਚਾਚੀ	ਉਮੀਦ ਹੈ ਕਿ ਹੁਣ ਤੂੰ ਠੀਕ ਹੈਂ ਕਿਉਂ ਕਿ ਅਸੀਂ ਅੱਜ ਸਰ੍ਹੋਂ ਦਾ ਸਾਗ ਤੇ ਮੱਕੀ ਦੀ ਰੋਟੀ ਬਣਾਈ ਹੈ। ਇਹ ਪੰਜਾਬ ਦੀ ਖ਼ਾਸ ਸੁਗਾਤ ਹੈ !
Aunt	umeed hai ki hunh toon theek hain kion ki aseen ajj sar-h-on daa saag te makkee dee rotee banhaaee hai. ih panjaab dee khaas sugaat hai!

Aunt	*How was your tour of Delhi?*
Jaspreet	*It was very nice. One day I went around Old Delhi. I saw the Red Fort and Sees Ganj Gurdwara. That was the best day I had. I also bought a sitar from Chandni Chowk market.*
Aunt	*What else did you buy?*
Jaspreet	*Aunty Ji, I bought clothes and shoes too!*
Aunt	*Simran, what did you do?*
Simran	*I ate every type of food, but I fell ill. Then I went to the doctor and he gave me some medicine.*
Aunt	*I hope you're fine now since today we've made **sarhon daa saag** and **makkee dee rotee**. This is a speciality of Panjab!*

ਸ਼ਬਦਾਵਲੀ   **shabdaavalee   Vocabulary**

ਸੈਰ	sair	*tour, trip* (f.)
ਸੁਹਣੀ	suhnhee	*nice, pretty* (v.)
ਪੁਰਾਣੀ	puraanhee	*old* (v.)
ਪੁਰਾਣੀ ਦਿੱਲੀ	puraanhee dillee	*Old Delhi* (f.)
ਕਿਲ੍ਹਾ	kilhaa	*fort* (m.)
ਚੰਗਾ	changaa	*good* (v.)
ਗੁਜ਼ਰਨਾ	guzarnhaa	*to be spent, to go by*
ਚਾਂਦਨੀ	chaandanee	*moonlight*
ਚੌਂਕ	chaunk	*roundabout, circle, centre* (m.)
ਬਜ਼ਾਰ	bazaar	*bazaar* (m.)
ਖ਼ਰੀਦਨਾ	khareednhaa	*to buy*
ਕੀ ਕੁਝ	kee kujh	*what else*
ਕਪੜੇ	kaprhe	*clothes* (m.)
ਜੁੱਤੀ	juttee	*shoes* (f.)
ਹਰ	har	*each, every*

ਕਿਸਮ	kisam	*type*
ਹਰ ਕਿਸਮ ਦੇ ਖਾਣੇ	har kisam de khaanhe	*every type of food*
ਪਰ	par	*but*
ਉਮੀਦ	umeed	*hope, wish* (f.)
ਕਿਉਂ ਕਿ	kion ki	*because, since*
ਸਰੋਂ ਦਾ ਸਾਗ	sarhon daa saag	*mustard leaves* (m.)
ਮੱਕੀ ਦੀ ਰੋਟੀ	makkee dee rotee	*unleavened corn bread* (f.)
ਬਣਾਉਣਾ	banhaaunhaa	*to make*
ਖ਼ਾਸ	khaas	*special*
ਸੁਗਾਤ	sugaat	*gift* (f.)
ਖ਼ਾਸ ਸੁਗਾਤ	khaas sugaat	*speciality* (f.)

☑ ਅਭਿਆਸ   abhiaas   Exercises

After reading the dialogue and/or listening to the audio tape, try to do the following exercises.

1. True or false?

a. ਚਾਚੀ ਜਸਪ੍ਰੀਤ ਤੇ ਸਿਮਰਨ ਨੂੰ ਦਿੱਲੀ ਦੀ ਸੈਰ ਬਾਰੇ ਪੁੱਛ ਰਹੀ ਸੀ।   True / False
chaachee jaspreet te simran noon dillee dee sair baare puchch rahee see.

b. ਚਾਚੀ ਨੇ ਕੁੜੀਆਂ ਨੂੰ ਕਿਹਾ ਕਿ ਜ਼ਿਆਦਾ ਪੈਸਾ ਨਹੀਂ ਖ਼ਰਚਣਾ ਚਾਹੀਦਾ   True / False
chaachee ne kurheeaan noon kihaa ki ziaadaa paisaa naheen kharchnhaa chaaheedaa.

c. ਸਿਮਰਨ ਮੌਸਮ ਕਰ ਕੇ ਬਿਮਾਰ ਹੋ ਗਈ ਸੀ।   True / False
simran mausam kar ke bimaar ho gaee see.

2. Match the responses appropriate to the questions

a) ਤੂੰ ਹੋਰ ਕੀ ਕੁਝ ਖ਼ਰੀਦਿਆ ?
toon hor kee kujh khareediaa?

i) ਬਹੁਤ ਸੁਹਣੀ ਰਹੀ
bahut suhnhee rahee

b) ਤੂੰ ਬਿਮਾਰ ਕਿਉਂ ਹੋ ਗਈ ਸੀ ?
toon bimaar kiun ho gaee see?

ii) ਮੈਂ ਹਰ ਕਿਸਮ ਦੇ ਖਾਣੇ ਖਾਧੇ
main har kisam de khaanhe khadhe

c) ਦਿੱਲੀ ਦੀ ਸੈਰ ਕਿਵੇਂ ਰਹੀ ?
dillee dee sair kiven rahee?

iii) ਮੈਂ ਕਪੜੇ ਖ਼ਰੀਦੇ ਤੇ ਜੁੱਤੀ ਵੀ ਖ਼ਰੀਦੀ
main kaprhe khareede te juttee vee khareedee

d) ਦਿੱਲੀ ਵਿਚ ਤੁਸੀਂ ਕੀ ਕੁਝ ਦੇਖਿਆ ?
dillee vich tuseen kee kujh dekhiaa?

iv) ਮੈਂ ਲਾਲ ਕਿਲ੍ਹਾ ਅਤੇ ਸੀਸ ਗੰਜ ਗੁਰਦਵਾਰਾ ਦੇਖਿਆ
main laal kilhaa ate sees ganj gurdavaaraa dekhiaa

Passage: A day in the village

ਪੈਰਾ: ਇੱਕ ਦਿਨ ਪਿੰਡ ਵਿਚ

pairaa: ikk ḏin piṉḏ vich

Jaspreet and Simran have gone to their mother's family's village after having seen their father's relatives in Jalandhar. The following passage is a page from Jaspreet's diary. She has written about the day that she and her sister spent in the village.

ਸ਼ਬਦਾਵਲੀ   shab<u>d</u>aavalee   Vocabulary

28 Joon

aseen ajj jalandhar ho ke naanke pind gaeeaan. saare saanoon piaar naal mile. saade

maamaa jee naanaa jee te naanee jee de kol rahinde han. uhnaan ne saanoon saaraa

pind dikhaaiaa. aseen taraiktar te charhneeaan ate khetaan vich ghunmeeaan. aseen

khooh te ruke. main khooh pahilee vaaree vekhiaa. simran majhjh noon dekh ke dar

gaee te ikk dam daurh gaee. khooh de naal ikk bandaa ganne de ras ton gurh banhaa

rihaa see. shaam noon jadon aseen vaapas aae taan maamee jee ne saanoon rotee

khuaaee. us ton baa-a-d vihrhe vich aseen naanee jee kolon puraanheeaan kahaanheeaan

sunheeaan. raat noon saariaa ne garam dudhdh peetaa ate phir saun gae. pind daa

maahaul mainoon bahut pasand hai.

28 June

Today, after having been to Jalandhar, we went to our mother's family's village. Everyone met us

with affection. Our mother's brother lives with grandfather and grandmother. He showed us the

entire village. We rode on a tractor and went around the fields. We stopped at the well. It was

the first time that I had seen a well. Simran saw buffalo, got scared and immediately ran

away. Next to the well there was a man who was making Gurh (a sweet delicacy) from the juice

of the sugarcane. In the evening when we arrived, mami ji fed us. After that we all sat in the

courtyard and heard old stories from grandmother. At night everyone drank hot milk and then

went to sleep. I like the atmosphere of the village a lot.

ਅਭਿਆਸ   **abhiaas**   **Exercises**

ਨਾਨਕੇ ਪਿੰਡ	naanke pind	*mother's family's village*
ਪਿਆਰ	piaar	*love, affection* (m.)
ਮਿਲਣਾ	milnhaa	*to meet*
ਟਰੈਕਟਰ	taraiktar	*tractor* (m.)
ਚੜ੍ਹਨਾ	charhhnhaa	*to climb, to ride*

ਖੇਤ	khet	land, field (m.)
ਖੂਹ	khooh	water well (m.)
ਪਹਿਲੀ ਵਾਰੀ	pahilee vaaree	first time
ਮੱਝ	majhjh	buffalo (f.)
ਡਰਨਾ	darnaa	to be scared
ਇੱਕ ਦਮ	ikk dam	immediately, at once
ਦੌੜ	daurh	to run
ਬੰਦਾ	bandaa	man (m.)
ਗੰਨਾ	gannaa	sugarcane (m.)
ਗੁੜ	gurh	brown sugar cake (m.)
ਵਾਪਸ	vaapas	return, back to
ਤਾਂ	taan	then
ਰੋਟੀ	rotee	food (literally: unleavened bread which is part of the staple diet of Panjab) (f.)
ਖੁਆਈ	khuaaee	to feed
ਉਸ ਤੋਂ ਬਾਅਦ	us ton baa-a-d	after that
ਵਿਹੜਾ	vihrhaa	courtyard (m.)
ਕਹਾਣੀ	kahaanhee	story (f.)
ਗਰਮ	garam	warm, hot
ਦੁੱਧ	dudhdh	milk (m.)
ਸੌਣਾ	saunhaa	to sleep
ਮਾਹੌਲ	maahaul	atmosphere, environment (m.)

After reading the passage and/or listening to the audio tape, try to do the following exercises.

1. Answer the following questions about the passage

a. ਜਸਪ੍ਰੀਤ ਤੇ ਸਿਮਰਨ ਦੇ ਮਾਮਾ ਜੀ ਕਿਹਨਾਂ ਕੋਲ ਰਹਿੰਦੇ ਹਨ ?

jaspreet te simran de maamaa jee kihnaan kol rahinde han?

b. ਜਿਹੜਾ ਬੰਦਾ ਖੂਹ ਦੇ ਕੋਲ ਸੀ, ਉਹ ਕੀ ਬਣਾ ਰਿਹਾ ਸੀ ?

jihrhaa bandaa khooh de kol see, uh kee banhaa rihaa see?

c. ਰੋਟੀ ਖਾਣ ਤੋਂ ਬਾਅਦ ਕੁੜੀਆਂ ਨੇ ਕੀ ਕੀਤਾ ?

rotee khaanh ton baa-a-d kurheeaan ne kee keetaa?

d. ਸੌਣ ਤੋਂ ਪਹਿਲੇ ਸਾਰਿਆਂ ਨੇ ਕੀ ਪੀਤਾ ?

saunh ton pahile saariaan ne kee peetaa?

2. Complete the table

ਪਿੰਡ		
	khooh	
ਵਿਹੜਾ		
		fields
	ga<u>nn</u>aa	

ਬੋਲੀ ਬਾਰੇ   **bolee baare**   **Language points**

The past tense

You have already been introduced to the simple past tense in Unit 6. Verbs in the simple past tense were shown to agree with the number and gender of the subject. To help you remember, here are examples of the verbs ਆਉਣਾ **aaunhaa** (*to come*), ਰੋਣਾ **ronhaa** (*to cry*), ਬੋਲਣਾ **bolnhaa** (*to speak*), ਹੋਣਾ **honhaa** (*to be*) and ਦੱਸਣਾ **<u>d</u>assnhaa** (*to tell*) in their past perfect forms:

Masculine singular	Masculine plural	Feminine singular	Feminine plural	
ਆਇਆ aaiaa	ਆਏ aae	ਆਈ aaee	ਆਈਆਂ aaeeaa<u>n</u>	*came*
ਰੋਇਆ roiaa	ਰੋਏ roe	ਰੋਈ roee	ਰੋਈਆਂ roeeaa<u>n</u>	*cried*
ਬੋਲਿਆ boliaa	ਬੋਲੇ bole	ਬੋਲੀ bolee	ਬੋਲੀਆਂ boleeaa<u>n</u>	*spoke*
ਦੱਸਿਆ <u>d</u>assiaa	ਦੱਸੇ <u>d</u>asse	ਦੱਸੀ <u>d</u>assee	ਦੱਸੀਆਂ <u>d</u>asseeaa<u>n</u>	*told*
ਹੋਇਆ hoiaa	ਹੋਏ hoe	ਹੋਈ hoee	ਹੋਈਆਂ hoeeaa<u>n</u>	*happened*

In the past perfect tenses in Panjabi, all verbs can be categorised into two groups: intransitive and transitive. Intransitive verbs do not rely upon an object to dictate the form of the verb. This literally means that the form of the verb is unchanging except, of course, in relation to the subject of the sentence. Intransitive verbs generally do not take a direct object. Transitive verbs, are those verbs which do take a direct object, and are more flexible. In such cases where an object is present, the ending of the verb will agree with the object. In the examples given above, *cried* and *spoke* are both intransitive verbs, meaning that the act of crying and speaking can stand alone without the requirement of an object. *Told*, on the other hand, can require the presence of an object such as *he told me a story* with *story* being the direct object. The following examples illustrate how the transitive verb is affected by the presence of a direct object:

ਮੈਂ ਕੇਲਾ ਖਾਧਾ	main kelaa khaadhaa	*I ate a banana.*
ਮੈਂ ਕੇਲੇ ਖਾਧੇ	main kele khaadhe	*I ate bananas.*
ਮੈਂ ਨਾਸ਼ਪਾਤੀ ਖਾਧੀ	main naashpaatee khaadhee	*I ate a pear.*
ਮੈਂ ਨਾਸ਼ਪਾਤੀਆਂ ਖਾਧੀਆਂ	main naashpaateeaan khaadheeaan	*I ate pears.*

You will notice that the first two examples both have the same object, except that the first is singular and the second is plural. Therefore, ਖਾਧਾ **khaadhaa** in the first example reflects the singular masculine nature of *banana* and ਖਾਧੇ **khaadhe** refers to the plural masculine nature of *bananas*. The third and fourth examples show a similar pattern for the feminine object *pear* with ਖਾਧੀ **khaadhee** and ਖਾਧੀਆਂ **khaadheeaan** corresponding to the respective singular and plural forms.

The main point to remember when using verbs in the past tense is that some verbs are subject inflected (meaning that they change according to the subject), while others are object inflected (i.e. change according to the object of the sentence). However, some verbs can be in either category. There are transitive verbs which behave like intransitive verbs when there is no direct object present, such as ਸਮਝਣਾ **samajhnhaa** (*to understand*) and ਪੜ੍ਹਨਾ **parhhnaa** (*to read*). There are also intransitive verbs which can behave as transitive verbs, such as ਕਹਿਣਾ **kahinhaa** (*to say*), ਪੁੱਛਣਾ **puchchanhaa** (*to ask*), and ਥੁੱਕਣਾ **thuknhaa** (*to spit*). However, there is no convention for knowing when a verb is intransitive or transitive apart from the nature of the verb and the presence of an object.

The 'agentive' postposition ਨੇ ne

Nearly all transitive verbs in the past tenses are affected by the postposition **ne** ਨੇ which directs the action of the verb towards the subject. In usual circumstances ਨੇ follows the subject of the sentence. However, in the example ਮੈਂ ਨਾਸ਼ਪਾਤੀ ਖਾਧੀ **main naashpaatee khaadhee**, ਨੇ **ne** is implicit and does not appear. The use of ਨੇ **ne** is illustrated in the table. Note that for some pronouns in the third person, the use of ਨੇ **ne** is optional as is indicated in parentheses:

Pronouns in the ਨੇ construction

Direct pronouns			In the ਨੇ (ne) construction	
1st	ਮੈਂ	main	ਮੈਂ	no change
person	ਅਸੀਂ	aseen	ਅਸੀਂ	no change
2nd	ਤੁਸੀਂ	tuseen	ਤੁਸੀਂ	no change
person	ਤੂੰ	toon	ਤੂੰ	no change

3rd	ਇਹ (sing)	ih	ਇਹ ਨੇ	ਨੇ ne required
person	ਇਹ (sing)	is	ਇਸ (ਨੇ)	ਨੇ ne optional
	ਉਹ (sing)	uh	ਉਹ ਨੇ	ਨੇ ne required
	ਉਹ (sing)	us	ਉਸ (ਨੇ)	ਨੇ ne optional
	ਇਹ (formal, plural)	ih	ਇਹਨਾਂ ihnaan (ਨੇ)	ਨੇ ne optional
	ਉਹ (formal, plural)	uh	ਉਹਨਾਂ uhnaan (ਨੇ)	ਨੇ ne optional
	ਕੌਣ (sing)	kaunh	ਕਿਸ kis (ਨੇ)	ਨੇ ne optional
	ਕੌਣ (formal, plural)	kaunh	ਕਿਹਨਾਂ kihnaan (ਨੇ)	ਨੇ ne optional

In cases where no direct object is present or the direct object is already followed by a postposition, the verb is made 'neutral'. The neutral verb is always in the singular masculine form. Most commonly, the postposition ਨੂੰ **noon** follows the object of the sentence, thus making the verb neutral. Here are some examples of transitive verbs in the ਨੇ, **ne** construction as well as with the postposition ਨੂੰ **noon**.

ਮੈਂ ਦਰਖ਼ਤ* ਨੂੰ ਕਟਿਆ	main darakhat noon katiaa	*I cut the tree.*
ਮੈਂ ਟਾਹਣੀ* ਨੂੰ ਕਟਿਆ	main taahanhee noon katiaa	*I cut the branch.*
ਮੈਂ ਦਰਖ਼ਤਾਂ ਨੂੰ ਕਟਿਆ	main darakhataan noon katiaa	*I cut the trees.*
ਮੈਂ ਟਾਹਣੀਆਂ ਨੂੰ ਕਟਿਆ	main taahanheeaan noon katiaa	*I cut the branches.*

* ਦਰਖ਼ਤ is grammatically masculine
* ਟਾਹਣੀ is grammatically feminine

Here are more examples of the use of transitive verbs:

ਅਮਰ ਨੇ ਕਹਾਣੀ ਸੁਣੀ	amar ne kahaanhee sunhee	*Amar heard the story.*
ਅਮਰ ਨੇ ਤਿੰਨ ਕਹਾਣੀਆਂ ਸੁਣੀਆਂ	amar ne tinn kahaanheeaan sunheeaan	*Amar heard three stories.*
ਅਮਰ ਨੇ ਸੁਣਿਆ	amar ne sunhiaa	*Amar heard.*
ਅਮਰ ਨੇ ਇਸ ਕਹਾਣੀ ਨੂੰ ਸੁਣਿਆ	amar ne is kahaanhee noon sunhiaa	*Amar heard this story.*
ਅਮਰ ਨੇ ਇਹਨਾਂ ਕਹਾਣੀਆਂ ਨੂੰ ਸੁਣਿਆ	amar ne ihnaan kahaanheeaan noon sunhiaa	*Amar heard these stories.*

You will recall from Unit 8 that pronouns and nouns change to their oblique forms when followed by postpositions. Taking the same examples:

ਇਹ ਕਹਾਣੀ   ih kahaanhee   *this story*

changes to ਇਸ ਕਹਾਣੀ is **kahaanhee** in the sentence

ਅਮਰ ਨੇ ਇਸ ਕਹਾਣੀ ਨੂੰ amar ne is kahaanhee noo<u>n</u>   *Amar heard this story.*
ਸੁਣਿਆ   sunhiaa

This story in the English is identical in both examples. In Panjabi, however, *this story* in the first example is in the direct form while *this story* in
the second example is in the oblique form.

Many verbs can fall within either category of transitive or intransitive
making the past tense in Panjabi less straightforward than, say, the present
or future tenses which are not reliant upon the object's relationship with
the verb. For instance, the verb ਕਰਨਾ **karnaa** *to do* and ਸਮਝਣਾ **samjhnhaa**
to understand can act as intransitive verbs when not followed by an object
or can behave as transitive verbs when an object is present. The same is
true for ਪੜ੍ਹਨਾ **parhhnaa** which can take the ਨੇ **ne** construction when used
in the sense *to read* or can stand alone when meaning *to study*. Often, ਨੇ
ne can be invisible, meaning that the sentence may be dictated by the ਨੇ
ne construction but that it is simply understood. This, however, occurs
with only a few verbs, so you should be cautious when applying these
rules. The best way of illustrating transitive verbs with ਨੇ **ne** is through
examples:

ਅਸੀਂ ਕਿਰਨ ਨੂੰ ਅੰਮ੍ਰਿਤਸਰ ਵੇਖਿਆ	asee<u>n</u> kiran (f.) noo<u>n</u> amritsar vekhiaa	*We met Kiran in Amritsar.*
ਅਸੀਂ ਤਾਰਿਕ ਨੂੰ ਲੰਡਨ ਵੇਖਿਆ	asee<u>n</u> taarik (m.) noo<u>n</u> la<u>n</u>dan vekhiaa	*We saw Tariq in London.*

Note that the verb did not change in these examples even though the
gender of the object does because of the presence of ਨੂੰ **noo<u>n</u>**. In the
following examples you will see how the ending of the verb in the past
tense corresponds with the gender and number of the objects:

ਉਹਨਾਂ (ਨੇ) ਬਹੁਤ ਕੇਲੇ ਖਾਧੇ	uhnaa<u>n</u> ne bahu<u>t</u> kele khaa<u>dh</u>e	*They ate many bananas.*
ਤੁਸੀਂ ਇਹ ਕਮੀਜ਼ਾਂ ਕਿਉਂ ਖ਼ਰੀਦੀਆਂ ?	<u>t</u>usee<u>n</u> ih kameezaa<u>n</u> kiu<u>n</u> <u>kh</u>areedeeaa<u>n</u>?	*Why did you buy these shirts?*

ਕਿਸ ਨੇ ਗੱਡੀ ਨੂੰ ਸਾਫ਼ ਕੀਤਾ ਸੀ ?	kis ne gaddee noo<u>n</u> saaf kee<u>t</u>aa see?	*Who cleaned the car?*
ਰਾਮ ਨੇ ਮੇਰੀ ਗੱਲ ਸਮਝੀ	raam ne meree gall samajhee	*Ram understood what I said.*

Compound verbs

Compound verbs are formed when the stem of a main verb is followed by an auxiliary verb. These constructions are very common in Panjabi and are the equivalent of two verbs coming together in English such as in the expression *to go to sleep*. In Unit 9 you learned how to express *can* and *already* through the uses of ਸਕਣਾ **saknhaa** and ਚੁਕਣਾ **chuknhaa** which, when combined with other verb stems, form compound verb constructions. In a similar way, other verbs are used as auxiliary verbs to emphasise or give an added meaning to the verb stem. Whereas ਸਕਣਾ **saknhaa** and ਚੁਕਣਾ **chuknhaa** have very specific meanings, this is not the case for most other compound constructions which are less simple to define. A helpful hint regarding compound verbs, however, is that the auxiliary verb loses its own meaning when it accompanies the stem of another verb. Often it is the context of the sentence and the meaning of the main verb that will tell you about the emphasis that the auxiliary verb has added.

The most common auxiliary verbs are ਜਾਣਾ **jaanhaa** (*to go*), ਦੇਣਾ **denhaa** (*to give*) and ਲੈਣਾ **lainhaa** (*to take*). When an intransitive verb is the main verb, ਜਾਣ **janhaa** (*to go*) is generally used to give the sense of completeness or change. To show how the meaning of the main verb is affected by the auxiliary ending, here are a few examples:

ਆਉਣਾ	aaunhaa	*to come*	ਆ ਜਾਣਾ	aa jaanhaa	*to arrive*
ਸੌਣਾ	saunhaa	*to sleep*	ਸੌਣ ਜਾਣਾ	saunh jaanhaa	*to go to sleep*
ਖਾਣਾ	khaanhaa	*to eat*	ਖਾ ਜਾਣਾ	khaa jaanhaa	*to eat up*
ਪੀਣਾ	peenhaa	*to drink*	ਪੀ ਜਾਣਾ	pee jaanhaa	*to drink up*

The following sentences illustrate how these compound verbs with ਜਾਣਾ **jaanhaa** (*to go*) can be used in sentences:

ਚਾਚੀ ਪਿੰਡ ਤੋਂ ਆ ਗਈ ਸੀ	chaachee pi<u>n</u>d <u>t</u>on aa gaee see	*Aunt had come from the village.*
ਮੈਂ ਬਾਰਾਂ ਵਜੇ ਸੌਣ ਜਾਵਾਂ ਗੀ	mai<u>n</u> baar-h-aa<u>n</u> vaje saunh jaavaa<u>n</u> gee	*I will go to sleep at 12 o'clock.*

| ਉਹ ਐਨਾ ਭੁੱਖਾ ਸੀ ਕਿ ਉਹ ਸਭ ਕੁਝ ਖਾ ਗਿਆ ! | uh ainaa bhukhkhaa see ki uh sabh kujh khaa giaa! | *He was so hungry that he ate everything up!* |
| ਬਿੱਲੀ ਸਾਰਾ ਦੁੱਧ ਪੀ ਗਈ | billee saaraa dudhdh pee gaee | *The cat drank (up) all the milk.* |

Of the transitive verbs, the auxiliaries of **ਲੈਣਾ lainhaa** (*to take*) and **ਦੇਣਾ denhaa** (*to give*) are the most common. The effects of each upon the main verb can be best described in terms of the direction of the action. **ਲੈਣਾ lainhaa** tends to give the sense that the action is being done towards or for the benefit of the performer while **ਦੇਣਾ denhaa** indicates that the action is being directed away from the performer. The difference between the two can often be quite subtle:

ਇਹ ਕਿਤਾਬ ਰੱਖ ਲੈ	ih kitaab rakhkh lai	*Keep this book (with you).*
ਇਹ ਕਿਤਾਬ ਮੇਜ਼ ਤੇ ਰੱਖ ਦੇ	ih kitaab mez te rakhkh de	*Put this book on the table.*
ਉਹ ਪੰਜਾਬੀ ਪੜ੍ਹ ਲੈਂਦੀ ਹੈ	uh panjaabee parhh laindee hai	*She reads Panjabi.*
ਉਹ ਚਿੱਠੀ ਪੜ੍ਹ ਦੋਂਦੀ ਹੈ	uh chiththee parhh dendee hai	*She reads out the letter.*

ਲੈਣਾ lainhaa and **ਦੇਣਾ denhaa**, in addition to directing the action, also add a feeling of completeness.

ਮੈਂ ਕੰਮ ਜਲਦੀ ਕਰ ਲਿਆ ਸੀ	main kanm jaldee kar liaa see	*I [had] finished the job quickly.*
ਸਿਮਰਨ ਨੇ ਜੁੱਤੀ ਖ਼ਰੀਦ ਲਈ	simran ne juttee khareed laee	*Simran bought shoes.*
ਡਾਕਟਰ ਨੇ ਸਿਮਰਨ ਨੂੰ ਦਵਾਈ ਦੇ ਦਿੱਤੀ	daaktar ne simran noon davaaee de dittee	*The doctor gave Simran medicine.*
ਟੈਕਸੀ ਵਾਲੇ ਨੇ ਸਮਾਨ ਗੱਡੀ ਵਿਚ ਰੱਖ ਦਿੱਤਾ	taiksee vaale ne samaan gaddee vich rakhkh dittaa	*The taxi driver put the luggage in the car.*

The particle -ਕੇ ke

The particle -ਕੇ **ke** resembles the conjunction *and* in English. In English two verbs can be joined by *and* such as in the case *he came (home) and* *ate*. In Panjabi the first verb is followed by -ਕੇ **ke** to denote that the first action occurred first. In this example, the literal meaning would be *having come (home), he ate*. Therefore, the literal meaning of -ਕੇ ke is *having*. In the passage from Jaspreet's diary, you will recall that she says *Simran saw a buffalo and ran away*. In Panjabi this would be translated as: *Having seen a buffalo, Simran ran away*. Here are a few more examples of how -ਕੇ **ke** is used:

ਰਾਜਿੰਦਰ ਨੂੰ ਬੁਲਾ ਕੇ ਉਹ ਨੂੰ ਦੱਸੋ	raajindar noon bulaa ke uh noon dasso	*Call Rajinder and tell him.*
ਕੰਮ ਖਤਮ ਕਰ ਕੇ ਤੂੰ ਘਰ ਨੂੰ ਚਲੇ ਜਾ	kanm khatam kar ke toon ghar noon chale jaa	*After finishing work, go home.*
ਦੁਕਾਨ ਤੇ ਜਾ ਕੇ ਮੱਖਣ ਲਿਆਓ	dukaan te jaa ke makhkhanh liaao	*Go to the shop and bring some butter.*

-ਕੇ **ke** can be used with more idiomatic expressions as well, which are often not easily translated into English but which are useful ways of expressing what might otherwise be lengthy sentences. Here are some examples of the usage of -ਕੇ **ke** in idiomatic phrases as well as in adverbial expressions (i.e. expressions which describe actions) which will help you to understand its functions better.

Adverbial phrases

ਅੱਗੇ ਚਲ ਕੇ	agge chal ke	*from now on, in the future*
ਸੋਚ ਕੇ	soch ke	*after thinking*
ਹੱਸ ਕੇ	hass ke	*laughingly*
ਡਰ ਕੇ	dar ke	*being scared*

Idiomatic uses of -ਕੇ

ਚੰਡੀਗੜ੍ਹ ਤੋਂ ਹੋ ਕੇ ਜਾਣਾ	chandeegarh ton hoke jaanhaa	*Go via Chandigarh.*
ਪਿਤਾ ਜੀ ਨੇ ਮੈਨੂੰ ਜਾਣ ਕੇ ਨਹੀਂ ਦੱਸਿਆ	pitaa jee ne mainoon jaanh ke naheen dassiaa	*Father purposely didn't tell me.*
ਇੱਕ ਘਰ ਛੱਡ ਕੇ ਸਾਡਾ ਹੈ	ikk ghar chadd ke saadaa hai	*The house after the next one is ours.*

The particle -ਕੇ ke is also used when expressing the time of the day. You will recall from Unit 7 that the verb ਵੱਜਣਾ vajjnhaa (*to strike, to chime*) is used to tell the time. The times of quarter past, half past, quarter to, and times on the hour which are regularly used were illustrated to you in this unit. When you wish to show that the time is a few minutes before or after the hour, then the particle -ਕੇ ke is combined with ਵੱਜਣਾ vajjnhaa. Therefore, ਵਜ ਕੇ vaj ke means *having struck*. ਵਜਣ ਵਿਚ vajnh vich means *before the hour*. The following examples illustrate how -ਕੇ ke and ਵਿਚ vich are used to express such times:

ਪੰਜ ਵਜਣ ਵਿਚ ਦੋ ਮਿੰਟ ਹਨ	pan̲j vajanh vich d̲o min̲t han	*It is two minutes to five.*
ਪੰਜ ਵਜ ਕੇ ਦੋ ਮਿੰਟ ਹਨ	panj vaj ke d̲o min̲t han	*It is two minutes past five.*
ਬਾਰਾਂ ਵਜਣ ਵਿਚ ਅਠਾਰਾਂ ਮਿੰਟ ਹਨ	baar-haa̲n vajanh vich athaar-haa̲n min̲t han	*It is eighteen minutes to twelve.*
ਬਾਰਾਂ ਵਜ ਕੇ ਅਠਾਰਾਂ ਮਿੰਟ ਹਨ	baar-haa̲n vaj ke athaar-haa̲n min̲t han	*It is eighteen minutes past twelve.*

ਵਿਆਖਿਆ   viaakhiaa   Commentary

Rural Panjab

Panjab's predominantly rural society has had a profound impact on the development of the Panjabi language. On the one hand there is a great deal of local diversity, such that dialects and pronunciations can change over small distances. On the other, there is a richness in the language which comes from rural idioms. Conversations in Panjabi are often peppered with these sayings and it is difficult to relate them without some knowledge of village life. As with all rural settings, day-to-day life in a village is dominated by the agricultural economy which is in turn related to the changing seasons.

Panjab is renowned in the whole of India as the 'bread basket' of the country. In the 1970s the region benefited enormously from the introduction of genetically engineered wheat seeds which resulted in much larger crop returns. This phenomenon has been called the 'Green Revolution' and resulted in Panjab having the greatest per capita income of all the states in the Indian Union.

☑ ਅਭਿਆਸ   abhiaas   Exercises

After reading the dialogue and/or listening to the audio tape, try to do the
following exercises.

1. Use the particle -ਕੇ ke to express the sentences in Panjabi

a) *Having eaten, we all went to sleep.*
b) *Go to the shop and bring some milk.*
c) *After completing the task, go home.*
d) *Go to Amritsar via Jalandhar.*

2. Insert the appropriate past tense forms

Write the appropriate past form of the verbs given to you in parentheses.
Remember the rules about transitive and intransitive verbs!

a) ਮੈਂ ਦੋ ਕੇਲੇ _____ (ਖਾਣਾ)
   main do kele _____ (khaanhaa)
b) ਬੱਚੀ _____ (ਰੋਣਾ)
   bachchee _____ (ronhaa)
c) ਨਾਨੀ ਜੀ ਨੇ ਸਾਨੂੰ ਕਹਾਣੀ _____ (ਸੁਣਾਉਣਾ)
   naanee jee ne saanoon kahaanhee _____ (sunhaaunhaa)
d) ਮੈਂ ਦਰਖ਼ਤ ਨੂੰ _____ (ਕੱਟਣਾ)
   main darakhat noon _____ (katnhaa)

▥ 3. Responses in Panjabi

The following is a conversation between you and your aunt. You are
visiting her in London and she is asking you about your trip to central
London today. Respond to her questions in Panjabi with the answers given
to you in English.

Aunt   ਤੁਹਾਡੀ ਲੰਡਨ ਦੀ ਸੈਰ ਕਿਵੇਂ ਰਹੀ ?
           tuhaadee landan dee sair kiven rahee?
You   *It was very nice. I went to Trafalgar Square and saw Nelson's
           Column. I also went to Buckingham Palace.*
Aunt   ਤੁਸੀਂ ਹੋਰ ਕੀ ਕੀਤਾ ?
           tuseen hor kee keetaa?
You   *I went to Oxford Circus and bought some clothes.*
Aunt   ਤੁਸੀਂ ਕੀ ਕੁਝ ਖਾਧਾ ?
           tuseen kee kujh khaadhaa?

You *I only ate some pizza.*

Aunt ਉਮੀਦ ਹੈ ਕਿ ਤੁਹਾਨੂੰ ਭੱਖ ਲੱਗੀ ਹੈ ਕਿਉਂ ਕਿ ਅੱਜ ਅਸੀਂ ਮੱਛੀ ਤੇ ਚਿਪਸ ਬਣਾਏ ਹਨ। ਇਹ ਹੈ ਇੰਗਲੈਂਡ ਦੀ ਖ਼ਾਸ ਸੁਗਾਤ !

umee<u>d</u> hai ki <u>t</u>uhaanoo<u>n</u> bhukhkh laggee hai kiu<u>n</u> ki ajj asee<u>n</u> ma<u>chch</u>ee <u>t</u>e chips banhaae han. ih hai <u>inglaind d</u>ee <u>kh</u>aas sugaat!

4. Name the numbered objects in Panjabi

1. Water well   2. Buffalo   3. Sugarcane   4. House   5. Fields

11 ਹਰਿਮੰਦਰ ਸਾਹਿਬ

harma<u>nd</u>ar saahib

The Golden Temple

In this unit you will learn:

- how to make enquiries and collect information
- how to buy train tickets
- about the Golden Temple

1 Shan-e-Panjab

ਗੱਲ ਬਾਤ ੧ ਸ਼ਾਨੇ ਪੰਜਾਬ

gall baa<u>t</u> 1 shaane pa<u>nj</u>aab

Both sisters are at Jalandhar railway station early in the morning. After visiting their relatives, they are now on their way to pay homage to Harmandar Sahib, the Golden Temple in Amritsar.

ਜਸਪ੍ਰੀਤ	ਅੰਮ੍ਰਿਤਸਰ ਜਾਣ ਲਈ ਸਭ ਤੋਂ ਚੰਗੀ ਗੱਡੀ ਕਿਹੜੀ ਹੈ ?
ਟਿਕਟ ਬਾਬੂ	ਸ਼ਾਨੇ ਪੰਜਾਬ। ਬਹੁਤ ਸਾਰੇ ਸੈਲਾਨੀ ਇਸ ਗੱਡੀ ਵਿਚ ਸਫਰ ਕਰਦੇ ਹਨ।
ਜਸਪ੍ਰੀਤ	ਅਸੀਂ ਦੋਨੋਂ ਅੱਜ ਜਾਣਾ ਚਾਹੁੰਦੀਆਂ ਹਾਂ। ਕੀ ਸਾਨੂੰ ਫਰਸਟ ਕਲਾਸ ਵਿਚ ਸੀਟ ਮਿਲ ਜਾਏ ਗੀ ?
ਟਿਕਟ ਬਾਬੂ	ਕੀ ਤੁਹਾਨੂੰ ਵਾਪਸੀ ਟਿਕਟ ਚਾਹੀਦੀ ਹੈ ਜਾਂ ਇੱਕ ਪਾਸੇ ਦੀ ?
ਸਿਮਰਨ	ਇੱਕ ਪਾਸੇ ਦੀ। ਗੱਡੀ ਕਿੰਨੇ ਵਜੇ ਚਲਦੀ ਹੈ ?
ਟਿਕਟ ਬਾਬੂ	ਗੱਡੀ ਗਿਆਰਾਂ ਵਜੇ ਸਵੇਰੇ ਚਲਦੀ ਹੈ, ਅਤੇ ਚਾਈ ਵਜੇ ਬਾਅਦ ਦੁਪਹਿਰ ਨੂੰ ਤੁਹਾਨੂੰ ਅੰਮ੍ਰਿਤਸਰ ਪਹੁੰਚਾ ਦੇਂਦੀ ਹੈ।
ਸਿਮਰਨ	ਅੱਛਾ, ਸਾਨੂੰ ਦੋ ਟਿਕਟਾਂ ਦੇ ਦੇਵੋ।
ਟਿਕਟ ਬਾਬੂ	ਨਵੀਆਂ ਥਾਂਵਾਂ ਦੇਖਣਾ ਚੰਗੀ ਗੱਲ ਹੈ। ਇਹ ਹਨ ਤੁਹਾਡੀਆਂ ਦੋ ਟਿਕਟਾਂ।
ਜਸਪ੍ਰੀਤ	ਧੰਨਵਾਦ।
ਟਿਕਟ ਬਾਬੂ	ਸੁਰੱਖਿਅਤ ਸਫਰ ਲਈ ਸ਼ੁਭ ਇਛਾਵਾਂ।

Jaspreet	*Which is the best train to Amritsar?*
Booking clerk	*The Shan-e-Panjab [the pride of Panjab]. A lot of tourists travel on this train.*

Jaspreet	*The two of us want to go today. Will we be able to get a seat in first class?*
Booking clerk	*Do you want return or single?*
Simran	*Single. What time does the train leave?*
Booking clerk	*The train leaves at eleven in the morning and gets you to Amritsar at two thirty in the afternoon.*
Simran	*Okay, can we have [lit. give us] two tickets.*
Booking clerk	*It is good to see new places. Here are your two tickets.*
Jaspreet	*Thanks.*
Booking clerk	*Best wishes for a safe journey.*

ਸ਼ਬਦਾਵਲੀ   shab<u>d</u>aavalee   Vocabulary

ਗੱਡੀ	gaddee	*automobile, train (f.)*
ਬਹੁਤ ਸਾਰੇ	bahu<u>t</u> saare	*a lot, many*
ਸੈਲਾਨੀ	sailaanee	*tourists (m./f.)*
ਸਫ਼ਰ ਕਰਨਾ	safar karnaa	*to travel*
ਮਿਲ ਜਾਣਾ	mil jaanhaa	*to get, to receive*
ਬਾਅਦ ਦੁਪਹਿਰ	baa-a-<u>d</u> dupahir	*afternoon*
ਪਹੁੰਚਾ ਦੇਣਾ	pahun<u>ch</u>aa <u>d</u>enhaa	*to deliver, to cause to arrive*
ਸੁਰੱਖਿਅਤ ਸਫ਼ਰ	surakhkhia<u>t</u> safar	*safe journey*
ਸ਼ੁਭ ਇਛਾਵਾਂ	shubh i<u>ch</u>aavaan	*best wishes*

ਅਭਿਆਸ   abhiaas   Exercises

After reading the dialogue and/or listening to the audio tape, try to do the following exercises.

1. Identify the speaker

The following phrases have been taken from the dialogue. Identify who said each of the phrases.

a) ਬਹੁਤ ਸਾਰੇ ਸੈਲਾਨੀ ਇਸ ਗੱਡੀ ਵਿਚ ਸਫ਼ਰ ਕਰਦੇ ਹਨ।   _____

b) ਅੰਮ੍ਰਿਤਸਰ ਜਾਣ ਲਈ ਸਭ ਤੋਂ ਚੰਗੀ ਗੱਡੀ ਕਿਹੜੀ ਹੈ ?   _____

c) ਨਵੀਆਂ ਥਾਂਵਾਂ ਦੇਖਣਾ ਚੰਗੀ ਗੱਲ ਹੈ।   _____

d) ਗੱਡੀ ਕਿੰਨੇ ਵਜੇ ਚਲਦੀ ਹੈ ?   _____

e) ਸਾਨੂੰ ਫ਼ਰਸਟ ਕਲਾਸ ਵਿਚ ਸੀਟ ਮਿਲ ਜਾਏ ਗੀ ?   _____

2. Rewrite in the correct word order

a) ਅਸੀਂ ਹਾਂ ਜਾਣਾ ਅੱਜ ਚਾਹੁੰਦੀਆਂ

b) ਹੈ ਗੱਲ ਚੰਗੀ ਦੇਖਣਾ ਥਾਂਵਾਂ ਨਵੀਆਂ

c) ਇਹ ਟਿਕਟਾਂ ਦੋ ਹਨ ਤੁਹਾਡੀਆਂ

2 The Golden Temple

ਗੱਲ ਬਾਤ ੨ ਹਰਿਮੰਦਰ ਸਾਹਿਬ

gall baat 2 harma<u>nd</u>ar saahib

Simran and Jaspreet are visiting the Golden Temple in Amritsar. They are accompanied by a guide provided by the temple management committee.

ਗਾਇਡ	ਸਿੱਖਾਂ ਦੇ ਚੌਥੇ ਗੁਰੂ, ਰਾਮਦਾਸ ਜੀ ਨੇ ਅੰਮ੍ਰਿਤਸਰ ਸ਼ਹਿਰ ਵਸਾਇਆ ਸੀ ਅਤੇ ਪੰਜਵੇਂ ਗੁਰੂ, ਅਰਜਨ ਦੇਵ ਜੀ ਨੇ ਹਰਿਮੰਦਰ ਸਾਹਿਬ ਬਣਵਾਇਆ ਸੀ।
ਸਿਮਰਨ	ਅੰਮ੍ਰਿਤਸਰ ਦਾ ਅਰਥ ਕੀ ਹੈ ?
ਗਾਇਡ	ਇਸ ਦਾ ਲਫ਼ਜ਼ੀ ਅਰਥ ਹੈː ਅੰਮ੍ਰਿਤ ਦਾ ਸਰੋਵਰ।
ਜਸਪ੍ਰੀਤ	ਹਰਿਮੰਦਰ ਸਾਹਿਬ ਨੂੰ ਸੁਨਹਿਰੀ ਮੰਦਰ ਕਿਉਂ ਕਿਹਾ ਜਾਂਦਾ ਹੈ ?
ਗਾਇਡ	ਕਿਉਂ ਕਿ ਗੁੰਬਦਾਂ ਤੇ ਬਹੁਤ ਸਾਰਾ ਸੋਨਾ ਲੱਗਾ ਹੋਇਆ ਹੈ। ਇਹ ਮਹਾਰਾਜਾ ਰਣਜੀਤ ਸਿੰਘ ਨੇ ਲੱਗਵਾਇਆ ਸੀ।
ਸਿਮਰਨ	ਲਗਾਤਾਰ ਹੋ ਰਿਹਾ ਕੀਰਤਨ ਮਨ ਨੂੰ ਸ਼ਾਂਤੀ ਦੇਂਦਾ ਹੈ ਅਤੇ ਸਾਰਾ ਮਾਹੌਲ ਸਵਰਗ ਵਰਗਾ ਹੈ।
ਗਾਇਡ	ਇਸ ਕਰ ਕੇ ਦਰਸ਼ਕ ਨਾ ਕੇਵਲ ਭਾਰਤ ਤੋਂ ਇੱਥੇ ਆਉਂਦੇ ਹਨ ਬਲਕਿ ਸਾਰੀ ਦੁਨੀਆਂ ਤੋਂ ਆਉਂਦੇ ਹਨ।

Guide	*The town of Amritsar was founded by the fourth Guru of the Sikhs, Ram Das, and the fifth Guru Arjun Dev had Harmandar Sahib built.*
Simran	*What does the word Amritsar mean?*
Guide	*The literal meaning is 'a pool of nectar'.*
Jaspreet	*Why is the Harmandar Sahib called the Golden Temple?*
Guide	*Because the domes are covered in a lot of gold. This gold was put on by Maharaja Ranjit Singh.*
Simran	*The continuous recitation of religious hymns gives peace of mind and the entire atmosphere is heavenly.*
Guide	*That is why visitors come here not only from India but from all over the world.*

ਸ਼ਬਦਾਵਲੀ   shab<u>d</u>aavalee   Vocabulary

ਸਿੱਖਾਂ ਦੇ	sikhkhaa<u>n</u> <u>d</u>e	*of the Sikhs*
ਚੌਥੇ ਗੁਰੂ	chau<u>the</u> guroo	*fourth Guru* (m.)
ਸ਼ਹਿਰ	shahir	*city* (m.)
ਵਸਾਉਣਾ	vasaaunhaa	*to establish, to found*
ਪੰਜਵਾਂ	panjvaa<u>n</u>	*fifth*
ਬਣਵਾਉਣਾ	banhvaaunhaa	*to get built*
ਅਰਥ	ar<u>th</u>	*meaning*
ਲਫ਼ਜ਼ੀ	lafzee	*literal*
ਅੰਮ੍ਰਿਤ	a<u>n</u>mrit	*nectar, holy water* (m.)
ਸਰੋਵਰ	sarovar	*pool* (m.)
ਹਰਿਮੰਦਰ ਸਾਹਿਬ	harma<u>nd</u>ar saahib	*Golden Temple* (m.)
ਸੁਨਹਿਰੀ	sunahiree	*golden*
ਕਿਉਂ	kiu<u>n</u>	*why*
ਕਿਹਾ ਜਾਂਦਾ ਹੈ	kihaa jaa<u>nd</u>aa hai	*is said, is called*
ਕਿਉਂ ਕਿ	kiu<u>n</u> ki	*because*
ਗੁੰਬਦ	gu<u>nbad</u>	*dome* (m.)
ਸੋਨਾ	sonaa	*gold* (m.)
ਲੱਗਣਾ	laggnhaa	*to be covered, laden*
ਲੱਗਵਾਉਣਾ	laggvaaunhaa	*to get covered*
ਲਗਾਤਾਰ	lagaataar	*continuously*
ਕੀਰਤਨ	keerta<u>n</u>	*singing of hymns* (m.)
ਮਨ	man	*mind* (m.)
ਸ਼ਾਂਤੀ	shaa<u>n</u>tee	*peace* (f.)
ਦੇਣਾ	<u>d</u>enhaa	*to give*
ਸਾਰਾ ਮਾਹੌਲ	saaraa maahaul	*whole atmosphere* (m.)
ਸਵਰਗ	savarag	*heaven* (m.)
ਵਰਗਾ	vargaa	*like* (v.)
ਇਸ ਕਰ ਕੇ	is kar ke	*that's why*
ਦਰਸ਼ਕ	<u>d</u>arshak	*visitors* (m./f.)
ਨਾ ਕੇਵਲ	naa keval	*not only*
ਬਲਕਿ	balki	*but also*
ਦੁਨੀਆਂ	<u>d</u>uneeaa<u>n</u>	*world* (f.)

ਅਭਿਆਸ   abhiaas   Exercises

After reading the dialogue and/or listening to the audio tape, try to do the following exercises.

1. Matching

Match the questions with the appropriate answers.

ਸਵਾਲ *savaal* Question	ਜਵਾਬ *javaab* Answer
a) ਅੰਮ੍ਰਿਤਸਰ ਦਾ ਅਰਥ ਕੀ ਹੈ ?	i) ਛੱਥੇ ਗੁਰੂ ਜੀ ਨੇ।
b) ਹਰਿਮੰਦਰ ਸਾਹਿਬ ਕਿਸ ਨੇ ਬਣਵਾਇਆ ਸੀ ?	ii) ਅੰਮ੍ਰਿਤਸਰ ਦਾ ਸਰੋਵਰ।
c) ਅੰਮ੍ਰਿਤਸਰ ਸ਼ਹਿਰ ਕਿਸ ਨੇ ਵਸਾਇਆ ਸੀ ?	iii) ਮਹਾਰਾਜਾ ਰਣਜੀਤ ਸਿੰਘ ਨੇ।
d) ਗੁੰਬਦਾਂ ਤੇ ਕਿਸ ਨੇ ਸੋਨਾ ਲਗਵਾਇਆ ਸੀ ?	iv) ਪੰਜਵੇਂ ਗੁਰੂ ਜੀ ਨੇ।

2. Crossword

Complete the crossword in English using the clues given in Panjabi. Can you figure out what the 'mystery word' is in the shaded boxes?

੧. ਸੋਨਾ

੨. ਗੁੰਬਦ

੩. ਦਰਸ਼ਕ

੪. ਦੁਨੀਆਂ

੫. ਸ਼ਹਿਰ

੬. ਗੁਰੂ

ਬੋਲੀ ਬਾਰੇ   **bolee baare**   **Language points**

Conjunct verbs

Conjunct verbs have meanings which are specified by the nouns or adjectives that they include. Conjunct verbs are formed by combining a noun or adjective with an infinitive (either in its simple form or as a verb tense). For example, *to clean* in English merely requires the infinitive. In Panjabi *to clean* would require two words: ਸਾਫ਼ (*clean*, adjective) and ਕਰਨਾ (*to do*, infinitive). The adjective specifies the type or nature of the action while the infinitive directs the action. The most common infinitives used in conjunct constructions are ਕਰਨਾ (*to do*) and ਹੋਣਾ (*to be*). Here are some examples of common conjunct verbs using both adjectives and nouns.

With nouns

ਪਿਆਰ ਕਰਨਾ	to love
ਪਸੰਦ ਕਰਨਾ	to like, to prefer
ਕੰਮ ਕਰਨਾ	to work
ਸ਼ੁਰੂ ਕਰਨਾ	to begin, to commence
ਮੱਦਦ ਕਰਨਾ	to help
ਕੋਸ਼ਿਸ਼ ਕਰਨਾ	to try

With adjectives

ਸਾਫ਼ ਕਰਨਾ	to clean
ਖ਼ਤਮ ਕਰਨਾ	to finish, to complete
ਠੀਕ ਕਰਨਾ	to fix, to correct
ਬੰਦ ਕਰਨਾ	to close
ਘੱਟ ਕਰਨਾ	to reduce, to lessen

Here are a few examples to illustrate how conjunct verbs are used:

1 ਕੰਮ ਸਵੇਰੇ ਸ਼ੁਰੂ ਹੁੰਦਾ ਹੈ। *Work begins in the morning.*
 [ਸ਼ੁਰੂ ਹੋਣਾ *to begin* is an intransitive verb formed with the noun ਕੰਮ.]

2 ਮੈਂ ਤੁਹਾਡੀ ਉਡੀਕ ਕਰਾਂ ਗੀ। *I will wait for you.*
 [Here ਉਡੀਕ ਕਰਨਾ *to wait* is a transitive verb with ਉਡੀਕ as a noun.
 This is an example of a verbal expression which is formed exactly
 as a conjunct verb. However, the noun retains its own meaning and
 sense.]

3. ਮੇਰਾ ਵਿਆਹ ੧੯੬੪ ਵਿਚ ਹੋਇਆ ਸੀ *I got married in 1964.*

There are some conjunct verbs in which neither ਕਰਨਾ nor ਹੋਣਾ are involved.

ਦਿਖਾਈ ਦੇਣਾ	to be visible
ਯਾਦ ਆਉਣਾ	to come to mind
ਯਾਦ ਰੱਖਣਾ	to bear in mind, to remember

Causative verbs

Causative verbs are groups of related verbs which share a similar
meaning, but which differ in terms of who is carrying out the action. You
have already come across such related verbs in Unit 10, in the first
dialogue when Simran says to Chaachee:

ਮੈਂ ਹਰ ਕਿਸਮ ਦੇ ਖਾਣੇ ਖਾਧੇ   *I ate every type of food.*

In the diary passage in Unit 10, Jaspreet writes:

ਮਾਮੀ ਜੀ ਨੇ ਸਾਨੂੰ ਰੋਟੀ ਖੁਆਈ   *Aunt fed us.*

As you can see from these examples, ਖੁਆਣਾ *to feed* and ਖਾਣਾ *to eat* are
clearly related to one another. However, the difference lies in who the
agent or 'doer' of the action is. Not all verbs are grouped into causative
pairs. However, there are a large number of verbs which can be placed into
such groups. Causative pairs and groupings are formed by a pattern of
adding a suffix (or ending) to the stem of the verb as the action moves
further away from the subject.

ਕਰਨਾ	*to do*
ਕਰਾਉਣਾ	*to cause to be done*
ਕਰਵਾਉਣਾ	*to cause to be done by someone else*
ਦੇਖਣਾ	*to see*
ਦਿਖਣਾ	*to be shown, to appear*
ਦਿਖਾਉਣਾ	*to show*
ਬਣਨਾ	*to make, to build*
ਬਣਾਉਣਾ	*to be made, to be built*
ਬਣਵਾਉਣਾ	*to have made or built (from/by someone else)*
ਪਕਾਉਣਾ	*to cook*
ਪਕਣਾ	*to be cooked*
ਪਕਵਾਉਣਾ	*to have cooked (by someone else), to cause to be cooked*
ਜਾਗਣਾ	*to wake*
ਜਗਾਉਣਾ	*to awaken*
ਜਗਵਾਉਣਾ	*to cause to wake*

The infinitive as a verbal noun

The simple verb, or infinitive, was explained in Unit 3 as the base of all
Panjabi verbs. To refresh your memory, the infinitive of Panjabi verbs is
formed by the root of the verb plus the ending -ਣਾ or -ਨਾ. By now you
should be familiar with the various tenses of the Panjabi verb. In addition
to being the base of all verb tenses, the infinitive can also be used as a
noun. You will recall in the first dialogue that the booking clerk says to
Jaspreet and Simran:

ਨਵੀਆਂ ਥਾਂਵਾਂ ਦੇਖਣਾ ਚੰਗੀ ਗੱਲ ਹੈ   *It's good seeing [to see] new places.*

Notice that the infinitive ਦੇਖਣਾ is not the verb of the sentence (ਹੋਣਾ is the verb) but that it is a verbal noun indicating an action (which behaves as a noun) within the sentence. Here are a few more examples of the infinitive as a verbal noun:

ਜਲਦੀ ਉਠਣਾ ਜ਼ਰੂਰੀ ਹੈ	*Waking up [to wake up] early is necessary.*
ਜ਼ਿਆਦਾ ਬੋਲਣਾ ਚੰਗਾ ਨਹੀਂ ਲੱਗਦਾ	*Talking [to talk] too much doesn't look good.*
ਪੜ੍ਹਨਾ ਸੌਖਾ ਹੈ, ਲਿਖਣਾ ਮੁਸ਼ਕਲ	*Reading [to read] is easy, writing [to write] is difficult.*

When the infinitive has an object, it will correspond to the gender and number of that noun. Since the infinitive already has a masculine/singular appearance with the -ਆ ending, it does not change when the object is masculine and singular. However, when the object is masculine/plural it will take the ending -ਏ and when the object is feminine, then the ending changes to -ਈ, -ਈਆਂ if plural. Note the following examples:

ਨੌਕਰੀ ਕਰਨੀ	*working* (to work, to have a job)
ਕਿਤਾਬਾਂ ਪੜ੍ਹਨੀਆਂ	*reading* (to read) books
ਖਾਣਾ ਬਣਾਉਣਾ	*cooking* (to cook, to make food)
ਦਰਵਾਜ਼ੇ ਖੋਲ੍ਹਣੇ	*opening* (to open) the doors

Like other nouns, the infinitive is also affected by postpositions. The ending of the infinitive in the oblique, therefore, changes to the shortened form as discussed in Unit 8. Here are some examples of verbal nouns in the oblique:

ਮੈਂ ਹਾਲੇ ਬਾਹਰ ਜਾਣ ਨੂੰ ਤਿਆਰ ਨਹੀਂ ਹਾਂ	*I am not ready to go out yet.*
ਉਹਨਾਂ ਦੇ ਇੱਥੇ ਆਉਣ ਨਾਲ ਮੇਰਾ ਸਮਾਂ ਜ਼ਾਇਆ ਹੋ ਗਿਆ	*Their coming here wasted my time.*
ਚਾਹ ਪੀਣ ਦਾ ਮੌਕਾ ਨਹੀਂ ਮਿਲਿਆ	*There wasn't an opportunity to drink tea.*

The passive voice

In English 'I said' is in the active voice (i.e. the subject of the verb is directly carrying out the action) and 'it was said' is in the passive voice (i.e. the subject is on the receiving end of the action). The same distinction is also true in Panjabi. The passive voice can be formed in two ways. In the first form the passive verb (the participle [see Unit 12] and the form of ਜਾਣ) agrees with the subject:

ਲੁਧਿਆਣੇ ਵਿਚ ਪੰਜਾਬੀ ਬੋਲੀ ਜਾਂਦੀ ਹੈ   *Panjabi is spoken in Ludhiana.*
ਕਿਹਾ ਜਾਂਦਾ ਹੈ ਕਿ ਅੰਮ੍ਰਿਤਸਰ   *It is said that Amritsar is the city of the*
   ਸਿੱਖਾਂ ਦਾ ਸ਼ਹਿਰ ਹੈ   *Sikhs.*

ਕੱਲ੍ ਤਕ ਸਾਰਾ ਕੰਮ ਕਰ ਲਿਆ ਜਾਏਗਾ   *By tomorrow all of the work will be done.*

The passive voice can also be expressed by using the postpositions ਤੋਂ and ਕੋਲੋਂ to indicate by whom the action was done. In this form the verb of the sentence agrees with the object. Note the following examples:

ਕਪ ਮੇਰੇ ਤੋਂ ਟੁੱਟ ਗਿਆ   *The cup was broken by me.*
ਕੁਰਸੀ ਮੇਰੇ ਤੋਂ ਟੁੱਟ ਗਈ   *The chair was broken by me.*
ਗਲਤੀ ਪਿਤਾ ਜੀ ਕੋਲੋਂ ਹੋਈ   *The mistake was made by father.*

You will recall from earlier in this unit that causative verbs are groups of related verbs. Active intransitive verbs and passive transitive verbs (see Unit 10) can both be used to express the passive voice. For example, the verb ਬਣਨਾ *to be made* and ਬਣਾਉਣਾ *to make* can both be used to give the sense *is/are made*.

ਜੁੱਤੀਆਂ ਇੱਥੇ ਬਣਦੀਆਂ ਹਨ   *Shoes are made here.*
ਜੁੱਤੀਆਂ ਇੱਥੇ ਬਣਾਈਆਂ ਜਾਂਦੀਆਂ ਹਨ   *Shoes are made here.*

ਵਰਗਾ 'like'

The postposition ਵਰਗਾ is used when comparing objects or people with one another in terms of quality, size, colour, etc. You will recall in Dialogue 2 that the guide described the atmosphere of the Golden Temple: ਮਾਹੌਲ ਸਵਰਗ ਵਰਗਾ ਹੈ (*the atmosphere is heavenly (lit. like heaven)*). ਵਰਗਾ is affected by the gender and number of the person or object being likened to, so that the ending of ਵਰਗਾ is masculine, in this example, since *heaven* is a masculine noun. Note in the following examples how the ending of ਵਰਗਾ changes accordingly:

ਇਹ ਕੁੜੀ ਪਰੀ ਵਰਗੀ ਹੈ   *This girl is like a fairy.*
ਇਹ ਕੁੜੀਆਂ ਪਰੀਆਂ ਵਰਗੀਆਂ ਹਨ   *The girls are like fairies.*
ਉਸ ਦਾ ਮਕਾਨ ਮੱਹਲ ਵਰਗਾ ਵੱਡਾ ਹੈ   *His house is big like a palace.*
ਉਹ ਮੁੰਡੇ ਦੈਂਤਾਂ ਵਰਗੇ ਹਨ   *Those boys are like giants.*
ਉਹ ਦਵਾਈ ਖੰਡ ਵਰਗੀ ਮਿੱਠੀ ਹੈ   *That medicine is sweet like sugar.*

There are also other words for describing likeness in Panjabi: ਜਿਹਾ (jihaa), ਵਾਂਗੂੰ (vaa<u>ng</u>oo<u>n</u>) and ਤਰ੍ਹਾਂ (<u>t</u>ar-h-aa<u>n</u>). These words all appear in this book.

ਵਿਆਖਿਆ viaakhiaa Commentary

1. Railways

India has one of the largest railway networks in the world. Trains may be both the most luxurious and most uncomfortable way to travel in India, but they are always entertaining. The fastest trains to Panjab from Delhi are the Shan-e-Panjab and the Shatabdi. However, almost all trains heading north from Delhi will pass through Panjab. There is also a train called the Samjota Express which crosses the India–Pakistan border from East to West Panjab at Attari.

2. The city of Amritsar

The city of Amritsar is one of the central towns in the corridor to India for those travelling by land to and from Central Asia. Amritsar is a cultural and religious centre not only in the state of Panjab but also in South Asia. Founded over 400 years ago, Amritsar has become the political and cultural centre of the region and is the religious centre for the Sikh faith. At the time of the annexation of Panjab by the British in 1849, Amritsar was the largest city in Panjab. However, other larger cities such as Lahore and Ludhiana have now surpassed Amritsar in terms of size and economic dynamism since the partition in 1947. Today Amritsar is still the most significant religious centre for the Sikhs, being the home of the Golden Temple, and continues to be regarded as one of the main tourist attractions of Panjab.

☑ ਅਭਿਆਸ   abhiaas   Exercises

After reading the dialogue and/or listening to the audio tape, try to do the following exercises.

1. Fill in the blanks

a. ਜਿਹੜੀ ਗੱਡੀ ਜਲੰਧਰ ਤੋਂ ਅੰਮ੍ਰਿਤਸਰ ਜਾਂਦੀ ਹੈ ਉਸ ਦਾ ਨਾਮ _____ ਹੈ।

b. ਬਹੁਤ ਸਾਰੇ _____ ਉਸ ਗੱਡੀ ਵਿਚ _____ ਹਨ।

c. ਅੰਮ੍ਰਿਤਸਰ ਦਾ _____ ਅਰਥ ਹੈ: '_____'।

d. ਲਗਾਤਾਰ _____ ਮਨ ਨੂੰ _____ ਦੇਂਦਾ ਹੈ ਅਤੇ ਸਾਰਾ ਮਾਹੌਲ _____ ਵਰਗਾ ਹੈ।

⊟ 2. Answer the following questions in Panjabi

a. Who was the founder of the city of Amritsar?

b. What is the meaning of Amritsar?

c. Why is Harmandar Sahib known as the Golden Temple?

⊟ 3. Listening

You are standing at the ticket counter at Amritsar railway station speaking with the booking clerk about your planned journey to Delhi. Listen to the tape and converse with the ticket master by translating the English sentences given to you.

You	*I want to go to Delhi today. Which is the best train to Delhi?*
Ticket master	ਸ਼ੇਤਾਬਦੀ ਐਕਸਪ੍ਰੈਸ ਸਭ ਤੋਂ ਚੰਗੀ ਹੈ। ਬਹੁਤ ਲੋਕ ਉਸ ਵਿਚ ਸਫਰ ਕਰਦੇ ਹਨ।
You	*Will I be able to get a seat in 2nd class?*
Ticket master	ਹਾਂ ਜੀ ਕੀ ਤੁਹਾਨੂੰ ਸਿਰਫ ਇੱਕ ਪਾਸੇ ਦੀ ਟਿਕਟ ਚਾਹੀਦੀ ਹੈ ?
You	*No, I want a return ticket. What time does the train leave from Amritsar?*
Ticket master	ਗੱਡੀ ਅੰਮ੍ਰਿਤਸਰ ਤੋਂ ਢਾਈ ਵਜੇ ਚਲਦੀ ਹੈ ਅਤੇ ਦਿੱਲੀ ਅੱਠ ਵਜੇ ਰਾਤ ਨੂੰ ਪਹੁੰਚਦੀ ਹੈ।
You	*OK, give me one 2nd-class ticket.*
Ticket master	ਸੁਰੱਖਿਅਤ ਸਫਰ ਲਈ ਸ਼ੁਭ ਇਛਾਵਾਂ।

12 ਘਰ ਨੂੰ ਚਿੱਠੀ
ghar noo<u>n</u> chiththee
A letter home

In this unit you will learn:

■ how to write a letter
■ how to express *how did it go?*
■ how to talk about where you've visited
■ how to construct sentences beginning with *if*

1 Changing money

ਗੱਲ ਬਾਤ ੧ ਪੈਸੇ ਬਦਲਣਾ

gall baa<u>t</u> 1 paise ba<u>d</u>alnhaa

Simran and Jaspreet are in the Air India office in Chandigarh waiting to get their tickets confirmed. While they are there a German tourist, Paul, strikes up a conversation with them.

ਪੌਲ	ਮੇਰਾ ਨਾਮ ਪੌਲ ਹੈ। ਮੈਂ ਜਰਮਨ ਹਾਂ। ਮੈਨੂੰ ਅੰਗਰੇਜ਼ੀ ਨਹੀਂ ਆਉਂਦੀ ਪਰ ਮੈਂ ਪੰਜਾਬੀ ਬੋਲ ਸਕਦਾ ਹਾਂ।
ਸਿਮਰਨ	ਅਸੀਂ ਅਮਰੀਕਨ ਹਾਂ। ਅਸੀਂ ਵੀ ਪੰਜਾਬੀ ਬੋਲ ਸਕਦੀਆਂ ਹਾਂ। ਅਸੀਂ ਤਿੰਨ ਹਫ਼ਤਿਆਂ ਲਈ ਭਾਰਤ ਆਈਆਂ ਹਾਂ। ਸਾਨੂੰ ਬਹੁਤ ਹੀ ਚੰਗਾ ਲੱਗਾ ਹੈ।
ਪੌਲ	ਮੈਂ ਅੱਜ ਹੀ ਅੰਮ੍ਰਿਤਸਰ ਤੋਂ ਵਾਪਸ ਆਇਆ ਹਾਂ। ਜੇ ਅਸੀਂ ਪਹਿਲੇ ਮਿਲਦੇ ਤਾਂ ਅਸੀਂ ਇਕੱਠੇ ਘੁੰਮਦੇ। ਤੁਸੀਂ ਕਿੱਥੇ ਕਿੱਥੇ ਗਈਆਂ ?
ਜਸਪ੍ਰੀਤ	ਅਸੀਂ ਬਹੁਤ ਜਗ੍ਹਾ ਦੇਖੀਆਂ ਹਨ। ਤੁਹਾਨੂੰ ਕਿਹੜੀ ਜਗ੍ਹਾ ਸਭ ਤੋਂ ਚੰਗੀ ਲੱਗੀ ?
ਪੌਲ	ਤਾਜ ਮਹੱਲ ਮੈਂ ਪਹਿਲੇ ਦੇਖ ਚੁੱਕਾ ਸੀ। ਹੁਣ ਮੈਂ ਹਰਿਮੰਦਰ ਸਾਹਿਬ ਦੇਖਿਆ ਹੈ। ਹਰਿਮੰਦਰ ਸਾਹਿਬ ਦਾ ਕੋਈ ਮੁਕਾਬਲਾ ਨਹੀਂ।

ਜਸਪ੍ਰੀਤ ਤੇ ਸਿਮਰਨ ਅਸੀਂ ਤੁਹਾਡੇ ਨਾਲ ਸਹਿਮਤ ਹਾਂ।

ਪੌਲ	ਮੈਂ ਪੈਸੇ ਬਦਲਣਾ ਚਾਹੁੰਦਾ ਹਾਂ। ਮੇਰੇ ਕੋਲ ਯੂ.ਐਸ. ਡਾਲਰ ਹਨ। ਮੈਨੂੰ ਕੀ ਕਰਨਾ ਚਾਹੀਦਾ ਹੈ ?

ਸਿਮਰਨ	ਤੁਸੀਂ ਕਿਸੇ ਬੈਂਕ ਜਾਓ। ਡਾਲਰ ਦੇ ਕੇ ਰੁਪਏ ਲੈ ਲਵੋ। ਇਹ ਕੰਮ ਸੌਖਾ ਹੈ।
ਪੌਲ	ਜੇ ਮੈਂ ਬੈਂਕ ਦੇ ਰੇਟ ਤੋਂ ਜ਼ਿਆਦਾ ਲੈਣਾ ਚਾਹਵਾਂ ?
ਜਸਪ੍ਰੀਤ	... ਤਾਂ ਤੁਹਾਨੂੰ ਕਿਸੇ ਦੁਕਾਨਦਾਰ ਨੂੰ ਪੁੱਛਣਾ ਚਾਹੀਦਾ ਹੈ।
ਪੌਲ	ਧੰਨਵਾਦ। ਮੇਰੀ ਵਾਰੀ ਆ ਗਈ ਹੈ। ਉਮੀਦ ਹੈ ਕਿ ਫਿਰ ਮਿਲਾਂ ਗੇ।

Paul	*My name is Paul. I'm German. I don't know any English but I can speak Panjabi.*
Simran	*We are American. We can also speak Panjabi. We've come to India for three weeks. We like it very much.*
Paul	*I have just come from Amritsar today. Had we met before, we could have travelled together. Where have you been?*
Jaspreet	*We have seen many places. Which one did you like the most?*
Paul	*I had already seen the Taj Mahal. Now I have seen Harmandar Sahib. There is no comparison with Harmandar Sahib.*
Jaspreet and Simran	*We agree with you.*
Paul	*I want to change some money. I have US dollars. What should I do?*
Simran	*Go to any bank. Get rupees by giving dollars. This is not difficult to do [lit. an easy task].*
Paul	*And if I want a higher rate than the bank?*
Jaspreet	*... then you should ask any shopkeeper.*
Paul	*Thanks. My turn has come now. Hope we'll meet again.*

🔑 ਸ਼ਬਦਾਵਲੀ   shabda̲avalee   Vocabulary

ਵਾਪਸ	vaapas	return, back
ਜੇ	je	if
ਮਿਲਣਾ	milnhaa	to meet
ਪਹਿਲੇ	pahile	before
ਇਕੱਠੇ	ikaththe	together (v.)
ਤਾਂ	ta̲an	then
ਜਗ੍ਹਾ	jag-h-aa	place (f.)
ਦੇਖਣਾ	de̲khnhaa	to see
ਮੁਕਾਬਲਾ	mukaablaa	comparison, competition (m.)

ਸਹਿਮਤ	sahima<u>t</u>	*agree*
ਬਦਲਣਾ	ba<u>d</u>alnhaa	*to change, exchange*
ਕੰਮ	ka<u>n</u>m	*job, work, task* (m.)
ਸੌਖਾ	saukhaa	*easy, simple* (v.)
ਉਮੀਦ	umee<u>d</u>	*hope* (f.)
ਫਿਰ	phir	*again*

✔ ਅਭਿਆਸ　　　**abhiaas**　　　**Exercises**

After reading the dialogue and/or listening to the audio tape, try to do the following exercises.

1. True or false?

a. ਜਸਪ੍ਰੀਤ ਤੇ ਸਿਮਰਨ ਅਮਰੀਕਨ ਹਨ ਪਰ ਉਹਨਾਂ ਨੂੰ ਪੰਜਾਬੀ ਨਹੀਂ
　　ਆਉਂਦੀ ।　　　　　　　　　　　　　　　　　　True / False

b. ਪੌਲ ਨੇ ਕਿਹਾ ਕਿ ਜੇ ਉਹ ਪਹਿਲੇ ਮਿਲਦੇ ਤਾਂ ਉਹ ਇਕੱਠੇ ਘੁੰਮਦੇ।　True / False

c. ਜਦੋਂ ਪੌਲ ਨੇ ਦੋਨਾਂ ਭੈਣਾਂ ਨੂੰ ਪੈਸੇ ਬਦਲਣ ਬਾਰੇ ਪੁੱਛਿਆ ਤਾਂ ਉਹਨਾਂ ਨੇ　True / False
　　ਜਵਾਬ ਦਿੱਤਾ ਕਿ ਇਹ ਕੰਮ ਬਹੁਤ ਮੁਸ਼ਕਲ ਹੈ।

d. ਜਸਪ੍ਰੀਤ ਤੇ ਸਿਮਰਨ ਨੇ ਪੌਲ ਨੂੰ ਕਿਹਾ ਕਿ ਜੇ ਉਹ ਬੈਂਕ ਦੇ ਰੇਟ ਤੋਂ ਜ਼ਿਆਦਾ
　　ਲੈਣਾ ਚਾਹੁੰਦਾ ਹੈ ਤਾਂ ਫਿਰ ਕਿਸੇ ਦੁਕਾਨਦਾਰ ਨੂੰ ਪੁੱਛਣਾ ਚਾਹੀਦਾ ਹੈ।　True / False

2. Fill in the blanks

a. ਪੌਲ _____ ਹੈ ਤੇ ਉਸ ਨੂੰ _____ ਨਹੀਂ ਆਉਂਦੀ ਪਰ ਉਹ _____ ਬੋਲ ਸਕਦਾ ਹੈ।

b. ਪੌਲ _____ ਪਹਿਲੇ ਦੇਖ ਚੁਕਾ ਸੀ।

c. ਜਸਪ੍ਰੀਤ, ਸਿਮਰਨ ਤੇ ਪੌਲ _____ ਹਨ ਕਿ ਹਰਿਮੰਦਰ ਸਾਹਿਬ ਦਾ ਕੋਈ _____
ਨਹੀਂ।

d. ਪੌਲ ਅੱਜ ਹੀ _____ ਤੋਂ ਵਾਪਸ ਆਇਆ ਹੈ।

A letter home　ਘਰ ਨੂੰ ਚਿੱਠੀ　**ghar noo<u>n</u> chiththee**

ਪਿਆਰੇ ਪਿਤਾ ਤੇ ਮਾਤਾ ਜੀ,　　　　　　　　੪ ਜੁਲਾਈ

　　　ਸਤਿ ਸ੍ਰੀ ਅਕਾਲ

ਸਾਨੂੰ ਉਮੀਦ ਹੈ ਕਿ ਤੁਸੀਂ ਠੀਕ ਠਾਕ ਹੋ। ਅਸੀਂ ਇੱਥੇ ਖ਼ੁਸ਼ ਹਾਂ। ਅਸੀਂ ਪਿੰਡ ਗਈਆਂ
ਸੀ ਤੇ ਉਹ ਮਕਾਨ ਦੇਖਿਆ ਜਿੱਥੇ ਤੁਸੀਂ ਰਹਿੰਦੇ ਹੁੰਦੇ ਸੀ। ਪਿੰਡ ਦੇ ਲੋਕਾਂ ਨੇ ਸਾਨੂੰ

ਬਹੁਤ ਪਿਆਰ ਦਿਖਾਇਆ, ਪਰ ਗਰਮੀ ਬਹੁਤ ਸੀ। ਇੱਕ ਵਾਰੀ ਤਿੰਨ ਦਿਨ ਲਗਾਤਾਰ
ਬਾਰਸ਼ ਹੁੰਦੀ ਰਹੀ ਸੀ। ਇੱਥੇ ਆ ਕੇ ਸਾਡੀ ਪੰਜਾਬੀ ਦੀ ਸ਼ਬਦਾਵਲੀ ਬਹੁਤ ਵੱਧ ਗਈ
ਹੈ। ਅਸੀਂ ਹੈਰਾਨ ਹੋਈਆਂ ਹਾਂ ਕਿ ਇੱਥੇ ਐਨੀ ਅਬਾਦੀ ਤੇ ਟਰੈਫ਼ਿਕ ਹੈ। ਅਸੀਂ ਤੁਹਾਡੇ
ਲਈ ਬਹੁਤ ਸੁਗਾਤਾਂ ਖ਼ਰੀਦੀਆਂ ਹਨ। ਅਸੀਂ ਚਾਹੁੰਦੀਆਂ ਸੀ ਕਿ ਤੁਸੀਂ ਸਾਡੇ ਨਾਲ ਹੁੰਦੇ।

ਸ਼ੁਭ ਇਛਾਵਾਂ

ਤੁਹਾਡੀਆਂ ਪਿਆਰੀਆਂ ਬੇਟੀਆਂ

ਜਸਪ੍ਰੀਤ ਤੇ ਸਿਮਰਨ

Dear Dad and Mum,   4 July

Sat sri akal.

*We hope that you are fine. We are happy here. We went to the village
and saw the house where you used to live. The people of the village
have shown us tremendous affection but it was very hot. Once, it
rained for three days without stopping. Our Panjabi vocabulary has
increased a lot by coming here. We are astonished to see so many
people and so much traffic. We have bought many presents for you.
We wish you were here with us.*

With best wishes,

Your loving daughters,

Jaspreet and Simran

🔑 ਸ਼ਬਦਾਵਲੀ　　shabdaavalee　　Vocabulary

ਪਿਆਰੇ	piaare	*dear, beloved* (v.)
ਕਿ	ki	*that*
ਖ਼ੁਸ਼	<u>kh</u>ush	*happy*
ਮਕਾਨ	makaan	*house* (m.)
ਜਿੱਥੇ	<u>jiththe</u>	*where*
ਲੋਕ	lok	*people* (m.)
ਪਿਆਰ	piaar	*love, affection* (m.)
ਦਿਖਾਉਣਾ	<u>d</u>ikhaaunhaa	*to show*
ਗਰਮੀ	garmee	*heat, warmth (hot, war<u>m</u>)* (f.)

ਵਾਰੀ	vaaree	*turn, instance* (f.)
ਅਬਾਦੀ	abaa<u>d</u>ee	*population* (f.)
ਲਗਾਤਾਰ	lagaa<u>t</u>aar	*continuously, ongoing*
ਬਾਰਸ਼	baarash	*rain* (f.)

ਅਭਿਆਸ   abhiaas   Exercises

After reading the dialogue and/or listening to the audio tape, try to do the following exercises.

1. Complete the box

ਲਗਾਤਾਰ		
	piaare	
ਖ਼ੁਸ਼		
		warmth
	vaaree	

2. Answer the questions about Jaspreet and Simran's letter home

a. ਜਸਪ੍ਰੀਤ ਤੇ ਸਿਮਰਨ ਨੇ ਪਿੰਡ ਵਿਚ ਕੀ ਦੇਖਿਆ ?
b. ਇੱਕ ਵਾਰੀ ਤਿੰਨ ਦਿਨ ਲਗਾਤਾਰ ਕੀ ਹੁੰਦੀ ਰਹੀ ਸੀ ?
c. ਜਸਪ੍ਰੀਤ ਤੇ ਸਿਮਰਨ ਕਿਉਂ ਹੈਰਾਨ ਹੋਈਆਂ ਹਨ ?
d. ਜਸਪ੍ਰੀਤ ਤੇ ਸਿਮਰਨ ਨੇ ਆਪਣੇ ਮਾਤਾ ਜੀ ਤੇ ਪਿਤਾ ਜੀ
    ਲਈ ਕੀ ਖ਼ਰੀਦਿਆ ?

2 Simran at the post office

ਗੱਲ ਬਾਤ ੨ ਸਿਮਰਨ ਡਾਕਖ਼ਾਨੇ ਤੇ

gall baa<u>t</u> 2 simran daak<u>kh</u>aane <u>t</u>e

ਸਿਮਰਨ	ਮੈਂ ਇਹ ਚਿੱਠੀ ਅਮਰੀਕਾ ਭੇਜਣੀ ਹੈ।
ਡਾਕਬਾਬੂ	ਕੀ ਤੁਸੀਂ ਸਮੁੰਦਰੀ ਡਾਕ ਰਾਹੀਂ ਭੇਜਣੀ ਹੈ ਜਾਂ ਹਵਾਈ ਡਾਕ ਰਾਹੀਂ ?
ਸਿਮਰਨ	ਹਵਾਈ ਡਾਕ ਰਾਹੀਂ।

| ਡਾਕਬਾਬੂ | ਇਸ ਤੇ ੧੨ ਰੁਪਏ ਦੀਆਂ ਟਿਕਟਾਂ ਲਾਓ। |
| ਸਿਮਰਨ | ਅੱਛਾ ਜੀ। ਧੰਨਵਾਦ। |

Simran	*I want to send this letter to America.*
Postal worker	*Do you want to send the letter by sea or by air mail?*
Simran	*By air mail.*
Postal worker	*Put 12 rupees worth of stamps on it [the letter].*
Simran	*Okay. Thanks.*

ਸ਼ਬਦਾਵਲੀ   shabdaavalee   Vocabulary

ਚਿੱਠੀ	chiththee	*letter* (f.)
ਭੇਜਣਾ	bhejnhaa	*to send, to post*
ਸਮੁੰਦਰ	samundar	*sea* (m.)
ਡਾਕ	daak	*mail, post* (f.)
ਸਮੁੰਦਰੀ ਡਾਕ	samundaree daak	*sea mail* (f.)
ਰਾਹੀਂ	raaheen	*via, by*
ਹਵਾਈ	havaaee	*by air*
ਹਵਾਈ ਡਾਕ	havaaee daak	*air mail* (f.)
ਟਿਕਟ	tikat	*stamp* (f.)

ਬੋਲੀ ਬਾਰੇ   bolee baare   Language points

The perfect tenses

The perfect tenses describe actions which have been completed.

Present prefect

The present perfect tense in Panjabi refers to those actions which have just occurred, such as *I have eaten*. It is generally used when one is concerned with the present effects of something which happened in the recent past. You will recall from Unit 9 that the verb ਚੁਕਣਾ is used to express *to have already done* or *to have finished doing*. The stem that is used with ਚੁਕਣਾ represents the action in the present perfect tense that has already occurred. The present perfect of ਖਾਣਾ *to eat* is as follows:

Masculine singular	ਮੈਂ ਖਾ ਚੁਕਾ/ ਚੁਕਿਆ ਹਾਂ	*I have eaten*
Feminine singular	ਮੈਂ ਖਾ ਚੁਕੀ ਹਾਂ	*I have eaten*
Masculine plural	ਅਸੀਂ ਖਾ ਚੁਕੇ ਹਾਂ	*we have eaten*
Feminine plural	ਅਸੀਂ ਖਾ ਚੁਕੀਆਂ ਹਾਂ	*we have eaten*
Masculine informal singular	ਤੂੰ ਖਾ ਚੁਕਾ/ਚੁਕਿਆ ਹੈਂ	*you have eaten*
Feminine informal singular	ਤੂੰ ਖਾ ਚੁਕੀ ਹੈਂ	*you have eaten*
Formal masculine plural	ਤੁਸੀਂ ਖਾ ਚੁਕੇ ਹੋ	*you have eaten*
Masculine singular	ਇਹ/ਉਹ ਖਾ ਚੁਕਾ/ਚੁਕਿਆ ਹੈ	*he has eaten*
Feminine singular	ਇਹ/ਉਹ ਖਾ ਚੁਕੀ ਹੈ	*she has eaten*
Formal Masculine plural	ਇਹ/ਉਹ ਖਾ ਚੁਕੇ ਹਨ	*he/has/they have eaten*
Feminine plural	ਇਹ/ਉਹ ਖਾ ਚੁਕੀਆਂ ਹਨ	*she has/ they have eaten*

Past perfect

The past perfect tense is used when the effects of an action in the remote past is being referred to in the more recent past. In English *to eat* in the past perfect would be expressed as *had eaten*. The past perfect tense in Panjabi is formed similarly to the present perfect tense as just shown, except that the present auxiliary verbs are used in the present perfect while the past perfect tense is formed with the past form of the auxiliary verbs. The following examples show *to eat* ਖਾਣਾ in the past perfect tense:

Masculine singular	ਮੈਂ ਖਾ ਚੁਕਾ/ ਚੁਕਿਆ ਸੀ	*I had eaten*
Feminine singular	ਮੈਂ ਖਾ ਚੁਕੀ ਸੀ	*I had eaten*
Masculine plural	ਅਸੀਂ ਖਾ ਚੁਕੇ ਸੀ	*we had eaten*

Feminine plural	ਅਸੀਂ ਖਾ ਚੁਕੀਆਂ ਸੀ	*we had eaten*
Masculine informal singular	ਤੂੰ ਖਾ ਚੁਕਾ/ਚੁਕਿਆ ਸੀ	*you had eaten*
Feminine informal singular	ਤੂੰ ਖਾ ਚੁਕੀ ਸੀ	*you had eaten*
Masculine singular	ਇਹ/ਉਹ ਖਾ ਚੁਕਾ/ਚੁਕਿਆ ਸੀ	*he had eaten*
Feminine singular	ਇਹ/ਉਹ ਖਾ ਚੁਕੀ ਸੀ	*she had eaten*
Formal Masculine plural	ਇਹ/ਉਹ ਖਾ ਚੁਕੇ ਸਨ	*he/they had eaten*
Feminine plural	ਇਹ/ਉਹ ਖਾ ਚੁਕੀਆਂ ਸਨ	*she/they had eaten*

Compound constructions with ਲੈਣਾ, ਦੇਣਾ and ਜਾਣਾ can also be used to express the present and past perfect, most commonly when there is an object present. Notice the following examples:

ਮੈਂ ਖਾਣਾ ਖਾ ਲਿਆ ਹੈ	*I have eaten food.*
ਉਸ ਨੇ ਸਾਨੂੰ ਸੁਗਾਤ ਦੇ ਦਿੱਤੀ ਹੈ	*He has given us a gift.*

The present perfect continuous and the past perfect continuous are expressed in the same manner as the present and past continuous tenses except that an indication of time is used to denote whether or not the action is in the perfect tense.

present continuous	ਬਾਰਸ਼ ਹੋ ਰਹੀ ਹੈ	*It is raining.*
present perfect continuous	ਬਾਰਸ਼ ਦੋ ਦਿਨ ਤੋਂ ਹੋ ਰਹੀ ਹੈ	*It has been raining for two days.*
past continuous	ਬਾਰਸ਼ ਹੋ ਰਹੀ ਸੀ	*It was raining.*
past perfect continuous	ਬਾਰਸ਼ ਦੋ ਦਿਨ ਤੋਂ ਹੋ ਰਹੀ ਸੀ	*It had been raining for two days.*

How did it go?

In Panjabi, *how did it go?* is expressed through the use of the continuous form of ਰਹਿਣਾ. You have already been introduced to ਰਹੀ/ਰਿਹਾ as the continuous tense form of ਰਹਿਣਾ *to stay, to live* equivalent to the English -ing. In Unit 5 Geeta asks Sita: ਤੂੰ ਕੀ ਕਰ ਰਹੀ ਹੈਂ? literally meaning *What are you doing?* The continuous form of ਰਹਿਣਾ can have another quite different sense as *how did it go?*. Although the form of ਰਹਿਣਾ is in the continuous, the sense of the sentence refers to the past:

ਤੁਹਾਡੀ ਇੰਡੀਆ ਦੀ ਫੇਰੀ ਕਿਵੇਂ ਰਹੀ ? *How was your tour of India?*
ਤੁਹਾਡਾ ਦਿਨ ਕਿਵੇਂ ਰਿਹਾ ?   *How was your day?*

ਰਹੀ/ਰਿਹਾ in these examples means outcome or conclusion. Therefore, this sentence has the sense *How did your trip to India go?* and *How did your day go?*. Notice that the form of ਰਹਿਣਾ corresponds with the gender/ number character of the object being described, in this case ਫੇਰੀ (trip, tour) which is feminine. *How did it go?* is a colloquial phrase which you will find useful when informally asking someone about their day or trip.

The subjunctive

The subjunctive mood (set of verb tenses) is commonly used when there is a sense of possibility, vagueness or indefiniteness. When the exact time or state of an action is uncertain, the subjunctive is used. The present subjunctive is formed in a way similar to the future tense, except that the -ਗਾ/ -ਗੀ/-ਗੇ/-ਗੀਆਂ endings are left out. In English we rarely use the subjunctive mood, but learners of other European languages will be aware of this system of verbal constructions.

ਮੈਂ ਕਰਾਂ
ਅਸੀਂ ਬੋਲੀਏ
ਤੂੰ ਕਰੇਂ
ਤੁਸੀਂ ਬੋਲੋ
ਇਹ/ਉਹ ਬੋਲੇ
ਇਹ/ਉਹ ਬੋਲਣ

The range of situations in which the present subjunctive is used can be best compared with the future tense, as in the following examples:

Future

ਉਹ ਕਿੱਥੇ ਜਾਏਗੀ ?   *Where will she go?*
ਮੈਂ ਕੁਝ ਕਵਾਂਗੀ   *I will say something.*
ਅਸੀਂ ਕੀ ਕਰਾਂਗੇ ?   *What will we do?*

Present subjunctive

ਉਹ ਕਿੱਥੇ ਜਾਏ ?   *Where shall he/she go?*
ਮੈਂ ਕੁਝ ਕਵਾਂ ?   *Shall/may I say something?*
ਅਸੀਂ ਕੀ ਕਰੀਏ ?   *What might we do?*

The examples of the future tense show that an action is to occur sometime in the future while the present subjunctive gives a sense that an action *may* happen. The past subjunctive expresses that an action might have happened in the past, but that it did not occur. It is formed in exactly the same way as the present imperfect tense which you learned in Unit 4, and, unlike the present subjunctive, is affected by gender:

past subjunctive

ਮੈਂ ਕਰਦਾ/ਕਰਦੀ
ਅਸੀਂ ਕਰਦੇ/ਕਰਦੀਆਂ
ਤੂੰ ਕਰਦਾ/ਕਰਦੀ
ਤੁਸੀਂ ਕਰਦੇ
ਇਹ/ਉਹ ਕਰਦਾ/ਕਰਦੀ
ਇਹ/ਉਹ ਕਰਦੇ/ਕਰਦੀਆਂ

The past subjunctive will be illustrated in the following section where conditional sentences will be introduced. The subjunctive is also used when there is a feeling of possibility, commonly expressed through perhaps ਸ਼ਾਇਦ or it is possible ਹੋ ਸਕਦਾ ਹੈ।

ਸ਼ਾਇਦ ਉਹ ਆਵੇ, ਸ਼ਾਇਦ ਨਾ ਆਵੇ *Perhaps he'll come, perhaps he won't come.*
ਹੋ ਸਕਦਾ ਹੈ ਕਿ ਬੱਚੇ ਬਾਹਰ ਹੋਣ   *It is possible that the children are outside.*

More complex sentences can be constructed by combining the present tense or present continuous tense to express the nature of the action in question such as *perhaps he might be coming* in which *coming* is in the continuous tense while the sense of possibility is expressed through the subjunctive form of ਹੋਣਾ which is ਹੋਣ.

ਸ਼ਾਇਦ ਮੁੰਡੇ ਗੁਜਰਾਤੀ ਸਿੱਖ ਰਹੇ ਹੋਣ *Perhaps the boys are learning Gujarati.*
ਸ਼ਾਇਦ ਪਿਤਾ ਜੀ ਆਉਂਦੇ ਹੋਣ   *Perhaps father might be coming.*

The subjunctive is also used in a number of other situations in which necessity, command or obligation are being expressed. Notice such instances in the following examples:

ਜ਼ਰੂਰੀ ਹੈ ਕਿ ਅਸੀਂ ਠੀਕ ਸਮੇਂ ਤੇ ਨਿਕਲੀਏ *It is necessary that we leave on time.*
ਉਹ ਨੂੰ ਦੱਸ ਕਿ ਚੁੱਪ ਰਵੇ !   *Tell him to be quiet!*

Conditional sentences

Conditional sentences (i.e. where an action is dependent on a *condition*) in Panjabi are formed by using a sequence of ਜੇ *if* and ਤਾਂ *then*. In English conditional sentences also follow a similar pattern: *if he comes, then I won't go*. In Panjabi this sentence would be ਜੇ ਉਹ ਆਏ ਗਾ ਤਾਂ ਮੈਂ ਨਹੀਂ ਜਾਵਾਂ ਗਾ. If the conditional action being referred to is in the future, such as in this example, the verb tense of the *if* clause will be in the future. However, when the action in an *if* clause is not definite or certain, it must be expressed in the subjunctive mood. In the following examples both the future tense and the subjunctive mood are used:

Future

ਜੇ ਉਹ ਆਏ ਗਾ ਤਾਂ ਮੈਂ ਸੌਂਵਾਂ ਗਾ   *If he comes (will come), then I'll sleep.*

Subjunctive

ਜੇ ਅਸੀਂ ਸੱਤ ਵਜੇ ਨਿਕਲੀਏ ਤਾਂ ਕਿੰਨੇ   *If we leave at 7 o'clock, (then) what time*
ਵਜੇ ਘਰ ਪਹੁੰਚਾਂ ਗੇ ?   *will we reach home?*
ਜੇ ਟੈਕਸੀ ਨਾ ਮਿਲੇ ਤਾਂ ਬਸ ਫੜੋ   *If you don't get a taxi, then catch a bus.*

The present tense can be used in the *if* clause when the action being referred to is in the past. In the first dialogue in this unit, Paul says to Jaspreet and Simran: ਜੇ ਅਸੀਂ ਪਹਿਲੇ ਮਿਲਦੇ ਤਾਂ ਅਸੀਂ ਇਕੱਠੇ ਘੁੰਮਦੇ meaning *If we had met before, then we would have travelled together.*

ਜੇ ਉਹ ਆਉਂਦਾ ਤਾਂ ਮੈਂ ਸੌਂਦਾ   *If he had come, I would have slept.*
ਜੇ ਤੁਸੀਂ ਸਾਡੇ ਨਾਲ ਹੁੰਦੇ ਤਾਂ ਜ਼ਿਆਦਾ   *If you had been with us, we would have*
ਮਜ਼ਾ ਆਉਂਦਾ   *enjoyed it more.*

ਵਿਆਖਿਆ   viaakhiaa   Commentary

Letter writing

Letter writing in Panjabi is similar to English. As *Dear* in English is used, in Panjabi ਪਿਆਰੇ (which translates literally as *dear* or *beloved*) is generally used to address people who are relatively familiar to the writer. For more formal letters ਪਿਆਰੇ is often too intimate an address, so ਮਾਨਯੋਗ (respected) followed by the name of the person or ਸ੍ਰੀਮਾਨ ਜੀ (Dear Sir) are often more appropriate when writing to someone not known to you.

Greetings (see Unit 1) such as ਸਤਿ ਸ੍ਰੀ ਅਕਾਲ, ਨਮਸਕਾਰ and ਅੱਸਲਾਮ ਅਲੈਕਮ are commonly placed after the initial address on the line below, according to the religion of the addressee. The body of the letter follows no specific rules. However, a letter is generally concluded with the equivalent of the appropriate endings such as ਪਿਆਰ ਨਾਲ *with affection*, ਤੁਹਾਡਾ ਦੋਸਤ *your friend,* ਤੁਹਾਡੀਆਂ ਬੇਟੀਆਂ *your daughters* (as Jaspreet and Simran finish their letter to their parents), or whichever ending is fitting.

Doaba

Jaspreet and Simrans's trip to Jalandhar is no surprise when considering the pattern of migration from Panjab. The doaba region of which Jalandhar is a central town, is the main area in India from which migration has taken place. People from this region can be found in the four corners of the world. In fact the 'doaba' dialect is what you are most likely to encounter if you are learning and using Panjabi in the west. It is often said that there is no family in the doaba without a relative in the USA, UK, Far East or the Gulf.

☑ ਅਭਿਆਸ   abhiaas   Exercises

After reading the dialogue and/or listening to the audio tape, try to do the following exercises.

1. Write in Panjabi

Make the following statements in Panjabi according to the directions in parentheses:

a. I have eaten (singular/male)
b. I have eaten (singular/female)
c. They had spoken (plural/male)
d. He had been speaking for ten minutes (singular/masculine)

2. Listening

Paul is at the bank changing some money. Listen to the dialogue between Paul and the bank teller on the audio tape. Answer the following questions about the dialogue:

ਪੌਲ ਕੋਲ ਕਿਹੜੇ ਦੇਸ਼ ਦੇ ਪੈਸੇ ਹਨ ?
ਪੌਲ ਕਿੰਨੇ ਪੈਸੇ ਬਦਲਣਾ ਚਾਹੁੰਦਾ ਹੈ ?
ਅੱਜ ਦਾ ਰੇਟ ਕੀ ਹੈ ?
ਕੀ ਰੁਪਇਆਂ ਦਾ ਰੇਟ ਕੱਲ੍ਹ ਤੋਂ ਘੱਟ ਹੈ ਜਾਂ ਵੱਧ ?
ਪੌਲ ਕੋਲ ਕਿਹੜਾ ਪਾਸਪੋਰਟ ਹੈ ?

3. Writing a postcard

You are writing a postcard to your friend Sonia about your stay in Panjab.
Some words are missing. Select the appropriate words from the list to
complete the postcard.

_____ ਸੋਨੀਆ, ਜੀ

ਸਤਿ ਸ੍ਰੀ ਅਕਾਲ। ਮੇਰੀ ਪੰਜਾਬ ਦੀ _____ ਅੱਛੀ

ਰਹੀ ਹੈ। ਮੈਂ ਬਹੁਤ _____ ਦੇਖੀਆਂ ਹਨ ਪਰ

_____ ਮੈਨੂੰ ਸਭ ਤੋਂ ਚੰਗਾ ਲੱਗਾ। ਉਸ ਦਾ ਕੋਈ

_____ ਨਹੀਂ। ਇੱਥੇ ਆ ਕੇ ਮੇਰੀ ਪੰਜਾਬੀ ਦੀ _____

ਵੱਧ ਗਈ ਹੈ। ਜੇ ਤੁਸੀਂ ਮੇਰੇ ਨਾਲ _____, _____

ਜ਼ਿਆਦਾ ਮਜ਼ਾ _____.

25 c./.   ਮਾਰਕ

To

Sonia Kaur
222 Carl Road
Apt 31
Marion, Ohio
43302 U.S.A

- ਤਾਂ   ■ ਜਗ੍ਹਾ   ■ ਪਿਆਰੇ   ■ ਹੁੰਦੇ   ■ ਫੇਰੀ   ■ ਮੁਕਾਬਲਾ
- ਸ਼ਬਦਾਵਲੀ   ■ ਆਉਂਦਾ   ■ ਹਰਿਮੰਦਰ ਸਾਹਿਬ

13 | ਵਿਆਹ ਦੀਆਂ ਰਸਮਾਂ
viaah deeaan rasmaan
Marriage customs

In this unit you will learn:

- more about Panjabi marriage customs
- how to tell the date and month of year
- how to express *sort of*, *rather*

Matrimonial advertisement ਵਿਆਹ ਸਬੰਧੀ viaah sabandhee

The following paragraph is a matrimonial advertisement taken from a widely read Panjabi newspaper in Britain called *Des Pardes* (*Home and Abroad*). The parents of a young man have placed the advertisement in order to find a partner for their son.

ਲੁਧਿਆਣੇ ਤੋਂ ਪਤਵੰਤੇ ਹਿੰਦੂ ਖਤਰੀ ਮਾਪਿਆਂ ਦੇ ਲੜਕੇ ਲਈ ਯੋਗ ਰਿਸ਼ਤੇ ਦੀ ਲੋੜ ਹੈ। ਲੜਕਾ ਪੜ੍ਹਿਆ ਲਿਖਿਆ, ਪੇਸ਼ਾਵਰ, ਸੱਚੀ ਮੁੱਚੀ ਸੁਹਣਾ ਤੇ ਨਰਮ ਸੁਭਾ ਦਾ ਹੈ। ਲੜਕੇ ਦਾ ਕੱਦ ੫ ਫੁੱਟ ੮ ਇੰਚ ਤੇ ਉਮਰ ੨੮ ਸਾਲ ਹੈ। ਲੜਕੀ ਪਤਲੀ, ਗੋਰੀ, ਸੁਹਣੀ, ਬ੍ਰਿਟਿਸ਼ ਸ਼ਹਿਰੀਅਤ ਵਾਲੀ, ਪੜ੍ਹੀ ਲਿਖੀ, ਵਿਹਾਰੀ ਨੌਕਰੀ ਤੇ ਲੱਗੀ ਹੋਣੀ ਚਾਹੀਦੀ ਹੈ। ਪੂਰਬ ਤੇ ਪੱਛਮ ਦੀਆਂ ਕਦਰਾਂ ਨੂੰ ਸਮਝਣ ਵਾਲੀ ਹੋਣੀ ਚਾਹੀਦੀ ਹੈ। ਲੜਕੀ ਦੀ ਉਮਰ ੨੫ ਸਾਲ ਤੋਂ ਵੱਧ ਨਾ ਹੋਵੇ। ਫੋਟੋ ਵਾਪਸ ਭੇਜ ਦਿੱਤੀ ਜਾਏ ਗੀ। ਤਲਾਕ ਸ਼ੁਦਾ ਕੁੜੀਆਂ ਨੂੰ ਲਿਖਣ ਦੀ ਲੋੜ ਨਹੀਂ। ਸੰਪਰਕ ਕਰੋ: Box number 2961 c/o ਦੇਸ ਪਰਦੇਸ।

Respectable Hindu Khatri parents from Ludhiana seek suitable match for their son. The boy is educated, a professional, genuinely handsome and kind natured. The boy is 5 ft 8 inches tall and he is 28 years old. The girl should be slim, fair, beautiful, a British citizen, educated and professionally employed. Should understand Eastern and Western values and be not more than 25 years of age. Photo returnable. Divorcees need not apply. Contact: Box number 2961 c/o Des Pardes.

ਸ਼ਬਦਾਵਲੀ   shab<u>d</u>aavalee   **Vocabulary**

ਪਤਵੰਤੇ	pa<u>t</u>van<u>te</u>	*respectable* (v.)
ਖਤਰੀ	kha<u>t</u>ree	*Khatri* (m./f.) (*caste*)
ਮਾਪਿਆਂ	maapiaa<u>n</u>	*parents* (m.)
ਰਿਸ਼ਤਾ	rish<u>t</u>aa	*(marriage) relation* (m.)
ਜੋਗ	yog	*suitable*
ਲੋੜ	lorh	*require, necessity, wanted*
ਪੜ੍ਹਿਆ ਲਿਖਿਆ	parhhiaa likhiaa	*educated* (v.)
ਪੇਸ਼ਾਵਰ	peshaavar	*professional* (m./f.)
ਸੱਚੀ ਮੁੱਚੀ	sachchee muchchee	*genuinely*
ਸੁਹਣਾ	suhnhaa	*handsome* (v.)
ਨਰਮ ਸੁਭਾ	naram subhaa	*kind natured* (m.)
ਕੱਦ	ka<u>dd</u>	*height* (m.)
ਉਮਰ	umar	*age* (f.)
ਪਤਲੀ	pa<u>t</u>lee	*thin, slim* (v.)
ਗੋਰੀ	goree	*fair, white* (v.)
ਸ਼ਹਿਰੀਅਤ	shahireea<u>t</u>	*citizen* (f.)
ਵਿਹਾਰੀ ਨੌਕਰੀ	vihaaree naukaree	*professionally employed* (f.)
ਨੌਕਰੀ	naukaree	*job, employment* (f.)
ਪੂਰਬ	poorab	*east* (m.)
ਪੱਛਮ	pa<u>chch</u>am	*west* (m.)
ਕਦਰਾਂ	ka<u>d</u>raa<u>n</u>	*values* (f.)
ਵਾਪਸ	vaapas	*return*
ਭੇਜਣਾ	bhejnhaa	*to send*
ਤਲਾਕ	<u>t</u>alaak	*divorce* (m.)
ਸੰਪਰਕ	sa<u>n</u>parak	*contact* (m.)

ਅਭਿਆਸ   abhiaas   **Exercises**

After reading the passage and/or listening to the audio tape, try to do the following exercises.

1. Answer the questions about the passage

a. ਕੀ ਲੜਕੇ ਦੇ ਮਾਪੇ ਹਿੰਦੂ ਹਨ ?

b. ਕੀ ਲੜਕਾ ਪੜ੍ਹਿਆ ਲਿਖਿਆ ਹੈ ?

c. ਕੀ ਲੜਕੀ ੨੦ ਸਾਲ ਤੋਂ ਘੱਟ ਹੋਵੇ ?

2. Reply to matrimonial advertisement

The following is a reply to the matrimonial advertisement. From the personal information given, decide whether or not the couple are a suitable match (i.e. they have at least five of the qualities that were specified in the advertisement). It's up to you to decide!

> Box number 2961 c/o ਦੇਸ ਪਰਦੇਸ:
>
> ਦਿੱਲੀ ਤੋਂ ਮਾਪੇ ਆਪਣੀ ਲੜਕੀ ਲਈ ਰਿਸ਼ਤਾ ਲੱਭ ਰਹੇ ਹਨ। ਲੜਕੀ ਸੁਹਣੀ ਤੇ ਪਤਲੀ ਹੈ। ਪੜ੍ਹੀ ਲਿਖੀ ਹੈ ਪਰ ਨੌਕਰੀ ਨਹੀਂ ਕਰਦੀ ਹੈ। ਭਾਰਤੀ ਸ਼ਹਿਰੀਅਤ ਵਾਲੀ ਹੈ। ਪੂਰਬ ਤੇ ਪੱਛਮ ਦੀਆਂ ਕਦਰਾਂ ਸਮਝਣ ਵਾਲੀ ਹੈ ਅਤੇ ਉਸ ਦੀ ਉਮਰ ੨੯ ਸਾਲਾਂ ਦੀ ਹੈ। ਵਿਆਹ ਇੱਕ ਵਾਰੀ ਹੋ ਚੁਕਾ ਹੈ।

3. Say or write in the correct word order

a. ਵਿਹਾਰੀ ਨੌਕਰੀ ਹੈ ਲੜਕੀ ਚਾਹੀਦੀ ਤੇ ਹੋਣੀ ਲੱਗੀ
b. ਤਲਾਕ ਸ਼ੁਦਾ ਲਿਖਣ ਨੂੰ ਲੜਕੀਆਂ ਲੋੜ ਦੀ ਨਹੀਂ
c. ਉਮਰ ਦੀ ਲੜਕੀ ੨੫ ਸਾਲ ਹੋਵੇ ਵੱਧ ਨਾ ਤੋਂ
d. ਲੜਕਾ ਸੁਹਣਾ ਸੱਚੀ ਮੁੱਚੀ ਹੈ

🔊 A wedding invitation

🖾 ਗੱਲ ਬਾਤ ਸੱਦਾ ਪੱਤਰ

gall baat saddaa pattar

Debra has received an invitation to attend a Panjabi wedding. Since she has never been to a Panjabi wedding, she has gone to her friend Darshana to ask her what the ceremonies will be like.

ਡੈਬਰਾ   ਮੇਰੀ ਸਹੇਲੀ ਜੀਤੀ ਦੇ ਵਿਆਹ ਦਾ ਸੱਦਾ ਪੱਤਰ ਆਇਆ ਹੈ। ਵਿਆਹ ੨੯
            ਜਨਵਰੀ ਨੂੰ ਹੈ। ਮੈਨੂੰ ਮਹਿੰਦੀ ਬਾਰੇ ਕੁਝ ਦੱਸ।
ਦਰਸ਼ਨਾ   ਮਹਿੰਦੀ ਪਰਵਾਰਕ ਰਸਮ ਹੈ। ਕੁੜੀਆਂ ਆਪਣੇ ਹੱਥਾਂ ਤੇ ਮਹਿੰਦੀ ਲਗਾਉਂਦੀਆਂ
                                        ਹਨ। ਕਈ ਤਰ੍ਹਾਂ ਦੇ ਨਮੂਨੇ
ਬਣਾਦੀਆਂ ਹਨ ਅਤੇ ਵਿਆਹ ਦੇ ਗੀਤ ਵੀ ਗਾਏ ਜਾਂਦੇ   ਹਨ।
ਡੈਬਰਾ   ਕੀ ਆਦਮੀ ਇਸ ਰਸਮ ਵਿਚ ਸ਼ਾਮਲ ਹੁੰਦੇ ਹਨ ?
ਦਰਸ਼ਨਾ   ਨਹੀਂ, ਇਹ ਕੇਵਲ ਔਰਤਾਂ ਲਈ ਹੈ। ਆਦਮੀ ਬਰਾਤ ਵਿਚ ਸ਼ਾਮਲ ਹੁੰਦੇ ਹਨ।
ਡੈਬਰਾ   ਬਰਾਤ ਦਾ ਕੀ ਮਤਲਬ ਹੈ ?

ਦਰਸ਼ਨਾ	ਬਰਾਤ ਵਿਚ ਲਾੜੇ ਦੇ ਰਿਸ਼ਤੇਦਾਰ ਅਤੇ ਦੋਸਤ ਸ਼ਾਮਲ ਹੁੰਦੇ ਹਨ। ਇਹ ਛੋਟਾ ਜੇਹਾ ਜਲੂਸ ਹੁੰਦਾ ਹੈ। ਮੁੰਡਾ ਘੋੜੀ ਤੇ ਚੜ੍ਹਿਆ ਹੁੰਦਾ ਹੈ ਅਤੇ ਅੱਗੇ ਅੱਗੇ ਵਾਜੇ ਵਾਲੇ ਹੁੰਦੇ ਹਨ। ਜਾਂਝੀ ਭੰਗੜਾ ਪਾਉਂਦੇ ਹਨ।
ਡੇਬਰਾ	ਸੱਦਾ ਪੱਤਰ ਤੇ ਲਿਖਿਆ ਹੋਇਆ ਹੈ ਕਿ ਡੋਲੀ ਚਾਰ ਵਜੇ ਤੁਰੇਗੀ। ਇਹ ਕੀ ਰਸਮ ਹੈ ?
ਦਰਸ਼ਨਾ	ਡੋਲੀ ਦਾ ਮਤਲਬ ਹੈ ਕਿ ਕੁੜੀ ਦਾ ਪੇਕੇ ਛੱਡ ਕੇ ਸਹੁਰੇ ਜਾਣਾ। ਇਹ ਮੌਕਾ ਖ਼ੁਸ਼ੀ ਤੇ ਗ਼ਮੀ ਦਾ ਮੇਲ ਹੈ।
ਡੇਬਰਾ	ਇਹ ਗੱਲ ਬੜੀ ਦਿਲਚਸਪ ਲੱਗਦੀ ਹੈ। ਮੈਂ ਵਿਆਹ ਤੇ ਜਾਣ ਲਈ ਉਤਸੁਕ ਹਾਂ।

Debra *My friend Jeeti's wedding invitation has come. The wedding is on the 28th of January. Tell me something about* **mehndi**.

Darshana **Mehndi** *is a family custom. Girls put henna on their hands. They draw different designs and wedding songs are sung.*

Debra *Are men present during this ritual?*

Darshana *No. This is just for the women. Men are present at the* **baraat**.

Debra *What is the meaning of* **baraat**?

Darshana *At the* **baraat** *the groom's relatives and friends are present. This is a sort of small procession. The boy is on a mare and in front are some musicians. The wedding party performs* **bhangra** *(a folk dance of Panjab).*

Debra *It's written on the invitation that the* **doli** *will leave at four o'clock. What is this custom?*

Darshana **Doli** *means that the girl leaves her family's home to go to her in-laws. This time is a happy and sad occasion.*

Debra *This seems interesting. I look forward to going to the wedding!*

ਸ਼ਬਦਾਵਲੀ   shab<u>d</u>aavalee   Vocabulary

ਸਹੇਲੀ	sahelee	*friend* (f.)
ਸੱਦਾ ਪੱਤਰ	sa<u>dd</u>aa pa<u>tt</u>ar	*invitation* (m.)
ਮਹਿੰਦੀ	mahi<u>nd</u>ee	*henna* (f.)
ਜਾਣਨਾ	jaanhnaa	*to know*
ਆਪਣਾ	aapnhaa	*one's own*
ਪਰਵਾਰਕ	parvaarak	*family (relating to family)*
ਰਸਮ	rasam	*custom, ritual* (f.)
ਕਈ ਤਰ੍ਹਾਂ	kaee <u>t</u>ar-h-aa<u>n</u>	*different types*
ਨਮੂਨਾ	namoonaa	*pattern, design* (m.)
ਗੀਤ	gee<u>t</u>	*song* (m.)
ਗਾਣਾ	gaanhaa	*to sing*

ਸ਼ਾਮਲ	shaamal	to be present, to join or participate
ਬਰਾਤ	baraat	procession of the groom's relatives and friends (f.)
ਮਤਲਬ	matlab	meaning, definition (m.)
ਲਾੜਾ	laarhaa	groom (m.)
ਰਿਸ਼ਤੇਦਾਰ	rishtedaar	relatives (m./f.)
ਜਿਹਾ	jihaa	sort of, rather
ਜਲੂਸ	jaloos	procession, parade (m.)
ਘੋੜੀ	ghorhee	mare (f.)
ਚੜ੍ਹਨਾ	charhhnaa	to be upon, to ride
ਵਾਜੇ ਵਾਲੇ	vaaje vaale	band of musicians (m.)
ਜਾਂਞੀ	jaannjee	members of groom's wedding party (m./f.)
ਭੰਗੜਾ	bhangrhaa	bhangra (m.) (style of Panjabi dance) (see Commentary Unit 16)
ਡੋਲੀ	dolee	ceremony (f.) bidding farewell to the bride (see Commentary)
ਤੁਰਨਾ	turnaa	to walk, to depart, to leave
ਪੇਕੇ	peke	bride's family, bride's parents (m.)
ਛੱਡਨਾ	chaddnaa	to leave
ਸਹੁਰੇ	sahure	in-laws (m.)
ਮੌਕਾ	maukaa	opportunity, occasion (m.)
ਖ਼ੁਸ਼ੀ	khushee	happiness (f.)
ਗ਼ਮੀ	ghamee	sadness (f.)
ਮੇਲ	mel	meeting, combination (m.)
ਦਿਲਚਸਪ	dilchasp	interesting
ਉਤਸੁਕ	utsuk	anxious, awaiting

ਅਭਿਆਸ abhiaas Exercises

After reading the dialogue and/or listening to the audio tape, try to do the following exercises.

1. Match the questions with the correct answer

1. ਮਹਿੰਦੀ ਦੀ ਰਸਮ ਕੀ ਹੈ ?
2. ਵਿਆਹ ਕਿਸ ਤਾਰੀਖ਼ ਨੂੰ ਹੈ ?
3. ਬਰਾਤ ਵਿਚ ਕੌਣ ਸ਼ਾਮਲ ਹੁੰਦਾ ਹੈ?
4. ਡੋਲੀ ਕੀ ਹੁੰਦੀ ਹੈ ?

a. ਵਿਆਹ ੨੯ ਜਨਵਰੀ ਨੂੰ ਹੈ
b. ਕੁੜੀਆਂ ਆਪਣੇ ਹੱਥਾਂ ਤੇ ਮਹਿੰਦੀ ਲਗਾਉਂਦੀਆਂ ਹਨ
c. ਕੁੜੀ ਦਾ ਪੇਕੇ ਛੱਡ ਕੇ ਸਹੁਰੇ ਜਾਣ ਨੂੰ ਡੋਲੀ ਕਿਹਾ ਜਾਂਦਾ ਹੈ
d. ਲੜਕੇ ਦੇ ਦੋਸਤ ਅਤੇ ਰਿਸ਼ਤੇਦਾਰ ਸ਼ਾਮਲ ਹੁੰਦੇ ਹਨ

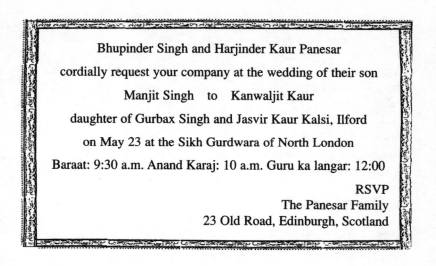

Bhupinder Singh and Harjinder Kaur Panesar

cordially request your company at the wedding of their son

Manjit Singh   to   Kanwaljit Kaur

daughter of Gurbax Singh and Jasvir Kaur Kalsi, Ilford

on May 23 at the Sikh Gurdwara of North London

Baraat: 9:30 a.m. Anand Karaj: 10 a.m. Guru ka langar: 12:00

RSVP
The Panesar Family
23 Old Road, Edinburgh, Scotland

2. Answer the questions about the wedding invitation

a. ਮੁੰਡੇ ਦੇ ਮਾਪੇ ਕਿੱਥੇ ਰਹਿੰਦੇ ਹਨ ?
b. ਕੁੜੀ ਦੇ ਮਾਪੇ ਕਿੱਥੋਂ ਦੇ ਹਨ ?
c. ਮੁੰਡੇ ਦਾ ਨਾਮ ਕੀ ਹੈ ?
d. ਕੁੜੀ ਦਾ ਨਾਮ ਕੀ ਹੈ ?
e. ਕੁੜੀ ਦੇ ਮਾਪਿਆਂ ਦੇ ਨਾਮ ਕੀ ਹਨ ?
f. ਵਿਆਹ ਕਿਹੜੇ ਸ਼ਹਿਰ ਵਿਚ ਹੋ ਰਿਹਾ ਹੈ ?
g. ਵਿਆਹ ਕਿਹੜੀ ਤਾਰੀਖ਼ ਨੂੰ ਹੈ ?
h. ਬਰਾਤ ਕਿੰਨੇ ਵਜੇ ਤੁਰੇਗੀ ?
i. ਅਨੰਦ ਕਾਰਜ ਕਦੋਂ ਸ਼ੁਰੂ ਹੋਣਾ ਹੈ ?
j. ਗੁਰੂ ਕਾ ਲੰਗਰ ਕਿੰਨੇ ਵਜੇ ਵਰਤੇ ਗਾ ?

ੴ ਬੋਲੀ ਬਾਰੇ   bolee baare   Language points

Participial uses

A participle is a verb which is used to describe an object or an action. Therefore, participle constructions in Panjabi can either be used adjectively to describe nouns or adverbially to describe actions. You will remember from the matrimonial advertisement that the boy is described as *educated*. In Panjabi this was expressed as **ਪੜ੍ਹਿਆ ਲਿਖਿਆ**. Both verbs **ਪੜ੍ਹਨਾ**

and ਲਿਖਣਾਂ are combined in their perfect forms in agreement with ਲੜਕਾ. Similarly, the prospective girl was said to be *educated*, expressed as ਪੜ੍ਹੀ ਲਿਖੀ, also showing agreement with the object being described. Often, the perfect forms of ਹੋਣਾ can also be used to strengthen the participial expression. Here are some more examples of how the participle can be used in Panjabi:

Adjective participles

ਮੈਂ ਉਬਲੇ ਹੋਏ ਅੰਡੇ ਨਹੀਂ ਖਾਂਦਾ	*I don't eat boiled eggs.*
ਉਹ ਬੈਠਾ ਹੋਇਆ ਆਦਮੀ ਕੌਣ ਹੈ ?	*Who is that man sitting down (i.e. seated)?*
ਮਾਤਾ ਜੀ ਨੇ ਡਰੀ ਹੋਈ ਕੁੜੀ ਨੂੰ ਚੁੱਕ ਲਿਆ	*Mum picked up the scared girl.*

Adverbial participles

ਉਹ ਮੁਸਕਰਾਂਦਾ ਹੋਇਆ ਲਤੀਫ਼ਾ ਸੁਣਾ ਰਿਹਾ ਸੀ	*He was telling a joke smilingly.*

Another use of the participle is in order to emphasise the on-going nature or repetitiveness of the action being described. This can be done in two ways: by repeating the verb in the simple present tense or by using the past participle with a form of ਜਾਣਾ, both forms agreeing with the subject.

ਪੜ੍ਹਦੇ ਪੜ੍ਹਦੇ ਅਸੀਂ ਥੱਕ ਗਏ ਹਾਂ	*We are tired from constantly studying.*
ਰਸਤੇ ਵਿਚ ਜਾਂਦੇ ਜਾਂਦੇ ਮੈਨੂੰ ਮਿਲਣਾ	*As you go (along) the way, come and see me.*
ਛੋਟੀ ਲੜਕੀ ਬੋਲੀ ਜਾਂਦੀ ਹੈ	*The little girl keeps on talking.*

The particle ਜਿਹਾ

ਜਿਹਾ is a particle which is added after an adjective in order to give it a modest or diluted sense. In English the sense of a description is diluted in a number of different ways, most commonly by using such words as rather, sort of, quite, and the suffix -ish. The form of ਜਿਹਾ is affected by the gender and number of the noun being described and can therefore also appear in the following forms: ਜਿਹੀ, ਜਿਹੇ and ਜਿਹੀਆਂ.

ਛੋਟਾ ਜਿਹਾ ਘਰ	*rather a small house.*
ਥੋੜ੍ਹਾ ਜਿਹਾ	*quite a small (amount).*
ਪੁਰਾਣੀ ਜਿਹੀ ਗੱਡੀ	*an old-ish car.*

The opposite of ਜਿਹਾ, in this sense, is ਸਾਰਾ. This is used to exaggerate rather than dilute a description, such as in Unit 11 when the booking clerk is telling the girls how popular the train to Amritsar, Shan-e-Panjab, is: ਬਹੁਤ ਸਾਰੇ ਸੈਲਾਨੀ ਇਸ ਗੱਡੀ ਵਿਚ ਸਫ਼ਰ ਕਰਦੇ ਹਨ *A lot of tourists travel on this train.*

The particle -ਜਿਹਾ can also follow a noun in order to give the sense *like*. Therefore, the noun preceding -ਜਿਹਾ represents what the description is being likened to. For example:

ਪਟਾਕਾ -ਜਿਹਾ   *like a firecracker.*

When asking the question *what sort of?* or *what is it like?* then ਕਿਹੋ is combined with ਜਿਹਾ.

ਕਿਹੋ ਜਿਹਾ ਮਕਾਨ ?   *what sort of house?*
ਕਿਹੋ ਜਿਹੇ ਕਪੜੇ ?   *what sort of clothes?*

Reflexive adjectives and pronouns

In English *myself* and *themselves* are reflexive pronouns indicating that the action is directed towards or belongs to the subject of the sentence. In Panjabi the reflexive adjective ਆਪਣਾ means *one's own* and is defined by the noun or pronoun being affected by the reflexive nature of the sentence. Like other adjectives, it also changes according to the gender and number of the object that it is describing as well as in the oblique form.

ਉਹ ਆਪਣੇ ਘਰ ਵਿਚ ਰਹਿੰਦਾ ਹੈ   *He lives in his own house.*
ਉਹ ਆਪਣੇ ਭਰਾ ਨਾਲ ਆਇਆ ਹੈ   *He has come with his (own) brother*
ਹਰ ਚੀਜ਼ ਆਪਣੀ ਜਗ੍ਹਾ ਤੇ ਹੋਣੀ ਚਾਹੀਦੀ ਹੈ   *Everything should be in its proper place.*
ਆਪਣੀਆਂ ਲੜਕੀਆਂ ਕੀ ਕਰਦੀਆਂ ਹਨ ?   *What do your (own) daughters do?*

Reflexive pronouns, unlike reflexive adjectives, do not rely upon another noun or adjective to be defined. If you recall from Unit 2, pronouns were introduced as naming words. The reflexive pronouns, in a similar way, are also naming words which are used to represent a person. The most common reflexive pronoun is ਆਪ which translates as *by oneself*. ਖ਼ੁਦ which is borrowed from Persian, can also be used to give the same sense. Note the following examples:

ਮੈਂ ਇਹ ਕੰਮ ਆਪ ਕਰਾਂ ਗਾ   *I will do this work myself.*
ਮੈਂ ਸਾਰਾ ਖਾਣਾ ਖ਼ੁਦ ਬਣਾਇਆ ਹੈ   *I have made all the food myself.*
ਉਹ ਨੇ ਆਪ ਜਾ ਕੇ ਫਲ ਖ਼ਰੀਦਿਆ   *She went and bought fruit herself.*

The reflexive adjective ਆਪਣਾ and the reflexive pronoun ਆਪ can be combined to give another meaning: *on one's own* or *without anyone's help* ਆਪਣੇ ਆਪ.

ਕਿਰਨ ਆਪਣੇ ਆਪ ਪੰਜਾਬੀ ਪੜ੍ਹਦੀ ਹੈ   *Kiran studies Panjabi on her own*
                   (without anyone else's help).
ਸੰਜੀਵ ਆਪਣੇ ਆਪ ਨੂੰ ਬਹੁਤ ਸਮਝਦਾ ਹੈ *Sanjeev thinks highly of himself.*

ਆਪਸ, meaning *fraternity*, is used to express situations of mutuality or reciprocity with the postposition ਵਿਚ to form *among or between.*

ਅਸੀਂ ਆਪਸ ਵਿਚ ਗੱਲ ਕਰ ਰਹੇ ਸੀ   *We were talking among ourselves.*
ਬੱਚੇ ਆਪਸ ਵਿਚ ਖੇਡ ਰਹੇ ਸਨ   *The children were playing among*
                   themselves.

Finally, ਆਪਾਂ is used specifically with a group of people otherwise referred to as ਅਸੀਂ *us*. Therefore, the new meaning given by the reflexive pronoun is *let's* or *all of us.*

ਆਪਾਂ ਚਲੀਏ   let's go

ਵਿਆਖਿਆ   viaakhiaa   Commentary

1. What's the date today?

When asking someone today's date in Panjabi, you would say ਅੱਜ ਕੀ ਤਾਰੀਖ਼ ਹੈ ? This is different from asking someone the day or day of the week, as explained in Unit 7 with the words ਦਿਨ *day* and ਵਾਰ *day of the week*. ਤਾਰੀਖ਼ literally means *date* and the reply to your question would be a numerical figure of the date accompanied by the month of the year: ਅੱਜ ਅਠਾਰ੍ਹਾਂ ਜੂਨ ਹੈ. *Today is the 18th of June.* It is also not uncommon to use ordinal numbers for the first three or four days of the month: ਅੱਜ ਮਹੀਨੇ ਦੀ ਤੀਜੀ ਤਾਰੀਖ਼ ਹੈ. *It is the third day of the month.*

Months of the year

ਜਨਵਰੀ	janvaree	*January*
ਫਰਵਰੀ	farvaree	*February*
ਮਾਰਚ	maarch	*March*
ਅਪਰੈਲ	aprail	*April*
ਮਈ	maee	*May*
ਜੂਨ	joon	*June*
ਜੁਲਾਈ	julaaee	*July*
ਅਗਸਤ	aga<u>st</u>	*August*
ਸਤੰਬਰ	sata<u>n</u>bar	*September*
ਅਕਤੂਬਰ	ak<u>t</u>oobar	*October*
ਨਵੰਬਰ	nava<u>n</u>bar	*November*
ਦਸੰਬਰ	<u>d</u>asa<u>n</u>bar	*December*

The four seasons of the year in English are spring, autumn, winter and summer which describe the weather of the period. In Panjabi there are terms less influenced by English (as the months of the year) to denote the seasons which, in Pakistan and North India, are quite distinctive.

ਬਸੰਤ	basa<u>nt</u>	*spring*
ਗਰਮੀ	garmee	*summer*
ਬਰਸਾਤ	barsaa<u>t</u>	*rainy season*
ਪੱਤਝੜ	pa<u>tt</u>jharh	*autumn*
ਸਰਦੀ	sar<u>d</u>ee	*winter*

2. Marriage customs

Panjabi weddings are lavish affairs with numbers of guests usually in the hundreds, sometimes in the thousands, and large amounts of food and decoration. Weddings are seen as social occasions and signify the coming together of two families rather than of two individuals, as is traditionally the case in western marriages. It is this aspect of Panjabi – and most other South Asian – weddings that leads to them often being labelled as 'arranged'. Usually the families arrange the weddings of their offspring, in that families are present at the meeting of the man and woman. There is a huge variety in the process of arranging marriages from one extreme where the man and woman do not meet until the wedding day (which is rare in the diaspora) to a situation where the man and woman see each other and make their own decision about whether they wish to marry or not. It is this latter version that is more usual in the diaspora.

When families are involved in the selection of the partner, they take into account a range of factors, such as those outlined in the advert at the beginning of this unit. Alongside education and other social aspects, the advert specifies a particular caste group, in this case **Khatri**. Caste is a form of social grouping and organisation which is based upon occupational traditions as well as kinship ties. Even in the diaspora, caste affiliations are still adhered to and most advertisements of this kind carry some sort of caste affiliation. Some common castes are **Jat, Ramgharia** and **Brahmin**.

The wedding ceremonies that we described in this unit are religion-neutral in the Panjabi context and most Sikh, Hindu and Muslim weddings share these customs. The actual wedding vows, however, are of a religious nature and for Sikhs this is called the **Anand Karaj**, for Hindus it is the **Vivaah** and for Muslims the **Nikah**. For all Panjabis, however, weddings are major social events and involve spectacles of emotion, family participation and financial expenditure.

A common Panjabi wedding will involve a **mehndi** ritual, where the bride is adorned on her hands and feet with exquisite patterns in dye. The groom arrives on horseback with his relatives at the bride's house and the wedding ceremony takes place here. The ceremony is followed by a feast. The saddest occasion is when the bride is seen off at the end of the ceremony. This is called the **doli** and often involves protracted crying and sadness. Each of the events of the Panjabi wedding is accompanied by music.

ਅਭਿਆਸ   abhiaas   Exercises

After reading the dialogue and/or listening to the audio tape, try to do the
following exercises.

1. Write a matrimonial advertisement

Prepare a matrimonial advertisement in Panjabi on behalf of the parents
of a girl giving the following information:

a. The parents are Sikhs living in London.
b. The girl is beautiful, educated and working in a bank.
c. The girl is 25 years of age and is 5' 3" tall.
d. The boy should be from a respectable family, be a British citizen and
   professionally employed.

2. Complete the sentences

Use the appropriate forms of ਆਪਣਾ and ਜਿਹਾ.

a. ਥੋੜ੍ਹਾ _____ ਹੋਰ ਦੁੱਧ ਦੇਵੋ।   *Give me a little more milk.*
b. ਮੈਂ _____ ਪਿਤਾ ਜੀ ਨਾਲ ਆਇਆ ਹਾਂ।   *I have come with my father.*
c. ਮੇਰੀਆਂ _____ ਭੈਣਾਂ ਵਿਆਹ ਤੇ ਨਹੀਂ ਗਈਆਂ।   *My own sisters didn't go to
                                                      the wedding.*
d. ਉਹ ਕਿਹੋ _____ ਲੋਕ ਸਨ ?   *What sort of people were they?*

3. Fill in the blanks

Use the appropriate participle expressions.

a. _____ _____ ਅੰਡੇ   *boiled eggs*
b. _____ _____ ਮੁੰਡਾ   (*scared boy*)
c. _____ _____ ਲੜਕਾ   (*educated boy*)

4. Listening

The following passage has been recorded on the audio tape. Listen to it
and then answer the questions in Panjabi.

ਡੇਬਰਾ ਨੂੰ ਜੀਤੀ ਦੇ ਵਿਆਹ ਦਾ ਸੱਦਾ ਪੱਤਰ ਆਇਆ ਹੈ। ਵਿਆਹ ੨੮ ਜਨਵਰੀ ਨੂੰ ਹੈ। ਡੇਬਰਾ
ਪਹਿਲੇ ਕਦੇ ਕਿਸੇ ਪੰਜਾਬੀ ਵਿਆਹ ਤੇ ਨਹੀਂ ਗਈ। ਉਹ ਵਿਆਹ ਦੀਆਂ ਰਸਮਾਂ ਬਾਰੇ ਜਾਣਨਾ
ਚਾਹੁੰਦੀ ਹੈ। ਇਸ ਲਈ ਉਹ ਆਪਣੀ ਸਹੇਲੀ ਦਰਸ਼ਨਾ ਕੋਲ ਗਈ ਹੈ।

a. ਵਿਆਹ ਦਾ ਸੱਦਾ ਪੱਤਰ ਕਿਸ ਨੂੰ ਆਇਆ ਹੈ ?
b. ਵਿਆਹ ਕਿਸ ਦਾ ਹੈ ?
c. ਕੀ ਡੇਬਰਾ ਕਦੀ ਪੰਜਾਬੀ ਵਿਆਹ ਤੇ ਗਈ ਹੈ ?
d. ਵਿਆਹ ਕਿਹੜੀ ਤਾਰੀਖ਼ ਹੈ ?
e. ਡੇਬਰਾ ਦਰਸ਼ਨਾ ਕੋਲ ਕਿਉਂ ਗਈ ਹੈ ?

14 | ਉਹਨਾਂ ਨੇ ਮੇਰੇ ਬਾਰੇ ਕੀ ਕਿਹਾ ਸੀ ?

uhnaa<u>n</u> ne mere baare kee kihaa see?

What did they say about me?

In this unit you will learn:

- how to have a conversation about school
- how to speak with a police officer and a social worker
- how to use purpose clauses with *so that*

1 Did you meet my class teacher?

ਗੱਲ ਬਾਤ ੧ ਕੀ ਤੁਸੀਂ ਮੇਰੇ ਸ਼੍ਰੇਣੀ ਅਧਿਆਪਕ ਨੂੰ ਮਿਲੇ ਸੀ ?

gall baa<u>t</u> 1 kee <u>t</u>usee<u>n</u> mere shrenhee a<u>dh</u>iaapak noo<u>n</u> mile see?

Mr Lall has just attended his son Ramesh's parents' evening at his school. Mr Lall has come home and is talking to Ramesh.

ਰਮੇਸ਼	ਪਾਪਾ ਜੀ ! ਕੀ ਤੁਸੀਂ ਮੇਰੇ ਸ਼੍ਰੇਣੀ ਅਧਿਆਪਕ ਨੂੰ ਮਿਲੇ ਸੀ ?
ਮਿਸਟਰ ਲਾਲ	ਹਾਂ, ਮੈਂ ਉਸ ਤੋਂ ਇਲਾਵਾ ਤੇਰੇ ਦੂਜੇ ਮਜ਼ਮੂਨਾਂ ਦੇ ਅਧਿਆਪਕਾਂ ਨੂੰ ਵੀ ਮਿਲਿਆ ਸੀ।
ਰਮੇਸ਼	ਉਹਨਾਂ ਨੇ ਮੇਰੇ ਬਾਰੇ ਕੀ ਕਿਹਾ ਸੀ ?
ਮਿਸਟਰ ਲਾਲ	ਹਿਸਾਬ ਦੇ ਅਧਿਆਪਕ ਨੇ ਕਿਹਾ ਕਿ ਤੂੰ ਘਰ ਦਾ ਕੰਮ ਕਰਨ ਵਿਚ ਲਾਪਰਵਾਹ ਹੈਂ ਅਤੇ ਕਲਾਸ ਵਿਚ ਗਾਲੜੀ ਹੈਂ।
ਰਮੇਸ਼	ਉਹ ਮੈਨੂੰ ਪਸੰਦ ਨਹੀ ਕਰਦਾ। ਅੰਗਰੇਜ਼ੀ ਦੇ ਅਧਿਆਪਕ ਨੇ ਕੀ ਕਿਹਾ ?
ਮਿਸਟਰ ਲਾਲ	ਉਸ ਨੇ ਕਿਹਾ ਕਿ ਰਮੇਸ਼ ਵਿਚ ਲਿਆਕਤ ਹੈ ਪਰ ਉਹ ਵਰਤਦਾ ਨਹੀਂ।
ਰਮੇਸ਼	ਉਹ ਸਾਨੂੰ ਚੰਗੀ ਤਰ੍ਹਾਂ ਪੜ੍ਹਾਂਦਾ ਨਹੀਂ।
ਮਿਸਟਰ ਲਾਲ	ਖ਼ੈਰ ! ਤੈਨੂੰ ਪੜ੍ਹਾਈ ਵਿਚ ਮਿਹਨਤ ਕਰਨੀ ਚਾਹੀਦੀ ਹੈ ਤਾਂ ਕਿ ਤੂੰ ਚੰਗੇ ਗਰੇਡ ਲੈ ਕੇ ਡਾਕਟਰ ਬਣ ਸਕੇਂ।

Ramesh	*Dad! Did you meet my class teacher?*
Mr Lall	*Yes and apart from him I also met your other subject teachers.*

Ramesh	*What did they say about me?*
Mr Lall	*The maths teacher said that you were careless in doing your homework and talkative in class.*
Ramesh	*He doesn't like me. What did the English teacher say?*
Mr Lall	*He said that Ramesh has the ability but does not use it.*
Ramesh	*He does not teach us properly.*
Mr Lall	*Anyway! You should study hard so that you get good grades and can become a doctor.*

ਸ਼ਬਦਾਵਲੀ   shab<u>d</u>aavalee   Vocabulary

ਸ਼੍ਰੇਣੀ	shrenhee	*class* (f.)
ਅਧਿਆਪਕ	adhiaapak	*teacher* (m./f.)
ਤੋਂ ਇਲਾਵਾ	<u>t</u>on ilaavaa	*apart from, besides*
ਦੂਜੇ	<u>d</u>ooje	*others*
ਮਜ਼ਮੂਨਾਂ	mazmoonaa<u>n</u>	*subjects* (m.)
ਹਿਸਾਬ	hisaab	*maths* (m.)
ਘਰ ਦਾ ਕੰਮ	ghar <u>d</u>aa kan<u>m</u>	*homework* (m.)
ਲਾ ਪਰਵਾਹ	laa parvaah	*careless*
ਗਾਲੜੀ	gaalrhee	*talkative*
ਲਿਆਕਤ	liaaka<u>t</u>	*ability* (f.)
ਵਰਤਣਾ	var<u>t</u>nhaa	*to use*
ਤਰ੍ਹਾਂ	<u>t</u>ar-h-aa<u>n</u>	*way, style*
ਪੜ੍ਹਾਉਣਾ	parhhaaunhaa	*to teach*
ਖ਼ੈਰ	<u>kh</u>air	*anyway*
ਪੜ੍ਹਾਈ	parhhaaee	*studies* (f.)
ਤਾਂ ਕਿ	taa<u>n</u> ki	*so that*
ਗਰੇਡ	gared	*grade* (m.)
ਬਣਨਾ	banhnaa	*to become*

ਅਭਿਆਸ   abhiaas   Exercises

After reading the dialogue and/or listening to the audio tape, try to do the following exercises.

1. Insert the missing vowels

The vowel signs in the following sentences are missing. Rewrite them after inserting the vowels and joining the letters.

a. ਪਪ ਜ ! ਕ /ਤ ਸੰ /ਮ ਰ /ਸੂ ਣ /ਅ ਧ ਆ ਪ ਕ / ਨੰ /ਮ ਲ /ਸ ?

b. ਓ ਹ / ਸ ਨੂੰ /ਚੰ ਗ / ਤ ਰੰੁ / ਪ ੜੰ ਦ / ਨ ਹੰ ।

c. ਤ ਨੰੂ /ਪ ੜ੍ ਣ / ਵ ਚ /ਮ ਹ ਨ ਤ /ਕ ਰ ਨ / ਚ ਹ ਦ / ਹ ।

2. Crossword

Complete the crossword in English using the clues given in Panjabi.

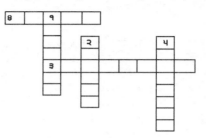

੧. ਅਧਿਆਪਕ

੨. ਰਮੇਸ਼

੩. ਘਰ ਦਾ ਕੰਮ

੪. ਹਿਸਾਬ

੫. ਲਾ ਪਰਵਾਹ

2 Yes, officer

ਗੱਲ ਬਾਤ ੨ ਹਾਂ ਜੀ ਅਫ਼ਸਰ ਸਾਹਿਬ

gall baaṯ 2 haan jee, afsar saahib

Sheela has been stopped by a police officer for using her mobile phone while driving her car.

ਪੁਲਿਸ ਅਫ਼ਸਰ	ਬੀਬੀ ਜੀ, ਕਾਰ ਇੱਕ ਪਾਸੇ ਖੜ੍ਹੀ ਕਰੋ ਅਤੇ ਮੋਬਾਇਲ ਫ਼ੋਨ ਬੰਦ ਕਰੋ ਤਾਂ ਕਿ ਤੁਸੀਂ ਮੈਨੂੰ ਸੁਣ ਸਕੋ।
ਸ਼ੀਲਾ	ਹਾਂ ਜੀ ਅਫ਼ਸਰ ਸਾਹਿਬ
ਪੁਲਿਸ ਅਫ਼ਸਰ	ਤੁਸੀਂ ਅਪਰਾਧ ਕਰ ਰਹੇ ਹੋ। ਤੁਹਾਡੇ ਤੇ ਕਾਰ ਚਲਾਦਿਆਂ ਮੋਬਾਇਲ ਫ਼ੋਨ ਦੀ ਵਰਤੋਂ ਕਰਨ ਦਾ ਦੋਸ਼ ਲਗਾਇਆ ਜਾਂਦਾ ਹੈ।
ਸ਼ੀਲਾ	ਮੈਂ ਕੇਵਲ ਇਕ ਮਿੰਟ ਲਈ .ਫ਼ੋਨ ਵਰਤ ਰਹੀ ਸੀ
ਪੁਲਿਸ ਅਫ਼ਸਰ	ਤੁਸੀਂ ਪਿਛਲੇ ਦਸ ਮਿੰਟ ਤੋਂ ਗੱਲਾਂ ਕਰ ਰਹੇ ਸੀ। ਤੁਸੀਂ ਕਾਰ ਤੋਂ ਬਾਹਰ ਆਓ ਅਤੇ ਆਪਣਾ ਲਾਇਸੈਂਸ ਦਿਖਾਓ।
ਸ਼ੀਲਾ	ਅਫ਼ਸਰ ਸਾਹਿਬ, ਕਿਰਪਾ ਕਰ ਕੇ ਇਸ ਵਾਰੀ ਮੈਨੂੰ ਮਾਫ਼ ਕਰ ਦੇਵੋ।
ਪੁਲਿਸ ਅਫ਼ਸਰ	ਤੁਸੀਂ ਕਾਨੂੰਨ ਦੀ ਉਲੰਘਣਾ ਕੀਤੀ ਹੈ। ਇਹ ਤੁਹਾਡੀ ਟਿਕਟ ਹੈ। ਹਫ਼ਤੇ ਅੰਦਰ ਆਪਣੇ ਕਾਰ ਦੇ ਕਾਗ਼ਜ਼ਾਤ ਪੇਸ਼ ਕਰੋ।

Police officer	*Madam, please pull the car over to one side and stop using the telephone so that you can listen to me.*
Sheela	*Yes, officer.*

Police officer	*You are committing an offence. I am charging you [lit. you are charged] for using a mobile phone while driving.*
Sheela	*I was only using the phone for one minute.*
Police officer	*You've been talking for the last ten minutes. Please get out of the car and show me your licence.*
Sheela	*Officer, please let me off this time.*
Police officer	*You have broken the law. Here is your ticket. Please produce your car documents within one week.*

ਸ਼ਬਦਾਵਲੀ   shab<u>d</u>aavalee   Vocabulary

ਬੀਬੀ	beebee	*madame* (f.)
ਇੱਕ ਪਾਸੇ	ikk paase	*one side*
ਖੜਨਾ	kharhhnhaa	*to stand, to park*
ਬੰਦ	ba<u>nd</u>	*closed, off*
ਅਪਰਾਧ	apraa<u>dh</u>	*offence* (m.)
ਦੋਸ਼	<u>d</u>osh	*charge* (m.)
ਗੱਲਾਂ	gallaa<u>n</u>	*speech, conversation* (f.)
ਲਾਇਸੈਂਸ	laaisai<u>n</u>s	*licence* (m.)
ਇਸ ਵਾਰੀ	is vaaree	*this time*
ਮਾਫ਼	maaf	*pardon, excuse*
ਕਾਨੂੰਨ	kaanoo<u>n</u>n	*law* (m.)
ਉਲੰਘਨਾ	ula<u>n</u>ghnhaa	*to disobey, to break*
ਕਾਗਜ਼ਾਤ	kaa<u>gh</u>zaa<u>t</u>	*papers, documents* (m.)
ਪੇਸ਼ ਕਰਨਾ	pesh karnaa	*to present, to produce*

☑ ਅਭਿਆਸ   abhiaas   Exercises

After reading the dialogue and/or listening to the audio tape, try to do the following exercises.

1. Complete the table

ਕਾਨੂੰਨ		law
	beebee	
		documents
ਮਾਫ਼		
	ula<u>n</u>ghnhaa	

2. Loan words

Make a list of five words borrowed from English used in Dialogue 2.

3 I am a social worker
ਗੱਲ ਬਾਤ 3 ਮੈਂ ਸਮਾਜ ਸੇਵਕ ਹਾਂ

gall baat 3 main samaaj sevak haan

A social worker, Mrs Kaur, visits Kuldeep's house. She is following a complaint that under-aged children have been left unattended for long periods in the house.

ਸਮਾਜ ਸੇਵਕ	ਹੈਲੋ। ਮੈਂ ਸਮਾਜ ਸੇਵਕ ਹਾਂ ਅਤੇ ਮੇਰਾ ਨਾਮ ਮਿਸਜ਼ ਕੌਰ ਹੈ। ਇਹ ਮੇਰਾ ਸ਼ਨਾਖ਼ਤੀ ਕਾਰਡ ਹੈ। ਮੈਂ ਤੁਹਾਡੇ ਨਾਲ ਗੱਲ ਕਰਨ ਆਈ ਹਾਂ।
ਕੁਲਦੀਪ	ਅੰਦਰ ਆ ਜਾਓ। ਕੀ ਗੱਲ ਹੈ ?
ਸਮਾਜ ਸੇਵਕ	ਤੁਹਾਡੇ ਖ਼ਿਲਾਫ਼ ਸਾਡੇ ਦਫ਼ਤਰ ਵਿਚ ਇੱਕ ਸ਼ਿਕਾਇਤ ਪਹੁੰਚੀ ਹੈ।
ਕੁਲਦੀਪ	ਕੀ ਹੋ ਗਿਆ ਹੈ ? ਕੀ ਮੈਂ ਕੋਈ ਗ਼ਲਤ ਕੰਮ ਕਰ ਬੈਠੀ ਹਾਂ।
ਸਮਾਜ ਸੇਵਕ	ਤੁਸੀਂ ਆਪਣੇ ਦੋਨਾਂ ਬੱਚਿਆਂ ਨੂੰ ਇੱਕਲੇ ਘਰ ਦੇ ਅੰਦਰ ਛੱਡ ਕੇ, ਕੰਮ ਤੇ ਚਲੇ ਜਾਂਦੇ ਹੋ। ਇਹ ਇੱਕ ਖ਼ਤਰਨਾਕ ਸਥਿਤੀ ਬਣ ਸਕਦੀ ਹੈ।
ਕੁਲਦੀਪ	ਮੈਂ ੫ ਵਜੇ ਜਾਂਦੀ ਹਾਂ। ਮੇਰੇ ਪਤੀ ੭ ਵਜੇ ਆਉਂਦੇ ਹਨ। ਸਿਰਫ਼ ਦੋ ਘੰਟੇ ਦੀ ਗੱਲ ਹੈ।
ਸਮਾਜ ਸੇਵਕ	ਇਹਨਾਂ ਦੋ ਘੰਟਿਆਂ ਵਿਚ ਕੁਝ ਵੀ ਹੋ ਸਕਦਾ ਹੈ। ਕੰਮ ਦੇ ਘੰਟੇ ਬਦਲੋ ਜਾਂ ਕੋਈ ਹੋਰ ਇੰਤਜ਼ਾਮ ਕਰੋ।
ਕੁਲਦੀਪ	ਇਹ ਮੇਰੇ ਲਈ ਮੁਸ਼ਕਲ ਹੈ। ਮੈਂ ਕੰਮ ਨਹੀਂ ਛੱਡ ਸਕਦੀ।
ਸਮਾਜ ਸੇਵਕ	ਕੋਈ ਬੇਬੀ ਸਿਟਰ ਲੱਭੋ।
ਕੁਲਦੀਪ	ਮੈਂ ਪੂਰੀ ਕੋਸ਼ਿਸ਼ ਕਰਾਂ ਗੀ।

Social worker	*Hello, I am a social worker and my name is Mrs Kaur. Here is my identity card. I have come to talk to you.*
Kuldip	*Please come in. What is the matter?*
Social worker	*We have received a complaint in our office against you.*
Kuldip	*What has happened? Have I done anything wrong?*
Social worker	*You leave both of your children alone in the house and go to work. This is a potentially dangerous situation.*
Kuldip	*I leave at 5 o'clock. My husband comes home at 7 o'clock. It is only a matter of two hours.*
Social worker	*Anything can happen in those two hours. Either change your hours of work or make alternative arrangements.*

Kuldip	*This is difficult for me. I can't leave work.*
Social worker	*Find a baby sitter.*
Kuldip	*I will try my best.*

ਸ਼ਬਦਾਵਲੀ   shabdaavalee   Vocabulary

ਸਮਾਜ ਸੇਵਕ	samaaj sevak	*social worker* (m./f.)
ਸ਼ਨਾਖ਼ਤੀ ਕਾਰਡ	shanaakhtee kaard	*identity card* (m.)
ਖ਼ਿਲਾਫ਼	khilaaf	*against*
ਦਫ਼ਤਰ	daftar	*office* (m.)
ਸ਼ਿਕਾਇਤ	shikaait	*complaint* (f.)
ਗ਼ਲਤ	ghalat	*wrong*
ਖ਼ਤਰਨਾਕ	khatarnaak	*dangerous*
ਸਥਿਤੀ	sathitee	*situation* (f.)
ਇੰਤਜ਼ਾਮ	intzaam	*arrangements* (m.)
ਬੇਬੀ ਸਿਟਰ	bebee sitar	*baby sitter* (m./f.)
ਲੱਭਣਾ	labhbhnhaa	*to find*

ਅਭਿਆਸ   abhiaas   Exercises

After reading the dialogue and/or listening to the audio tape, try to do the following exercises.

1. Write or say in the correct word order

a. ਹਾਂ ਸੇਵਕ ਸਮਾਜ ਮੈਂ   b. ਹੈ ਕੀ ਗੱਲ ?

c. ਜਾਓ ਆ ਅੰਦਰ   d. ਹੈ ਲਈ ਮੇਰੇ ਇਹ ਮੁਸ਼ਕਲ

2. Complete the sentences

Choose the correct word from the bracket to complete the sentence according to the specifications of gender and number. Remember that the verb changes according to the subject.

a. ਮੈਂ ਤੁਹਾਡੇ ਨਾਲ ਗੱਲ ਕਰਨ (ਆਈ / ਆਇਆ) ਹਾਂ।   [masculine/singular]
I have come to talk to you.

b. ਮੈਂ ਕੰਮ ਨਹੀਂ ਛੱਡ (ਸਕਦੀ/ ਸਕਦਾ)।   [feminine/singular]
I can't leave work.

c. ਤੁਸੀਂ ਕੰਮ ਤੇ (ਚਲੇ ਜਾਂਦੇ / ਚਲੀ ਜਾਂਦੇ) ਹੋ।   [formal/singular]
You go to work.

d. ਮੈਂ ਪੂਰੀ ਕੋਸ਼ਿਸ਼ (ਕਰਾਂ ਗੇ / ਕਰਾਂ ਗੀ)   [feminine/singular]
I will try my best.

ਬੋਲੀ ਬਾਰੇ   **bolee baare**   **Language points**

Purpose clauses

In Unit 7 infinitives in the oblique were shown to express purpose such as
ਮੈਂ ਦੋਸਤ ਨੂੰ ਮਿਲਣ ਆਇਆ ਹਾਂ, *I have come to meet a friend.* Another way of
expressing purpose is through the use of ਤਾਂ ਕਿ, *so that, in order to.* The
verb in the purpose clause is normally in the subjunctive (since the action
is often indefinite or uncertain).

ਸਿਮਰਨ ਨੇ ਦਵਾਈ ਲੈ ਲਈ ਤਾਂ ਕਿ ਬੁਖ਼ਾਰ ਉਤਰ ਜਾਏ	*Simran took medicine so that her fever would come down.*
ਮੈਂ ਦਰਵਾਜ਼ਾ ਬੰਦ ਕੀਤਾ ਸੀ ਤਾਂ ਕਿ ਬਿੱਲੀ ਅੰਦਰ ਨਾ ਆ ਸਕੇ	*I closed the door so that the cat couldn't come inside.*
ਇਮਰਾਨ ਉਰਦੂ ਪੜ੍ਹ ਰਿਹਾ ਹੈ ਤਾਂ ਕਿ ਉਹ ਪਾਕਿਸਤਾਨ ਵਿਚ ਆਪਣੇ ਰਿਸ਼ਤੇਦਾਰਾਂ ਨਾਲ ਗੱਲ ਕਰ ਸਕੇ	*Imran is studying Urdu so that he can speak with his relatives in Pakistan.*

Compound postpositions

In Unit 4 simple postpositions such as ਵਿਚ *in*, ਤੋਂ *from* and ਨੂੰ *to* were
introduced. Postpositions having more than one word are called
compound postpositions, most commonly using the postposition ਦੇ *of*.
Compound postpositions behave in the same way as simple postpositions
by requiring the words preceding them to be in the oblique case. Here are
some commonly used compound postpositions:

ਦੇ ਅੰਦਰ	*inside*	ਦੇ ਵਾਸਤੇ	*for*
ਦੇ ਉੱਪਰ	*above, upon*	ਦੇ ਲਈ	*for*
ਦੇ ਪਿੱਛੇ	*behind*	ਦੀ ਜਗ੍ਹ	*in place of*
ਦੇ ਥੱਲੇ	*below*	ਦੇ ਸਾਹਮਣੇ	*opposite, facing*
ਤੋਂ ਪਹਿਲੇ	*before*	ਦੇ ਬਾਹਰ	*outside*
ਤੋਂ ਬਾਅਦ	*after*	ਤੋਂ ਇਲਾਵਾ	*apart from*
ਦੇ ਨੇੜੇ	*near*	ਤੋਂ ਬਿਨਾਂ / ਬਗ਼ੈਰ	*without*
ਦੇ ਬਾਰੇ	*about, concerning*	ਦੇ ਬਾਵਜੂਦ	*in spite of*

Indirect speech

So far in this book we have focused on direct speech, when sentences and
phrases have been directly spoken or reproduced. Indirect speech occurs
when another action or speech is being reported or conveyed, such as in
English: *She told me to call him,* ਉਸ ਨੇ ਮੈਨੂੰ ਕਿਹਾ ਕਿ ਉਹ ਨੂੰ ਬੁਲਾਓ. Indirect

speech in Panjabi is expressed with the particle ਕਿ *that* to denote what was actually said or done.

Indirect speech is used when the verb of thought or speech occurred before the thought or speech being conveyed.

ਮੈਂ ਆਪਣੇ ਆਪ ਵਿਚ ਸੋਚਿਆ ਕਿ ਮੈਂ   *I thought to myself that I would*
ਜ਼ਰੂਰ ਜਿੱਤਾਂ ਗੀ   *definitely win.*
ਜਗਜੀਤ ਨੇ ਕਿਹਾ ਕਿ ਇਹ ਕਿਤਾਬ   *Jagjit said that this book is worth*
ਪੜ੍ਹਨ ਵਾਲੀ ਹੈ   *reading.*
ਕਿਸੇ ਨੇ ਮੈਨੂੰ ਦੱਸਿਆ ਕਿ ਮਿਸਜ਼ ਸ਼ਰਮਾ *Someone told me that Mrs Sharma has*
ਭਾਰਤ ਚਲੀ ਗਈ ਹੈ   *gone to India.*

When the speech being conveyed is a command.

ਉਸ ਨੇ ਬੱਚਿਆਂ ਨੂੰ ਕਿਹਾ ਕਿ ਚੁੱਪ ਰਹੋ   *He told the children to be quiet.*
ਮੈਂ ਸਾਰਿਆਂ ਨੂੰ ਕਿਹਾ ਕਿ ਘਰ ਵਾਪਸ   *I told everyone to go back home.*
ਚਲੇ ਜਾਓ

☑ ਅਭਿਆਸ   abhiaas   Exercises

After reading the dialogue and/or listening to the audio tape, try to do the following exercises.

1. Fill in the blanks with the appropriate compound postpositions

a. ਸਾਡਾ ਘਰ ਸਕੂਲ _____ ਹੈ।   *Our house is near the school.*
b. ਬਿੱਲੀ ਡੱਬੇ _____ ਹੈ।   *The cat is inside the box.*
c. ਉਹ ਰੋਟੀ ਖਾਣ _____ ਆਵੇ ਗਾ।   *He will come after eating.*
d. ਤਸਵੀਰ_____ ਕੁਝ ਹੋਰ ਚਾਹੀਦਾ ਹੈ।   *There should be something else in place of the picture.*

2. Match the pairs

The following eight sentences need to be joined with ਤਾਂ ਕਿ. Match the correct pairs of sentences with one another.

a) ਮੈਂ ਦਰਵਾਜ਼ਾ ਬੰਦ ਕੀਤਾ		i) ... ਸਵੇਰੇ ਜਲਦੀ ਉਠ ਸਕੋ
b) ਅਸੀਂ ਪੰਜਾਬੀ ਬੋਲਾਂ ਗੇ	ਤਾਂ ਕਿ	ii) ... ਕੁੱਤਾ ਅੰਦਰ ਨਾ ਆ ਸਕੇ
c) ਤੈਨੂੰ ਜਲਦੀ ਆਉਣਾ ਚਾਹੀਦਾ ਹੈ		iii) ... ਸਾਰੇ ਸਮਝ ਜਾਣ
d) ਤੁਸੀਂ ਜਲਦੀ ਸੌਂ ਜਾਓ		iv) ... ਅਸੀਂ ਬਸ ਫੜ ਸਕੀਏ

3. Listening

Sheela is telling her story to her friend Meena about how she was stopped by the police officer for using her mobile phone while driving. Listen to the tape and answer the following questions. You may answer the questions with short or full answers.

a. ਸ਼ੀਲਾ ਆਪਣੀ ਕਾਰ ਵਿਚ ਕਿੱਥੇ ਜਾ ਰਹੀ ਸੀ ?
b. ਉਹ ਕਿੰਨੀ ਦੇਰ ਤੋਂ ਮੋਬਾਈਲ ਤੇ ਗੱਲਾਂ ਕਰ ਰਹੀ ਸੀ ?
c. ਕੀ ਸ਼ੀਲਾ ਨੇ ਅਫਸਰ ਅੱਗੇ ਸੱਚ ਬੋਲਿਆ ?
d. ਇੱਕ ਹਫਤੇ ਦੇ ਅੰਦਰ ਸ਼ੀਲਾ ਨੂੰ ਕੀ ਕਰਨਾ ਪੈਣਾ ਹੈ ?

4. Alphabetical order

Rearrange the following words into alphabetical order, considering only the first letter of each word.

ਪਾਪਾ	ਵਰਤਣਾ	ਡਾਕਟਰ	ਅਧਿਆਪਕ	ਬਾਰੇ
ਪੜ੍ਹਉਣਾ	ਮਜ਼ਮੂਨਾਂ	ਦੂਜੇ	ਹਿਸਾਬ	ਕਲਾਸ
ਲਿਆਕਤ	ਕੰਮ	ਮਿਹਨਤ	ਸ਼੍ਰੇਣੀ	ਇਲਾਵਾ

15 | ਵੈਸਾਖੀ
vaisaakhee
Vaisakhi

In this unit you will:

■ learn about the Vaisakhi festival
■ be introduced to Panjabi poetry and music
■ express *to allow*

▥ The Vaisakhi fair

ਵੈਸਾਖੀ ਦਾ ਮੇਲਾ

vaisaakhee ḏaa melaa

The following extract is a news report from the BBC Asian Network reporting on the events of the Vaisakhi festival in Birmingham, UK.

ਨੀਲੂ	ਮੈਂ ਨੀਲੂ ਹਾਂ ਤੇ ਮੈਂ ਬੀ. ਬੀ. ਸੀ. ਰੇਡੀਓ ਲਈ ਹੈਂਡਜ਼ਵਰਥ ਪਾਰਕ ਤੋਂ ਰਿਪੋਰਟ ਪੇਸ਼ ਕਰ ਰਹੀ ਹਾਂ। ਇਸ ਸਾਲ ਵੈਸਾਖੀ ਦਾ ਤਿਉਹਾਰ ਬੜੀ ਧੂਮ ਧਾਮ ਨਾਲ ਮਨਾਇਆ ਜਾ ਰਿਹਾ ਹੈ। ਅੱਜ ਲੱਗਦਾ ਹੈ ਜਿਵੇਂ ਸਾਰੇ ਸ਼ਹਿਰ ਦੇ ਪੰਜਾਬੀ ਲੋਕ ਪਹੁੰਚੇ ਹੋਏ ਹਨ। ਹੁਣੇ ਮੈਂ ਅੰਕਲ ਜੀ ਨੂੰ ਪੁੱਛਿਆ ਹੈ ਕਿ ਉਹਨਾਂ ਨੂੰ ਮੇਲਾ ਕਿਵੇਂ ਲੱਗ ਰਿਹਾ ਹੈ।
ਅੰਕਲ	ਮੈਨੂੰ ਆਪਣਾ ਪੇਂਡੂ ਜੀਵਨ ਯਾਦ ਆ ਰਿਹਾ ਹੈ। ਸਾਡੇ ਲਈ ਇਹ ਫ਼ਸਲਾਂ ਕਟਣ ਦੀ ਖੁਸ਼ੀ ਦਾ ਤਿਉਹਾਰ ਹੈ।
ਨੀਲੂ	... ਨਾਲੇ ਵੈਸਾਖ ਪੰਜਾਬੀ ਸਾਲ ਦਾ ਪਹਿਲਾ ਮਹੀਨਾ ਵੀ ਹੈ। ਅੱਛਾ ਆਂਟੀ ਜੀ, ਤੁਸੀਂ ਇੱਥੇ ਅੱਜ ਕਿਉਂ ਆਏ ਹੋ ?
ਆਂਟੀ	ਬੇਟੀ, ਵੈਸਾਖੀ ਸਿੱਖ ਕੌਮ ਦਾ ਜਨਮ ਦਿਨ ਹੈ। ਜਿੱਥੇ ਅਸੀਂ ਖਲੋਤੇ ਹਾਂ, ਉੱਥੇ ਨਗਰ ਕੀਰਤਨ ਆਉਣ ਵਾਲਾ ਹੈ। ਅੱਗੇ ਅੱਗੇ ਨੌਜੁਆਨ ਗਤਕਾ ਖੇਡ ਰਹੇ ਹਨ। ਪਿੱਛੇ ਗੁਰੂ ਗਰੰਥ ਸਾਹਿਬ ਦੀ ਸਵਾਰੀ ਹੈ।
ਨੀਲੂ	ਮੈਂ ਹੁਣ ਲੰਗਰ ਹਾਲ ਵੱਲ ਜਾ ਰਹੀ ਹਾਂ। ਦੇਖੋ! ਜਲੇਬੀਆਂ, ਪਕੌੜੇ ਅਤੇ ਹੋਰ ਕਈ ਚੀਜ਼ਾ ਸੇਵਾਦਾਰ ਮੁਫ਼ਤ ਵਰਤਾ ਰਹੇ ਹਨ। ਬੱਚਿਆਂ ਨੂੰ ਲੰਗਰ ਪਹਿਲੇ ਲੈਣ ਦੇਵੋ।
ਕਾਕਾ	ਨੀਲੂ ਆਂਟੀ ! ਮੈਂ ਲੰਗਰ ਛਕਣ ਤੋਂ ਬਾਅਦ ਝੂਟੇ ਲਵਾਂ ਗਾ। ਬੱਚਿਆਂ ਦੇ ਮਨਪਰਚਾਵੇ ਲਈ ਬਹੁਤ ਕੁਝ ਹੈ।

ਨੀਲੂ	ਅੱਛਾ ਬੇਟਾ। ਝੂਟਿਆਂ ਤੋਂ ਇਲਾਵਾ ਨੁਮਾਇਸ਼ ਵੀ ਲੱਗੀ ਹੋਈ ਹੈ। ਭੰਗੜਾ ਸ਼ੁਰੂ ਹੋਣ ਲੱਗਾ ਹੈ। ਹੁਣ ਮੈਨੂੰ ਇਜਾਜ਼ਤ ਦੇਵੋ। ਸਾਰਿਆਂ ਨੂੰ ਬੀ। ਬੀ। ਸੀ। ਵੱਲੋਂ ਵੈਸਾਖੀ ਦੀ ਵਧਾਈ !

Neelu   *I'm Neelu and I'm reporting for BBC Radio from Handsworth Park. The* **Vaisakhi** *festival this year is being celebrated with a 'bang'. It seems today that all the Panjabi people of the city have come here. I have just asked Uncle how he feels about the fair.*

Uncle   *I am remembering my village life. For us this is a happy festival of harvest.*

Neelu   **Vaisakh** *is also the first month of the Panjabi calendar. Well, Auntie, why have you come here?*

Auntie   **Vaisakhi** *is the birthday of the Sikh nation. The religious procession is due to arrive where we are standing. In front of the procession young people are playing* **gatka***. It is followed by the installation of the* **Guru Granth Sahib***.*

Neelu   *I am going towards the* **langar** *hall. Look!* **Jalebeeaan, pakaurhe** *and many other things are being served by volunteers free of charge. Please allow the children to have* **langar** *first.*

Young boy   *Auntie Neelu! I will go on the rides after I've had* **langar***. There is a lot of entertainment for the children.*

Neelu   *OK, son. Apart from the rides, there is also an exhibition.* **Bhangra** *is about to begin. Now, please excuse me. To everyone from BBC Radio, happy* **Vaisakhi!**

◀ ਸ਼ਬਦਾਵਲੀ   **shab<u>d</u>aavalee   Vocabulary**

ਪੇਸ਼	pesh	*to present*
ਵੈਸਾਖੀ	vaisaakhee	Vaisakhi, *one of the Sikh festivals* (f.)
ਮੇਲਾ	melaa	*fair* (m.)
ਧੂਮ ਧਾਮ	<u>dh</u>oom <u>dh</u>aam	*bang, pomp and show* (f.)
ਮਨਾਉਣਾ	manaaunhaa	*to celebrate*
ਦਰਸ਼ਕ	<u>d</u>arshak	*participant, visitor* (m./f.)
ਪੁੱਛਣਾ	pu<u>chch</u>nhaa	*to ask*
ਪੇਂਡੂ	pe<u>n</u>doo	*of the village, village-like*
ਜੀਵਨ	jeevan	*life* (m.)
ਫ਼ਸਲਾਂ	fasalaa<u>n</u>	*crops* (f.)
ਕਟਣ	katanh	*to cut*

ਤਿਉਹਾਰ	tiuhaar	celebration, festival (m.)
ਵੈਸਾਖ	vaisaakh	one of the Indian months (m.)
ਕੌਮ	kaum	nation, community (f.)
ਜਨਮ ਦਿਨ	janam din	birthday (m.)
ਖਲੋਣਾ	khalonhaa	to be stood, to stand
ਨਗਰ ਕੀਰਤਨ	nagar keertan	religious procession (m.)
ਗਤਕਾ	gatkaa	a Sikh martial art like fencing (m.)
ਖੇਡਣਾ	khednhaa	to play
ਗੁਰੂ ਗਰੰਥ	guroo garanth	Guru Granth; Holy book of the Sikhs (m.)
ਸਵਾਰੀ	savaaree	installation (f.)
ਲੰਗਰ	langar	community kitchen (m.)
ਸੇਵਾਦਾਰ	sevaadaar	volunteer (m./f.)
ਮੁਫ਼ਤ	mufat	free
ਵਰਤਾਉਣਾ	vartaaunhaa	to serve
ਛਕਣਾ	chaknhaa	to take, to consume
ਝੂਟੇ	jhoote	rides (m.)
ਮਨਪਰਚਾਵੇ	manparchaave	entertainment, enjoyment (m.)
ਨੁਮਾਇਸ਼	numaaish	exhibition (f.)
ਵੱਲੋਂ	vallon	on behalf of
ਵਧਾਈ	vadhaaee	congratulations (f.)

☑ ਅਭਿਆਸ   abhiaas   Exercises

After reading the dialogue and/or listening to the audio tape, try to do the following exercises.

1. Answer in Panjabi

Answer the questions in Panjabi in either full sentences or in short form answers. The answers to the questions can be found in the dialogue. The first one has been done for you.

a. *What is the name of the radio presenter?*
   ਪੇਸ਼ ਕਰਤਾ ਦਾ ਨਾਮ ਨੀਲੂ ਹੈ। (full sentence) or ਨੀਲੂ (short answer)
b. *What is the report about?*
c. *What are the main things associated with the Vaisakhi festival?*
   (*name two*)
d. *What is being served in the community kitchen?*
e. *What is the name of the game being played in front of the procession?*
f. *What are the main activities taken place at the Vaisakhi fair?*
   (*name any two*)

2. Identify the appropriate answers

The Vaisakhi festival is associated with:

- ■ village people
- ■ harvest season
- ■ Sikh religion
- ■ candles
- ■ the new year

3. True or false?

Langar *means community kitchen.*	True / False
Guru Granth *is the holy book of the Sikhs.*	True / False
Gatka *is a group dance.*	True / False
Nagar Kirtan *is singing.*	True / False

Folk song: My spinning wheel is of many colours

ਲੋਕ ਗੀਤ: ਚਰਖਾ ਮੇਰਾ ਰੰਗਲਾ

lok ge̲e̲t: charkhaa meraa ra̲nglaa

The following is a traditional Panjabi folk song. Listen to the song on the tape while reading the verses of the song.

ਚਰਖਾ ਮੇਰਾ ਰੰਗਲਾ ਵਿਚ ਸੋਨੇ ਦੀਆਂ ਮੇਖਾਂ
ਵੇ ਮੈਂ ਤੈਨੂੰ ਯਾਦ ਕਰਾਂ ਜਦ ਚਰਖੇ ਵੱਲ ਵੇਖਾਂ

ਚਰਖੇ ਦੇ ਸ਼ੀਸ਼ਿਆਂ 'ਚ ਦਿਸੇ ਤੇਰਾ ਮੁੱਖ ਵੇ
ਵੇਖ ਵੇਖ ਮਿਟ ਦੀ ਨਾ ਅੱਖੀਆਂ ਦੀ ਭੁੱਖ ਵੇ
ਸੀਨੇ ਵਿਚ ਨੇ ਰੜਕ ਦੀਆਂ ਇਹ ਚਰਖੇ ਦੀਆਂ ਮੇਖਾਂ

ਦਿਨ ਰਾਤ ਤੇਰੀਆਂ ਰਾਹਾਂ ਵੱਲ ਜਾਵਾਂ ਝਾਕੀ ਵੇ
ਤੇਰੇ ਬਿਨ ਅਸੀਂ ਕੀ ਮਨਾਉਣੀ ਏ ਵੈਸਾਖੀ ਵੇ
ਸੌ ਸੌ ਪੀਰ ਮਨਾਵਾਂ ਨਾਲੇ ਥਾਂ ਥਾਂ ਮੱਥੇ ਟੇਕਾਂ
ਵੇ ਮੈਂ ਤੈਨੂੰ ਯਾਦ ਕਰਾਂ ਜਦ ਚਰਖੇ ਵੱਲ ਵੇਖਾਂ

My spinning wheel is of many colours, studded with gold nails
Oh! I remember you, when I look at the spinning wheel

I see your face in the mirror work of the spinning wheel
Continuously looking does not satisfy my eyes' desire
The studded nails of this spinning wheel prick my heart

Day and night I keep watch on the road for your return
Without you, what kind of *Vaisakhi* am I to celebrate?
For your return I pray to a hundred holy men
and bow my head at many holy places
Oh! I remember you, when I look at the spinning wheel

🔑 ਸ਼ਬਦਾਵਲੀ   **shab<u>d</u>aavalee**   **Vocabulary**

ਚਰਖਾ	charkhaa	*spinning wheel* (m.)
ਰੰਗਲਾ	ra<u>n</u>glaa	*colourful* (v.)
ਸੋਨਾ	sonaa	*gold* (m.)
ਮੇਖ	mekh	*nail* (f.)
ਵੇ	ve	*subjunctive particle*

ਵੱਲ	vall	*towards*
ਵੇਖਣਾ	vekhnhaa	*to see*
ਸ਼ੀਸ਼ਾ	sheeshaa	*mirror* (m.)
ਦਿਸਣਾ	<u>d</u>isnhaa	*to be visible, to be seen*
ਮੁੱਖ	mukhkh	*face* (m.)
ਮਿਟਣਾ	mitnhaa	*to finish, to vanish*
ਭੁੱਖ	bhukhkh	*hunger* (f.)
ਸੀਨਾ	seenaa	*bosom, heart* (m.)
ਰੜਕਣਾ	rarhkanhaa	*to prick, to rub against*
ਰਾਹਾਂ	raahaa<u>n</u>	*roads, routes* (f.)
ਝਾਕਣਾ	jhaaknhaa	*to stare, to look at*
ਪੀਰ	peer	*holy man* (m.)
ਮਨਾਉਣਾ	manaaunhaa	*to pray, to believe*
ਟੇਕਣਾ	teknhaa	*to bow down*

✍ ਅਭਿਆਸ   abhiaas   Exercises

After reading the folk song and/or listening to the audio tape, try to do the following exercise.

Answer the questions (yes or no)

> My spinning wheel is many-coloured.
> It is studded with nails of gold.
> I remember you whenever I look at it.
> These nails make me suffer in love.

ਮੇਰਾ ਚਰਖਾ ਕਈ ਰੰਗਾਂ ਵਾਲਾ ਹੈ।
ਇਸ ਵਿਚ ਸੋਨੇ ਦੀਆਂ ਮੇਖਾਂ ਲੱਗੀਆਂ ਹੋਈਆਂ ਹਨ।
ਜਦੋਂ ਮੈਂ ਇਸ ਵੱਲ ਵੇਖਦੀ ਹਾਂ, ਉਦੋਂ ਤੈਨੂੰ ਯਾਦ ਕਰਦੀ ਹਾਂ।
ਇਹ ਮੇਖਾਂ ਮੈਨੂੰ ਪਿਆਰ ਵਿਚ ਤੜਫਾਂਦੀਆਂ ਹਨ।

ਕੀ ਇਹ ਗੀਤ ਪਿਆਰ ਬਾਰੇ ਕੁਝ ਦੱਸ ਰਿਹਾ ਹੈ ?
ਕੀ ਚਰਖੇ ਵਿਚ ਲੋਹੇ (iron) ਦੀਆਂ ਮੇਖਾਂ ਹਨ ?
ਜਦੋਂ ਔਰਤ ਚਰਖੇ ਵੱਲ ਵੇਖਦੀ ਹੈ ਕੀ ਉਦੋਂ ਆਪਣੇ ਪਿਆਰ ਨੂੰ ਭੁੱਲ ਜਾਂਦੀ ਹੈ ?
ਕੀ ਚਰਖੇ ਦਾ ਸਿਰਫ਼ ਇੱਕ ਰੰਗ ਹੈ ?

੬ ਬੋਲੀ ਬਾਰੇ   bolee baare   Language points

Relative–correlatives

You have already been introduced to the most common relative pronoun, ਜਿਹੜਾ which means *that* (see Unit 9 for a review of how sentences with relative pronouns are formed). Relative–correlatives are relative pronouns which are paired with their correlating counterparts. The correlating counterpart of the relative pronoun ਜਿਹੜਾ can be either ਇਹ or ਉਹ (*that ... which*). In English, the sentence *I will go when he comes* contains only one relative pronoun *when*. However, the same sentence would be expressed in Panjabi as *when he comes, then I will go* with the relative pronoun *when* and its correlative *then*. There are a number of such pairings, that can be used to indicate place, time, quantity and likeness. For example:

Relative		Correlative	
ਜਿਹੜਾ	who, which	ਉਹ	he, she, it, that
ਜਿਹੜਾ	who, which	ਇਹ	he, she, it, this
ਜਦੋਂ	when	ਉਦੋਂ	then
ਜਦ ਤਕ	as long as	ਤਦ ਤਕ	until then
ਜਿਵੇਂ	in such a way	ਉਵੇਂ	in that way
ਜਿੰਨਾਂ	as many, however much	ਓਨਾਂ	that much, that many
ਜਿੰਨਾਂ	as many, however much	ਇੰਨਾਂ	this much, this many
ਜਿੱਥੇ	where	ਉੱਥੇ	there

ਜਿੱਥੇ ਅਸੀਂ ਰਹਿੰਦੇ ਹਾਂ ਉੱਥੇ ਪੰਜਾਬੀ ਬੋਲੀ ਜਾਂਦੀ ਹੈ   Panjabi is spoken where we live.
(lit. *Where we live, Panjabi is spoken there.*)

ਜਿਵੇਂ ਤੁਸੀਂ ਚਾਹੁੰਦੇ ਹੋ ਉਵੇਂ ਅਸੀਂ ਕਰਾਂ ਗੇ   We'll do as you like.
(lit. *As you like, that is the way we will do.*)

ਜਿਹੜਾ ਬੰਦਾ ਲਾਹੌਰ ਜਾ ਚੁਕਾ ਹੈ ਉਹ ਨੂੰ ਰਸਤਾ ਪੁੱਛੋ   Ask directions from the man who has been to Lahore.
(lit. *The man who has been to Lahore, ask the way from him.*)

ਜੱਦ ਤਕ ਤੂੰ ਪੰਜਾਬ ਨਹੀਂ ਜਾਂਦਾ ਤੱਦ ਤਕ ਤੈਨੂੰ ਚੰਗੀ ਪੰਜਾਬੀ ਨਹੀਂ ਆਏ ਗੀ	*You won't learn good Panjabi until you go to Panjab.* (lit. *As long as you don't go to Panjab, until then you won't learn good Panjabi.*)
ਜਿੰਨਾਂ ਜ਼ਿਆਦਾ ਕੰਮ ਕਰੋ ਗੇ ਓਨੇ ਜ਼ਿਆਦਾ ਪੈਸੇ ਕਮਾ ਸਕੋ ਗੇ	*The more you work, the more money you can earn.* (lit. *As much work as you will do, that much more money you will earn.*)

The subjunctive particle ਵੇ

You will recall from Unit 12 that the subjunctive mood is used to indicate uncertainty or indefiniteness. The particle ਵੇ is associated with the endings of the subjunctive mood. It is not, however, uncommon to see the particle ਵੇ on its own, particularly in poetic language and songs. It can appear as part of the verb in the subjunctive or on its own in the phrase or sentence. In the passage of the song **ਚਰਖਾ ਮੇਰਾ ਰੰਗਲਾ** the particle ਵੇ occurs at the beginning of the second line:

ਵੇ ਮੈਂ ਤੈਨੂੰ ਯਾਦ ਕਰਾਂ   *(Oh!) I remember you.*

The vocative case, as you learned in Unit 8, is a projection of an address to someone similar to the English *oh!* or *hey!*. ਵੇ is a colloquial form of address in friendly and informal situations.

The verb ਲੱਗਣਾ

The verb ਲੱਗਣਾ has occured a number of times throughout the units so far. In Unit 9 Simran asks Jaspreet about the cloth: **ਤੈਨੂੰ ਕਿਹੜਾ ਵਧੇਰੇ ਚੰਗਾ ਲਗਦਾ ਹੈ?**, *Which one do you like better?* In the second dialogue of Unit 9 Simran says to the doctor: **ਮੈਨੂੰ ਠੰਡ ਲੱਗ ਰਹੀ ਹੈ**, *I am feeling cold.* The basic definition of ਲੱਗਣਾ is *to be applied to*, however it can also carry slightly different meanings. In the first example it means *to seem* or *to appear* and in the second example it has the sense *to be struck.* In fact ਲੱਗਣਾ is used in a wide range of situations and it is therefore always necessary to take the context of the sentence into account. Here are some examples of these different, yet related, senses of the verb ਲੱਗਣਾ:

ਲੱਗਣਾ meaning *to seem, to like, to be struck*

ਨਿਆਣੇ ਨੂੰ ਠੰਡ ਲੱਗੇ ਗੀ	*The child will feel cold.*
ਅਮਰੀਕਾ ਰਹਿਣਾ ਮੈਨੂੰ ਅੱਛਾ ਲੱਗਦਾ ਹੈ	*I like living in America.* (lit. *Living in America seems good to me.*)
ਘਰ ਨੂੰ ਅੱਗ ਲੱਗੀ ਹੋਈ ਸੀ	*The house was on* (lit. *struck by*) *fire.*

ਲੱਗਣਾ to mean *time taken* or *to cost*

ਅੰਮ੍ਰਿਤਸਰ ਪਹੁੰਚਣ ਨੂੰ ਕਿੰਨਾ ਚਿਰ ਲੱਗੇ ਗਾ ?	*How long will it take to get to Amritsar?*
ਮੈਨੂੰ ਸਿਰਫ਼ ਦਸ ਮਿੰਟ ਲੱਗੇ	*It only took me ten minutes.*
ਇੱਕ ਟਿਕਟ ਲਈ ਕਿੰਨੇ ਪੈਸੇ ਲੱਗਦੇ ਹਨ ?	*How much money does one ticket cost?* (lit. *it take*)

ਲੱਗਣਾ following an oblique infinitive

In this case, its meaning changes to give the sense *to begin.*

ਬਾਰਸ਼ ਹੋਣ ਲੱਗੀ	*It began to rain.*
ਮੈਂ ਕੰਮ ਸ਼ੁਰੂ ਕਰਨ ਲੱਗਾ ਸੀ	*I was about to begin work.*
ਉਹ ਸੋਚਣ ਲੱਗਾ ਕਿ ਸਾਰੇ ਚਲੇ ਗਏ ਹਨ	*He began to think that everyone had left.*

Oblique infinitives with ਦੇਣਾ

The general use of ਦੇਣਾ in compound constructions was discussed in Unit 9. ਦੇਣਾ can also be used with oblique infinitives to give the meaning of *to allow to* or *to permit*. Similar to the way in which ਲੱਗਣਾ changes its meaning to *to begin* when following oblique infinitives, ਦੇਣਾ with the oblique infinitive also changes its meaning.

ਕੁੱਤੇ ਨੂੰ ਅੰਦਰ ਆਉਣ ਦੇ	*Let the dog come inside.*
ਪਿਤਾ ਜੀ ਨੇ ਮੈਨੂੰ ਗੱਡੀ ਚਲਾਉਣ ਨਹੀਂ ਦਿੱਤੀ	*Father did not allow me to drive the car.*
ਉਹ ਆਪਣੇ ਬੱਚੇ ਨੂੰ ਬਾਹਰ ਖੇਡਣ ਦੇਂਦੇ ਹਨ	*They allow their child to play outside.*

ਵਿਆਖਿਆ   viaakhiaa   Commentary

1. Media

There are many opportunities, living in the West, to interact with Panjabi speakers and to hear the language being spoken. In particular there has been a growth in media output. In most big towns and cities in England, and the major cities in North America, there are radio stations which either produce programming totally in Panjabi or have specific Panjabi language programmes. In Toronto, Canada, a mainstream cable television channel broadcasts six hours of Panjabi programming every day. Generally, most satellite and cable TV channels catering for a South Asian audience will have some Panjabi programmes in addition to Hindi/Urdu, Gujarati and Bengali programming.

Much of the programming on these TV channels is taken up with films. The Indian sub-continent produces more films every year than Hollywood. Bombay (Mumbai) is the centre of the Indian film industry and to mark this fact it is affectionately called 'Bollywood'. However, regional film makers are also very significant in the overall production and consumption of cinema in South Asia. In fact the Telegu film industry matches – in terms of number of films produced – that of Mumbai. Despite the presence of large numbers of Panjabi actors and directors – in fact the Kapoor family has dominated Indian films over the last forty years – the Panjabi language film industry is not well developed in East Panjab. The majority of Panjabi language films are produced in Lahore (also called 'Lollywood') and are high in action but low in quality, both cinematically and in terms of language use. However, there are a few films to be recommended which are useful to watch in order to pick up the language. These films are available in any South Asian area in England, Canada and beyond. Wherever a South Asian community is settled, there is always an outlet for videos and, more recently, cinema halls showing films from the sub-continent.

2. Poetry

Panjab is renowned for folk poetry, particularly for the tradition of Sufi-inspired poems. Poetry flourished in medieval times with poets such as Bulleh Shah and Warish Shah making indelible implants on the social consciousness of the Panjabi *literati*. In the modern period, Bhai Vir Singh and Amrita Pritam are two poets worthy of mention. Poetry is popular primarily because of its sung form. The folk song given earlier in this unit is a good example of a form of poetic verse. Much of this music has become professionalised and Panjab is the foremost producer of folk music in India and Pakistan.

☑ ਅਭਿਆਸ   abhiaas   Exercises

After reading the dialogue and/or listening to the audio tape, try to do the following exercises.

1. Fill in the blanks

In this unit you have learned about relative–correlatives in the language points section. Fill in the blanks with the appropriate relative–correlative pairs.

a. ____ ਦੌੜੇ ਗਾ, ____ ਇਨਾਮ ਜਿਤੇ ਗਾ
   The person who runs will win the prize.

b. ____ ਤੁਸੀਂ ਚਾਹੁੰਦੇ ਹੋ, ____ ਅਸੀਂ ਕਰਾਂ ਗੇ
   We will do as you like.

c. ____ ਤੁਸੀਂ ਰਹਿੰਦੇ ਹੋ, ____ ਪੰਜਾਬੀ ਬੋਲੀ ਜਾਂਦੀ ਹੈ
   Panjabi is spoken where you live.

d. ____ ਮੈਂ ਦਵਾਈ ਖਾਧੀ, ____ ਹੀ ਆਰਾਮ ਆ ਗਿਆ
   When I took the medicine I felt relief immediately.

2. Complete the sentences

Complete the sentences in Panjabi with the appropriate expressions of *to allow to*. The first one has been done for you.

a. ਉਸ ਨੂੰ ਅੰਦਰ (ਆਉਣ ਦੇ)   *Let him come inside.*
b. ਕੁੱਤੇ ਨੂੰ _____   *Let the dog go out.*
c. ਮੈਨੂੰ ਜੂਸ _____   *Let me drink juice.*
d. ਬੀਬੀ ਜੀ ਨੂੰ ਟੀ ਵੀ _____   *Allow the lady to watch TV.*

3. Write sentences using the verb ਲੱਗਣਾ

a. It takes fifteen minutes to get to work.
b. How much does one first-class ticket cost ?
c. I am feeling hot.
d. It started to rain.
e. We were about to go out.

16 | ਪੰਜਾਬ ਦੇ ਲੋਕ ਨਾਚ
panjaab de lok naach
Folk dances of Panjab

In this unit you will learn:

- about the folk dances of Panjab
- about experiences of the Panjabi diaspora
- phrases of choice

1 Folk dances of Panjab

ਗੱਲ ਬਾਤ ੧ ਪੰਜਾਬ ਦੇ ਲੋਕ ਨਾਚ

gall baat 1 panjaab de lok naach

It is the end of Mr Singh's Panjabi class. He has taken all the students to a cultural programme in the Southall Community Centre to see a range of folk dances. As they enter the hall they hear the sound of drums and see the dancers.

ਮਿਸਟਰ ਸਿੰਘ	ਉਹ ਮੁੰਡੇ ਸਟੇਜ ਤੇ ਪੰਜਾਬ ਦਾ ਲੋਕ ਨਾਚ ਭੰਗੜਾ ਪਾ ਰਹੇ ਹਨ। ਉਹਨਾਂ ਨੇ ਚਮਕੀਲੇ ਰੰਗਦਾਰ ਕਪੜੇ ਪਾਏ ਹੋਏ ਹਨ। ਉਹਨਾਂ ਦੇ ਹੱਥਾਂ ਵਿਚ ਡਾਂਗਾਂ ਹਨ।
ਡੇਵਿਡ	ਇੱਕ ਬੰਦੇ ਨੇ ਬੋਲ ਚੁੱਕਿਆ ਹੋਇਆ ਹੈ।
ਮਿਸਟਰ ਸਿੰਘ	ਬੋਲ ਦੇ ਵੱਜਣ ਨਾਲ ਸਿਰਫ ਪੈਰ ਨਹੀਂ ਸਗੋਂ ਦਿਲ ਵੀ ਨੱਚਣ ਲੱਗ ਪੈਂਦਾ ਹੈ।
ਜੇਨ	ਭੰਗੜੇ ਵਾਲਿਆਂ ਦੀਆਂ ਬੋਲੀਆਂ ਪੁਰਾਣੀਆਂ ਹਨ। ਮੈਨੂੰ ਨਵੇਂ ਤੇ ਅਜੋਕੇ ਗੀਤ ਚੰਗੇ ਲੱਗਦੇ ਹਨ ਜਿਹੜੇ ਇੱਥੋਂ ਦੇ ਜੰਮਪਲ ਨੌਜੁਆਨਾਂ ਨੇ ਰਚੇ ਹਨ।
ਮਿਸਟਰ ਸਿੰਘ	ਮੰਨੋ ਜਾਂ ਨਾ ਮੰਨੋ, ਭੰਗੜਾ ਅੰਤਰ ਰਾਸ਼ਟਰੀ ਨਾਚ ਬਣ ਗਿਆ ਹੈ। ਭਾਵੇਂ ਤੁਸੀਂ ਪੰਜਾਬ ਜਾਂ ਬਾਹਰ ਹੋ, ਭੰਗੜਾ ਦੇਖ ਸਕਦੇ ਹੋ।
ਜੇਨ	ਕੀ ਸਿਰਫ ਮੁੰਡੇ ਭੰਗੜਾ ਪਾਉਂਦੇ ਹਨ ?
ਮਿਸਟਰ ਸਿੰਘ	ਪੁਰਾਣੇ ਜ਼ਮਾਨੇ ਵਿਚ ਭੰਗੜਾ ਮੁੰਡਿਆਂ ਲਈ ਸੀ ਤੇ ਗਿੱਧਾ ਕੁੜੀਆਂ ਲਈ ਸੀ। ਹੁਣ ਸਭ ਕੁਝ ਰਲ ਮਿਲ ਗਿਆ ਹੈ। ਦੇਖੋ ! ਗਿੱਧਾ ਸ਼ੁਰੂ ਹੋ ਗਿਆ ਹੈ।
ਡੇਵਿਡ	ਉਹਨਾਂ ਵਿੱਚੋ ਇੱਕ ਕੁੜੀ ਚੋਲਕੀ ਵਜਾ ਰਹੀ ਹੈ ਅਤੇ ਦੂਜੀ ਚੋਲਕੀ ਤੇ ਚਮਚਾ ਮਾਰ ਰਹੀ ਹੈ।
ਜੇਨ	ਹਰ ਕੋਈ ਚੜ੍ਹਦੀ ਕਲਾ ਵਿਚ ਹੈ। ਆਓ, ਆਪਾਂ ਨੱਚੀਏ !

Mr Singh	*Those boys on the stage are performing* **bhangra**, *a folk dance of Panjab. They are wearing sparkling, colourful clothes. They are carrying long wooden poles in their hands.*
David	*One man is carrying a big drum.*
Mr Singh	*With the beat of the drum, it is not only the feet but also the heart that starts dancing.*
Jane	*The verses of* **bhangra** *are old fashioned. I like the new, modern songs which are composed by young people born and raised here.*
Mr Singh	*Believe it or not,* **bhangra** *has become an international dance. Whether you are in Panjab or abroad, you can always see* **bhangra**.
Jane	*Do only boys perform* **bhangra**?
Mr Singh	*In the old times,* **bhangra** *was for the boys and* **gidha** *was for the girls. Now everything is mixed up. Look! The* **gidha** *has started.*
David	*One of the girls is playing a small drum and the other girl is tapping the small drum with a spoon.*
Jane	*Everyone is in high spirits. Come on, let's dance!*

ਸ਼ਬਦਾਵਲੀ   shab<u>d</u>aavalee   Vocabulary

ਲੋਕ ਨਾਚ	lok naach	*folk dance* (m.)
ਚਮਕੀਲਾ	chamkeelaa	*glittering, shining, sparkling* (v.)
ਰੰਗਦਾਰ	ra<u>ng</u>daar	*colourful*
ਡਾਂਗ	daa<u>ng</u>	*long wooden pole* (f.)
ਢੋਲ	dhol	*big drum* (m.)
ਵੱਜਣਾ	vajjnhaa	*to be played, to be beaten*

ਪੈਰ	pair	*feet* (m.)
ਸਗੋਂ	sagon	*but also*
ਦਿਲ	dil	*heart* (m.)
ਨੱਚਣਾ	nachchnhaa	*to dance*
ਬੋਲੀਆਂ	boleeaan	*folk verse couplets* (f.)
ਅਜੋਕਾ	ajokaa	*modern*
ਜੰਮਪਲ	janmpal	*raised, born and bred*
ਨੌਜੁਆਨ	naujuaan	*youth* (m.)
ਰਚਨਾ	rachnaa	*composition* (f.)
ਮੰਨੋ ਜਾਂ ਨਾ ਮੰਨੋ	manno jaan naa manno	*believe it or not*
ਅੰਤਰ ਰਾਸ਼ਟਰੀ	antarr aashtaree	*international*
ਜ਼ਮਾਨਾ	zamaanaa	*times* (m.)
ਗਿੱਧਾ	gidhdhaa	*women's folk dance* (m.)
ਰਲ ਮਿਲਣਾ	ral milnhaa	*to be mixed*
ਵਿੱਚੋਂ	vichchon	*from within*
ਢੋਲਕੀ	dholkee	*small drum* (f.)
ਵਜਾਉਣਾ	vajaaunhaa	*to play (music), to beat*
ਚਮਚਾ	chamchaa	*spoon* (m.)
ਮਾਰਨਾ	maarnaa	*to hit, to tap*
ਚੜ੍ਹਦੀ ਕਲਾ	charhhdee kalaa	*high spirits*

ਅਭਿਆਸ   abhiaas   Exercises

After reading the dialogue and/or listening to the audio tape, try to do the following exercises.

1. True or false?

a. ਪੁਰਾਣੇ ਜ਼ਮਾਨੇ ਵਿਚ ਭੰਗੜਾ ਸਿਰਫ਼ ਮੁੰਡਿਆਂ ਲਈ ਸੀ   True / False
b. ਜੋਨ ਨੂੰ ਉਹ ਗੀਤ ਚੰਗੇ ਲੱਗਦੇ ਹਨ ਜਿਹੜੇ ਪੁਰਾਣੇ ਤੇ ਪੰਜਾਬ ਦੇ ਹਨ   True / False
c. ਢੋਲਕੀ ਤੇ ਕੁੜੀਆਂ ਡਾਂਗਾਂ ਮਾਰਦੀਆਂ ਹਨ   True / False
d. ਭੰਗੜਾ ਅੰਤਰ ਰਾਸ਼ਟਰੀ ਨਾਚ ਬਣ ਗਿਆ ਹੈ   True / False

2. Write or say the sentences in Panjabi

a. *I like* **bhangra**.
b. *I like* **bhangra** *more than* **gidha**.
c. *Whether you're in Panjab or abroad, you can see* **bhangra**.
d. *Come on, let's dance!*

3. Try to identify the items from the descriptions given in the dialogue

a.   b.   c.

▶ 2 Avtar's life story

📷 ਗੱਲ ਬਾਤ ੨ ਅਵਤਾਰ ਦੀ ਜੀਵਨ ਕਹਾਣੀ

gall baat 2 avtaar dee jeevan kahaanhee

Two men, Avtar and Tarlok, are sitting on a park bench in Vancouver enjoying the sunny day. Avtar is reminiscing about his family's history and how he came to settle in Vancouver.

ਅਵਤਾਰ	ਕੀ ਸਾਨੂੰ ਆਪਣੇ ਬਚਪਨ ਵਿਚ ਕਦੀ ਖ਼ਿਆਲ ਸੀ ਕਿ ਅਸੀਂ ਇਸ ਉਮਰ ਵਿਚ ਕੈਨੇਡਾ ਰਹਿ ਰਹੇ ਹੋਵਾਂ ਗੇ ? ਮੇਰਾ ਪੜਦਾਦਾ ਅੰਗਰੇਜ਼ਾਂ ਦੇ ਰਾਜ ਵੇਲੇ ਫ਼ੌਜ ਵਿਚ ਭਰਤੀ ਹੋ ਗਿਆ ਤੇ ਉਸ ਨੂੰ ਮਲੇਸ਼ੀਆ ਭੇਜ ਦਿੱਤਾ ਗਿਆ। ਮੇਰੇ ਦਾਦੇ ਦਾ ਜਨਮ ਉੱਥੇ ਹੋਇਆ। ਜਦੋਂ ਉਹ ਵਾਪਸ ਪਰਤਿਆ ਤਾਂ ਅਜ਼ਾਦੀ ਲਈ ਜੱਦੋ ਜਹਿਦ ਸ਼ੁਰੂ ਹੋ ਗਈ ਸੀ। ਮੇਰਾ ਦਾਦਾ ਗ਼ਦਰ ਪਾਰਟੀ ਵਿਚ ਸ਼ਾਮਲ ਹੋ ਕੇ ਵੈਨਕੂਵਰ ਆ ਗਿਆ।
ਤਰਲੋਕ	ਕੀ ਤੇਰਾ ਜਨਮ ਕੈਨੇਡਾ ਹੋਇਆ ਸੀ ?
ਅਵਤਾਰ	ਕਹਾਣੀ ਲੰਬੀ ਹੈ। ਸਾਡੇ ਵੱਡਕਿਆਂ ਨੇ ਬਾਂ ਬਾਂ ਦਾ ਪਾਣੀ ਪੀਤਾ ਹੈ। ਸਮਾਂ ਪਾ ਕੇ ਮੇਰਾ ਦਾਦਾ ਪੰਜਾਬ ਮੁੜ ਗਿਆ। ਫਿਰ ੧੯੪੭ ਵਿਚ ਪੰਜਾਬ ਦਾ ਬਟਵਾਰਾ ਹੋ ਗਿਆ। ਉਦੋਂ ਮੇਰੇ ਪਿਤਾ ਜੀ ਲਾਇਲਪੁਰ ਸਨ ਤੇ ਸਾਰੇ ਪਰਵਾਰ ਨੂੰ ਜਲੰਧਰ ਜਾਣਾ ਪਿਆ। ਮੇਰਾ ਜਨਮ ਜਲੰਧਰ ਹੋਇਆ ਸੀ।
ਤਰਲੋਕ	ਮੇਰੇ ਦਾਦਾ ਜੀ ਈਸਟ ਅਫ਼ਰੀਕਾ ਰੇਲਵੇ ਬਣਾਉਣ ਚਲੇ ਗਏ। ਮੇਰਾ ਜਨਮ ਅਸਥਾਨ ਯੂਗੰਡਾ ਹੈ। ੧੯੭੧ ਵਿਚ ਛੱਡ ਛੱਡਾ ਕੇ ਅਸੀਂ ਪਹਿਲੇ ਇੰਗਲੈਂਡ ਗਏ ਤੇ ਫਿਰ ਕੈਨੇਡਾ ਆ ਗਏ।
ਅਵਤਾਰ	ਇਸ ਦਾ ਮਤਲਬ ਇਹ ਹੈ ਕਿ ਤੁਸੀਂ ਪੰਜਾਬ ਤੋਂ ਕਾਫ਼ੀ ਦੇਰ ਤੋਂ ਉਖੜੇ ਹੋਏ ਹੋ।
ਤਰਲੋਕ	ਹਾਂ। ਪਰ ਹੁਣ ਮੇਰਾ ਦਿਲ ਲੱਗ ਗਿਆ ਹੈ, ਭਾਵੇਂ ਅਸੀਂ ਪੰਜਾਬ ਤੋਂ ਦੂਰ ਹਾਂ। ਇੱਥੇ ਆਪਣੀ ਅਬਾਦੀ ਕਾਫ਼ੀ ਹੈ। ਮਾਹੌਲ ਪੰਜਾਬ ਵਾਂਗੂ ਹੈ।
ਅਵਤਾਰ	ਦੁਨੀਆਂ ਵਿਚ ਕਿਸੇ ਵੀ ਜਗਾਹ ਚਲੇ ਜਾਓ, ਭਾਵੇਂ ਕੈਨੇਡਾ ਭਾਵੇਂ ਇੰਗਲੈਂਡ ਜਾਂ ਅਮਰੀਕਾ, ਕੋਈ ਨ ਕੋਈ ਆਪਣਾ ਪੰਜਾਬੀ ਬੰਦਾ ਤੈਨੂੰ ਮਿਲ ਜਾਏ ਗਾ।
ਤਰਲੋਕ	ਪਰ ਸਿਆਣੇ ਲੋਕ ਕਹਿੰਦੇ ਹਨ ਕਿ ਧੋਬੀ ਦਾ ਕੁੱਤਾ ਨਾ ਘਰ ਦਾ ਨਾ ਘਾਟ ਦਾ !
ਅਵਤਾਰ	ਇਹ ਅਖਾਣ ਪੁਰਾਣਾ ਹੈ। ਹੁਣ ਸਾਰੀ ਦੁਨੀਆਂ ਤੁਹਾਡੀ ਹੈ। ਵਾਹਿਗੁਰੂ ਭਲੀ ਕਰੇ ਗਾ ।

Avtar *Did we ever dream in our childhood that at this age we would be living in Canada? My great grandfather joined the army during the time of British rule and he was sent to Malaysia. My grandfather was born there. When he returned home, the struggle for independence had started. My grandfather joined the Gadar Party and came to Vancouver.*

Tarlok *So, were you born in Canada?*

Avtar *It's a long story. Our forefathers have been to many places [lit. our forefathers drank water from many different places]. After a while, my grandfather returned to Panjab. Then in 1947 Panjab was partitioned. At that time my father was in Lyallpur and the whole family had to go to Jalandhar. I was born in Jalandhar.*

Tarlok *My grandfather went to East Africa to build the railways. My birthplace is Uganda. In 1971 we left everything and went first to England and then came to Canada.*

Avtar *This means that you have been uprooted from Panjab for a long time.*

Tarlok *Yes. But even though we are far away from Panjab, I am now happily settled [lit. my heart has been applied or fixed]. There are quite a lot of our own people here. The atmosphere is just like Panjab.*

Avtar *Go anywhere in the world, whether it's Canada, England or America, and you will meet a Panjabi person.*

Tarlok *But wise men say that immigrants belong to no one place. [Proverb: the dog of a washerman belongs neither at home nor at the washing place.]*

Avtar *This is an old proverb. Now the whole world belongs to you. God will watch over you.*

ਸ਼ਬਦਾਵਲੀ- shab<u>d</u>aavalee   Vocabulary

ਜੀਵਨ	jeevan	*life* (m.)
ਬਚਪਨ	bachpan	*childhood* (m.)
ਪੜਦਾਦਾ	par<u>hd</u>aa<u>d</u>aa	*great grandfather* (m.)
ਰਾਜ	raaj	*rulership, kingdom* (m.)
ਵੇਲੇ	vele	*period, time* (m.)
ਫੌਜ	fauj	*military* (f.)
ਭਰਤੀ	bhar<u>t</u>ee	*join*
ਜਨਮ	janam	*birth* (m.)

ਪਰਤਨਾ	partnhaa	*to return*
ਅਜ਼ਾਦੀ	azaa<u>d</u>ee	*freedom, independence* (f.)
ਜਦੋ ਜਹਿਦ	ja<u>d</u>o jahi<u>d</u>	*struggle* (f.)
ਅਜ਼ਾਦੀ ਲਈ ਜਦੋ ਜਹਿਦ	azaa<u>d</u>ee laee ja<u>d</u>o jahid	*struggle for independence*
ਗ਼ਦਰ	<u>gh</u>a<u>d</u>ar	*mutiny* (m.)
ਗ਼ਦਰ ਪਾਰਟੀ	<u>gh</u>a<u>d</u>ar paartee	*Gadar Party* (f.) (an anti-colonial political movement in Panjab in the early 20th century which had strong connections with Vancouver because of the large number of exiles from Panjab who went there)
ਲੰਬਾ	la<u>n</u>baa	*long, lengthy* (v.)
ਵਡੱਕਿਆਂ	vadkkiaa<u>n</u>	*ancestors, forefathers* (m.)
ਥਾਂ ਥਾਂ	<u>th</u>aa<u>n</u> <u>th</u>aa<u>n</u>	*each and every place* (m.)
ਸਮਾਂ ਪਾ ਕੇ	samaa<u>n</u> paa ke	*after a while, after some time*
ਮੁੜਨਾ	murhnaa	*to turn around, to return*
ਬਟਵਾਰਾ	batvaaraa	*division, partition* (m.)
ਈਸਟ ਅਫ਼ਰੀਕਾ	eest afreekaa	*East Africa* (m.)
ਯੂਗੰਡਾ	yooga<u>n</u>daa	*Uganda* (m.)
ਜਨਮ ਅਸਥਾਨ	janam as<u>th</u>aan	*birthplace* (m.)
ਉਖੜਨਾ	ukharhnaa	*to be displaced, to be uprooted*
ਦਿਲ ਲੱਗਣਾ	<u>d</u>il laggnhaa	*to feel at home, to be settled, to live happily*
ਕੋਈ ਨ ਕੋਈ	koee na koee	*some one or another*
ਸਿਆਣਾ	siaanhaa	*wise, mature* (v.)
ਧੋਬੀ	<u>dh</u>obee	*washerman* (m.)
ਕੁੱਤਾ	ku<u>t</u>taa	*dog* (m.)
ਘਾਟ	ghaat	*place where clothes are washed on the bank of the river or canal* (m.)
ਅਖਾਣ	akhaanh	*proverb, saying* (m.)
ਭਲੀ	bhalee	*look after, watch over*

◢ ਅਭਿਆਸ   abhiaas   Exercises

After reading the dialogue and/or listening to the audio tape, try to do the following exercises.

1. Name four countries mentioned in the dialogue

2. Answer the questions

Answer the following questions in Panjabi either in short form or in full sentences. You may lift the answers from the dialogue.

a. ਜਿਹੜੇ ਦੋਨੋਂ ਦੋਸਤ ਆਪਸ ਵਿਚ ਗੱਲਾਂ ਕਰ ਰਹੇ ਹਨ, ਉਹਨਾਂ ਦੇ ਨਾਮ ਕੀ ਹਨ ?

b. ਅਵਤਾਰ ਦੇ ਦਾਦੇ ਦਾ ਜਨਮ ਕਿੱਥੇ ਹੋਇਆ ਸੀ ?

c. ਜਦੋਂ ਪੰਜਾਬ ਦਾ ਬਟਵਾਰਾ ਹੋ ਗਿਆ, ਅਵਤਾਰ ਦਾ ਪਿਤਾ ਕਿੱਥੇ ਸੀ ?

d. ਤਰਲੋਕ ਦਾ ਜਨਮ ਅਸਥਾਨ ਕਿੱਥੇ ਹੈ ?

e. ਸਿਆਣੇ ਬੰਦੇ ਕੀ ਕਹਿੰਦੇ ਹਨ ?

3. Give the reasons why Avtar and Tarlok's families migrated to each place

a. ਅਵਤਾਰ ਦੇ ਪੜਦਾਦਾ ਜੀ ਮਲੇਸ਼ੀਆ ਕਿਉਂ ਗਏ ਸੀ ?

b. ਅਵਤਾਰ ਦੇ ਦਾਦਾ ਜੀ ਵੈਨਕੂਵਰ ਕਿਉਂ ਗਏ ਸੀ ?

c. ੧੯੪੭ ਵਿਚ ਅਵਤਾਰ ਦੇ ਸਾਰੇ ਪਰਵਾਰ ਨੂੰ ਜਲੰਧਰ ਕਿਉਂ ਜਾਣਾ ਪਿਆ ?

d. ਤਰਲੋਕ ਦੇ ਦਾਦਾ ਜੀ ਈਸਟ ਅਫਰੀਕਾ ਕਿਉਂ ਗਏ ਸੀ ?

▧ ਬੋਲੀ ਬਾਰੇ   bolee baare   Language points

Future continuous

The future continuous is used when an ongoing action in the future is being described, similar to the usage in the English sentence *I will be going*. This would be expressed in Panjabi as ਮੈਂ ਜਾ ਰਿਹਾ ਹੋਵਾਂ ਗਾ. The future continuous can also be used in situations when the on-going action in the future was not certain at the time of contemplation. For example, at the beginning of the second dialogue, when Avtar says to Tarlok ਕੀ ਸਾਨੂੰ ਕਦੀ ਖ਼ਿਆਲ ਸੀ ਕਿ ਅਸੀਂ ਕੈਨੇਡਾ ਰਹਿ ਰਹੇ ਹੋਵਾਂ ਗੇ ?, *Did we ever dream that we would be living in Canada?* In English the uncertainty of the sentence would be expressed through the use of *would* rather than *will*. In Panjabi the future continuous tense can be used for both types of situations.

In previous units you were introduced to both the present continuous tense and the future tense. The future continuous tense can be most simply understood as a combination of the present continuous and the future tenses. Notice in the following examples how the future continuous combines the two tenses:

Future tense	ਮੈਂ ਜਾਵਾਂ ਗਾ	*I will go*
Present continuous	ਮੈਂ ਜਾ ਰਿਹਾ ਹਾਂ	*I am going*
Future continuous	ਮੈਂ ਜਾ ਰਿਹਾ ਹੋਵਾਂ ਗਾ	*I will/would be going*
Future tense	ਅਸੀਂ ਖਾਵਾਂ ਗੇ	*We will eat*
Present continuous	ਅਸੀਂ ਖਾ ਰਹੇ ਹਾਂ	*We are eating*
Future continuous	ਅਸੀਂ ਖਾ ਰਹੇ ਹੋਵਾਂ ਗੇ	*We will/would be eating*

The continuous action in the sentence takes the present continuous form such as in these examples with *going* represented through the stem ਜਾ and *eating* with the stem ਖਾ, and with the appropriate forms of ਰਿਹਾ. You should have noticed that the auxiliary verb that comes at the end of the present continuous tense does not appear in the future continuous. Instead, the verb ਹੋਣਾ is in the future form with the respective -ਗਾ endings.

Phrases of choice

In English, phrases of choice are expressed through such words as *either ... or*, *neither ... nor* and *not only ... but also*. In Panjabi there are similar types of constructions to express choice most commonly using the following:

ਭਾਵੇਂ ... ਭਾਵੇਂ	*either ... or, whether or not*
ਚਾਹੇ .. .ਚਾਹੇ	*either ... or, whether or not*
ਨਾ ... ਨਾ	*neither ... nor*
ਨਾ ਸਿਰਫ਼ ... ਸਗੋਂ	*not only ... but*
ਜਾਂ ... ਨਾ	*may or not*

Some examples of these words in use:

ਭਾਵੇਂ ਤੁਸੀਂ ਜਾਓ ਭਾਵੇਂ ਨਾ ਜਾਓ, ਮੈਂ ਇੱਥੇ ਰਵਾਂ ਗੀ	*Whether you go or not, I will stay here.* (lit. *Whether you go or whether you do not go, I will stay here.*)
ਚਾਹੇ ਸਾਡੇ ਨਾਲ ਆਓ ਚਾਹੇ ਉਹਨਾਂ ਨਾਲ ਜਾਓ, ਤੁਹਾਨੂੰ ਜਲਦੀ ਨਿਕਲਣਾ ਪੈਣਾ	*Whether you come with us or (whether you) go with them, you'll have to get out quickly.*
ਸਾਡੇ ਕੋਲ ਨਾ ਕਿਤਾਬਾਂ ਹਨ ਨਾ ਕਾਗਜ਼ ਹੈ	*We have neither books nor paper.*
ਲੋਕ ਨਾ ਸਿਰਫ਼ ਭਾਰਤ ਤੋਂ ਆਉਂਦੇ ਹਨ ਸਗੋਂ ਸਾਰੀ ਦੁਨੀਆਂ ਤੋਂ ਆਉਂਦੇ ਹਨ	*People come not only from India, but from all over the world.*
ਮੰਨੋ ਜਾਂ ਨਾ ਮੰਨੋ ਇਹ ਜਗ੍ਹਾ ਸਭ ਤੋਂ ਸੁਹਣੀ ਹੈ	*You may or may not agree but this is the nicest place.*

ਹੈ ਗਾ and ਸੀ ਗਾ

In colloquial Panjabi, the verb ਹੋਣਾ is often expressed with the ending -ਗਾ when there is an added emphasis. The ending -ਗਾ merely indicates definiteness or confirmation, and must agree with the number and gender of the subject that it is referring to followed by the appropriate present form of ਹੋਣਾ. In Unit 3 Jane and Henry went to the sweets shop with Mr Singh. Jane asked the shopkeeper ਕੀ ਕੋਈ ਨਮਕੀਨ ਚੀਜ਼ ਹੈ ?, *Is there anything salty?* This question is general in nature. If Jane had wished to put further emphasis on the definite availability of something salty, she could have said: ਕੀ ਕੋਈ ਨਮਕੀਨ ਚੀਜ਼ ਹੈ ਗੀ ਏ ?, *Is there anything salty (available)?* The shopkeeper could have then replied ਹਾਂ ਜੀ, ਹੈ ਗੀ ਏ; *Yes, there (definitely) is.* Note that the feminine singular form is used (-ਗੀ) in agreement with ਚੀਜ਼, although in the shopkeeper's response the subject is omitted as it is simply understood. Since ਹੈ ਗਾ is only used in informal speech, the auxiliary verb ਹੋਣਾ also appears in its informal form, hence ਏ instead of ਹੈ.

When one wants to express the same type of definiteness in the past, then ਸੀ (was) is followed by the ending -ਗਾ. Again, the number and gender of the subject will determine the ending of -ਗਾ. Some examples are as follows:

ਜਸਪ੍ਰੀਤ ਤੇ ਸਿਮਰਨ ਘਰ ਸੀ ਗੀਆਂ	*Jaspreet and Simran were (definitely) at home.*
ਤੁਸੀਂ ਚੁੱਪ ਚਾਪ ਸੀ ਗੇ	*You (certainly) were quiet.*

You will come across ਹੈ ਗਾ and ਸੀ ਗਾ frequently in spoken colloquial conversation, though rarely in the written form.

ਵਿਆਖਿਆ viaakhiaa Commentary

Folk music

Folk music is an integral part of cultural expression not only in Panjab, but in the three Panjabs: East Panjab in India, West Panjab in Pakistan and the Panjabi diaspora all over the world. In fact, music is one of the main factors that links Panjabis across religious, national and caste divisions. **Bhangra** music, in particular, has come to prominence in the last twenty years in the west. The picture of the two boys on the cover of this book actually shows the traditional costume of **bhangra** dancers. This active and incessant dance music form is a vital part of a global expression of youth culture as well as a particular link between **des** (*home*) and **pardes** (*abroad*) for many Panjabis.

As we saw in the previous unit, there are many other musical forms from Panjab which focus on the relationship between music and poetry which are less related to the robust dance style of **bhangra** and more to the film music and **ghazal** (*ballad*) form. A wide range of Panjabi music from westernised dance music to slow ballads is widely available in the South Asian shopping centres of London, New York, Toronto and Melbourne.

ਅਭਿਆਸ abhiaas Exercises

After reading the dialogue and/or listening to the audio tape, try to do the following exercises.

1. Complete the sentences

Complete the sentences (verbally or in written form) with the help of the vocabulary given. The first one has been done for you.

a. ਸਾਡੇ ਕੋਲ ਨਾ ਕਿਤਾਬਾਂ ਹਨ, ਨਾ ਕਾਗ਼ਜ਼ ਹੈ।
   We have neither books nor paper.

b. ਸਾਡੇ ਕੋਲ ਨਾ _____ ਹਨ, ਨਾ _____ ਹੈ।
c. ਸਾਡੇ ਕੋਲ ਨਾ _____ ਹਨ, ਨਾ _____ ਹੈ।
d. ਸਾਡੇ ਕੋਲ ਨਾ _____ ਹਨ, ਨਾ _____ ਹੈ।

| ਪੈਂਸਲਾਂ | pencils | ਕਾਪੀ | exercise book | ਘੜੀਆਂ | watches |
| ਰੇਡੀਓ | radio | ਬੋਤਲਾਂ | bottles | ਪਾਣੀ | water |

2. Say or write the sentences in Panjabi

a. ਮੰਨੋ ਜਾਂ ਨਾ ਮੰਨੋ, ਇਹ ਜਗ੍ਹਾ ਸੋਹਣੀ ਹੈ।
   Believe it or not, this place is beautiful.
b. Not only is this book long, but it is also difficult.
c. Not only do we like **bhangra**, but we also like **gidha**.
d. Whether you live in Panjab or abroad, you can see **bhangra**.
e. You may or may not agree, but Vancouver's atmosphere is just like Panjab.

3. Tick the boxes which correspond with Tarlok and Avtar's respective life histories

	ਇੰਗਲੈਂਡ	ਮਲੇਸ਼ੀਆ	ਕੈਨੇਡਾ	ਲਾਇਲਪੁਰ	ਸੁਗੀਡਾ	ਜਲੰਧਰ
ਤਰਲੋਕ						
ਅਵਤਾਰ						

APPENDIX 1

Consonants			Velar	Palatal	Retroflex	Dental	Labial
Plosives	Voiceless	Unaspirated	ਕ	ਚ	ਟ	ਤ	ਪ
		Aspirated	ਖ	ਛ	ਠ	ਥ	ਫ
	Voiced	Unaspirated	ਗ	ਜ	ਡ	ਦ	ਬ
		Aspirated	ਘ	ਝ	ਢ	ਧ	ਭ
	Nasals		ਙ	ਞ	ਣ	ਨ	ਮ
Fricatives	Voiceless		ਖ਼	ਸ਼		ਸ	ਫ਼
	Voiced		ਗ਼			ਜ਼	
Flapped and Tapped sounds					ੜ	ਰ	
Aspirate, semi-vowel and liquid				ਹ	ਯ		ਲ	ਵ

APPENDIX 2

Comparison of tongue positions

a. Pronunciation of t and d in English. Tongue against the teeth ridge.

b. Pronunciation of ਤ t̲ and ਦ d̲. Tongue against the base of upper incisors.

c. Pronunciation of ਟ t and ਡ d. Tongue against the back hard palate.

KEY TO EXERCISES

Reading and writing

Lesson 4 Exercise 2 a. ਰਿੱਛ b. ਕਿੱਲ c. ਹਿਰਨ Lesson 5 Exercise 2 a. ਸੀਟੀ b. ਬਿੱਲੀ c. ਵਲੀ Lesson 6 Exercise 2 a. ਚੱਕਣ b. ਜਬਾਨ c. ਉੱਨ Lesson 7 Exercise 2 a. ਊਠ b. ਸੂਰ c. ਝਾੜੂ Lesson 8 Exercise 2 a. ਲੇਲੇ b. ਭੇਡ c. ਸੇਬ Lesson 9 Exercise 2 a. ਭੇਟ b. ਐਤਵਾਰ c. ਐਨਕ Lesson 10 Exercise 2 a. ਘੋੜਾ b. ਮੋਟਾ c. ਖੋੜਾ Lesson 11 Exercise 2 a. ਚੌਲ b. ਖਿਡੌਣੇ c. ਫੌਜੀ Lesson 12 Exercise 2 a. ਜੰਘ b. ਲੰਗਾ c. ਵਤਾਊਂ

Unit 1

Dialogue 1 exercises

1. a. True b. True c. False 2. a. ਮੇਰਾ ਨਾਂ ਡੇਵਿਡ ਹੈ। meraa naa<u>n</u> devid hai. b. ਤੁਹਾਡਾ ਕੀ ਨਾਮ ਹੈ? <u>t</u>uhaadaa kee naam hai? c. ਤੇਰਾ ਕੀ ਨਾਂ ਏ? <u>t</u>eraa kee naa<u>n</u> e?

Dialogue 2 exercises

1. a. ਅੱਸਲਾਮ ਅਲੈਕਮ। asslaam alaikam. b. ਤੁਹਾਡਾ ਕੀ ਹਾਲ ਹੈ? <u>t</u>uhaadaa kee haal hai? c. ਕੀ ਪਰਵਾਰ ਠੀਕ ਹੈ? kee parvaar theek hai? 2. a. 2 b. 3   c. 1

End exercises

1. 1st line, 2nd letter; 3rd line, 1st letter; 5th line, 4th letter 2. a. ਨਮਸਤੇ namas<u>t</u>e b. ਵਾਲੈਕਮ ਅੱਸਲਾਮ vaalaikam asslaam c. ਸਤਿ ਸ੍ਰੀ ਅਕਾਲ sa<u>t</u> sree akaal 3. a. ਤੁਹਾਡਾ <u>t</u>uhaadaa b. ਤੇਰਾ <u>t</u>eraa c. ਤੇਰਾ <u>t</u>eraa 4. You: ਸਤਿ ਸ੍ਰੀ ਅਕਾਲ। ਮੇਰਾ ਨਾਮ _____ ਹੈ। ਤੁਹਾਡਾ ਕੀ ਨਾਮ ਹੈ? sa<u>t</u> sree akaal. meraa naam _____ hai. <u>t</u>uhaadaa kee naam hai? You: ਮੈਂ ਠੀਕ ਹਾਂ। ਤੁਸੀਂ ਕਿਵੇਂ ਹੋ? mai<u>n</u> theek haa<u>n</u>. <u>t</u>usee<u>n</u> kive<u>n</u> ho? You: ਰੱਬ ਰਾਖਾ। rabb raakhaa.

Unit 2

Dialogue 1 exercises

1. a. False   b. False   c. True 2. Jeevan – Panjabi John – English Ram – Gujarati

Dialogue 2 exercises

1. Ashok: ਹਾਂ ਜੀ, ਮੈਂ ਅਸ਼ੋਕ ਹਾਂ।   haan jee, main ashok haan. Mrs Sharma: ਮੇਰਾ ਹਾਲ ਠੀਕ ਹੈ।   meraa haal theek hai. Kiran: ਨਹੀਂ, ਮੇਰੇ ਮਾਤਾ ਜੀ ਇੱਥੇ ਨਹੀਂ ਹਨ। naheen, mere maataa jee iththe naheen han. 2. a. ਮੈਂ ਕਿਰਨ ਹਾਂ। main kiran haan. b. ਕੀ ਤੁਸੀਂ ਅਸ਼ੋਕ ਹੋ? kee tuseen ashok ho? c. ਉਹ ਇੱਥੇ ਨਹੀਂ ਹਨ uh iththe naheen han. 3. 1. Panjabi 2. English 3. Class 4. Mrs Sharma 5. Hindu

End exercises

1. are, hai, ਹੋ 2. a. ਕੀ ਤੁਸੀਂ ਅਸ਼ੋਕ ਹੋ? kee tuseen ashok ho? b. ਕੀ ਤੁਸੀਂ ਕਿਰਨ ਹੋ? kee tuseen kiran ho? c. ਮੈਂ ਕਿਰਨ ਹਾਂ main kiran haan d. ਉਹ ਅਸ਼ੋਕ ਹੈ uh ashok hai 3. a. ਹੈਂ hain b. ਹਾਂ haan c. ਹਨ han 4. 1st line 2nd letter 3rd line 1st letter 4th line 2nd letter

Unit 3

Dialogue 1 exercises

1. a. False b. False c. True d. False e. True 2. ਕਰੇਲਾ karelaa ਸ਼ਲਗਮ shalgam ਭਿੰਡੀ bhindee ਗੋਭੀ gobhee ਟਮਾਟਰ tamaatar ਮਟਰ matar

Dialogue 2 exercises

1. miththaa, bitter, ਸੁਆਦ 2. a. ਇਹ ਦੁਕਾਨ ਹੈ। ih dukaan hai. b. ਇਹ ਚੰਗੀ ਦੁਕਾਨ ਹੈ। ih changee dukaan hai. c. ਇਹ ਮਿਠਿਆਈ ਦੀ ਦੁਕਾਨ ਹੈ। ih mithiaaee dee dukaan hai. d. ਇਹ ਚੰਗੀ ਮਿਠਿਆਈ ਦੀ ਦੁਕਾਨ ਹੈ। ih changee mithiaaee dee dukaan hai.

End exercises

1. a. ਛੋਟਾ chotaa b. ਵੱਡਾ vaddaa c. ਛੋਟੀ chotee d. ਵੱਡੀ vaddee e. ਛੋਟਾ chotaa f. ਵੱਡਾ vaddaa 2. Mr Singh: samosaa, pakaurhe, bhindee Jane: samosaa, laddoo, pakaurhe Henry: rasmalaaee, bhindee, gobhee 3. a. ਗੁਲਾਬ ਜਾਮਣ gulaab jaamanh b. ਬਰਫੀ barfee c. ਸਮੋਸਾ samosaa d. ਪਕੌੜੇ pakaurhe 4. a. ਉਹਨਾਂ ਦੇ uhnaan de b. ਮੇਰੇ mere c. ਸਾਡੀਆਂ saadeeaan d. ਤੁਹਾਡੀਆਂ tuhaadeeaan

Unit 4

Dialogue 1 exercises

1. b. ਕੀ ਇਹ ਸੀਟ ਖ਼ਾਲੀ ਹੈ? kee ih seet <u>kh</u>aalee hai? ਹਾਂ ਜੀ, ਖ਼ਾਲੀ ਹੈ। haa<u>n</u> jee, <u>kh</u>aalee hai. c. ਮੈਂ ਅਧਿਆਪਕਾ ਹਾਂ। mai<u>n</u> adhiaapkaa haa<u>n</u>. d. ਤੁਸੀਂ ਕੀ ਕਰਦੇ ਹੋ? <u>t</u>usee<u>n</u> kee kar<u>d</u>e ho? 2. a. ਮੈਂ ਵੀ ਬਰਮਿੰਘਮ ਰਹਿੰਦਾ ਹਾਂ mai<u>n</u> vee barmi<u>n</u>gham rahi<u>nd</u>aa haa<u>n</u>. b. ਮੈਂ ਦਿੱਲੀ ਤੋਂ ਹਾਂ mai<u>n</u> dillee <u>t</u>on haa<u>n</u>. c. ਤੁਸੀਂ ਕੀ ਕਰਦੇ ਹੋ? <u>t</u>usee<u>n</u> kee kar<u>d</u>e ho? 3. 1. c 2. a 3. b 4. e 5. d

Dialogue 2 exercises

1. a. True b. True c. False 2. a. ਮੇਰਾ ਨਾਮ (_____) ਹੈ। meraa naam (_____) hai. b. ਮੈਂ (_____) ਹਾਂ mai<u>n</u> (_____) haa<u>n</u>. c. ਮੈਂ (_____) ਤੋਂ ਹਾਂ mai<u>n</u> (_____) <u>t</u>on haa<u>n</u>. d. ਮੈਂ (_____) ਰਹਿੰਦਾ/ ਰਹਿੰਦੀ ਹਾਂ। mai<u>n</u> (_____) rahi<u>nd</u>aa/rahi<u>nd</u>ee haa<u>n</u>.

End exercises

1. a. True b. False c. False d. False 2. a. Mrs Sharma b. Mrs Khan c. Dr Singh 3. a. direct b. oblique c. direct d. oblique e. oblique 4. b. ਮੇਰੀਆਂ ਬੇਟੀਆਂ ਸਕੂਲ ਵਿਚ ਪੜ੍ਹਦੀਆਂ ਹਨ। mereeaa<u>n</u> beteeaa<u>n</u> sakool vich parhh<u>d</u>eeaa<u>n</u> han. *My daughters study in school.* c. ਤੁਹਾਡੇ ਲੜਕੇ ਕਿੱਥੇ ਰਹਿੰਦੇ ਹਨ? <u>t</u>uhaade larhke ki<u>thth</u>e rahi<u>nd</u>e han? *Where do your sons live?* d. ਕੀ ਉਹ ਮੁੰਡੇ ਪੰਜਾਬੀ ਬੋਲਦੇ ਹਨ? kee uh mu<u>nd</u>e pa<u>n</u>jaabee bol<u>d</u>e han? *Do those boys speak Panjabi?*

Unit 5

Dialogue 1 exercises

1. a. ਨਮਸਤੇ, ਤੂੰ ਕੀ ਕਰ ਰਹੀ ਹੈਂ? namas<u>t</u>e, <u>t</u>oon kee kar rahee hai<u>n</u>? b. ਮੈਂ ਜੇਬਾਂ ਲਗਾ ਰਹੀ ਹਾਂ। mai<u>n</u> jebaa<u>n</u> lagaa rahee haa<u>n</u>. c. ਮੈਨੇਜਰ ਸਾਡੀ ਤਨਖ਼ਾਹ ਨਹੀਂ ਵਧਾ ਰਿਹਾ। mainejar saadee <u>t</u>an<u>kh</u>aah naheen vadhaa rihaa. 2. 1. machine 2. work 3. salary 4. pockets 5. time 6. needle

Dialogue 2 exercises

1. 1st line 2nd letter 2nd line 1st letter 3rd line 3rd letter 4th line 2nd letter 2. a. ਸੁਮੀਤ ਫ਼ਿਲਮ ਦੇਖ ਰਹੀ ਸੀ। sumee<u>t</u> filam <u>d</u>ekh rahee see. b. ਬੱਚੇ ਖੇਡ ਰਹੇ ਸਨ। bachche khed rahe san. c. ਸੁਮੀਤ ਦਾ ਪਤੀ ਕਾਰ ਧੋ ਰਿਹਾ ਸੀ। sumee<u>t</u> <u>d</u>aa pa<u>t</u>ee kaar <u>dh</u>o rihaa see.

End exercises

1. a. ਤੁਸੀਂ ਸਮਾਂ ਜ਼ਾਇਆ ਕਰ ਰਹੇ ਹੋ। ṯuseen̲ samaan̲ zaaiaa kar rahe ho. b. ਤੁਸੀਂ ਕੰਮ ਕਿਉਂ ਛੱਡ ਰਹੇ ਹੋ? ṯuseen̲ kan̲m kiun̲ c̲hadd rahe ho? c. ਤੁਸੀਂ ਠੀਕ ਕਹਿ ਰਹੇ ਹੋ। ṯuseen̲ theek kahi rahe ho. 2. paṯee, house/home, ਕੱਲ੍ਹ 3. b. ਤੁਸੀਂ ਕੀ ਪੁੱਛ ਰਹੇ ਸੀ? ṯuseen̲ kee puc̲hch rahe see? *What were you asking*? c. ਉਹ ਕੀ ਕਰ ਰਹੇ ਸਨ? uh kee kar rahe san? *What were they doing*? d. ਉਹ ਕਾਰ ਧੋ ਰਿਹਾ ਸੀ। uh kaar d̲ho rihaa see. *He was washing the car*. 4. a. ਗੀਤਾ ਟੈਨਸ ਖੇਡ ਰਹੀ ਹੈ। geeṯaa tainas khed rahee hai. *Geeta is playing tennis*. b. ਅਵਤਾਰ ਖਾਣਾ ਖਾ ਰਿਹਾ ਹੈ। avṯaar khaanhaa khaa rihaa hai. *Avtar is eating food*. c. ਸੀਤਾ ਤੇ ਗੀਤਾ ਪੰਜਾਬੀ ਬੋਲ ਰਹੀਆਂ ਹਨ। seeṯaa ṯe geeṯaa panjaabee bol raheeaan̲ han. *Sita and Geeta are speaking Panjabi*. d. ਮੁੰਡਾ ਕਿਤਾਬ ਪੜ੍ਹ ਰਿਹਾ ਹੈ। mun̲daa kiṯaab parhh rihaa hai. *The boy is reading a book*.

Unit 6

Dialogue 1 exercises

1. a. ਪਵਨ ਲੰਡਨ ਸੀ। pavan lan̲dan see. *Pavan was in London*. b. ਪਵਨ ਦੀ ਭਤੀਜੀ ਦਾ ਵਿਆਹ ਸੀ। pavan d̲ee bhaṯeejee d̲aa viaah see. *It was Pavan's niece's wedding*. c. ਮਾਨਚੈਸਟਰ maanchaisṯar *Manchester* d. ਤਕਰੀਬਨ ੧੦੦ ਬੰਦੇ ṯakreeban 100 ban̲d̲e *about 100 people* 2. a. ਤੁਸੀਂ ਐਤਵਾਰ ਕਿੱਥੇ ਸੀ? ṯuseen̲ aiṯvaar kiṯh̲the see? b. ਤੁਸੀਂ ਕੱਲ੍ਹ ਕਿੱਥੇ ਸੀ? ṯuseen̲ kallh kiṯhthe see? c. ਤੁਸੀਂ ਹਫ਼ਤੇ ਦੇ ਅਖੀਰ ਕਿੱਥੇ ਸੀ? ṯuseen̲ hafṯe d̲e akheer kiṯhthe see?

Dialogue 2 exercises

1. ਇਸਤਰੀ, woman ਇਕੱਠ, gathering ਪ੍ਰਾਹੁਣੇ, praahunhe ਕਾਲਜ, college ਭਾਬੀ, bhaabee 2. a. informal b. informal c. formal

End exercises

1.

2. a. 2 b. 3 c. 1 3. a. True b. False c. True 4. b. ਉਹ ਹਫ਼ਤੇ ਦੇ ਅਖੀਰ ਲੰਡਨ ਨਹੀਂ ਗਏ ਸਨ। uh haf<u>te de</u> a<u>kh</u>eer la<u>n</u>dan naheen gae san. ਕੀ ਉਹ ਹਫ਼ਤੇ ਦੇ ਅਖੀਰ ਲੰਡਨ ਗਏ ਸਨ ? kee uh haf<u>te de</u> a<u>kh</u>eer la<u>n</u>dan gae san? c. ਅਸੀਂ ਇਕੱਠੇ ਟੈਨਸ ਨਹੀਂ ਖੇਡਦੇ ਸੀ। aseen ikaththe tainas naheen <u>kh</u>ed<u>de</u> see. ਕੀ ਅਸੀਂ ਇਕੱਠੇ ਟੈਨਸ ਖੇਡਦੇ ਸੀ ? kee aseen ikaththe tainas <u>kh</u>ed<u>de</u> see? d. ਉਹ ਪੰਜਾਬੀ ਨਹੀਂ ਬੋਲਦੀ ਹੁੰਦੀ ਸੀ। uh pan<u>j</u>aabee naheen boldee hu<u>n</u>dee see ਕੀ ਉਹ ਪੰਜਾਬੀ ਬੋਲਦੀ ਹੁੰਦੀ ਸੀ ? kee uh pan<u>j</u>aabee boldee hu<u>n</u>dee see?

Unit 7

Dialogue 1 exercises

1. a. ਜ਼ਰੂਰ zaroor b. ਕੱਲ੍ਹ kallh c. ਕਿੰਨੇ ਵਜੇ ki<u>nn</u>e vaje 2. 4. 2. 3. 1.

Dialogue 2 exercises

1. a. ਤੁਸੀਂ ਕੀ ਪੀਓ ਗੇ ? tuseen kee peeo ge? b. ਕੀ ਤੁਸੀਂ ਟੀ ਵੀ ਦੇਖੋ ਗੇ ? kee <u>t</u>useen tee vee <u>d</u>ekho ge? c. ਕੀ ਤੁਸੀਂ ਰਸ ਲਵੋ ਗੇ ਜਾਂ ਚਾਹ ? kee <u>t</u>useen ras lavo ge jaa<u>n</u> chaah? 2. 1st line 1st letter 3rd line 3rd letter 5th line 2nd letter

End exercises

1. a. ਤੂੰ ਸੁਣ <u>t</u>oon sunh b. ਤੁਸੀਂ ਸੁਣੋ <u>t</u>useen sunho c. ਤੁਸੀਂ ਸੁਣੋ ਜੀ <u>t</u>useen sunho jee d. ਜ਼ਰਾ ਸੁਣਨਾ ਜੀ zaraa sunhnaa jee 2. 1. ਦਸ ਵਜੇ ਹਨ <u>d</u>as vaje han 2.ਢਾਈ ਵਜੇ ਹਨ dhaaee vaje han 3. ਪੌਣੇ ਛੇ ਵਜੇ ਹਨ paunhe <u>ch</u>e vaje han 4. ਸਵਾ ਅੱਠ ਵਜੇ ਹਨ savaa aththth vaje han 5. ਬਾਰਾਂ ਵਜੇ ਹਨ baar-h-aa<u>n</u> vaje han 6. ਸੱਤ ਵਜੇ ਹਨ sa<u>tt</u> vaje han 3. a. ਮੈਂ ਚਾਹ ਪੀਵਾਂ ਗਾ main chaah peevaa<u>n</u> gaa b. ਮੈਂ ਚਾਹ ਪੀਵਾਂ ਗੀ main chaah peevaa<u>n</u> gee c. ਅਸੀਂ ਚਾਹ ਪੀਵਾਂ ਗੇ aseen chaah peevaa<u>n</u> ge d. ਅਸੀਂ ਚਾਹ ਪੀਵਾਂ ਗੀਆਂ aseen chaah peevaa<u>n</u> geeaa<u>n</u> 4. a. ਹਾਂ ਜੀ, ਧੰਨਵਾਦ haa<u>n</u> jee, <u>dh</u>annvaad b. ਹਾਂ, ਕੱਲ੍ਹ ਮੈਂ ਆਵਾਂ ਗਾ haa<u>n</u>, kallh main aavaa<u>n</u> gaa c. ਨਹੀਂ ਮੈਂ ਕਾਹਲ ਵਿਚ ਹਾਂ naheen main kaahal vich haa<u>n</u> d. ਚੰਗਾ ਫਿਰ, ਮੈਂ ਉਡੀਕਾਂ ਗਾ changaa phir, main udeekaa<u>n</u> gaa

Unit 8

Dialogue 1 exercises

1. 1. ਸਿਤਾਰ si<u>t</u>aar 2. ਡਾਲਰ daalar 3. ਖ਼ਰਚਾ <u>kh</u>archaa 4. ਫਿਰਨਾ phirnaa 2. a. 2 b. 3 c. 1

Dialogue 2 exercises

1. a. ਸਾਨੂੰ ਥੋੜੀ ਬਹੁਤੀ ਪੰਜਾਬੀ ਆਉਂਦੀ ਹੈ। saanoon thorhee bahutee panjaabee aaun dee hai. b. ਅਸੀਂ ਕਨਾਟ ਪਲੇਸ ਜਾਣਾ ਚਾਹੁੰਦੀਆਂ ਹਾਂ। aseen kanaat pales jaanhaa chaahundeeaan haan. c. ਜੀ ਕੀ ਤੁਸੀਂ ਦੋ ਮਹੀਨੇ ਰਹਿਣ ਦੀ ਆਗਿਆ ਦੇਵੋ ਗੇ। jee kee tuseen do maheene rahinh dee aagiaa devo ge. 2. a. ਤੁਸੀਂ ਦੋ ਸਵਾਰੀਆਂ ਹੋ ਤੇ ਸਮਾਨ ਵੀ ਬਹੁਤ ਹੈ। tuseen do savaareeaan ho te samaan vee bahut hai. b. ਸਾਡੇ ਕੋਲ ਕੇਵਲ ਇੱਕ ਮਹੀਨੇ ਦਾ ਵੀਜ਼ਾ ਹੈ। saade kol keval ikk maheene daa veezaa hai. c. ਅਨੰਦ ਮਾਣੋ! anand maanho!

End exercises

1. a. ਚਾਹੀਦੀ chaaheedee b. ਚਾਹੀਦਾ chaaheedaa c. ਵਜਾਉਣ vajaaunh 2. a. ਉਸ ਨੂੰ ਕੀ ਚਾਹੀਦਾ ਹੈ? us noon kee chaaheedaa hai? b. ਧੀਓ, ਤੁਹਾਨੂੰ ਕੀ ਚਾਹੀਦਾ ਹੈ? dheeo, tuhaanoon kee chaaheedaa hai? c. ਤੂ ਕਿਹਨਾਂ ਨੂੰ ਦੱਸਿਆ ਸੀ? toon kihnaan noon dassiaa see? d. ਕੀ ਸਾਨੂੰ ਜਾਣਾ ਚਾਹੀਦਾ ਹੈ? kee saanoon jaanhaa chaaheedaa hai? 3. a. ਘਰ ਵਾਲਾ ghar vaalaa b. ਟੈਕਸੀ ਵਾਲਾ taiksee vaalaa c. ਸਬਜ਼ੀ ਵਾਲਾ sabzee vaalaa 4. four Ashoka Hotel Rs50 agreed 10 miles none yes

Unit 9

Dialogue 1 exercises

1. a. ਮੈਨੂੰ ਫਿੱਕੇ ਰੰਗ ਦਾ ਕਪੜਾ ਚਾਹੀਦਾ ਹੈ। mainoon phikke rang daa kaprhaa chaaheedaa hai. b. ਮੈਨੂੰ ਮੋਟਾ ਅਤੇ ਹੰਢਣਸਾਰ ਕਪੜਾ ਚਾਹੀਦਾ ਹੈ। mainoon motaa ate handhanhsaar kaprhaa chaaheedaa hai. c. ਅੱਜ ਕੱਲ੍ਹ ਦੇ ਰਵਾਜ ਦੀ ਛਪਾਈ ਚਾਹੀਦੀ ਹੈ। ajj kallh de ravaaj dee chapaaee chaaheedee hai. d. ਕੀਮਤ ਬਹੁਤ ਜ਼ਿਆਦਾ ਨਹੀਂ ਹੋਣੀ ਚਾਹੀਦੀ। keemat bahut ziaadaa naheen honhee chaaheedee. 2. vadheeaa, good ਵਧੇਰੇ, vadhere ਕੀਮਤ, price mukaablaa, comparison ਸਭ ਤੋਂ ਵਧੀਆ, best

Dialogue 2 exercises

1. a. ਕੀ ਤਕਲੀਫ਼ ਹੈ? kee takleef hai? b. ਕੀ ਤੈਨੂੰ ਬੁਖ਼ਾਰ ਹੈ? kee tainoon bukhaar hai? c. ਹੁਣ ਮੈਂ ਸਮਝਿਆ। hunh main samajhiaa. 2. You: ਤਬੀਅਤ tabeeat Doctor: ਤਕਲੀਫ਼ takleef You: ਪੇਟ pet, ਦਰਦ dard, ਬੁਖ਼ਾਰ bukhaar Doctor: ਬੁਖ਼ਾਰ bukhaar, ਠੰਡ thand Doctor: ਦਵਾਈ davaaee, ਅਰਾਮ araam

End exercises

1. Horizontal: 1st line 1st letter 2nd line 2nd letter 3rd line 1st letter 4th line 3rd letter 5th line 2nd letter Vertical: 1st column 3rd letter 2nd column 2nd letter 3rd column 2nd letter 4th column 1st letter 5th column 1st letter 2. a. ਮੈਨੂੰ ਠੰਡ ਲੱਗਦੀ ਹੈ। mainoon thand laggdee hai. b. ਮੇਰਾ ਸਿਰ

ਦੁੱਖਦਾ ਹੈ। meraa sir <u>d</u>ukhkh<u>d</u>aa hai. c. ਮੇਰੇ ਪੇਟ ਵਿਚ ਦਰਦ ਹੈ। mere pet vich <u>d</u>ard hai. d. ਮੈਨੂੰ ਬੁਖ਼ਾਰ ਹੈ। mainoon <u>b</u>ukhaar hai. 3. a. ਮੈਂ ਕੱਲ੍ਹ ਨਹੀਂ ਆ ਸਕਦਾ/ਸਕਦੀ। mai<u>n</u> kallh naheen aa sak<u>d</u>aa/sak<u>d</u>ee. b. ਕੀ ਤੁਸੀਂ ਪੰਜਾਬੀ ਬੋਲ ਸਕਦੇ ਹੋ? kee <u>t</u>usee<u>n</u> panjaabee bol sak<u>d</u>e ho? c. ਅਸੀਂ ਪਹਿਲੇ ਉੱਥੇ ਜਾ ਚੁਕੇ ਹਾਂ। asee<u>n</u> pahile u<u>thth</u>e jaa chuke haa<u>n</u>. d. ਉਹ ਪਹਿਲੇ ਖਾ ਚੁਕੇ ਹਨ। uh pahile khaa chuke han. 4. a. ਜਿਹੜਾ jihrhaa b. ਜਿਸ jis c. ਜਿਹੜੇ jihrhe d. ਜੋ jo

Unit 10

Dialogue 1 exercises

1. a. True b. False c. False 2. 1. c 2. b 3. a 4. d

Dialogue 2 exercises

1. a. ਨਾਨਾ ਜੀ ਤੇ ਨਾਨੀ ਜੀ ਕੋਲ naanaa jee <u>t</u>e naanee jee kol b. ਗੁੜ gurh c. ਕਹਾਣੀਆਂ ਸੁਣੀਆਂ kahaanheeaa<u>n</u> sunheeaa<u>n</u> d. ਦੁੱਧ <u>d</u>ud<u>h</u>d<u>h</u> 2. pin<u>d</u>, village ਖੂਹ, water-well vihrhaa, court yard ਖੇਤ, khe<u>t</u> ਗੰਨਾ, sugarcane

End exercises

1. a. ਖਾਣਾ ਖਾ ਕੇ ਅਸੀਂ ਸੌਂ ਗਏ! khaanhaa khaa ke asee<u>n</u> sau<u>n</u> ge! b. ਦੁਕਾਨ ਤੇ ਜਾ ਕੇ ਦੁੱਧ ਲਿਆ! <u>d</u>ukaan <u>t</u>e jaa ke <u>d</u>ud<u>h</u>d<u>h</u> liaa! c. ਕੰਮ ਖ਼ਤਮ ਕਰ ਕੇ ਤੂੰ ਘਰ ਨੂੰ ਚਲੇ ਜਾ! ka<u>n</u>m <u>kh</u>a<u>t</u>am kar ke <u>t</u>oo<u>n</u> ghar noo<u>n</u> chale jaa! d. ਜਲੰਧਰ ਹੋ ਕੇ ਅੰਮ੍ਰਿਤਸਰ ਜਾਓ! jala<u>n</u>dhar ho ke a<u>n</u>mri<u>t</u>sar jaao! 2. a. ਖਾਧੇ khaa<u>dh</u>e b. ਰੋਈ roee c. ਸੁਣਾਈ sunhaaee d. ਕਟਿਆ katiaa 3. You: ਬਹੁਤ ਸਹੁਣੀ ਰਹੀ। ਮੈਂ ਟਰਾਫ਼ਲਗਰ ਸਕੁਆਰ (ਗਈ/ਗਿਆ) ਅਤੇ ਨੈਲਸਨ ਦਾ ਕਾਲਮ ਦੇਖਿਆ। ਮੈਂ ਬਕਿੰਘਮ ਪੈਲਸ ਵੀ (ਗਈ/ਗਿਆ)। bahu<u>t</u> suhnhee rahee. mai<u>n</u> taraafaalgar sakuar (gaee/giaa) a<u>t</u>e nailsan <u>d</u>aa kaalam <u>d</u>ekhiaa. mai<u>n</u> baki<u>n</u>gham pailas vee (gaee/giaa). You: ਮੈਂ ਔਕਸਫੋਰਡ ਸਰਕਸ (ਗਈ/ਗਿਆ) ਅਤੇ ਕੁਝ ਕਪੜੇ ਖ਼ਰੀਦੇ। mai<u>n</u> auksford sarkas (gaee/giaa) a<u>t</u>e kujh kaprhe <u>kh</u>aree<u>d</u>e. You: ਮੈਂ ਕੇਵਲ ਪੀਜ਼ਾ ਖਾਧਾ। mai<u>n</u> keval peezaa khaa<u>dh</u>aa. 4. 1. ਖੂਹ waterwell 2. ਮੱਝ majhjh 3. ਗੰਨਾ ga<u>n</u>naa 4. ਘਰ ghar 5. ਖੇਤ khe<u>t</u>

Unit 11

Dialogue 1 exercises

1. a. ਟਿਕਟ ਬਾਬੂ b. ਜਸਪ੍ਰੀਤ c. ਟਿਕਟ ਬਾਬੂ d. ਸਿਮਰਨ e. ਜਸਪ੍ਰੀਤ 2. a. ਅਸੀਂ ਅੱਜ ਜਾਣਾ ਚਾਹੁੰਦੀਆਂ ਹਾਂ। b. ਨਵੀਆਂ ਥਾਂਵਾਂ ਦੇਖਣਾ ਚੰਗੀ ਗੱਲ ਹੈ। c. ਇਹ ਹਨ ਤੁਹਾਡੀਆਂ ਦੋ ਟਿਕਟਾਂ।

Dialogue 2 exercises

1. 1. b 2. d 3. a 4. c 2. 1. gold 2. dome 3. visitors 4. world 5. city
6. guru Mystery word: Amritsar

End exercises

1. a. ਸ਼ਾਨੇ ਪੰਜਾਬ b. ਸੈਲਾਨੀ, ਜਾਂਦੇ c. ਲਫ਼ਜ਼ੀ, ਅੰਮ੍ਰਿਤ ਦਾ ਸਰੋਵਰ d.ਹੋ ਰਿਹਾ ਕੀਰਤਨ, ਸ਼ਾਂਤੀ,
ਸਵਰਗ 2. a. ਗੁਰੂ ਰਾਮ ਦਾਸ b. ਅੰਮ੍ਰਿਤ ਦਾ ਸਰੋਵਰ c. ਗੁੰਬਦਾਂ ਤੇ ਸੋਨਾ ਲੱਗਾ ਹੋਇਆ ਹੈ 3. You:
ਮੈਂ ਅੱਜ ਦਿੱਲੀ ਜਾਣਾ (ਚਾਹੁੰਦਾ) ਹਾਂ। ਸਭ ਤੋਂ ਚੰਗੀ ਦਿੱਲੀ ਜਾਣ ਵਾਲੀ ਗੱਡੀ ਕਿਹੜੀ ਹੈ ? You:
ਕੀ ਮੈਨੂੰ ਸੈਕੰਡ ਕਲਾਸ ਵਿਚ ਸੀਟ ਮਿਲ ਜਾਏ ਗੀ। You: ਨਹੀਂ, ਮੈਨੂੰ ਵਾਪਸੀ ਟਿਕਟ
ਚਾਹੀਦੀ ਹੈ। ਅੰਮ੍ਰਿਤਸਰ ਤੋਂ ਗੱਡੀ ਕਿੰਨੇ ਵਜੇ ਚਲਦੀ ਹੈ ? You: ਅੱਛਾ, ਮੈਨੂੰ ਇੱਕ ਸੈਕੰਡ ਕਲਾਸ ਦੀ
ਟਿਕਟ ਦੇਵੋ।

Unit 12

Dialogue exercises

1. a. False b. True c. False d. True 2. a. ਜਰਮਨ, ਅੰਗਰੇਜ਼ੀ, ਪੰਜਾਬੀ b. ਤਾਜ ਮੱਹਲ
c. ਸਹਿਮਤ, ਮੁਕਾਬਲਾ d. ਅੰਮ੍ਰਿਤਸਰ

Letter exercises

1. lagaataar, continuously ਪਿਆਰੇ, dear k͟hush, happy ਗਰਮੀ, garmee ਵਾਰੀ,
instance 2. a. ਉਹਨਾਂ ਨੇ ਉਹ ਮਕਾਨ ਦੇਖਿਆ ਜਿੱਥੇ ਉਹਨਾਂ ਦੇ ਮਾਤਾ ਪਿਤਾ ਰਹਿੰਦੇ ਹੁੰਦੇ ਸੀ
b. ਬਾਰਸ਼ c. ਅਬਾਦੀ ਤੇ ਟਰੈਫ਼ਿਕ ਬਹੁਤ ਹੈ d. ਬਹੁਤ ਸੁਗਾਤਾਂ

End exercises

1. a. ਮੈਂ ਖਾ ਚੁਕਾ ਹਾਂ। b. ਮੈਂ ਖਾ ਚੁਕੀ ਹਾਂ। c. ਉਹ ਬੋਲ ਚੁਕੇ ਸਨ। d. ਉਹ ਦਸ ਮਿੰਟ ਤੋਂ ਬੋਲ ਰਿਹਾ
ਸੀ। 2. ਯੂ. ਐਸ. ਡਾਲਰ ੪੦੦ ਡਾਲਰ ੩੫ ਰੁਪੇ ਵੱਧ ਅਮਰੀਕਨ 3. ਪਿਆਰੇ ਫੇਰੀ ਜਗ੍ਹਾ ਹਰਿਮੰਦਰ
ਸਾਹਿਬ ਮੁਕਾਬਲਾ ਸ਼ਬਦਾਵਲੀ ਹੁੰਦੇ ਤਾਂ ਆਉਂਦਾ

Unit 13

Exercises to matrimonial advertisement

1. a. Yes b. Yes c. No 2. Not a suitable match! 3. a. ਲੜਕੀ ਵਿਹਾਰੀ ਨੌਕਰੀ ਤੇ
ਲੱਗੀ ਹੋਣੀ ਚਾਹੀਦੀ ਹੈ। b. ਤਲਾਕ ਸ਼ੁਦਾ ਲੜਕੀਆਂ ਨੂੰ ਲਿਖਣ ਦੀ ਲੋੜ ਨਹੀਂ। c. ਲੜਕੀ ਦੀ ਉਮਰ
੨੫ ਸਾਲ ਤੋਂ ਵੱਧ ਨਾ ਹੋਵੇ। d. ਲੜਕਾ ਸੱਚੀ ਮੁੱਚੀ ਸੁਹਣਾ ਹੈ।

Dialogue exercises

1. a. 2 b. 1 c. 4 d. 3 2. a. Edinburgh b. Ilford c. Manjit Singh d. Kanwaljit Kaur e. Gurbax Singh and Jasvir Kaur Kalsi f. North London g. May 23 h. 9:30 a.m. i. 10:00 a.m. j. 12:00 noon

End exercises

1. Matrimonial advertisement ਲੰਡਨ ਵਿਚ ਰਹਿ ਰਹੇ ਸਿੱਖ ਮਾਪਿਆਂ ਦੀ ਲੜਕੀ ਲਈ ਰਿਸ਼ਤੇ ਦੀ ਲੋੜ ਹੈ। ਲੜਕੀ ਦੀ ਉਮਰ ੨੫ ਸਾਲ ਦੀ ਹੈ ਅਤੇ ਕੱਦ 5' 3" ਹੈ। ਲੜਕੀ ਸੁਹਣੀ ਤੇ ਪੜ੍ਹੀ ਲਿਖੀ ਹੈ। ਬੈਂਕ ਵਿਚ ਕੰਮ ਕਰਦੀ ਹੈ। ਲੜਕਾ ਪਤਵੰਤੇ ਪਰਵਾਰ ਦਾ, ਬ੍ਰਿਟਿਸ਼ ਸ਼ਹਿਰੀਅਤ ਵਾਲਾ ਅਤੇ ਵਿਹਾਰੀ ਨੌਕਰੀ ਤੇ ਲੱਗਾ ਹੋਵੇ। 2. a. ਜਿਹਾ b. ਆਪਣੇ c. ਆਪਣੀਆਂ d. ਜਿਹੇ 3. a. ਉਬਲੇ ਹੋਏ b. ਡਰਿਆ ਹੋਇਆ c. ਪੜ੍ਹਿਆ ਲਿਖਿਆ 4. a. ਡੇਬਰਾ b. ਜੀਤੀ ਦਾ c. ਨਹੀਂ d. ੨੯ ਜਨਵਰੀ e. ਉਹ ਵਿਆਹ ਦੀਆਂ ਰਸਮਾਂ ਬਾਰੇ ਜਾਣਨਾ ਚਾਹੁੰਦੀ ਹੈ

Unit 14

Dialogue 1 exercises

1. a. ਪਾਪਾ ਜੀ! ਕੀ ਤੁਸੀਂ ਮੇਰੇ ਸ਼੍ਰੇਣੀ ਅਧਿਆਪਕ ਨੂੰ ਮਿਲੇ ਸੀ? b. ਉਹ ਸਾਨੂੰ ਚੰਗੀ ਤਰ੍ਹਾਂ ਪੜ੍ਹਾਂਦਾ ਨਹੀਂ। c. ਤੈਨੂੰ ਪੜ੍ਹਾਈ ਵਿਚ ਮਿਹਨਤ ਕਰਨੀ ਚਾਹੀਦੀ ਹੈ। 2. 1. teacher 2. Ramesh 3. homework 4. maths 5. careless

Dialogue 2 exercises

1. kaanoo<u>nn</u> ਬੀਬੀ, madam ਕਾਗ਼ਜ਼ਾਤ, kaa<u>gh</u>zaa<u>t</u> maaf, pardon ਉਲੰਘਣਾ, to disobey 2. mobile phone officer licence minute car

Dialogue 3 exercises

1. a. ਮੈਂ ਸਮਾਜ ਸੇਵਕ ਹਾਂ। b. ਕੀ ਗੱਲ ਹੈ? c. ਅੰਦਰ ਆ ਜਾਓ। d. ਮੇਰੇ ਲਈ ਇਹ ਮੁਸ਼ਕਲ ਹੈ। 2. a. ਆਇਆ b. ਸਕਦੀ c. ਚਲੇ ਜਾਂਦੇ d. ਕਰਾਂ ਗੀ

End exercises

1. a. ਵੇ ਨੇੜੇ b. ਵੇ ਅੰਦਰ c. ਤੋਂ ਬਾਅਦ d. ਦੀ ਜਗਾ 2. a. 2 b. 3 c. 4 d. 1 3. a. ਦਫ਼ਤਰ b. ੧੦ ਮਿੰਟ c. ਨਹੀਂ d. ਕਾਗ਼ਜ਼ਾਤ ਪੇਸ਼ ਕਰਨੇ ਹਨ 4. ਅਧਿਆਪਕ, ਇਲਾਵਾ, ਹਿਸਾਬ, ਕੰਮ, ਕਲਾਸ, ਡਾਕਟਰ, ਦੂਜੇ, ਪੜ੍ਹਉਣਾ, ਪਾਪਾ, ਬਾਰੇ, ਮਜ਼ਮੂਨਾਂ, ਮਿਹਨਤ, ਲਿਆਕਤ, ਵਰਤਣਾ, ਸ਼੍ਰੇਣੀ

Unit 15

Dialogue 1 exercises

1. b. ਵੈਸਾਖੀ ਮੇਲਾ c.1. ਫ਼ਸਲਾਂ ਕਟਣਾ 2. ਸਿੱਖ ਕੌਮ ਦਾ ਜਨਮ ਦਿਨ d. ਜਲੇਬੀਆਂ ਅਤੇ ਪਕੌੜੇ e. ਗਤਕਾ f. 1. ਨੁਮਾਇਸ਼ 2. ਭੰਗੜਾ 2. village people harvest season Sikh religion the new year 3. True   True   False   False

Folk song exercise

Yes No No No

End exercises

1. a. ਜਿਹੜਾ, ਉਹ b. ਜਿਵੇਂ, ਉੱਵੇਂ c. ਜਿੱਥੇ, ਉੱਥੇ d. ਜਦੋਂ, ਉਦੋਂ 2. b. ਬਾਹਰ ਜਾਣ ਦੇਵੋ c. ਪੀਣ ਦੇ d. ਦੇਖਣ ਦੇਵੋ/ਦਿਓ 3. a. ਕੰਮ ਤੇ ਜਾਣ ਲਈ ੧੫ ਮਿੰਟ ਲੱਗਦੇ ਹਨ। b. ਇੱਕ ਫ਼ਰਸਟ ਕਲਾਸ ਟਿਕਟ ਲਈ ਕਿੰਨੇ ਪੈਸੇ ਲੱਗਦੇ ਹਨ ? c. ਮੈਨੂੰ ਗਰਮੀ ਲੱਗਦੀ ਹੈ। d. ਬਾਰਸ਼ ਹੋਣ ਲੱਗੀ। e. ਅਸੀਂ ਬਾਹਰ ਜਾਣ ਲੱਗੇ ਸੀ।

Unit 16

Dialogue 1 exercises

1. a. True b. False c. False d. True 2. a. ਮੈਨੂੰ ਭੰਗੜਾ ਪਸੰਦ ਹੈ। b. ਮੈਨੂੰ ਭੰਗੜਾ ਗਿੱਧੇ ਨਾਲੋਂ ਜ਼ਿਆਦਾ ਪਸੰਦ ਹੈ। c. ਭਾਵੇਂ ਤੁਸੀਂ ਪੰਜਾਬ ਜਾ ਬਾਹਰ ਹੋ, ਭੰਗੜਾ ਦੇਖ ਸਕਦੇ ਹੋ। d. ਆਓ ਆਪਾਂ, ਨੱਚੀਏ। 3. a. drum b. long wooden pole c. spoon

Dialogue 2 exercises

1. Canada Uganda Malaysia England 2. a. ਅਵਤਾਰ ਤੇ ਤਰਲੋਕ b. ਮਲੇਸ਼ੀਆ c. ਲਾਇਲਪੁਰ d. ਯੂਗੰਡਾ e. ਧੋਬੀ ਦਾ ਕੁੱਤਾ ਨਾ ਘਰ ਦਾ ਨਾ ਘਾਟ ਦਾ 3. a. ਕਿਉਂ ਕਿ ਉਹ ਫ਼ੌਜ ਵਿਚ ਭਰਤੀ ਹੋ ਗਏ ਸਨ। b. ਕਿਉਂ ਕਿ ਉਹ ਗ਼ਦਰ ਪਾਰਟੀ ਵਿਚ ਸ਼ਾਮਲ ਹੋ ਗਏ ਸਨ। c. ਕਿਉਂ ਕਿ ਪੰਜਾਬ ਦਾ ਬਟਵਾਰਾ ਹੋ ਗਿਆ ਸੀ। d. ਕਿਉਂ ਕਿ ਉਹ ਰੇਲਵੇ ਬਣਾਉਣ ਗਏ ਸਨ।

End exercises

1. b. ਸਾਡੇ ਕੋਲ ਨਾ ਪੈਂਸਲਾਂ ਹਨ, ਨਾ ਕਾਪੀ ਹੈ। c. ਸਾਡੇ ਕੋਲ ਨਾ ਘੜੀਆਂ ਹਨ, ਨਾ ਰੇਡੀਓ ਹੈ। d. ਸਾਡੇ ਕੋਲ ਨਾ ਬੋਤਲਾਂ ਹਨ, ਨਾ ਪਾਣੀ ਹੈ। 2. b. ਨਾ ਸਿਰਫ਼ ਇਹ ਕਿਤਾਬ ਲੰਬੀ ਹੈ, ਸਗੋਂ ਮੁਸ਼ਕਲ ਵੀ ਹੈ। c. ਨਾ ਸਿਰਫ਼ ਅਸੀਂ ਭੰਗੜਾ ਪਸੰਦ ਕਰਦੇ ਹਾਂ, ਸਗੋਂ ਗਿੱਧਾ ਵੀ ਪਸੰਦ ਕਰਦੇ ਹਾਂ। d. ਭਾਵੇਂ ਤੁਸੀਂ ਪੰਜਾਬ ਵਿਚ ਹੋ ਭਾਵੇਂ ਬਾਹਰ, ਤੁਸੀਂ ਭੰਗੜਾ ਦੇਖ ਸਕਦੇ ਹੋ। e. ਮੰਨੋ ਜਾਂ ਨਾ ਮੰਨੋ, ਵੈਨਕੁਵਰ ਦਾ ਮਾਹੌਲ ਪੰਜਾਬ ਵਾਂਗੂ ਹੈ। 3. ਤਰਲੋਕ: ਇੰਗਲੈਂਡ, ਕੈਨੇਡਾ, ਯੂਗੰਡਾ ਅਵਤਾਰ: ਮਲੇਸ਼ੀਆ, ਕੈਨੇਡਾ, ਲਾਇਲਪੁਰ, ਜਲੰਧਰ

TOPIC VOCABULARY

English	Transliteration	ਪੰਜਾਬੀ
Parts of the body	*sareer de ang*	ਸਰੀਰ ਦੇ ਅੰਗ
Arm	baan	ਬਾਂਹ
Back	piththh	ਪਿੱਠ
Beard	daarhhee	ਦਾੜ੍ਹੀ
Body	sareer/jisam	ਸਰੀਰ, ਜਿਸਮ
Chest	chaatee	ਛਾਤੀ
Ear	kann	ਕੰਨ
Eye	akhkh	ਅੱਖ
Face	moonh/chihraa	ਮੂੰਹ/ਚਿਹਰਾ
Finger	unglee	ਉਂਗਲੀ
Foot	pair	ਪੈਰ
Hair	vaal	ਵਾਲ
Hand	haththh	ਹੱਥ
Head	sir	ਸਿਰ
Knee	godaa	ਗੋਡਾ
Leg	latt	ਲੱਤ
Moustache	muchchaan	ਮੁੱਛਾਂ
Mouth	moonh	ਸੂੰਹ
Neck	gardan	ਗਰਦਨ
Nose	nakk	ਨੱਕ
Shoulder	modhaa	ਮੋਢਾ
Stomach	dhidd/pet	ਢਿੱਡ/ਪੇਟ
Throat	gal/galaa	ਗਲ/ਗਲਾ
Tongue	jeebh/zabaan	ਜੀਭ/ਜ਼ਬਾਨ
Tooth	dand	ਦੰਦ
Vegetables	*sabzeeaan*	ਸਬਜ਼ੀਆਂ
Bitter gourd	karelaa	ਕਰੇਲਾ
Brinjal/egg plant	vataaoon/bainganh	ਵਤਾਊਂ/ਬੈਂਗਣ
Cabbage	band gobhee	ਬੰਦ ਗੋਭੀ
Capsicum	shimlaa mirach	ਸ਼ਿਮਲਾ ਮਿਰਚ

Carrots	gaajar	ਗਾਜਰ
Cauliflower	gobhee	ਗੋਭੀ
Courgette	raam toree	ਰਾਮ ਤੋਰੀ
Mushrooms	khunbaan	ਖੁੰਬਾਂ
Mustard leaves	sar-h-on de patte (saag)	ਸਰੋਂ ਦੇ ਪੱਤੇ (ਸਾਗ)
Okra	bhindee	ਭਿੰਡੀ
Peas	matar	ਮਟਰ
Potato	aaloo	ਆਲੂ
Spinach	paalak	ਪਾਲਕ
Tomatoes	tamaatar	ਟਮਾਟਰ
Turnip	shalgam/ gongloo	ਸ਼ਲਗਮ (ਗੋਂਗਲੂ)

Fruit	*phal*	ਫਲ
Apple	seb	ਸੇਬ
Apricot	khurmaanee	ਖੁਰਮਾਨੀ
Banana	kelaa	ਕੇਲਾ
Grapes	angoor	ਅੰਗੂਰ
Lemon	ninboo	ਨਿੰਬੂ
Mango	anb	ਅੰਬ
Orange	santraa	ਸੰਤਰਾ
Peach	aarhoo	ਆੜੂ
Pear	naakh/naashpaatee	ਨਾਖ/ ਨਾਸ਼ਪਾਤੀ
Pineapple	anaanaas	ਅਨਾਨਾਸ
Plums	alooche/ aaloobukhaaraa	ਅਲੂਚੇ/ ਆਲੂਬੁਖ਼ਾਰਾ
Pomegranate	anaar	ਅਨਾਰ

Places	*thaanvaan*	ਥਾਂਵਾਂ
Church	girjaa	ਗਿਰਜਾ
College	mahaan vidiaalaa	ਮਹਾਂ ਵਿਦਿਆਲਾ
Community kitchen	langar	ਲੰਗਰ
Enquiry office	puchch gichch daa daftar	ਪੁੱਛ ਗਿੱਛ ਦਾ ਦਫ਼ਤਰ
Exhibition	numaaish, pardarshanee	ਨੁਮਾਇਸ਼, ਪਰਦਰਸ਼ਨੀ
Factory	kaarkhaanaa	ਕਾਰਖ਼ਾਨਾ
Fort	kilhaa	ਕਿਲ੍ਹਾ
Hindu place of worship (temple)	mandar	ਮੰਦਰ
Hospital	haspataal	ਹਸਪਤਾਲ

Library	pustakaalaa	ਪੁਸਤਕਾਲਾ
Market	mandee	ਮੰਡੀ
Museum	ajaaib ghar	ਅਜਾਇਬ ਘਰ
Muslim place of worship (mosque)	masjid	ਮਸਜਿਦ/ਮਸੀਤ
Office	daftar	ਦਫ਼ਤਰ
Palace	mahhal	ਮੱਹਲ
Park	baagh	ਬਾਗ਼
Police station	thaanhaa, pulas chaunkee	ਥਾਣਾ, ਪੁਲਸ ਚੌਂਕੀ
Post office	daakkhaanaa	ਡਾਕਖਾਨਾ
Roadside restaurant	dhaabaa	ਚਾਬਾ
School	vidiaalaa, madrasaa	ਵਿਦਿਆਲਾ, ਮਦਰਸਾ
Shop	dukaan, hattee	ਦੁਕਾਨ, ਹੱਟੀ
Sikh place of worship	gurdavaaraa, gurduaaraa	ਗੁਰਦਵਾਰਾ, ਗੁਰਦੁਆਰਾ
Zoo	chirheeaaghar	ਚਿੜੀਆ ਘਰ

Occupations	*peshe*	*ਪੇਸ਼ੇ*
Carpenter	tarkhaanh	ਤਰਖਾਣ
Cook/chef	laangree	ਲਾਂਗਰੀ
Doctor	daaktar	ਡਾਕਟਰ
Farmer	kisaan	ਕਿਸਾਨ
Gardener	maalee	ਮਾਲੀ
Judge	jajj	ਜੱਜ
Lawyer	vakeel	ਵਕੀਲ
Mechanic	mistaree	ਮਿਸਤਰੀ
Milkman	dudhdh vaalaa	ਦੁੱਧ ਵਾਲਾ
Policeman	pulas vaalaa	ਪੁਲਸ ਵਾਲਾ
Postman	daakeeaa	ਡਾਕੀਆ
Priest (Sikh)	garanthee	ਗਰੰਥੀ
Singer	gaaik	ਗਾਇਕ
Teacher	adhiaapak	ਅਧਿਆਪਕ
Writer	lekhak	ਲੇਖਕ

| *Colours* | *rang* | *ਰੰਗ* |
| Black | kaalaa | ਕਾਲਾ |

Blue	neelaa	ਨੀਲਾ
Brown	badaamee	ਬਦਾਮੀ
Gold/Golden	sunahiree	ਸੁਨਹਿਰੀ
Green	haraa/sabaz	ਹਰਾ/ਸਬਜ਼
Grey	saletee	ਸਲੇਟੀ
Khaki	khaakee	ਖ਼ਾਕੀ
Maroon	laakhaa	ਲਾਖਾ
Orange	santaree	ਸੰਤਰੀ
Pink	gulaabee	ਗੁਲਾਬੀ
Purple	jaamnee	ਜਾਮਨੀ
Red	laal	ਲਾਲ
Saffron	kesaree	ਕੇਸਰੀ
White	chittaa/safed	ਚਿੱਟਾ/ ਸਫ਼ੇਦ
Yellow	peelaa	ਪੀਲਾ

Directions	*dishaavaan*	ਦਿਸ਼ਾਵਾਂ
Behind	pichche	ਪਿੱਛੇ
Down	thalle	ਥੱਲੇ
East	poorab	ਪੂਰਬ
Far	door	ਦੂਰ
In front	agge	ਅੱਗੇ
Left side	khabbe	ਖੱਬੇ
Near	nerhe/nazdeek	ਨੇੜੇ/ਨਜ਼ਦੀਕ
North	uttar	ਉੱਤਰ
Right side	sajje	ਸੱਜੇ
South	dakhkhanh	ਦੱਖਣ
Straight	sidhdhaa, sidhdhe	ਸਿੱਧਾ/ ਸਿੱਧੇ
That side	us paase	ਉਸ ਪਾਸੇ
This side	is paase	ਇਸ ਪਾਸੇ
Up	uppar	ਉੱਪਰ
West	pachcham	ਪੱਛਮ

Animals	*jaanvar*	ਜਾਨਵਰ
Bear	richch	ਰਿੱਛ
Buffalo	majhjh	ਮੱਝ
Camel	ooth	ਊਠ
Cat	billee	ਬਿੱਲੀ
Cow	gaan	ਗਾਂ

Deer	hiran	ਹਿਰਨ
Dog	kuttaa	ਕੁੱਤਾ
Elephant	haathee	ਹਾਥੀ
Fox	loonbarh	ਲੂੰਬੜ
Horse	ghorhaa	ਘੋੜਾ
Monkey	baandar	ਬਾਂਦਰ
Mouse	choohaa	ਚੂਹਾ
Pig	soor	ਸੂਰ
Sheep	bhed	ਭੇਡ
Tiger	sher	ਸ਼ੇਰ

Moods	*birteeaan*	*ਬਿਰਤੀਆਂ*
Angry	gussaa	ਗੁੱਸਾ
Anxious	pareshaan	ਪਰੇਸ਼ਾਨ
Contented	santushat	ਸੰਤੁਸ਼ਟ
Curious	utsuk	ਉਤਸੁਕ
Depressed	udaas	ਉਦਾਸ
Determined	nishchit	ਨਿਸ਼ਚਿਤ
Disgusted	upraam	ਉਪਰਾਮ
Frightened	dariaa hoiaa	ਡਰਿਆ ਹੋਇਆ
Happy	khush	ਖ਼ੁਸ਼
Irritated	khijhiaa hoiaa	ਖਿਝਿਆ ਹੋਇਆ
Lazy	susat	ਸੁਸਤ
Loving	piaaraa	ਪਿਆਰਾ
Sad/unhappy	ghamgeen	ਗ਼ਮਗੀਨ
Surprised	hairaan janak	ਹੈਰਾਨ ਜਨਕ
Thoughtful	vichaarsheel	ਵਿਚਾਰਸ਼ੀਲ

Travel and transport	*safar te aavaajaaee*	*ਸਫ਼ਰ ਤੇ ਆਵਾਜਾਈ*
Aeroplane	havaaee jahaaz	ਹਵਾਈ ਜਹਾਜ
Airport	havaaee addaa	ਹਵਾਈ ਅੱਡਾ
Bicycle	saaikal	ਸਾਇਕਲ
Boat	berhee	ਬੇੜੀ
Booking clerk	tikat baaboo	ਟਿਕਟ ਬਾਬੂ
Bus	bas	ਬਸ
Bus station	basaan daa addaa	ਬਸਾਂ ਦਾ ਅੱਡਾ

Car	kaar/ gaddee	ਕਾਰ/ਗੱਡੀ
Fare	kiraaiaa	ਕਿਰਾਇਆ
Foot (on)	paidal	ਪੈਦਲ
Horse carriage	taangaa/ yakkaa	ਟਾਂਗਾ/ਯੱਕਾ
Journey	yaatraa/ safar	ਯਾਤਰਾ/ਸਫ਼ਰ
Passenger	savaaree	ਸਵਾਰੀ
Road	sarhak	ਸੜਕ
Rickshaw	rikshaa	ਰਿਕਸ਼ਾ
Ship	samundaree jahaaz	ਸਮੁੰਦਰੀ ਜਹਾਜ਼
Ticket	tikat	ਟਿਕਟ
Train	rel gaddee	ਰੇਲ ਗੱਡੀ
(To) travel	safar karnaa	ਸਫ਼ਰ ਕਰਨਾ
Traveller	yaatree	ਯਾਤਰੀ
Vehicle	vaahanh	ਵਾਹਣ
Waiting room	udeek ghar/ musaafar khaanaa	ਉਡੀਕ ਘਰ/ ਮੁਸਾਫ਼ਰ ਖ਼ਾਨਾ

Personal identification	*nijjee shanaakhat*	ਨਿੱਜੀ ਸ਼ਨਾਖ਼ਤ

Age	umar	ਉਮਰ
Birthday	janam din	ਜਨਮ ਦਿਨ
(To be) born	janmnhaa	ਜੰਮਣਾ
Caste	zaat	ਜ਼ਾਤ
Family name	got	ਗੋਤ
Height	kadd	ਕੱਦ
Maiden name	pekaa naan	ਪੇਕਾ ਨਾਂ
Man	aadmee	ਆਦਮੀ
(To be) married	viaahiaa honhaa	ਵਿਆਹਿਆ ਹੋਣਾ
Name	naam/ naan	ਨਾਮ/ ਨਾਂ
Nation	kaum	ਕੌਮ
Nationality	kaumeeat	ਕੌਮੀਅਤ
Place of Birth	janam asthaan	ਜਨਮ ਅਸਥਾਨ
Religion	dharam, mazhab	ਧਰਮ, ਮਜ਼੍ਹਬ
(To be) unmarried	kanvaaraa honhaa	ਕੰਵਾਰਾ ਹੋਣਾ
Young	javaan	ਜਵਾਨ

House and home	*makaan ṯe ghar*	ਮਕਾਨ ਤੇ ਘਰ
Bathroom	ghusal khaanaa/ ishnaan ghar	ਗੁਸਲ ਖ਼ਾਨਾ/ਇਸ਼ਨਾਨ ਘਰ
Bed	manjaa, palangh	ਮੰਜਾ/ਪਲੰਘ
Bedroom	saunh vaalaa kamraa	ਸੌਣ ਵਾਲਾ ਕਮਰਾ
Building	imaaraṯ	ਇਮਾਰਤ
Bungalow	banglaa	ਬੰਗਲਾ
Carpet	daree	ਦਰੀ
Ceiling	andarlee chatt	ਅੰਦਰਲੀ ਛੱਤ
Cooker	chullhaa	ਚੁੱਲ੍ਹਾ
Court yard	vihrhaa	ਵਿਹੜਾ
Dining room	khaanh vaalaa kamraa	ਖਾਣ ਵਾਲਾ ਕਮਰਾ
Door	darvaazaa	ਦਰਵਾਜ਼ਾ
Floor	farash	ਫ਼ਰਸ਼
Garden	baagheechaa	ਬਾਗ਼ੀਚਾ
Key	taalee, chaabee	ਤਾਲੀ, ਚਾਬੀ
Kitchen	rasoee	ਰਸੋਈ
Light	roshnee	ਰੋਸ਼ਨੀ
Lock	taalaa, jandraa	ਤਾਲਾ, ਜੰਦਰਾ
Roof	baaharlee chatt	ਬਾਹਰਲੀ ਛੱਤ
Room	kamraa	ਕਮਰਾ
Sink	chubachchaa	ਚੁਬੱਚਾ
Sitting Room	baithak	ਬੈਠਕ
Stairs	paurheeaan	ਪੌੜੀਆਂ
Storey	manzal	ਮੰਜ਼ਲ
Tap	nalkaa	ਨਲਕਾ
Utencils	bartan, bhaande	ਬਰਤਨ, ਭਾਂਡੇ
Wall	deevar/ kandh	ਦੀਵਾਰ/ ਕੰਧ
Window	baaree/ khirhkee	ਬਾਰੀ, ਖਿੜਕੀ
Nature	*kudraṯ*	ਕੁਦਰਤ
Climate	paunh paanhee	ਪੌਣ ਪਾਣੀ
Earth	dhartee	ਧਰਤੀ
Flowers	phull	ਫੁੱਲ
Forest	jangal	ਜੰਗਲ
Grass	ghaah	ਘਾਹ
Lake	jheel	ਝੀਲ

Land	zameen	ਜ਼ਮੀਨ
Lightning	bijlee dee chamak	ਬਿਜਲੀ ਦੀ ਚਮਕ
Moon	chann	ਚੰਨ
Mountains	parbat/pahaarh	ਪਰਬਤ/ਪਹਾੜ
River	dariaa	ਦਰਿਆ
Sea	samundar	ਸਮੁੰਦਰ
Seasons	ruttaan	ਰੁੱਤਾਂ
Sky	asmaan	ਆਸਮਾਨ
Star	taaraa	ਤਾਰਾ
Sun	sooraj	ਸੂਰਜ
Tree	darakhat	ਦਰਖ਼ਤ

Weather	*mausam*	ਮੌਸਮ
Breeze	havaa	ਹਵਾ
Cloud	baddal	ਬੱਦਲ
Cold	thand	ਠੰਡ
Drought	sokaa	ਸੋਕਾ
Drizzle	boondaa baandee	ਬੂੰਦਾ ਬਾਂਦੀ
Dry	khushak	ਖ਼ੁਸ਼ਕ
Flood	harhh	ਹੜ੍ਹ
Fog	dhund	ਧੁੰਦ
Frost	koraa	ਕੋਰਾ
Hail stones	garhe	ਗੜੇ
Heat wave	loo	ਲੂ
Hot	garmee	ਗਰਮੀ
Rain	baarash, meenh	ਬਾਰਸ਼, ਮੀਂਹ
Shade	chaan	ਛਾਂ
Snow	baraf	ਬਰਫ਼
Sunshine	dhupp	ਧੁੱਪ
Thunder	garaj	ਗਰਜ
Wet	sillaa	ਸਿੱਲਾ

Numerals	*ginhtee*	ਗਿਣਤੀ	
0	sifar	ਸਿਫ਼ਰ	੦
1	ikk	ਇੱਕ	੧
2	do	ਦੋ	੨
3	tinn	ਤਿੰਨ	੩

4	chaar	ਚਾਰ	੪
5	panj	ਪੰਜ	੫
6	che	ਛੇ	੬
7	satt	ਸੱਤ	੭
8	athth	ਅੱਠ	੮
9	naun	ਨੌਂ	੯
10	das	ਦਸ	੧੦
11	giaaraan	ਗਿਆਰਾਂ	੧੧
12	baar-h-aan	ਬਾਰਾਂ	੧੨
13	ter-h-aan	ਤੇਰਾਂ	੧੩
14	chaud-h-aan	ਚੌਦਾਂ	੧੪
15	pandraan	ਪੰਦਰਾਂ	੧੫
16	solhaan	ਸੋਲ੍ਹਾਂ	੧੬
17	sataar-h-aan	ਸਤਾਰਾਂ	੧੭
18	athaar-h-aan	ਅਠਾਰਾਂ	੧੮
19	unnee	ਉੱਨੀ	੧੯
20	veeh	ਵੀਹ	੨੦
21	ikkee	ਇੱਕੀ	੨੧
22	baaee	ਬਾਈ	੨੨
23	te-ee	ਤੇਈ	੨੩
24	chauvee	ਚੌਵੀ	੨੪
25	panjhee	ਪੰਝੀ	੨੫
26	chabbee	ਛੱਬੀ	੨੬
27	sataaee	ਸਤਾਈ	੨੭
28	athaaee	ਅਠਾਈ	੨੮
29	unattee	ਉਨੱਤੀ	੨੯
30	teeh	ਤੀਹ	੩੦
31	ikkatee	ਇੱਕਤੀ	੩੧
32	battee	ਬੱਤੀ	੩੨
33	tetee	ਤੇਤੀ	੩੩
34	chauntee	ਚੌਂਤੀ	੩੪
35	paintee	ਪੈਂਤੀ	੩੫
36	chattee	ਛੱਤੀ	੩੬
37	saintee	ਸੈਂਤੀ	੩੭
38	athattee	ਅਠੱਤੀ	੩੮
39	untaalee	ਉਨਤਾਲੀ	੩੯
40	chaalee	ਚਾਲੀ	੪੦
41	iktaalee	ਇਕਤਾਲੀ	੪੧

42	bataalee	ਬਤਾਲੀ	੪੨
43	tirtaalee	ਤਿਰਤਾਲੀ	੪੩
44	chutaalee	ਚੁਤਾਲੀ	੪੪
45	pantaalee	ਪੰਤਾਲੀ	੪੫
46	chitaalee	ਛਿਤਾਲੀ	੪੬
47	santaalee	ਸੰਤਾਲੀ	੪੭
48	athtaalee	ਅਠਤਾਲੀ	੪੮
49	unhnjaa	ਉਣੰਜਾ	੪੯
50	panjaah	ਪੰਜਾਹ	੫੦
51	ikvanjaa	ਇਕਵੰਜਾ	੫੧
52	bavanjaa	ਬਵੰਜਾ	੫੨
53	tarvanjaa	ਤਰਵੰਜਾ	੫੩
54	churanjaa	ਚੁਰੰਜਾ	੫੪
55	pachvanjaa	ਪਚਵੰਜਾ	੫੫
56	chivanjaa	ਛਿਵੰਜਾ	੫੬
57	satvanjaa	ਸਤਵੰਜਾ	੫੭
58	athvanjaa	ਅਠਵੰਜਾ	੫੮
59	unhaath	ਉਣਾਹਠ	੫੯
60	sathth	ਸੱਠ	੬੦
61	ikaahth	ਇਕਾਹਠ	੬੧
62	baahth	ਬਾਹਠ	੬੨
63	trehth	ਤ੍ਰੇਹਠ	੬੩
64	chaunhth	ਚੌਂਹਠ	੬੪
65	painhth	ਪੈਂਹਠ	੬੫
66	chiaahth	ਛਿਆਹਠ	੬੬
67	sataahth	ਸਤਾਹਠ	੬੭
68	athaahth	ਅਠਾਹਠ	੬੮
69	unhattar	ਉਨਹੱਤਰ	੬੯
70	sattar	ਸੱਤਰ	੭੦
71	ikhattar	ਇਕਹੱਤਰ	੭੧
72	bahattar	ਬਹੱਤਰ	੭੨
73	tihattar	ਤਿਹੱਤਰ	੭੩
74	chauhattar	ਚੌਹੱਤਰ	੭੪
75	pachattar	ਪਚੱਤਰ	੭੫
76	chihattar	ਛਿਹੱਤਰ	੭੬
77	satattar	ਸਤੱਤਰ	੭੭
78	athattar	ਅਠੱਤਰ	੭੮
79	unaasee	ਉਨਾਸੀ	੭੯

80	assee	ਅੱਸੀ	੮੦
81	ikaasee	ਇਕਾਸੀ	੮੧
82	biaasee	ਬਿਆਸੀ	੮੨
83	triaasee	ਤ੍ਰਿਆਸੀ	੮੩
84	churaasee	ਚੁਰਾਸੀ	੮੪
85	pachaasee	ਪਚਾਸੀ	੮੫
86	chiaasee	ਛਿਆਸੀ	੮੬
87	sataasee	ਸਤਾਸੀ	੮੭
88	athaasee	ਅਠਾਸੀ	੮੮
89	unhaanven	ਉਨਾਨਵੇਂ	੮੯
90	navve	ਨੱਵੇ	੯੦
91	ikaanven	ਇਕਾਨਵੇਂ	੯੧
92	baanven	ਬਾਨਵੇਂ	੯੨
93	triaanven	ਤ੍ਰਿਆਨਵੇਂ	੯੩
94	churaanven	ਚੁਰਾਨਵੇਂ	੯੪
95	pachaanven	ਪਚਾਨਵੇਂ	੯੫
96	chiaanven	ਛਿਆਨਵੇਂ	੯੬
97	sataanven	ਸਤਾਨਵੇਂ	੯੭
98	athaanven	ਅਠਾਨਵੇਂ	੯੮
99	narhinven	ਨਛਿਨਵੇਂ	੯੯
100	sau	ਸੌਂ	੧੦੦
1000	ikk hazaar	ਇੱਕ ਹਜ਼ਾਰ	੧੦੦੦
100 000	lakhkh	ਲੱਖ	੧੦੦ ੦੦੦
10 000 000	karorh	ਕਰੋੜ	੧੦ ੦੦੦ ੦੦੦

PANJABI–ENGLISH GLOSSARY

ਉਸ	us	that
ਉਹ	uh	he, she, that, they
ਉਖੜਨਾ	ukharhnaa	to be displaced, to be uprooted
ਉਡੀਕਣਾ	udeeknhaa	to wait
ਉਤਸੁਕ	utsuk	anxious awaiting
ਉੱਥੋਂ	uththon	from there
ਉਮਰ	umar	age (f.)
ਉਮੀਦ	umeed	hope (f.)
ਉਰਦੂ	urdoo	Urdu (m./f.)
ਉਲੰਘਣਾ	ulanghnhaa	to disobey, to break
ਊਠ	ooth	male camel (m.)
ਅੱਸਲਾਮ ਅਲੈਕਮ	asslaam alaikam	Muslim greeting
ਅਸੀਂ	aseen	we
ਅਸੀਂ ਸਾਰੇ	aseen saare	all of us, we all
ਅਸੀਂ ਦੋਨੋਂ	aseen donon	both of us
ਅਖਾਣ	akhaanh	proverb, saying (m.)
ਅਖੀਰ	akheer	end
ਅਗਲਾ	aglaa	next (v.)
ਅੰਗਰੇਜ਼	angrez	English (m./f.)
ਅੱਛਾ	achchaa	OK, alright
ਅੱਜ	ajj	today
ਅੱਜ ਕੱਲ੍ਹ	ajj kallh	these days
ਅਜ਼ਾਦੀ	azaadee	freedom, independence (f.)
ਅੰਤਰ ਰਾਸ਼ਟਰੀ	antar raashtaree	international
ਅੰਦਰ	andar	inside
ਅਤੇ	ate	and
ਅਜ਼ਾਦੀ ਲਈ ਜਦੋ ਜਹਿਦ	azaadee laee jado jahid	struggle for independence (f.)
ਅਜੋਕਾ	ajokaa	modern
ਅਨੰਦ ਮਾਣੋ	anand maanho	enjoy yourself
ਅਨਾਰਕਲੀ	anaarkalee	name of classic Urdu film (f.)

ਅਪਰਾਧ	apraadh	offence (m.)
ਅਫਸਰ	afsar	officer (m./f.)
ਅਫਸੋਸ	afsos	regret, sorry
ਅਬਾਦੀ	abaadee	population (f.)
ਅਮਰੀਕਾ	amreekaa	America (m.)
ਅੰਮ੍ਰਿਤ	anmrit	nectar, holy water (m.)
ਅਰਥ	arth	meaning (m.)
ਅਰਾਮ	araam	rest (m.)
ਆ ਜਾ	aajaa	come (informal request)
ਆਉਣਾ	aaunhaa	to come
ਆਓ	aao	come (formal)
ਆਸ ਪਾਸ	aas paas	around and about
ਆਗਿਆ	aagiaa	permission (f.)
ਆਪਣਾ	aapnhaa	one's own
ਆਲੂ	aaloo	potato/es (m.)
ਅਧਿਆਪਕ	adhiaapak	teacher (m./f.)
ਅਧਿਆਪਕਾ	adhiaapkaa	teacher (f.)
ਐਨੇ ਸਾਰੇ	aine saare	so much
ਐਤਵਾਰ	aitvaar	Sunday (m.)
ਇਸ	is	it, this
ਇਸ ਕਰ ਕੇ	is kar ke	that is why
ਇਸਤਰੀ	istaree	lady (f.)
ਇਸ ਵਾਰੀ	is vaaree	this time
ਇਹ	ih	he, she, it, this
ਇੱਕ	ikk	one, a
ਇੱਕ ਪਾਸੇ	ikk paase	one side
ਇੱਕ ਸੌ ਵੀਹ	ikk sau veeh	one hundred and twenty
ਇਕੱਠ	ikathth	gathering (m.)
ਇਕੱਠੇ	ikaththe	together
ਇੱਕੋ	ikko	same
ਇੰਤਜ਼ਾਮ	intzaam	arrangements (m.)
ਇੱਥੇ	iththe	here
ਇਨਸ਼ਾ ਅੱਲਾ	inshaa allaa	hopefully [lit: if God wishes]
ਈਸਟ ਅਫਰੀਕਾ	eest afreekaa	East Africa (m.)
ਏ	e	is (informal)
ਸਹਿਮਤ	sahimat	agree
ਸ਼ਹਿਰ	shahir	city (m.)
ਸ਼ਹਿਰੀਅਤ	shahireeat	citizen (f.)

ਸਹੁਰੇ	sahure	in-laws (m.)
ਸਹੇਲੀ	sahelee	friend (f.)
ਸਕਣਾ	saknhaa	can, to be able to
ਸਕੂਲ	sakool	school (m.)
ਸਗੋਂ	sagon	but also
ਸੱਚ	sachch	true, truth (v.)
ਸੱਚੀ ਮੁੱਚੀ	sachchee muchchee	genuinely
ਸਤਿ ਸ੍ਰੀ ਅਕਾਲ	sat sree akaal	Sikh greeting
ਸਥਿਤੀ	sathitee	situation (f.)
ਸੱਦਾ ਪੱਤਰ	saddaa pattar	invitation (m.)
ਸਨਿਚਰਵਾਰ	sanicharvaar	Saturday (m.)
ਸ਼ਨਾਖ਼ਤੀ ਕਾਰਡ	shanaakhtee kaard	identity card (m.)
ਸਪਤਾਹ	saptaah	week (m.)
ਸੰਪਰਕ	sanparak	contact (m.)
ਸਬਜ਼ੀ	sabzee	vegetable (f.)
ਸਫ਼ਰ ਕਰਨਾ	safar karna	to travel
ਸਬ	sabh	all, every
ਸਬ ਕੁਝ	sabh kujh	everything
ਸਬ ਪਾਸੇ	sabh paase	everywhere
ਸਬ ਤੋਂ ਵਧੀਆ	sabh ton vadheeaa	the best
ਸਮਝਣਾ	samjhnhaa	to understand/comprehend
ਸਮਾਂ	samaan	time (m.)
ਸਮਾਂ ਪਾ ਕੇ	samaan paa ke	after a while, after some time
ਸਮਾਜ ਸੇਵਕ	samaaj sevak	social worker (m./f.)
ਸਮਾਨ	samaan	luggage, things (m.)
ਸਮੁੰਦਰ	samundar	sea (m.)
ਸਮੁੰਦਰੀ ਡਾਕ	samundaree daak	sea mail (f.)
ਸਮੋਸਾ	samosaa	triangular stuffed pastry (m.)
ਸਰਦਾਰ ਸਾਹਿਬ	sardaar saahib	Mr (m.)
ਸਰਦੀ	sardee	winter (f.)
ਸ੍ਰੇਣੀ	shrenhee	class (f.)
ਸਰੋਵਰ	sarovar	pool (m.)
ਸ਼ਲਗਮ	shalgam	turnip (m.)
ਸਵਰਗ	savarag	heaven (m.)
ਸਵਾਰੀ	savaaree	installation (f.)
ਸਵਾਰੀਆਂ	savaareeaan	passengers, travellers (f.)
ਸਵੇਰੇ	savere	in the morning
ਸਾਹਿਬ	saahib	sir (m.)

ਸਾਡਾ	saadaa	our
ਸ਼ਾਂਤੀ	shaantee	peace (f.)
ਸਾਫ਼ ਕਰਨਾ	saaf karnaa	to clean
ਸ਼ਾਬਾਸ਼	shaabaash	well done
ਸ਼ਾਮਲ	shaamal	to be present, to join in, participate
ਸਾਲ	saal	year (m.)
ਸਾਰਾ ਮਾਹੌਲ	saaraa maahaul	whole atmosphere (m.)
ਸਾਰੇ	saare	everyone, all (v.)
ਸਾੜ੍ਹੀ ਵਾਲੀ	saarhhee vaalee	the one wearing the sari (f.)
ਸਿਆਣਾ	siaanhaa	wise, mature (v.)
ਸਿਹਤ	sihat	health (f.)
ਸ਼ਿਕਾਇਤ	shikaait	complaint (f.)
ਸਿੱਖਾਂ ਦੇ	sikhkhaan de	of the Sikhs
ਸਿਤਾਰ	sitaar	sitar (f.) (stringed classical musical instrument)
ਸੀਟ	seet	seat (f.)
ਸ਼ੀਸ਼ਾ	sheeshaa	mirror (m.)
ਸੀਨਾ	seenaa	bosom, heart (m.)
ਸੁਆਦ	suaad	taste (m.)
ਸੁਆਦੀ	suaadee	tasty
ਸੁਹਣਾ	suhnhaa	nice, pretty (v.)
ਸ਼ੁੱਕਰਵਾਰ	shukkarvaar	Friday (m.)
ਸ਼ੁਕਰੀਆ	shukreeaa	thank you (m.)
ਸੁਣਨਾ	sunhnaa	to listen
ਸੁਨਹਿਰੀ	sunahiree	golden
ਸ਼ੁਭ ਇਛਾਵਾਂ	shubh ichaavaan	best wishes (f.)
ਸੁਰੱਖਿਅਤ ਸਫ਼ਰ	surakhkhiat safar	safe journey
ਸ਼ੁਰੂ ਹੋਣਾ	shuroo honhaa	to start, to begin
ਸ਼ੁਰੂ ਕਰਨਾ	shuroo karnaa	to begin, to commence
ਸੂਈ	sooee	needle (f.)
ਸੇਵਾਦਾਰ	sevaadaar	volunteer (m./f.)
ਸੈਲਾਨੀ	sailaanee	tourist (m./f.)
ਸੋਚਣਾ	sochnhaa	to think
ਸੋਨਾ	sonaa	gold (m.)
ਸੋਮਵਾਰ	somvaar	Monday (m.)
ਸੌ (੧੦੦)	sau	one hundred
ਸ਼ੌਕ	shauk	fondness, enjoyment, like (m.)

ਸੌਖਾ	saukhaa	easy, simple (v.)
ਹਜ਼ਮ	hazam	digest
ਹੰਢਣਸਾਰ	handhanhsaar	durable, hardwearing
ਹਫ਼ਤਾ	haftaa	week (m.)
ਹਫ਼ਤਾ	haftaa	Saturday (m.)
ਹਫ਼ਤੇ ਦੇ ਅਖ਼ੀਰ	hafte de akheer	weekend (m.)
ਹਰ ਪਾਸੇ	har paase	everywhere
ਹਰਿਮੰਦਰ ਸਾਹਿਬ	harmandar saahib	Golden Temple (m.)
ਹਵਾਈ	havaaee	by air
ਹਵਾਈ ਅੱਡਾ	havaaee addaa	airport (m.)
ਹਵਾਈ ਡਾਕ	havaaee daak	air mail (f.)
ਹਾਲ	haal	condition (m.)
ਹਾਂ ਜੀ	haan jee	yes (polite)
ਹਿਸਾਬ	hisaab	maths (m.)
ਹਿੰਦੂ	hindoo	Hindu (m./f.)
ਹੁਣ	hunh	now
ਹੋਸਟਲ	hostal	hostel (m.)
ਹੋਣਾ	honhaa	to be
ਹੈ	hai	is
ਕਈ	kaee	several
ਕਈ ਤਰ੍ਹਾਂ	kaee tar-h-aan	different types
ਕਹਿਣਾ	kahinhaa	to speak
ਕਟਣਾ	katnhaa	to cut
ਕੱਦ	kadd	height (m.)
ਕਦਰਾਂ	kadraan	values (f.)
ਕਦੀ	kadee	sometimes
ਕਦੋਂ	kadon	when
ਕਪੜਾ	kaprhaa	cloth (m.)
ਕਮਰਾ	kamraa	room (m.)
ਕਮਜ਼ੋਰੀ	kamzoree	weakness (f.)
ਕੰਮ	kanm	job, work task (m.)
ਕੰਮ ਕਰਨਾ	kanm karnaa	to work
ਕਰਨਾ	karnaa	to do
ਕਰਾਰਾ	karaaraa	spicy (v.)
ਕਰੇਲਾ	karelaa	bitter gourd (m.)
ਕੱਲ੍ਹ	kallh	yesterday/tomorrow
ਕਲਾਸ	kalaas	class (f.)
ਕਾਹਲਾ	kaahlaa	impatient, hasty (v.)

ਕਾਹਲ ਵਿਚ	kaahalvich	in a hurry
ਕਾਗ਼ਜ਼ਾਤ	kaaghzaat	papers, documents (m.)
ਕਾਫੀ ਕੁਝ	kaafee kujh	quite a lot, plenty
ਕਾਨੂੰਨ	kaanoonn	law (m.)
ਕਾਰ	kaar	car (f.)
ਕਾਲਜ	kaalaj	college (m.)
ਕਿ	ki	that
ਕਿਉਂ	kiun	why
ਕਿਉਂ ਕਿ	kiun ki	because
ਕਿਹਾ ਜਾਂਦਾ ਹੈ	kihaa jaandaa hai	is said, is called
ਕਿਹੜਾ	kihrhaa	which
ਕਿੱਥੇ	kiththe	where
ਕਿੰਨਾ	kinnaa	how much
ਕਿੰਨੇ	kinne	how many
ਕਿੰਨਾ ਚਿਰ ਤੋਂ	kinnaa chir ton	since when, for how long
ਕਿੰਨੀ ਦੂਰ	kinnee door	how far
ਕਿੰਨੇ ਦਾ ਮੀਟਰ	kinne daa meetar	how much per metre
ਕਿੰਨੇ ਵਜੇ	kinne vaje	what time
ਕਿਰਪਾ	kirpaa	blessings (f.)
ਕਿਰਾਇਆ	kiraaiaa	rate, fare, rent (m.)
ਕਿਵੇਂ	kiven	how
ਕਿਵੇਂ ਰਿਹਾ	kiven rihaa	how did it go?
ਕੀ	kee	what
ਕੀਮਤ	keemat	price (f.)
ਕੀਨੀਆ	keeneeaa	Kenya (m.)
ਕੀਰਤਨ	keertan	singing of hymns (m.)
ਕੁੱਤਾ	kuttaa	dog (m.)
ਕੋਈ	koee	any
ਕੋਈ ਨ ਕੋਈ	koee na koee	some one or another
ਕੋਸ਼ਿਸ਼ ਕਰਨਾ	koshish karnaa	to try
ਕੋਲ	kol	with, next to, in possession of
ਕੌਣ	kaunh	who
ਕੌਮ	kaum	nation, community (f.)
ਕੌੜਾ/ਕਸੈਲਾ	kaurhaa/kasailaa	bitter (v.)
ਕੇਵਲ	keval	only
ਕੈਮਰਾ	kaimraa	camera (m.)
ਖ਼ਤਮ ਕਰਨਾ	khatam karnaa	to finish, to complete
ਖ਼ਤਰਨਾਕ	khatarnaak	dangerous

ਖਤਰੀ	kha<u>t</u>ree	Khatri (m./f.) (caste)
ਖਰਚਾ	<u>kh</u>archaa	expense, expenses (m.)
ਖਲੋਣਾ	khalonhaa	to be stood, to stand
ਖੜਨਾ	kharhhnaa	to stand, to park
ਖਾਸ	<u>kh</u>aas	special
ਖਾਣਾ	khaanhaa	to eat
ਖਾਲੀ	<u>kh</u>aalee	empty, vacant
ਖ਼ਿਲਾਫ਼	khilaaf	against
ਖੁਸ਼	khush	happy
ਖੁਸ਼ੀ	khushee	good (f.) (lit: happiness)
ਖ਼ੁਦਾ ਹਾਫ਼ਿਜ਼	<u>kh</u>udaa haafiz	Muslim departing phrase
ਖੁੱਲ੍ਹਾ	khullhaa	open, plenty (v.)
ਖੇਡਣਾ	khednhaa	to play
ਖ਼ੈਰ	<u>kh</u>air	anyway
ਗੱਡੀ	gaddee	car, vehicle (f.)
ਗੱਡੀ	gaddee	automobile, train (f.)
ਗਤਕਾ	ga<u>t</u>kaa	a Sikh martial art, like fencing (m.)
ਗ਼ਦਰ	<u>gh</u>a<u>d</u>ar	mutiny (m.)
ਗ਼ਦਰ ਪਾਰਟੀ	<u>gh</u>a<u>d</u>ar paartee	Gadar Party (f.)
ਗ਼ਮੀ	<u>gh</u>amee	sadness (f.)
ਗਰਮੀ	garmee	summer, heat (f.)
ਗਰੇਡ	gared	grade (m.)
ਗੱਲ	gall	matter, news (f.) (lit: talk)
ਗ਼ਲਤ	<u>gh</u>ala<u>t</u>	wrong
ਗੱਲਾਂ	gallaa<u>n</u>	speech, conversation (f.)
ਗਾਜਰ	gaajar	carrots (f.)
ਗਾਣਾ	gaanhaa	to sing
ਗਾਲੜੀ	gaalrhee	talkative
ਗਿੱਧਾ	gi<u>dh</u>dhaa	women's folk dance (m.)
ਗੀਤ	geet	song (m.)
ਗ਼ੁਸਲਖ਼ਾਨਾ	<u>gh</u>usal <u>kh</u>aanaa	bathroom (m.)
ਗੁਜਰਾਤੀ	gujraa<u>t</u>ee	a person from Gujarat or of Gujarati origin (m./f.)
ਗੁੰਬਦ	gun<u>b</u>ad	dome (m.)
ਗੋਭੀ	gobhee	cauliflower (f.)
ਗੋਰੀ	goree	fair, white (v.)
ਘਰ	ghar	house, home (m.)

ਘਰ ਦਾ ਕੰਮ	ghar daa kanm	homework (m.)
ਘਰਵਾਲਾ	gharvaalaa	husband (m.)
ਘੱਟ	ghatt	less, lower
ਘੱਟ ਕਰਨਾ	ghatt karnaa	to reduce, to lessen
ਘੱਟੋ ਘੱਟ	ghatto ghatt	at least
ਘਾਟ	ghaat	place where clothes are washed on the bay (m.)
ਘੁੰਮਣਾ	ghunmnhaa	to go around
ਘੁੰਮਣਾ ਫਿਰਨਾ	ghunmnhaa phirnaa	to travel around
ਘੋੜੀ	ghorhee	mare (f.)
ਚੰਗੀ	changee	good (v.)
ਚਮਕੀਲਾ	chamkeelaa	glittering, shining (v.)
ਚਮਚਾ	chamchaa	spoon (m.)
ਚਰਖਾ	charkhaa	spinning wheel (m.)
ਚਲਣਾ	chalnhaa	to go
ਚੜ੍ਹਦੀ ਕਲਾ	charhhdee kalaa	high spirits
ਚੜ੍ਹਨਾ	charhhnaa	to be upon, to ride
ਚਾਹੁਣਾ	chaahunhaa	to need, to want
ਚਾਚਾ ਜੀ	chaachaa jee	uncle (m.) (father's brother)
ਚਿੱਠੀ	chiththee	letter (f.)
ਚਿਰ	chir	length of time
ਚੀਜ਼	cheez	thing (f.)
ਚੁਕਣਾ	chuknhaa	to be settled, finished
ਚੁੱਕਣਾ	chukknhaa	to lift, to pick
ਚੋਣ	chonh	choice, selection (f.)
ਚੌਥੇ ਗੁਰੂ	chauthe guroo	fourth Guru (m.)
ਚੌੜਾ	chaurhaa	wide (v.)
ਛਕਣਾ	chaknhaa	to take, to consume
ਛੱਡਣਾ	chaddnhaa	to leave, to quit
ਛਪਾਈਵਾਲਾ	chapaaeevaalaa	the printed one (m.)
ਛੱਲੀ	challee	corn on the cob (f.)
ਛਾਪਾ	chaapaa	print (m.)
ਛੁੱਟੀਆਂ	chutteeaan	holidays (f.)
ਛੋਟਾ	chotaa	small (v.)
ਜਗ੍ਹਾ	jag-h-aa	place, location (f.)
ਜਦੋ ਜਹਿਦ	jado jahid	struggle (f.)
ਜਨਮ	janam	birth (m.)
ਜਨਮ ਅਸਥਾਨ	janam asthaan	birthplace (m.)

ਜਨਮ ਦਿਨ	janam din	birthday (m.)
ਜੰਮਪਲ	janmpal	raised, born and bred
ਜੰਮਣਾ	janmnhaa	to be born
ਜ਼ਮਾਨਾ	zamaanaa	times (m.)
ਜਰਮਨ	jarman	German (m./f.)
ਜ਼ਰੂਰ	zaroor	definitely
ਜਲੂਸ	jaloos	procession, parade (m.)
ਜਾਂ	jaan	or
ਜ਼ਾਇਆ ਕਰਨਾ	zaaiaa karnaa	to waste time
ਜਾ ਚੁਕਣਾ	jaa chuknhaa	have (already) been
ਜਾਂਞੀ	jaannjee	members of the groom's wedding party (m./f.)
ਜਾਣਨਾ	jaanhnaa	to know
ਜ਼ਿਆਦਾ	ziaadaa	too much
ਜਿਸ	jis	which (oblique)
ਜਿਹਾ	jihaa	sort of, rather
ਜਿਹੜਾ	jihrhaa	that, which
ਜਿੱਥੇ	jiththe	where
ਜੀ	jee	honorific particle signifying respect
ਜੀ ਆਇਆਂ ਨੂੰ	jee aaiaan noon	welcome
ਜੀਵਨ	jeevan	life (m.)
ਜੁਮਾ	jumaa	Friday (m.)
ਜੁਮੇਰਾਤ	jumeraat	Thursday (f.)
ਜੇ	je	if
ਜੇਬਾਂ	jebaan	pockets (m./f.)
ਝਾਕਣਾ	jhaaknhaa	to stare, to look at
ਝੂਟੇ	jhoote	rides (m.)
ਟਮਾਟਰ	tamaatar	tomato/es (m.)
ਟਿਕਟ	tikat	stamp (f.)
ਟੀ. ਵੀ.	tee vee	TV (television) (m.)
ਟੇਕਣਾ	teknhaa	to bow down
ਟੈਲੀਫ਼ੋਨ	taileefon	telephone (m.)
ਟੈਲੀਫ਼ੋਨ ਕਰਨਾ	taileefon karnaa	to call by telephone
ਠੰਡ	thand	cold (f.)
ਠਹਿਰਨਾ	thahirnaa	to stay
ਠੀਕ	theek	fine/OK/alright/right
ਠੀਕ ਕਰਨਾ	theek karnaa	to fix, to correct

ਠੀਕ ਠਾਕ	theek thaak	OK, fine
ਡਾਕ	daak	mail, post (f.)
ਡਾਕਟਰ	daaktar	doctor (m./f.)
ਡਾਂਗ	daang	long wooden pole (f.)
ਡਾਲਰ	daalar	dollar (m.)
ਡੋਲੀ	dolee	ceremony bidding farewell to the bride (f.)
ਢੋਲ	dhol	big drum (m.)
ਢੋਲਕੀ	dholkee	small drum (f.)
ਤਸ਼ਰੀਫ਼ ਰੱਖੋ ਜੀ	tashreef rakhkho jee	please have a seat
ਤਕਰੀਬਨ	takreeban	about, approximately
ਤਕਲੀਫ਼	takleef	trouble, irritation, bother (f.)
ਤਨਖ਼ਾਹ	tankhaah	pay, salary (f.)
ਤਬੀਅਤ	tabeeat	state of health, condition (f.)
ਤਰ੍ਹਾਂ	tar-h-aan	way, style
ਤਲਾਕ	talaak	divorce (m.)
ਤਾਂ	taan	then
ਤਾਂ ਕਿ	taan ki	so that
ਤਿਉਹਾਰ	tiuhaar	celebration, festival (m.)
ਤੁਸੀਂ	tuseen	you (formal)
ਤੁਹਾਡਾ	tuhaadaa	your (informal)
ਤੁਹਾਡਾ ਕੀ ਹਾਲ ਹੈ	tuhaadaa kee haal hai	How are you?
ਤੁਹਾਡੀ ਕਿਰਪਾ ਹੈ	tuhaadee kirpaa hai	by your blessings
ਤੁਹਾਡੇ ਬਾਰੇ	tuhaade baare	about you
ਤੁਰਨਾ	turnaa	to walk, to depart, to leave
ਤੂੰ	toon	you (informal)
ਤੇ	te	and, on
ਤੇਰਾ	teraa	your (informal)
ਤੋਂ	ton	from
ਤੋਂ ਇਲਾਵਾ	ton ilaavaa	apart from, besides
ਤੋਂ ਪਹਿਲੇ	ton pahile	before
ਤੋਂ ਬਾਅਦ	ton baa-a-d	after
ਤੋਂ ਬਿਨਾਂ/ਬਗ਼ੈਰ	ton binaan/baghair	without
ਥਾਂ ਥਾਂ	thaan thaan	each and every place (m.)
ਥੋੜੀ ਬਹੁਤੀ	thorhee bahutee	more or less, to some extent

ਦਫ਼ਤਰ	daftar	office (m.)
ਦਰਸ਼ਕ	darshak	participant, visitor (m./f.)
ਦਰਦ	dard	pain, hurt (f.)
ਦਵਾਈ	davaaee	medicine (f.)
ਦਾ	daa	of
ਦਿਸਣਾ	disnhaa	to be visible, to be seen
ਦਿਖਾਉਣਾ	dikhaaunhaa	to show
ਦਿਨ	din	day (m.)
ਦਿਲ	dil	heart (m.)
ਦਿਲਚਸਪ	dilchasp	interesting
ਦਿਲ ਲੱਗਣਾ	dil laggnhaa	to feel at home, to be settled, to live happily
ਦਿੱਲੀ	dillee	Delhi (f.)
ਦੀ ਜਗ੍ਹਾ	dee jag-h-aa	in place of
ਦੁਕਾਨ	dukaan	shop (f.)
ਦੁਕਾਨਦਾਰ	dukaandaar	shopkeeper (m.)
ਦੁਨੀਆਂ	duneeaan	world (f.)
ਦੂਜਾ ਦਿਨ	doojaa din	second day
ਦੂਜੇ	dooje	others
ਦੂਰ	door	far, distant
ਦੂਰਤੋਂ	door ton	far from/away from
ਦੇ ਉੱਪਰ	de uppar	above, upon
ਦੇ ਅੰਦਰ	de an dar	inside
ਦੇਸ਼	desh	country (m.)
ਦੇਸੀ	desi	Indian, Panjabi, home
ਦੇ ਸਾਹਮਣੇ	de saahmanhe	opposite, facing
ਦੇਖਣਾ	dekhnhaa	to see, to watch
ਦੇਣਾ	denhaa	to give
ਦੇ ਥੱਲੇ	de thalle	below
ਦੇ ਨੇੜੇ	de nerhe	near
ਦੇ ਪਿੱਛੇ	de pichche	behind
ਦੇ ਬਾਹਰ	de baahar	outside
ਦੇ ਬਾਵਜੂਦ	de baavjood	in spite of
ਦੇ ਬਾਰੇ	de baare	about, concerning
ਦੇ ਲਈ	de laee	for
ਦੇ ਵਾਸਤੇ	de vaaste	for
ਦੋਸ਼	dosh	charge (m.)
ਦੋਨੋਂ	donon	both

ਧੰਨਵਾਦ	dhannvaad	thanks (m.)
ਧੀਆਂ	dheeaan	daughters (f.)
ਧੂਮ ਧਾਮ	dhoom dhaam	bang, pomp and show
ਧੋਣਾ	dhonhaa	to wash
ਧੋਬੀ	dhobee	washerman (m.)
ਨਹੀਂ	naheen	no
ਨਗਰ ਕੀਰਤਨ	nagar keertan	religious procession (m.)
ਨੱਚਣਾ	nachchnhaa	to dance
ਨਮਕੀਨ	namkeen	salty
ਨਮੂਨਾ	namoonaa	pattern, design (m.)
ਨਰਮ ਸੁਭਾ	naram subhaa	kind natured
ਨਾਂ	naan	name (m.) (informal)
ਨਾ ਕੇਵਲ	naa keval	not only
ਨਾਮ	naam	name (m.) (formal)
ਨੀਲਾ	neelaa	blue (v.)
ਨੁਮਾਇਸ਼	numaaish	exhibition (f.)
ਨੌਕਰ	naukar	male servant (m.)
ਨੌਕਰੀ	naukaree	job, employment (f.)
ਨੌਜੁਆਨ	naujuaan	youth (m.)
ਪਸੰਦ	pasand	like, pleasing
ਪਕੌੜਾ	pakaurhaa	a type of deep-fried pastry similar to fritters (m.)
ਪਹਿਲੀ ਵਾਰੀ	pahilee vaaree	first time
ਪਹਿਲੇ	pahile	before
ਪਹੁੰਚਾ ਦੇਣਾ	pahunchaa denhaa	to deliver, to cause to arrive
ਪੰਜਵਾਂ	panjvaan	fifth
ਪੱਛਮ	pachcham	west (m.)
ਪੰਜ ਵਜੇ	panj vaje	five o'clock
ਪੰਜਾਬ	panjaab	Panjab (m.)
ਪੰਜਾਬੀ	panjaabee	a person from Panjab or of Panjabi origin (m./f.)
ਪੱਤਝੜ	pattjharh	autumn (f.)
ਪਤਨੀ	patnee	wife (f.)
ਪਤਲਾ	patlaa	thin, slim (v.)
ਪਤਵੰਤੇ	patvante	respectable (v.)
ਪਤਾ	pataa	to know
ਪਤੀ	patee	husband (m.)
ਪਰ	par	but

ਪਰਸੋਂ	parson	day before yesterday/day after tomorrow
ਪਰਤਣਾ	partnhaa	to return
ਪਰਵਾਰ	parvaar	family (m.)
ਪਰਵਾਰਕ	parvaarak	family (relating to family)
ਪ੍ਰਾਹੁਣੇ	praahunhe	guests (m.)
ਪਲੇਟ	palet	plate (f.)
ਪੜਦਾਦਾ	parhdaadaa	great grandfather (m.)
ਪੜ੍ਹਨਾ	parhhnaa	to read, to study
ਪੜ੍ਹਾਉਣਾ	parhhaaunhaa	to teach
ਪੜ੍ਹਾਈ	parhhaaee	studies (f.)
ਪੜ੍ਹਿਆ ਲਿਖਿਆ	parhhiaa likhiaa	educated (v.)
ਪਾਸਪੋਰਟ	paasport	passport (m.)
ਪਾਸੇ	paase	direction, way
ਪਿਆਰ	piaar	love, affection (m.)
ਪਿਆਰ ਕਰਨਾ	piaar karnaa	to love
ਪਿਆਰੇ	piaare	dear, beloved (v.)
ਪਿੰਡਵਾਲਾ	pindvaalaa	villager (m.)
ਪੀਣਾ	peenhaa	to drink
ਪੀਰ	peer	holy man (m.)
ਪੀਰ	peer	Monday (m.)
ਪੁੱਛਣਾ	puchchnhaa	to ask
ਪੁੱਤਰ	puttar	son (m.)
ਪੁਰਸ਼	purash	gentleman (m.)
ਪੂਰਬ	poorab	east (m.)
ਪੂਰੀਆਂ	pooreeaan	fulfilling
ਪੇਸ਼	pesh	to present
ਪੇਸ਼ ਕਰਨਾ	pesh karnaa	to present, to produce
ਪੇਸ਼ਾਵਰ	peshaavar	professional (m./f.)
ਪੇਕੇ	peke	bride's family, bride's parents (m.)
ਪੇਟ	pet	stomach, belly (m.)
ਪੇਂਡੂ	pendoo	of the village, village-like (m./f.)
ਪੈਂਸਲ	painsal	pencil (f.)
ਪੈਸੇਵਾਲੇ	paisevaale	wealthy people (m.)
ਪੈਣਾ	painhaa	to act (to fall)
ਪੌੜੀਆਂ	paurheeaan	stairs (f.)
ਫਸਲਾਂ	fasalaan	crops (f.)

ਫ਼ਿਕਰ	fikar	worry (m.)
ਫਿੱਕਾ	phikkaa	light, pale (v.)
ਫਿਰ	phir	again
ਫਿਰਨਾ	phirnaa	to travel
ਫ਼ਿਲਮ	filam	film (f.)
ਫ਼ੋਟੋ	foto	photograph (f.)
ਫ਼ੌਜ	fauj	military (f.)
ਬਸੰਤ	basant	spring (f.)
ਬਹੁਤ	bahut	very
ਬਹੁਤ ਅੱਛਾ	bahut achchaa	very good (v.)
ਬਹੁਤ ਸਾਰੇ	bahut saare	a lot, many
ਬਹੁਤ ਸੁਹਣਾ	bahut suhnhaa	very nice, excellent (v.)
ਬਹੁਤ ਜ਼ਿਆਦਾ	bahut ziaadaa	far too much
ਬਗੀਚਾ	bagheechaa	garden (m.)
ਬਚਪਨ	bachpan	childhood (m.)
ਬੱਚੇ	bachche	children (m.)
ਬਟਵਾਰਾ	batvaaraa	division, partition (m.)
ਬਣਨਾ	banhnaa	to become
ਬਣਵਾਉਣਾ	banhvaaunhaa	to get built
ਬਦਲਣਾ	badalnhaa	to change, to exchange
ਬੰਦ	band	closed, off
ਬੰਦ ਕਰਨਾ	band karnaa	to close
ਬੰਦੇ	bande	people (m.)
ਬਰਸਾਤ	barsaat	rainy season (f.)
ਬਰਮਿੰਘਮ	barmingham	Birmingham (m.)
ਬਰਾਤ	baraat	procession of the groom's relatives and friends (f.)
ਬਲਕਿ	balki	but also
ਬੜੀ	barhee	very (v.)
ਬਾਅਦ ਦੁਪਹਿਰ	baa-a-d dupahir	afternoon
ਬਾਹਰੋਂ	baahron	from outside/from abroad
ਬਾਰਸ਼	baarash	rain (f.)
ਬਾਲ	baal	male child (m.)
ਬਿਮਾਰ	bimaar	ill, sick
ਬਿਮਾਰ ਹੋਣ ਤੋਂ ਪਹਿਲੇ	bimaar honh ton pahile	before falling ill
ਬਿਲਕੁਲ	bilkul	absolutely, perfectly
ਬੀਬੀ	beebee	madam (f.)

ਬੁਖ਼ਾਰ	bu<u>kh</u>aar	fever/temperature (m.)
ਬੁੱਧਵਾਰ	bu<u>dhdh</u>vaar	Wednesday (m.)
ਬੇਟਾ	betaa	son (m.)
ਬੇਟੀ	betee	daughter (f.)
ਬੇਨਤੀ	ben<u>t</u>ee	request (f.)
ਬੇਬੀ ਸਿਟਰ	bebee sitar	baby sitter (m./f.)
ਬੈਠਕ	baithak	sitting room (f.)
ਬੈਠਣਾ	baithnhaa	to sit
ਬੈਠੋ ਜੀ	baitho jee	please sit down (formal)
ਬੋਰ ਹੋਣਾ	bor honhaa	to be bored, to feel bored
ਬੋਲਣਾ	bolnhaa	to speak
ਬੋਲੀ	bolee	language (f.)
ਬੋਲੀਆਂ	boleeaa<u>n</u>	folk verse couplets (f.)
ਭੰਗੜਾ	bha<u>n</u>grhaa	bhangra (m.) (style of Panjabi dance)
ਭਤੀਜੀ	bha<u>t</u>eejee	niece (f.)
ਭਰਤੀ	bhar<u>t</u>ee	join
ਭਰਾ	bharaa	brother (m.)
ਭਲਕ/ਭਲਕੇ	bhalak/bhalke	tomorrow
ਭਲੀ	bhalee	look after, watch over
ਭਾਈ ਸਾਹਿਬ	bhaaee saahib	brother (m.)
ਭਾਬੀ	bhaabee	sister-in-law (f.) (brother's wife)
ਭਾਰਤ	bhaara<u>t</u>	India (m.)
ਭਾਰਤੀ	bhaar<u>t</u>ee	Indian (m./f.)
ਭਿੰਡੀ	bhi<u>n</u>dee	okra (type of vegetable) (f.)
ਭੁੱਖ	bhu<u>kh</u>kh	hunger (f.)
ਭੇਜਣਾ	bhejnhaa	to send, to post
ਭੈਣ	bhainh	sister (f.)
ਮਹਿੰਗਾ	mahi<u>n</u>gaa	expensive, costly (v.)
ਮਸ਼ੀਨ	masheen	machine (f.)
ਮਹਿੰਦੀ	mahi<u>n</u>dee	henna (f.)
ਮਹੀਨਾ	maheenaa	month (m.)
ਮਕਾਨ	makaan	house (m.)
ਮੰਗਣਾ	ma<u>n</u>gnhaa	to request, to ask, to charge
ਮੰਗਲਵਾਰ	ma<u>n</u>galvaar	Tuesday (m.)
ਮੰਗਾਂ	ma<u>n</u>gaa<u>n</u>	demands (f.)
ਮਜ਼ਮੂਨ	mazmoon	subject (m.)
ਮਟਰ	matar	peas (m.)

ਮਤਲਬ	matlab	meaning, definition (m.)
ਮੱਦਦ ਕਰਨਾ	maddad karnaa	to help
ਮਨ	man	mind (m.)
ਮਨਪਰਚਾਵੇ	manparchaave	entertainment, enjoyment (m.)
ਮਨਾਉਣਾ	manaaunhaa	to pray, to believe, to celebrate
ਮੰਨੋ ਜਾਂ ਨਾ ਮੰਨੋ	manno jaan naa manno	believe it or not
ਮਾਤਾ ਜੀ	maataa jee	mother (f.)
ਮਾਫ਼	maaf	pardon, excuse
ਮਾਫ਼ ਕਰਨਾ	maaf karnaa	sorry, to pardon
ਮਾਨਚੈਸਟਰ	maanchaistar	Manchester (m.)
ਮਾਪੇ	maape	parents (m.)
ਮਾਰਨਾ	maarnaa	to hit
ਮਿਹਰਬਾਨੀ	miharbaanee	thanks, please (f.)
ਮਿਟਣਾ	mitnhaa	to finish, to vanish
ਮਿੰਟ	mint	minute (m.)
ਮਿੱਠਾ	miththaa	sweet (v.)
ਮਿਠਿਆਈ	mithiaaee	Panjabi sweet (f.)
ਮਿਲ ਜਾਣਾ	mil jaanhaa	to get, to receive
ਮਿਲਣਾ	milnhaa	to meet
ਮੁੱਖ	mukhkh	face (m.)
ਮੁਕਾਬਲਾ	mukaablaa	comparison, competition (m.)
ਮੁਫ਼ਤ	mufat	free
ਮੁੜਨਾ	murhnaa	to turn around, to return
ਮੇਖ	mekh	nail (f.)
ਮੇਰਾ	meraa	my
ਮੇਰੇ ਕੋਲ ਨਹੀਂ	mere kol naheen	not with me, not in my possession
ਮੇਰੇ ਨਾਲ	mere naal	with me
ਮੇਲ	mel	meeting, combination (m.)
ਮੇਲਾ	melaa	fair (m.)
ਮੈਂ	main	I
ਮੈਨੇਜਰ	mainejar	manager (m./f.)
ਮੋਚੀ	mochee	cobbler (m.)
ਮੋਟਾ	motaa	fat, thick (v.)
ਮੌਕਾ	maukaa	opportunity, occasion (m.)
ਮੌਜਾਂ ਕਰਨਾ	maujaan karnaa	to enjoy
ਯਾਦ	yaad	memory, remembrance (f.)

ਯੁਵਕ	yuvak	youth (m.)
ਯੂਗੰਡਾ	yoogandaa	Uganda (m.)
ਯੋਗ	yog	suitable
ਰਸ	ras	(fruit) juice (m.)
ਰਸਮ	rasam	custom, ritual (f.)
ਰਸੋਈ	rasoee	kitchen (f.)
ਰਹਿਣਾ	rahinhaa	to stay, to live
ਰੱਖਣਾ	rakhkhnhaa	to put
ਰੰਗ	rang	colour (m.)
ਰੰਗਦਾਰ	rangdaar	colourful
ਰੰਗਲਾ	ranglaa	colourful (v.)
ਰਚਨਾ	rachnaa	composition (f.)
ਰਲ ਮਿਲਣਾ	ral milnhaa	to be mixed
ਰਵਾਜ	ravaaj	fashion (m.)
ਰੜਕਣਾ	rarhkanhaa	to prick, to rub against
ਰਾਹਾਂ	raahaan	roads, routes (f.)
ਰਾਹੀਂ	raaheen	via, by
ਰਾਜ	raaj	rulership, kingdom (m.)
ਰਾਜਾ	raaja	king (m.)
ਰਿਸ਼ਤਾ	rishtaa	(marriage) relation (m.)
ਰਿਸ਼ਤੇਦਾਰ	rishtedaar	relatives (m./f.)
ਰੁਪਇਆ	rupaiaa	rupee (m.)
ਲਈ	laee	for, in order to
ਲੱਗਣਾ	laggnhaa	to be covered, laden, to feel
ਲਗਵਾਉਣਾ	lagvaaunhaa	to get covered
ਲੰਗਰ	langar	community kitchen (m.)
ਲਗਾਉਣਾ	lagaaunhaa	to stitch, to apply, to put on
ਲਗਾਤਾਰ	lagaataar	continuously, on going
ਲੰਡਨ	landan	London (m.)
ਲੱਡੂ	laddoo	a type of Panjabi sweet (m.)
ਲਫ਼ਜ਼ੀ	lafzee	literal
ਲੰਬਾ	lanbaa	long, lengthy (v.)
ਲੱਭਣਾ	labhbhnhaa	to find
ਲਾ ਪਰਵਾਹ	laa parvaah	careless
ਲਾਇਸੈਂਸ	laaisains	licence (m.)
ਲਾਹੌਰਵਾਲੀ ਔਰਤ	laahaurvaalee aurat	the woman from Lahore (f.)
ਲਾਲ	laal	red

ਲਾੜਾ	laarhaa	groom (m.)
ਲਿਖਣਾ	likhnhaa	to write
ਲਿਆਉਣਾ	liaaunhaa	to bring
ਲਿਆਕਤ	liaaka<u>t</u>	ability (f.)
ਲੈਣਾ	lainhaa	to take, to have
ਲੋਕ	lok	people (m.)
ਲੋਕ ਨਾਚ	lok naach	folk dance (m.)
ਲੋੜ	lorh	require, necessity, want (f.)
ਵੱਸ	vass	authority, jurisdiction (m.)
ਵਸਾਉਣਾ	vasaaunhaa	to establish, to habilitate
ਵਕਤ	vaka<u>t</u>	time (m.)
ਵੱਜਣਾ	vajjnhaa	to be played, to be beaten
ਵਜਾਉਣ ਦਾ ਸ਼ੋਕ	vajaaunh <u>d</u>aa shauk	fond of playing, enjoy playing
ਵਜਾਉਣਾ	vajaaunhaa	to play (music), to beat
ਵਡੱਕਿਆਂ	vadkkiaa<u>n</u>	ancestors, forefathers (m.)
ਵੱਡਾ	vaddaa	big, large (v.)
ਵੱਧ	va<u>dhdh</u>	high, more
ਵਧਾਉਣਾ	va<u>dh</u>aaunhaa	to increase
ਵਧਾਈ	va<u>dh</u>aaee	congratulations (f.)
ਵਧੀਆ	va<u>dh</u>eeaa	good quality
ਵਧੇਰੇ	va<u>dh</u>ere	more
ਵਰਗਾ	vargaa	like (v.)
ਵਰਤਣਾ	vara<u>t</u>nhaa	to use
ਵਰਤਾਉਣਾ	var<u>t</u>aaunhaa	to serve
ਵੱਲ	vall	towards
ਵੱਲੋਂ	vallo<u>n</u>	on behalf of
ਵਾਜਬੀ	vaajbee	reasonable, fair, right
ਵਾਜੇ ਵਾਲੇ	vaaje vaale	band of musicians (m.)
ਵਾਲੈਕਮ ਅੱਸਲਾਮ	vaalaikam asslaam	Response to Muslim greeting
ਵਾਪਸ	vaapas	return, back
ਵਾਰੀ	vaaree	turn, instance (f.)
ਵਿਆਹ	viaah	wedding (m.)
ਵਿਹਾਰੀ ਨੌਕਰੀ	vihaaree naukaree	professionally employed (f.)
ਵਿਕਣਾ	viknhaa	to be sold
ਵਿਚ	vich	in
ਵਿੱਚੋਂ	vichcho<u>n</u>	from within

ਵਿਦਿਆਰਥੀ	vidiaar<u>th</u>ee	student (m./f.)
ਵੀ	vee	also
ਵੀਹ (੨੦)	veeh	twenty
ਵੀਜ਼ਾ	veezaa	visa (m.)
ਵੀਰਵਾਰ	veervaar	Thursday (m.)
ਵੇ	ve	subjunctive particle
ਵੇਖਣਾ	vekhnhaa	to see
ਵੇਲੇ	vele	period, time (m.)
ਵੈਸਾਖ	vaisaakh	one of the Indian months (m.)
ਵੈਸਾਖੀ	vaisaakhee	a Sikh festival (f.)

Grammar and Verb Index